PROGRESS IN CONVERGENCE
Technologies for Human Wellbeing

ANNALS OF THE NEW YORK ACADEMY OF SCIENCES
Volume 1093

PROGRESS IN CONVERGENCE
Technologies for Human Wellbeing

*Edited by William Sims Bainbridge and
Mihail C. Roco*

*Published by Blackwell Publishing on behalf of the New York Academy of Sciences
Boston, Massachusetts
2006*

Library of Congress Cataloging-in-Publication Data

Progress in convergence : technologies for human wellbeing / edited
by William Sims Bainbridge and Mihail C. Roco.
  p. cm.
  Includes bibliographical references.
  ISBN-13: 978-1-57331-665-1 (alk. paper)
  ISBN-10: 1-57331-665-2 (alk. paper)
  1. Biotechnology–Social aspects. 2. Technology–Social aspects.
3. Technological innovations. 4. Medical technology.
5. Interdisciplinary research. I. Bainbridge, William Sims. II. Roco,
Mihail C.

  TP248.23.P76 2007
  600–dc22

                                          2006037033

The *Annals of the New York Academy of Sciences* (ISSN: 0077-8923 [print]; ISSN: 1749-6632 [online]) is published 28 times a year on behalf of the New York Academy of Sciences by Blackwell Publishing, with offices located at 350 Main Street, Malden, Massachusetts 02148 USA, PO Box 1354, Garsington Road, Oxford OX4 2DQ UK, and PO Box 378 Carlton South, 3053 Victoria Australia.

Information for subscribers: Subscription prices for 2006 are: Premium Institutional: $3850.00 (US) and £2139.00 (Europe and Rest of World).
Customers in the UK should add VAT at 5%. Customers in the EU should also add VAT at 5% or provide a VAT registration number or evidence of entitlement to exemption. Customers in Canada should add 7% GST or provide evidence of entitlement to exemption. The Premium Institutional price also includes online access to full-text articles from 1997 to present, where available. For other pricing options or more information about online access to Blackwell Publishing journals, including access information and terms and conditions, please visit www.blackwellpublishing.com/nyas.

Membership information: Members may order copies of the *Annals* volumes directly from the Academy by visiting www.nyas.org/annals, emailing membership@nyas.org, faxing 212-298-3650, or calling 800-843-6927 (US only), or +1 212-298-8640 (International). For more information on becoming a member of the New York Academy of Sciences, please visit www.nyas.org/membership.

Journal Customer Services: For ordering information, claims, and any inquiry concerning your institutional subscription, please contact your nearest office:
UK: Email: customerservices@blackwellpublishing.com; Tel: +44 (0) 1865 778315; Fax +44 (0) 1865 471775
US: Email: customerservices@blackwellpublishing.com; Tel: +1 781 388 8599 or 1 800 835 6770 (Toll free in the USA); Fax: +1 781 388 8232
Asia: Email: customerservices@blackwellpublishing.com; Tel: +65 6511 8000; Fax: +61 3 8359 1120
Members: Claims and inquiries on member orders should be directed to the Academy at email: membership@nyas.org or Tel: +1 212 838 0230 (International) or 800-843-6927 (US only).

Printed in the USA.
Printed on acid-free paper.

Mailing: The *Annals of the New York Academy of Sciences* are mailed Standard Rate. **Postmaster:** Send all address changes to *Annals of the New York Academy of Sciences*, Blackwell Publishing, Inc., Journals Subscription Department, 350 Main Street, Malden, MA 01248-5020. Mailing to rest of world by DHL Smart and Global Mail.

Annals are available to subscribers online at the New York Academy of Sciences and also at Blackwell Synergy. Visit www.annalsnyas.org or www.blackwell-synergy.com to search the articles and register for table of contents e-mail alerts. Access to full text and PDF downloads of *Annals* articles are available to nonmembers and subscribers on a pay-per-view basis at www.annalsnyas.org.

The paper used in this publication meets the minimum requirements of the National Standard for Information Sciences Permanence of Paper for Printed Library Materials, ANSI Z39.48-1984.

ISSN: 0077-8923 (print); 1749-6632 (online)
ISBN-10: 1-57331-665-2 (paper); ISBN-13: 978-1-57331-665-1 (paper)

A catalogue record for this title is available from the British Library.

Digitization of the *Annals of the New York Academy of Sciences*

An agreement has recently been reached between Blackwell Publishing and the New York Academy of Sciences to digitize the entire run of the *Annals of the New York Academy of Sciences* back to volume one.

The back files, which have been defined as all of those issues published before 1997, will be sold to libraries as part of Blackwell Publishing's Legacy Sales Program and hosted on the Blackwell Synergy website.

Copyright of all material will remain with the rights holder. Contributors: Please contact Blackwell Publishing if you do not wish an article or picture from the *Annals of the New York Academy of Sciences* to be included in this digitization project.

ANNALS OF THE NEW YORK ACADEMY OF SCIENCES

Volume 1093
December 2006

PROGRESS IN CONVERGENCE
Technologies for Human Wellbeing

Editors
WILLIAM SIMS BAINBRIDGE AND MIHAIL C. ROCO

This volume is the result of a meeting held on February 24–25, 2005 in Hawaii that has also been augmented and updated by invited papers.

CONTENTS

Part III. Informatics for Convergence

Part IV. Cognitive Enhancement

Part V. Social and Ethical Implications

Part VI. Appendices

Reality of Rapid Convergence

WILLIAM SIMS BAINBRIDGE[a] AND MIHAIL C. ROCO[b]

[a]Division of Information and Intelligent Systems National Science Foundation, Arlington, Virginia 22230, USA

[b]National Science Foundation, ENG, Arlington, Virginia 22230, USA

ABSTRACT: A major series of conferences, workshops, and research projects has established the crucial importance of convergence across all fields of science and technology. Central to this unification at the present time are the NBIC fields: nanotechnology, biotechnology, information technology and new technologies based on cognitive science. This book provides an overview of this crucial phase change in human culture, beginning with four chapters offering an overview, followed by four chapters about nanobioconvergence, two about the ways in which information infrastructure can promote convergence, four chapters on cognitive technologies, and four addressing the social and ethical implications of this profound revolution.

KEYWORDS: nanotechnology; biotechnology; information technology; cognitive science; convergence

BACKGROUND OF CONVERGENCE

Human progress has many dimensions—including economic, cultural, and moral—but, throughout history, technological progress has been a precondition for all other forms of improvement in human welfare. Today, technical progress means not merely "stepping forward," but also "getting in step together" and "being responsible" as previously disparate fields converge and increasingly affect society. On the basis of the unity of nature at the nanoscale, the progressive unification of science promotes the emergence of new boundary-spanning technologies, especially across the NBIC disciplines. There are the rapidly developing domains of nanotechnology, biotechnology, information technology, and new technologies based in cognitive science. This brings technology closer to serving human dimensions. The future welfare of humanity depends upon mastering these emerging technologies, and devoting them to positive applications.

Address for correspondence: William Sims Bainbridge, Division of Information and Intelligent System, National Science Foundation, Arlington, VA 22230. Voice: 703-292-7470.
e-mail: wbainbri@nsf.gov
The views expressed here are those of the authors and do not necessarily represent the views of the National Science Foundation or the United States.

Ann. N.Y. Acad. Sci. 1093: ix–xiv (2006). © 2006 New York Academy of Sciences.
doi: 10.1196/annals.1382.001

The crucial importance of technological convergence became crystal clear at the world's first major conference to consider the societal implications of nanotechnology, held at the National Science Foundation near Washington, D.C., September 28–29, 2000 (Roco and Bainbridge 2001). One scientist or engineer after another reported that nanotechnology could have significant impacts when combined with this or that other science-based technology. The field of nanobiotechnology (or bionanotechnology) drew great attention, as scientists discussed the machine-like qualities of the moving structures inside the living cell, or applied to biological questions research tools that were originally developed for nanoscience. All were aware that microelectronics was in the process of becoming nanoelectronics, and that computer-operated sensor systems could make good use of nano-enabled chemical and biological detection devices. Thus, nanotechnology seemed more like a Great Enabler, than like an isolated specialization. Similar findings about integration of emerging technologies originated from the fields of information technology (Information Technology Research initiative in U.S., another "Great Enabler"), modern biology (e.g., Biocomplexity initiative at NSF) and cognitive and social sciences (e.g., Human and Social Dynamics initiative at NSF).

Energized by such insights, the National Science Foundation and U.S. Department of Commerce organized a conference on Converging Technologies, held December 3–4, 2001, at NSF to focus this time on the interfaces between converging and emerging technologies and their system. Key goals were improving individual and collective outcomes, bringing technology closer to serve people, and involving social scientists and philosophers closer with physical scientists and engineers from the beginning of technology projects. The NSF–DOC report was first reviewed by leading scientists in the field and then made available over the World Wide Web for public comments from all over the world, and then published (Roco and Bainbridge 2003).

A second Converging Technologies conference (focused on NBIC), was held in Los Angeles, February 5–7, 2003, and the resulting book was published by the New York Academy of Sciences in the same series as the present volume (Roco and Montemagno 2004). The third conference was in New York, February 25–27, 2004 (Bainbridge and Roco 2006).

The second conference on societal implications of nanoscience and nanotechnology gave convergence and social dimensions increased prominence (Roco and Bainbridge 2006).

The organizers of all of these conferences and book-length reports sought a wide range of expert contributors and analytical viewpoints. From the very beginning, they recognized that diversity of perspective would be advantageous for convergence. The goal is not to create and enforce some kind of new "orthodoxy" in science and engineering, but, rather, to nurture all the legitimate connections between fields, to integrate creative researchers and designers into the broader intellectual community, and to encourage philosophers and social scientists to explore the societal implications of new developments across the entire map of technology.

No one can impose a uniform theory on science or set of goals on engineering, and it would be a waste of time to try. However, all across these vast realms, a phase change seems to have begun. Previously separate fields are coming together, employing similar transforming tools and applying comparable concepts. The implications for human well-being could hardly be greater. Multidisciplinary discovery and invention, especially based in convergence at the nanoscale, offers the primary opportunities for technology to continue to promote economic growth. Technical dimensions are prominent in the solutions to all the world's social and environmental problems. A unified scientific understanding of nature, of which the human species is an integral part, can be the basis for a universal world culture that supports mutually beneficial trade, understanding, and peace.

OUTLINE OF THIS BOOK

The first step in developing this book was a conference, *Converging Technologies for Improving Human Performance*, held February 24–25, 2005, at the Keauhou Bay Sheraton near Kailua-Kona, Hawaii. As in previous meetings, improving human performance was focused on every day activities, such as learning, working, health care, and aging while maintaining working capabilities and quality of life. However, this is not simply a volume of conference proceedings. Half of the articles were contributed by conference participants, but the other half were recruited afterward to expand the scope and fill in gaps in the coverage. The aim literally has been to chart the recent progress in convergence and identify opportunities for future progress. The authors report some of the latest developments in the United States, Europe, and Japan, not only in the technical methods for convergence, but also the emerging applications of the technology and their likely social or ethical implications.

Four articles provide an overall perspective on convergence, beginning with an overview of converging technologies governance based on Mihail Roco's experience with the National Nanotechnology Initiative, the International Risk Governance Council, and the early NBIC efforts. Convergence integrated from the nanoscale has synergistic effects all across science and technology, which means not only that the effects are likely to be very significant but also that they will be very difficult to predict. Therefore, the traditional approach of establishing fixed government regulations and enforcing them rigidly will not succeed in achieving the greatest net benefit for humanity, facilitating innovations that advance human welfare while protecting societal values. Instead, a new approach is needed, employing dynamic governance in the processes that determine how power is exercised, how important decisions are made, and how stakeholders are involved. Roco's article lays out the principles of dynamic governance, then identifies its four key roles: transformational, responsible, inclusive, and visionary.

William Bainbridge urges scientists to identify concepts (such as conservation, indecision, configuration, interaction, variation, evolution, information, and cognition) that can unite previously separate fields, and he illustrates the value of intellectual convergence in the work of such theorists as John Conway, Harrison White, George Kingsley Zipf, and John Archibald Wheeler. Ullica Segerstrale analyzes the intellectual career of highly influential convergenist Edward O. Wilson, from his early days helping to create sociobiology to his more recent work on general scientific consilience, with a special focus on the conflict Wilson sees between religion and fundamental scientific principles like evolution by natural selection. Robert Balmer reports the very successful convergence program established at Union College, based on a new paradigm that integrates cutting-edge science and technology with the arts and humanities, organized following a vision of how to transform academia inspired by a set of 10 guiding principles proposed by Joseph Zolner.

The next four articles emphasize nanobioconvergence, often with the aid of information technology. Osamu Takai explains how he and his colleagues create new biomimetic materials, drawing lessons from nature to manufacture artificial materials with precisely engineered characteristics, for example remarkable water-repellant surfaces inspired by the microscopic roughness of the lotus leaf that allows this living wonder to repel water. Fabio Pichierri describes an approach to nanoelectronics, inspired by biological signal transduction at the level of protein molecules, capable of both amplifying a signal and integrating two or more signals. Michael Hochella, writes about how geoscience and environmental science are currently drawing upon nanoscience, molecular biology, and information technologies to develop what might be called "nanogeoscience." Jia Ming Chen and Chih-Ming Ho outline many ways in which nanoscale convergence is developing new research tools for biological science and medicine, including optical nanoscopes (employing a superlens concept for improved resolution), precise manipulation of biological particles in fluids, and realtime monitoring of a single living cell.

The ways that informatics can promote convergence are the focus of the next two articles. Bruce Herr, Weixia Huang, Shashikant Penumarthy, and Katy Börner present their work developing two kinds of information technology that facilitate collaboration across fields, information visualization cyberinfrastructure and the network workbench, which are based on an open source specification integrating data sets, algorithms, tools, and computing resources. Gavin Clarkson and David DeKorte approach the issue of how to facilitate collaboration from a very different direction, considering how to use information technology to identity and overcome "patent thickets," dense webs of intellectual property rights that prevent companies from developing products for fear of violating laws against monopolistic patent pooling.

The cognitive sciences take center stage in the next four articles that examine human progress. Anders Sandberg and Nick Bostrom offer a comprehensive review of the near-term possibilities for cognitive enhancements that would amplify the abilities of the mind, emphasizing bio-info-cogno convergences. Rana el Kaliouby, Rosalind Picard and Simon Baron-Cohen report on preliminary research to develop assistive information technology that would help individuals with autism spectrum disorder, an example of the affective computing their laboratory has been developing to give computers and robots the ability to respond appropriately to human emotions. Lin Liao, Donald J. Patterson, Dieter Fox, and Henry Kautz demonstrate the potential of portable information technologies to assist cognitively disabled people who have difficulty finding their way around a city, with a system that not only knows where it is and how to get to a specified destination, but also learns the habits and haunts of its individual user. Francis Quek and David McNeill explore the importance of spatial imagery for mathematics learning, in order to develop technologies to help blind children master this crucial subject.

The final four articles address the social and ethical implications of converging technologies from a range of perspectives. Nigel de S. Cameron draws upon analogies with biotechnology to argue that the development of nanotechnology must be guided by a respect for the human condition and human nature, if it is to achieve both public acceptance and maximum benefit for people. With competitive sports as his motivating example, Andy Miah offers a critique of the legislative structures governing human enhancement, and a framework for understanding the social effects of technology. From the perspective of analytical philosophy, Julian Savulescu considers competing theories of the justice of enhancement in the light of alternative definitions of it, fairness-based objections to it, and the natural distribution of capabilities in human populations. Alan Ziegler approaches Converging Technologies from the perspective of a legal scholar, noting that citizens tend to reject economic cost–benefit analyses of risks to human health, and seeks the correct balance between the precautionary principle and innovating despite uncertainties.

The book concludes with a pair of appendices. The first is a glossary of words that are often used in multidisciplinary discussions of convergence, but that may be unfamiliar to readers who had not been involved in the particular areas. The second is an annotated bibliography describing 25 books that would constitute the core shelf of a convergence library. The book you hold in your hands would be the 26th, and it naturally serves as both preface and summation.

CONCLUSION

Convergence and integration of emerging technologies are already happening in industry, research laboratories, and classrooms. At the National Science Foundation, for illustration, earlier awards were made from program solicitations, such as those focused on integration of science and engineering from the nanoscale and on improving learning beginning with brain research, and currently most contributions are in the "core" programs with unsolicited proposals. Industry is changing organization and businesses to adapt to the implications of converging technologies. This volume presents several new dimensions of this rapid convergence and demonstrates how it can serve human needs and aspirations.

REFERENCES

BAINBRIDGE, W.S. and M.C. ROCO, eds. 2006. *Managing Nano-Bio-Info-Cogno Innovations: Converging Technologies in Society*. Berlin: Springer.

ROCO, M.C. and W.S. BAINBRIDGE, eds. 2001. *Societal Implications of Nanoscience and Nanotechnology*. Dordrecht, Netherlands: Kluwer.

ROCO, M.C. and W.S. BAINBRIDGE, eds. 2003. *Converging Technologies for Improving Human Performance*. Dordrecht, Netherlands: Kluwer.

ROCO, M.C. and W.S. BAINBRIDGE, eds. 2006. *Nanotechnology: Societal Implications*. 2 volumes. Berlin: Springer.

ROCO, M.C. and C.D. MONTEMAGNO eds. 2004. *The Coevolution of Human Potential and Converging Technologies*. New York: New York Academy of Sciences.

Progress in Governance of Converging Technologies Integrated from the Nanoscale

MIHAIL C. ROCO

National Science Foundation, Arlington, Virginia 22230, USA

ABSTRACT: It is expected that convergence of nanotechnology, modern biology, the digital revolution, and cognitive sciences will bring about tremendous improvements in transformative tools, generate new products and services, enable human personal abilities and social achievements, and in time reshape societal relationships. This article focuses on the progress made in governance of such converging, emerging technologies that are integrated with more traditional technologies. The proposed framework for governance calls for several key functions: supporting the transformative impact; advancing responsible development that includes health, safety, and ethical concerns; encouraging national and global partnerships; and commitment to long-term planning with effects on human development. Principles of good governance include participation of all those involved or affected by the new technologies, transparency, participant responsibility, and effective strategic planning. Introduction and management of converging technologies must be done with respect for immediate concerns (such as information technology privacy, access to medical advancements, and addressing toxicity of new nanomaterials) and longer-term concerns (such as human development and concern for human integrity, dignity, and welfare). Four levels of governance of converging technologies have been identified: (*a*) adapting existing regulations and organizations; (*b*) establishing new programs, regulations, and organizations specifically to handle converging technologies; (*c*) national policies and institutional capacity building; and (*d*) international agreements and partnerships.

KEYWORDS: nanotechnology; biotechnology; information technology; cognition; societal implications; EHS; ELSI; NBIC; education; risk governance

Address for correspondence: Mihail C. Roco, The National Science Foundation, 4201 Wilson Boulevard, Rm. 505 N, Arlington, VA 22230. Voice: 703-292-8301; fax: 703-292-9013.
e-mail: mroco@nsf.gov

Ann. N.Y. Acad. Sci. 1093: 1–23 (2006). © 2006 New York Academy of Sciences.
doi: 10.1196/annals.1382.002

GOVERNANCE OF CONVERGING TECHNOLOGIES

Converging Technologies refers to a combination of new and more traditional technologies. *Converging, emerging technologies* refers to the synergistic combination of nanotechnology, biotechnology, information technology, and cognitive sciences (NBIC), each of which is currently progressing at a rapid rate, experiencing qualitative advancements, and interacting with the more established fields, such as mathematics and environmental technologies (Roco and Bainbridge 2003). A main reason for advancing NBIC has been inclusion of cognitive and social sciences in the mainstream of emerging technologies, and identifying better ways for serving people's needs through technological advancements. Key requirements were respecting the human condition and a long-term planning approach based on factual information, scientific principles, and full awareness of societal issues. The original converging technologies report recommended that "ethical, legal, moral, economic, environmental, workforce development, and other societal implications, must be addressed from the beginning, including scientists and engineers, social scientists, and a broad coalition of professional and civic organizations" (Roco and Bainbridge 2003, p. xii). It is better to address early the long-term issues related to revolutionary implications of converging technologies in a responsible government-sponsored framework, than trying to adjust developments later. Main challenges are: understanding the complex interactions within and outside of the technology domain, evaluating its evolution, and adopting measures to shape the future developments. Research on converging technologies in the United States, Canada, and several countries in Asia and Europe have been reported for a variety of applications (Roco and Montemagno 2004). Management of converging technologies recently has been reviewed (Bainbridge and Roco 2006).

Reaching at the building blocks of matter for all manmade and living systems, with the broad nanotechnology platform, makes the transforming tools more powerful and the unintended consequences more important than for other technologies. Science based on the unified concepts of matter at the nanoscale provides a new foundation for knowledge creation, innovation, and technology integration. The integration of nanotechnology with biotechnology, information technology, and cognitive sciences increases the transforming power and potential risks even further. Despite the progress and promises for significant benefits, integration of converging technologies is not well understood. Now we are at earlier stages of development, and most benefits and risks are functions of respective applications. A main, long-term concern is a possible instability in development, for several reasons. First, the transforming tools may create perturbations that could be difficult to control after the fact. Second, some perturbations might be created that affect the very foundations of life. Third, the systems enabled with converging technologies are complex and may exhibit emergent behavior. This underlines the need for an anticipatory and adaptive governance approach at the national and global levels. An attempt is made here to identify the basic elements of a suitable governance approach for converging technologies. Several fragmented activities already identified would be brought closer together in this framework.

Governance includes the processes, conventions, and institutions that determine:

- how power is exercised in view of managing resources and interests;
- how important decisions are made and conflicts resolved; and
- how various stakeholders are accorded participation in these processes.

In the most common current usage of the term, "governance" implies a move away from the previous *government* approach (a top-down legislative approach that attempts to regulate the behavior of people and institutions in quite detailed and compartmentalized ways) to *governance* (which attempts to set the parameters of the system within which people and institutions behave so that self-regulation or the ecosystem achieves the desired outcomes), or put more simply, the replacement of traditional "powers over" with contextual "powers to." Integration needs to be done using a system approach and involving all stakeholders related to different converging technologies. In such a system, permeable and flexible system boundaries facilitate communication and support the achievement of higher-level goals, while the government role will continue in this context. These assumptions underline the switch from *government* alone to *governance* in debates about the modernization of policy systems, implying a transition from constraining to enabling types of policy or regulation (i.e., from "sticks" to "carrots," Lyall and Tait 2005).

Risk governance includes the totality of actors, rules, conventions, processes, and mechanisms concerned with how relevant risk information is collected, analyzed, and communicated and management decisions are taken (Renn and Roco 2006). Risk governance encompasses all the risk-relevant decisions and actions. It is of particular importance in situations where the nature of the risk requires collaboration and coordination between various stakeholders (no single decision-making authority available) related to the assembly of converging technologies. Risk governance does not rely upon rigid adherence to a set of strict rules, but calls for the consideration of contextual factors, such as: (*a*) institutional arrangements (e.g., the regulatory and legal framework and coordination mechanisms, such as markets, incentives, or self-imposed norms); and (*b*) sociopolitical culture and perceptions.

Governance and risk governance are important concepts for assessing and managing the implications of converging technologies. On the one hand, converging technologies promises revolutionary products and societal outcomes. On the other hand, there is genuine concern about the disruptive potential of interventions by the converging technologies, and especially by NBIC. These concerns about converging technologies resonate with long-standing social science analysis of technology running "out of control" (Winner 1977). Along with the relatively low levels of information about converging technologies available, and the low public trust in industry and government, these factors are leading to an increasing risk of poor public perception, especially in the preassessment phase of the possible implications. A particular concern is that insufficient formal and informal education will result in the misuse or inefficient application of converging technologies.

Technological convergence has several characteristics and long-term outcomes, which underline its potential and at the same time provides new issues for global risk governance:

- Can be described by complexity of large dynamic systems with many variables;
- Leads to powerful new tools;
- Offers a broad technology platform (for industry, biomedicine, communication, knowledge creation, environment, and an almost indefinite array of potential applications);
- Has broadened and changed manufacturing capabilities with the promise of more efficient outcomes;
- Reverses the trend of specialization of scientific disciplines, providing unifying concepts for research and education, and leading to system integration in engineering and technology;
- Has become one of the main drivers for technological and economic change, as well as industrial competition;
- Has influenced the speed and scope of research and development (R&D) that exceeds for now the capacity of regulators to assess human, environmental, and societal implications; and
- The key decision processes from knowledge to products to their implications to risk governance policies follow an open loop.

FIGURE 1 shows the decision processes in the open loop approach, in which each cycle generates new classes of products that determine different societal implications. This loop is similar to that of nanotechnology (Renn and Roco 2006) and is applicable to converging technologies. The first focus of convergence should be on benefits to individuals and their societal environment. Good indicators of success are the quality of life, health, safety, and how personalized and democratic is the distribution of benefits. An emphasis must be given to "evidence-based," global-view, and result-oriented "pragmatic" governance (Pielke 2002).

Core governance processes and actors involved or affected by converging technologies are shown in FIGURE 2. The integration process and collective effects of converging technologies bring particularities as compared to any single technology. We have identified several core governance strategies: commitment to a long-term view, transformative approaches, and inclusiveness with both the participants and those affected, integration of converging technolo-

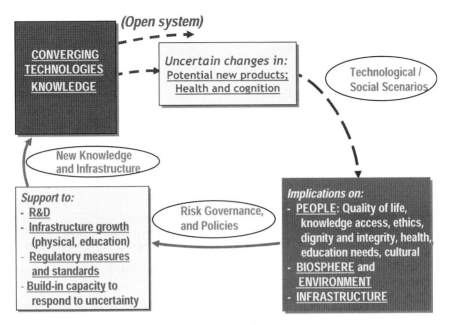

FIGURE 1. Governance of converging technologies.

gies, cross-converging technologies education, addressing societal dimensions, and earlier adopting of risk governance. Governance must deal with societal complexity, address multi-stakeholders, and use methodologies recognized globally for risk assessment and management.

The risk factors can be grouped into four categories, according to their sources:

- Technological (such as wireless communications, hybrid nanobiodevices, engineered and byproduct nanoparticles);
- Environmental (such as new viruses and bacteria, and sand storm);
- Societal (such as management and communication, and emotional response); and
- Dynamic evolution and interactions in the societal system (including reaction of interdependent networks, and government's corrective actions through norms and regulations).

Adaptive and corrective measures on the societal system are needed for risk governance of converging technologies. One must incorporate corrective holistic response into the complex societal system in addition to the linear, cause-and-effect approach currently used. The corrective actions need to have time scales comparable to the corresponding timescales of the disruptive events, and when possible be anticipatory (Roco 2005). Special focus must be on the interfaces between regulations, institutions, and risk communication where there is no clear jurisdiction or responsibilities overlap.

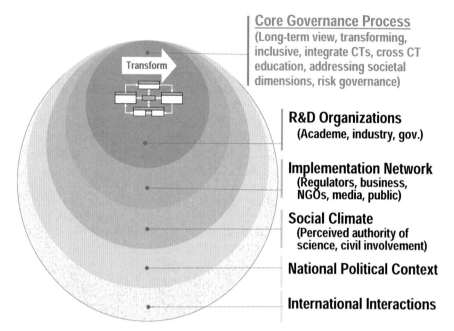

Core Governance Process
(Long-term view, transforming, inclusive, integrate CTs, cross CT education, addressing societal dimensions, risk governance)

Transform

R&D Organizations
(Academe, industry, gov.)

Implementation Network
(Regulators, business, NGOs, media, public)

Social Climate
(Perceived authority of science, civil involvement)

National Political Context

International Interactions

FIGURE 2. Overview of converging technologies governance.

The International Risk Governance Council provides an independent framework for identification, assessment, and mitigation of risk in general and as applied to nanotechnology (IRGC 2006a). The basic approach identifies two perception frames: one for the first generation of products (passive nanostructures) and another for future generations (active nanostructures and nanosystems) where the products with higher complexity have broader societal implications. The Converging Technologies Bar Association offers an integrative approach in addressing the legal aspects of introducing emerging technologies based on nanoscale science and engineering.[a]

An attempt to categorize the risk governance activities is presented in FIGURE 3 (with illustrations for nanotechnology). Issues related to system components typically can be addressed by adapting existing regulations and organizations. Issues related to changes in a technological system can be best addressed by new R&D programs, setting new regulations, and establishing new, suitable organizations. At the national level, typical actions are policies and legislative actions. At the international level, typical actions are international agreements, collaborative projects, and multi-stakeholder partnerships.

Governance has four key roles: *transformational*, *responsible*, *inclusive*, and *visionary development*. These components are discussed below, and several examples are provided in TABLE 1.

---

[a] www.convergingtechnologies.org

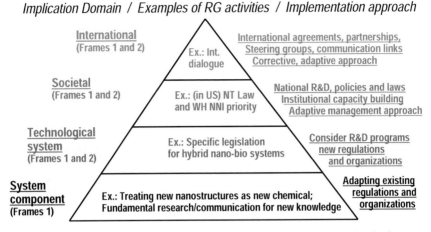

FIGURE 3. Multilevel structure of risk governance for converging technologies.

TRANSFORMATIONAL GOVERNANCE

The transformative function of governance is realized through four main mechanisms: (1) investment policies, (2) science and technology and business policies, (3) education and workforce training, and (4) supporting the needed transformational tools.

Investment Policies

The investment policies for converging technologies are generally fragmented, in a similar manner to how nanotechnology policies were before 2000. One needs to consider a system approach for technology and society, within the social and national framework for the respective economy. Investments must have reasonable return, the benefit-to-risk ratio must be justifiable and respect societal concerns. Key goals of investment policies are increasing productivity, quality of life, and equity. Several examples of investment policies are given below.

It is essential to establish a *broad and long-term R&D and infrastructure framework* for accelerated technoeconomical development using converging technologies. One must ensure the availability and synergism of investigative tools, knowledge creation, and production means supporting various converging technologies components. For example, large companies, or groups of smaller companies, would need to develop laboratories and facilities with multidisciplinary expertise to efficiently engineer and develop new products. The integration of converging technologies needs to be done using system analysis and design. Effective development and implementation of emerging

TABLE 1. Examples of recent developments in converging technologies (CT) governance

CT governance aspect	Example 1	Example 2	Example 3
(i) Investment policies	Support CT industries with high economic return and societal relevance	Support availability of natural resources (water, energy, food, clean environment)	Support priorities on human health and developing CT R&D infrastructure
(ii) Science, technology, and business policies	Support discoveries through competitive peer-reviewed, multidisciplinary programs	Support innovation in converging technologies (American Competitiveness Act, 2006)	Support CT integration; New organizational and business models (Radnor and Strauss 2003)
(iii) Education and training	Creating the pipeline for CT workers through earlier education (ex. NSF's Nanotechnology Center for Learning and Teaching)	Extending CT informal education to museums and internet (ex: NSF's Nanoscale Informal Science and Engineering network)	New university and community college curricula supporting CT
(iv) Economical transformation tools	Create integrative CT technology platforms	CT research clusters for various applications	Reducing the delay between inventions, technological development, and societal response
(v) EHS implications	U.S. Nanotechnology R&D Act of Dec 2003, including EHS policies	Identify research needs by diverse stakeholders	Develop new systemic knowledge for a life-cycle approach of CT products
(vi) ELSI+	Ethics of CT (Roco and Bainbridge 2001; NGOs, UNESCO reports 2006a)	Equitable benefits for developing countries (ETC 2005)	Nanotechnology for the poor (Meridian project 2006)
(vii) Methods for risk governance	Risk analysis including the social context	Multilevel risk governance	Including the international dimension (IRGC white paper 2006a)
(viii) Communication	Increase interactions between experts, users, and public at large	Public participation in the legislative process for CT funding	Coordination of regulatory agencies and research organizations
(ix) National capacity	Support interagency partnerships	Address societal infrastructure deficits for dealing with CT	Address social issues, such as workforce displacement
(x) Global capacity	International Dialogues on Responsible Nanotechnology (2004)	International Risk Governance Council reports	OECD working groups on emerging technologies
(xi) Long-term, global view	Strategic plans in U.S. for nanotechnology, information technology, health research, and neurosciences	Long-term effect of technology on human development (UNESCO reports)	Studies on changing societal interactions because of CT
(xii) Support human development	Research on brain and nervous system evolution	Research connecting brain functions, education, and mind	Provide feedback based on public and expert surveys

technologies may require broader foundations and longer-term commitments than classical technologies.

Converging technologies must serve with priority key sectors of the economy acting as *beneficiaries to the general population.* Examples are: supporting availability of natural resources (water, energy, food, materials, sustainable environment) driven by general public benefit (and not market focused); advance nanomanufacturing as a mean for social progress and welfare; and advance medical improvements for public health and benefit of all citizens.

Convergence can create *intelligent systems and environments* as a means for improving the quality of life and access of facilities to people with special needs. For example, with the use of wireless technology and nanoscale sensors, one may guide blind people and avoid car accidents.

New structures and methods of coordination are required for converging technologies, including those that promote participation of all those affecting and affected by the new technologies, new expertise and education domains, and new ways to structure the investments.

New indicators besides the Gross Domestic Product (GDP) must be used, including social benefits, societal accumulations, human development including education level, and security situation. We must identify *new evaluation criteria* to include the NBIC contribution in the national infrastructure. The criteria of progress must include infrastructure accumulations, increments in citizen education and training, improved working capabilities, and quality of life. Structuring the investments in new areas of NBIC will be a driver and enabler for the *knowledge society.*

The rates of investment in converging, emerging technologies are generally increasing faster than the GDP, and resources need to be planned accordingly for this purpose. For example, the worldwide GDP rate of increase was about 3.9% in 2005 and 2006, while the rate of increase for semiconductors was 8% and it is expected to be about 10% because of the increased semiconductor contents in new products (IC Insights 2006).

Science and Technology and Business Policies

Science and technology (S&T) and business policies play an important role in emerging technologies. Science is reaching closer to technological applications in emerging fields, and has an increased impact. A good example is the need to *support converging technologies integration* though long-term strategic planning, and systematically address the R&D gaps. Establishing coordinating groups at the national level, involving academia, industry, government, and civil organizations may play an important role. In the United States, the National Science Foundation (NSF), the National Aeronautics and Space Administration (NASA), the Environmental Protection Agency (EPA), the Department of Defense (DOD), the National Institutes of Health (NIH), the National Institute of Standards and Technology (NIST), and the Department of Energy (DOE) have R&D projects in the area of converging technologies. These projects are at the confluence of two or more NBIC domains, such as developing neuromorphic engineering, improving everyday human performance, "learning how to learn," and preparing for societal implications of converging technologies.

Encouraging discovery by competitive, peer-reviewed programs at the confluence of disciplines and areas of application in converging technologies is an effective approach. For example, the confluence of the research initiatives on Information Technology Research, the National Nanotechnology Initiative, Biocomplexity, the Human Genome Project, and social and behavioral sciences have stimulated innovative research. In United States, the American Competitiveness Act encourages innovation in emerging technologies. Other national programs for stimulating innovation have been adopted or are considered in EU, Japan, China, and other countries in 2006.

States and local organizations can contribute with specific actions to reach national goals. For instance, for nanotechnology, 19 U.S. states had enacted legislation on nanotechnology by January 2006 in support of NNI: either allocated funding directly (e.g., Illinois, California, New York, and Oregon), provided tax incentives (e.g., Arkansas and Michigan), created groups or boards to oversee the promotion of nanotechnology (12 states including Connecticut and Virginia), or implemented other measures to encourage interest in nanotechnology.

The different terminologies, methodologies, standards, and cultures of the various disciplines and applications involved in converging technologies constitute a barrier limiting rapid discovery, exchange, and assimilation of data and knowledge. Good governance should *lower those barriers* in science and technology communication by sponsored R&D studies, development of common databases and dictionaries, common measuring facilities, and metrology.

Support for developing and deploying *new business models* should aim at increasing productivity and other outcomes in the new context of accelerated global collaboration and competition. For example, one may consider, as suitable, transition from company centric to converging technologies network focused businesses, manage an ecosystem of diverse technologies businesses, create large databases for common use, develop collaborative capacity, and support business innovation networks. Spohrer and Engelbart (2004) show an increased connectivity between science and business for emerging technologies. Policies must encourage stewardship for the future, because markets cannot account well for the future. A good business model for encouraging innovation and increase productivity is the "open organization," including topics, such as open knowledge in R&D networks, open source for software, and pen communication.

Policies on intellectual property for converging technologies are necessary because of several particularities, including longer time interval before applications, more basic issues (genes, building blocks of matter, neural system, etc.), longer term from discovery to applications, and more powerful societal implications.

Education and Workforce Training

Qualified workers will need to handle new converging technologies knowledge, integrate, and promote innovation. Creating a pipeline through earlier education is essential. For illustration, the Nanoscale Center for Learning and Teaching at the Northwestern University funded by NSF is planned to reach 1 million students in its 5 years of operation. Another example of how informal education can be extended is Nanoscale Informal Science Education, an NSF funded network. Several universities reduced the disciplinary barriers through new curricula supporting converging technologies. Multidisciplinary projects must be supported, such as the NSF-NIH multidisciplinary workforce preparation, and the Science of Learning Centers.[b]

Technology and Economic Transformational Tools

Technological convergence requires the creation and development of integrative science, engineering and technology NBIC platforms, through priorities of infrastructure investments and production incentives. Such platforms are already in development at several companies (such as General Electric) and government laboratories (such as Sandia National Laboratories). Also valuable will be multifunctional research facilities and manufacturing capabilities (converging technologies clusters). New organizational and business models will also be needed, such as those in development through collaboration between the International Research Institute and National Science Foundation (NSF). The efficient introduction and development of converging new technologies will require new organizations and business models, as well as solutions for preparing the economy, such as multifunctional research facilities, integrative technology platforms, and global risk governance. It will be essential to reduce the usual delay between inventions, technological development, and societal response. The risks of science and engineering developments should be evaluated in the general context of potential benefits and pitfalls in the short and long terms. Harmonious introduction of technology should address societal acceptance, dialogue with the public, and research in response to societal needs.

RESPONSIBLE DEVELOPMENT

Societal implications of converging technologies should be judged *using a balanced approach* between the goals (leading to envisioned societal benefits)

---

[b] http://www.nsf.gov/news/news_summ.jsp?cntn_id=100454&org=NSF&from=news

and unexpected consequences (which could be a combination of unexpected benefits and risks). Implications apply in a variety of areas, including technological, economic, environmental, health, and educational, ethical, moral, and philosophical. Responsible development includes respect of life and ethics, support for improving quality of work and quality of life, sustainable development and overall respect to common resources, respect for human dignity, and physical integrity. Right to welfare and access to knowledge must be respected.

The responsible development function of governance implies addressing societal concerns in both the short term and long term. The coevolution of society and converging new technologies is a long-term trend. Several groups call for cultural changes and an international "code of conduct" for scientists, industry, and other stakeholders; however, the terms are not sufficiently well defined for possible implementation. A growing interest is on reducing the gap between developed and developing countries, and seeking how nanotechnology may bring benefits to the underdeveloped regions. In the shorter term, immediate environmental, health, and safety (EHS) issues must be addressed in research, societal studies, regulatory measures, and government policies. The people's needs and concerns should be addressed from various perspectives: knowledge society (intellectual drive), industrial society (help industry and other productive means), and civil society (help civil society goals). The International Risk Governance Council (IRGC 2006a, 2006b; Renn and Rocco 2006; www.irgc.org) is an example of international organizations aiming to address overarching risk assessment and management issues. IRGC goals are to develop an independent methodology framework for risk management and the principles for "good governance" for consideration by the national governments and international organizations.

Public and private accountability for various actions, and in particular for long-term effects, in governance is a main challenge because of limited references, complexity of the societal system, and continuity in job of those accountable.

EHS Issues

The potential benefits are large—but so are the perceived risks to EHS issues, which must be addressed early. Specific areas for assessing and managing potential EHS risks are: (a) instrumentation, metrology, and analytical methods; (b) effects on biological systems and human health; (c) effects on environment; (d) monitoring methods for health and environmental surveillance; and (e) risk assessment and management methods. Assessments must consider the entire life cycle of converging technologies products, including their eventual disposal, rather than just the effects of manufacturing and operating them. Open issues include the challenges of developing nomenclatures, definitions, and regulatory measures. Appraisal of research needs must include perspectives from government (see for illustration NNI 2006), industry (CBAN 2006), non-governmental organizations (NGOs), and civil groups.

Several earlier national governance activities have been established. For example, national level programs in nanotechnology have been created after 2000, notably in the United States (2000); countries in the EU and EC (2003), and Japan (2005). Regulations are based either on products (as in the United States) or processes (as in the EU). The converging, emerging technologies often cross existing jurisdictions and geographical boundaries. A clearer separation between science coupled with evidence-based advice versus political judgment needs to be made when adopting regulations.

International activities have been launched for various emerging technologies. For example, Asia-Pacific Economic Cooperation (APEC 2002; APEC Nanoforum 2006) and the Organization for Economic Cooperation and Development (OECD 2006) have supported studies and organized working groups on nanotechnology. In 2006, OECD established the "Working Party on Manufactured Nanomaterials" in the Environmental Directorate and a "Working Party on Development and Use of Nanotechnology Applications" in the Science, Technology, and Industry Directorate.

Ethical, Legal, and Social Issues

Extended ethical, legal, and social issues (ELSI+) include not only ethical, legal, and other social implications (ELSI), but also policy and security, and education gap issues. The concerns must be answered to the satisfaction of both the public and experts. Without professional ethics, it would not be possible to ensure efficient and harmonious development, cooperate between people and organizations, make the best investment choices, prevent harm to other people, and diminish undesirable socioeconomic implications.

There is a *dilemma of choices* in the complex societal system where converging technologies and social interactions develop. Beyond a few very simple principles, no single set of rules of ethical behavior is universally accepted. Also, policy toward a given technology is not a decision to be made necessarily by scientists using a systematic approach, but by elected leaders, and by civil and many other organizations tasked to make decisions about governance in a complex, evolving society. Should we give priority to societal benefits or individual rights? For example, it would be unethical to limit the development of basic needs of a large cross-section of population for the interest of smaller groups. However, it is unethical to affect others without consent. Democratic principles for equal opportunity, access to information, knowledge, and development are other challenges. Experts, the public, and others need information and must participate in order to make the best choices. Long-term progress cannot be derailed even if the road is not straight. Progress is faster with proper vision and when choices are guided by moral values, transformative goals, collective benefits, and professional ethics.

First, one should identify the moral values. Emerging technologies create imbalances in the first phase of development, and measures should be taken to address such unbalances. A system-oriented approach is needed to effectively address ethical and other social issues (Kushf 2004).

Cultural, ideological, and political influences color the scientific, NGO and government reports. One can observe such influences in the debates on stem cell research, increasing life span research, climate change, and even the original NBIC report itself. While the first report published in 2003 (Roco and Bainbridge 2003) is based on scientific evidence and underlines the need to respect the human condition, democracy, and serving human needs, subsequent reviews either underlined this direction and appreciated the transformative power of NBIC (in several countries in Europe; Japan; Korea; EC directorates), or made connections to the political positions in the respective countries and played down the message of the scientific contents of the NBIC report (one working group in the European Community; Netherlands Department of Justice). ELSI+ should not be used primarily as a "defensive approach" against concerns but as an approach to help innovation and positive outcomes by responsibly applying converging technologies. That report underlined the need for including human dimension and social scientist studies in technology development, as well as the need for anticipatory planning including for technology implications and for "upstream" public engagement discussed later in other reports (Wilston and Willis 2004). Dialogue between science, engineering, medicine, social and humanistic sciences must be reinforced earlier in the introduction of converging technologies in order to have synergistic outcomes and avoid mutual misunderstandings.

Examples of (ELSI+) issues include the need for science and data-based reporting in the public domain and transparency in all phases of the planning and execution. Privacy and confidentiality dominate information and medical-related issues.

Since there are no unique moral norms formally accepted at the global level, the positions taken by various organizations have different flavors. For instance, UNESCO prepared the report *The Ethics and Politics of Nanotechnology* (2006a, 2006b), with a cautionary approach to the development of emerging technologies. In its methodology, before taking potential actions, one first identifies the moral dimensions, then tests the relevancy of potential actions, and then enhances the political feasibility of potential actions. The Center on Nanotechnology in Society (IIT, Chicago) and Center for Responsible Nanotechnology (New York) are two NGOs that look to longer-term implications while others (Environmental Defense) are focused on more immediate concerns. The International Risk Governance Council attempts to address both short- and long-term aspects of governance of global, systemic risks.

A key concern is the equitable distribution of benefits, such as access to computers and Internet and sharing in natural resources (water, energy, food, and clean environment). In dealing with such difficult issues, one needs a neutral, constructive platform where all actors can interact. There is a need to adopt a balanced view, and avoid unjustifiable "utopian dreams and apocalyptic nightmares" (Gordjin 2003). The need of interactions among experts of various disciplines supporting converging technologies and between science and technology, creates a good ethical climate for cooperation. A little-noticed but noteworthy trend is a broadly based shift from mass production to mass personalization and distribution, with effects on more equitable distribution of benefits.

Multi-Stakeholder and Internationally Recognized Methods for Risk Governance

The policies and regulatory frameworks of the various countries have remained fragmented. International calls for addressing global challenges in R&D and for addressing the societal dimensions of emerging technologies at the international level have contributed to the collaborative developments, but have had a relatively limited effect on both converging technologies governance efforts and the harmonization of risk governance methods and structures. Given the opportunities, there is the danger that necessary risk governance precautions will not be taken internationally in the race to gain economic advantage and to grasp the economic benefits. Such an oversight could lead to an international backlash in emerging technologies development and diffusion if, due to lax standards and practice, an incident with negative repercussions on human health or the environment occurs. Given the high potential for social amplification by the media, such an incident could trigger worldwide attention and increase public concern. National regulatory agencies could feel propelled to tighten regulatory rules even if the incident occurred in a different country and would not have been possible or probable in any system with working standards and effective control. This problem is beginning to be recognized. Despite this increase in international interactions and developing knowledge for the safer use of converging technologies, an international accord toward harmonized regulation and standards is still lacking. The risk governance of emerging technologies, including risk policies and regulatory structures, continues to pursue separate paths in various countries. An illustration of progress made in bringing various stakeholders together to pursue coordinated governance methods is the report on nanotechnology prepared by IRGC (2006a), which extends the classical theories, such as of decision making (Hammond *et al.* 1999) to managing an emerging technology field. FIGURE 4 illustrates the steps in the IRGC risk assessment and management framework for nanotechnology. The initial framing of risk is important for public perception and decision makers. Eventual government regulations will be dedicated to various areas of application of converging technologies. In dealing with conflicts in risk management, it is preferable to adopt constructive solutions, such as changes in technology than additional regulations.

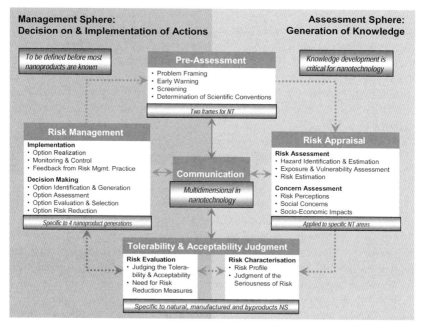

FIGURE 4. Steps in IRGC risk assessment and management framework for nanotechnology.

An example of an open issue is the question of combining formal meetings, such as those held under APEC, OECD, and United Nations aegis, and informal international meetings to set up the main issues in a creative manner with a diversity of stakeholders. For example, the series of conferences called International Conference on Nanotechnology Cooperation and Collaboration (INC) covers the nano-bio-info convergence with involvement from industry, government, and academia. Other issues include the variety of methods adopted by various international organizations and societies, and the priorities given to involving industry in elaborating and implementing legal and voluntary measures.

Communication and Participation

The goal is to include all those creating, using, and being affected by the converging technologies. The complexity of the subject, the different types of agency among and between the different actors, the scope of responsibilities and accountability, and the transboundary nature of converging technologies' many benefits and risks make it necessary that governmental, business, scientific, civil, and communication actors cooperate for the purpose of optimizing the converging technologies governance in all phases of its development. There is a perceived gap between science communities and manufacturers, regulators, the public, NGOs, business community, and the media. The following forms of communication should be included:

- *Documentation:* this serves transparency. In a democratic society it is absolutely essential that the publics not participating in the governance process learn of the reasons why the regulators opted for one policy and against another.
- *Information:* information serves to enlighten the communication partner. Information should be prepared and compiled in such a way that the target group can grasp, realize, and comprehend it, and can integrate its message into their everyday life. The role of media and Internet has increased in the last decade, even if the media focus has been mostly on the short term and news worthy information.
- *Two-way communication or dialogue*: this form of communication is aimed at two-way learning. There must be willingness on both sides to listen to and learn from the other. Mechanisms for improving the dialogue are needed.
- *Participation in risk analyses and management decisions*: in a pluralistic society people expect to be included adequately, directly or indirectly, in decisions that concern their lives. Not all affected people can participate in governance, but it must be ensured that the concerns of the stakeholders will be represented in the decision-making process and that the interests and values of those who will later have to live with the risk effects will be taken up appropriately and integrated into the decision-making process.

Communication between all stakeholders is essential. For example, the public should be informed about the principles and procedures used to test converging technologies products, to assess potential health or ecological impacts, and to monitor their effects. Perhaps large transnational companies should be required internationally to disclose information about health risks, even if some of the information is proprietary and connected to a company's competitive position. There is a need for risk communication training courses and exercises for scientists. Other issues are generating international standards, dictionaries for nomenclature and best practices applicable to both developing and developed countries. Communications should involve experts, regulators, legislators, the public, civil organizations, and media. Creating "open source" databases that are improved by users is an increasingly recommended approach. For example, the "Global Ethics Observatory" (UNESCO 2006b) is concerned with ethics for introduction of new technologies, and includes five databases: who's who, institutions, teaching programs, legislation and policies, and codes of conduct for scientists. Special educational activities are necessary in the context of the worldwide activities to enhance public understanding of sciences and humanities.

INCLUSIVENESS

Stakeholders involved in converging technologies are operating within a dynamic societal system with close dependencies. Rather than monitoring in detail the interactions, it is more efficient to support various parties to play their roles in the overall system, encourage partnerships, and facilitate mechanisms for interactions and conflict solving. Various stakeholders and levels of governance that are an inclusive part of the societal system are schematically presented in FIGURES 2 and 3. Multi-stakeholder partnerships at the national and international levels are sought from planning phase to execution. The current governance measures generally deal with a single event, cause-and-effect, and do not consider long time intervals, secondary effects, and interactions with other events. The governance organizations and measures are fragmented from the area of jurisdiction, type of product or process, intervention levels, and national and international harmonization of assessment and management procedures. An integrated governance approach for anticipatory and corrective measures is, however, necessary for an emerging technology that will have transboundary and global implications.

Building National Capacity to Govern Converging Technologies Development

Coordination is necessary for activities that are too big for a single region. For instance, the National Nanotechnology Initiative was conceived as an *inclusive process* in which various stakeholders would be involved. In 1999, "a grand coalition" of academic, industry, federal government, states, local organizations, and the public was envisioned that would advance nanotechnology and related technologies. The focus was on horizontal interdisciplinary research and education including most of the disciplines and areas of relevance.

Examples of challenges are developing corresponding infrastructure and institutional capacity, education and training, and coordinating all stakeholders in planning and implementation. An increased attention is necessary for involving civil organizations in key governance processes, including decision making.

Building International Capacity, Globalization, and Leveraging

While knowledge and products do not know borders, the policies and regulatory frameworks of the various countries have remained fragmented. Most of the wealth and capabilities to develop NBIC remain within developed countries. Formal and informal approaches are necessary for global governance. A special need is for more aligned global infrastructural initiatives and coordinated risk regulations. Developing countries, such as Brazil, China, and India have gained standing in converging technologies research because of better international communication (Internet, travel, etc.). For example, agreements on nomenclature and standards are in preparation by the International Standard Organization (ISO) and its national members, International American Society for Testing and Materials (ASTM), International Council on Nanotechnology (ICoN), American Institute of Mechanical Engineers (ASME), Institute of Electrical and Electronics Engineers (IEEE), and other organizations, particularly since 2004. Also, while work and dialogue is under way at various national and multinational patent offices, more progress is needed for uniform treatment of patents in converging technologies areas.

VISIONARY FUNCTION

Detecting early signs of change, development of scenarios, and commitment to long-term planning with human development in perspective are necessary for the complex development and integration of emerging technologies.

Long-Term and Global View in Planning, R&D, and Investments

The anticipatory role can be exercised by developing scientific, economic, and social scenarios and creating the capacity to address the identified issues, such as technology trends and economic cycles. For example, the World Economic Forum (WEF 2006) has developed scenarios for global risks in five interrelated areas: technological, economic, geopolitical, environmental, and societal. The identified highest technological risks were related to converging technologies, nanotechnology, electromagnetic fields, and pervasive computing. In another example, in 1999, *Nanotechnology Research Directions* (Roco *et al.* 1999) evaluated possible scenarios in the following decade.

Complementary views must be integrated into a holistic view. The technology view considers science and engineering advances, the innovation process, and potential changes in industry because of converging technologies. The macroeconomic view considers the economic growth and productivity changes. The social view considers interaction of technology with social factors. Scenarios may help identify issues, hypotheses, and possible paths in technology evolution.

National or international exercises for constructing scenarios that appear relevant to the context of the diffusion of converging technologies and the likely social reactions to it should also take place. Academic researchers, developers, potential users, and other important actors should be actively involved in this scenario building exercise in order to ensure the inclusion of an adequate representation of societal forces that ultimately shape the future of converging technologies. Successive changes ("cascade" effect) in a highly interactive and global environment need to be considered.

Support Human Development

This long-term goal is well described in *Human Development Report 2001* issued by the United Nations Development Programme (UNDP 2001). One begins with the effects of converging technologies on changes in the economy, organizations, quality of life, security, and environment. Optimizing human impact must be done in large technology projects. Examples of implications are understanding of aging, increasing life span, and including converging technologies in formal and informal education and preparation of the workforce. Resolving possible ideologically based conflicts generated by technological development need to be considered. In the longer term, one needs to explore evolution of human cognition and cultural trends.

Good governance should cover all four basic functions described above, in a balanced manner. Focusing the attention on one function may raise governance risks:

- Focusing only on the transforming function may raise risks to the human dimension and development.
- Focusing only on responsible development aspects may generate reactive approaches and delay economic benefits.
- Disregarding the inclusiveness function may lead to slower development and even isolationism.
- Focusing on short-term issues (not visionary) is not good for longer-term goals and future generations.

CONCLUDING REMARKS

Governance of converging technologies and particularly of the emerging components (NBIC) is essential for obtaining efficient outcomes in an environment with increased complexity and rapid changes. A main challenge is technology integration. Another challenge is development of exploratory cognitive technologies. There is a need for an adaptive, anticipatory, and corrective approach in the complex societal system in addressing implications for each major R&D program or project. Deliberate and proactive measures should be adopted in order to accelerate the benefits of converging technologies. User and civic group involvement is essential for taking better advantage of the technology and developing a complete picture of its societal implications. A multidisciplinary forum or a coordinating group should be established, involving academia, industry, government, and civil organizations from various countries in order to better address the NBIC scientific, technological, and infrastructure development challenges. Optimizing societal interactions, R&D policies, and risk governance for the converging new technologies can enhance economic competitiveness and democratization.

There are choices in deciding the governance objectives and respective approaches. A distinction must be made between scientific and fact-based or evidence-based governance on one side and ideologically based policies and advocacy on other side.

An important component in governance of converging technologies should be promoting innovation and entrepreneurship. The 2006 U.S. Competitiveness Initiative illustrates policies supporting such governance. A key focus should be on safety by considering the profound transformative implications of converging technologies and the need to avoid damage to third parties. The reaction of several NGOs in recent years is a useful tool for increasing awareness of civil society concerns in this regard.

Two main reasons for developing converging technologies are improving the quality of life and extending the limits of sustainable development. However, there are possible secondary negative implications and perception of risk in both these areas. Communicating with the public about the real and perceived implications of nanotechnology is important. Both benefits and potential risks need to be presented in a balanced manner.

Four levels of governance and risk governance of converging technologies in the dynamic societal system have been identified. Issues related to system components typically can be addressed by adapting existing regulations and organizations. Issues related to a technological system can be best addressed by new R&D programs, setting new regulations, and establishing new, suitable organizations. At the national level, typical actions are policies and legislative actions. At the international level, typical actions are international agreements and collaborative projects.

CONFLICT OF INTEREST STATEMENT

The opinions in this chapter reflect those of the author and do not necessarily represent those of National Science Foundation.

REFERENCES

APEC Nanoforum. 2006. Available at: http://www.cms.itri.org.tw/eng/APECNano Forum/

Asia-Pacific Economic Cooperation (APEC). 2002. *Nanotechnology: The Technology of the 21st Century (2 vols.)*, Bangkok, Thailand (ISBN 974-229-337-6).

BAINBRIDGE, W.S., and M.C. ROCO, eds. 2006. *Managing Nano-Bio-Info-Cogno Innovations: Converging Technologies in Society*. Berlin: Springer.

CBAN (Collaborative Board for Advancing Nanotechnology between NNI and industry). 2006. *Joint NNI-ChI CBAN and SRC CWG5 Nanotechnology EHS Research Needs Recommendations*. Washington, DC, January 20, 2006.

ETC Group. 2005. *The Potential Impact of Nanoscale Technologies on Commodity Markets: Implications for Commodity Dependent Developing Counties*. Ottawa,

Canada: ETC Group. Available at http://www.etcgroup.org/upload/publication/ 45/01/southcentre.commodities.pdf.

GORDJIN, B. 2003. Nanoethics: from utopian dreams and apocalyptic night-mares towards a more balanced view. Paris, France: UNESCO. Available at http://portal.unesco.org/shs/en/ev.php-URL_ID=6603&ampURL_DO=DO_TOPIC&URL_SECTION=201.html.

HAMMOND, J., R. KEENEY, and H. RAIFFA. 1999. *Smart Choices: A Practical Guide to Making Better Decisions.* Cambridge, Massachusetts: Harvard Business School Press.

IC Insights. 2006. Optoelectronics sales will barely top discrete semiconductors in 2006, press release October 26. Available at http://www.icinsights.com/ news/releases/press20061026.html

International Risk Governance Council (IRGC). 2006a. *White Paper on Risk Gover-nance of Nanotechnology.* Geneva: IRGC.

International Risk Governance Council (IRGC). 2006b. Surveys on *Risk Governance of Nanotechnology.* Geneva: IRGC.

KUSHF, G. 2004. Systems theory and the ethics of human enhancement. Pp. 124–149 in M.C. ROCO and C. MONTEMAGNO (eds.), *The Coevolution of Human Potential and Converging Technologies.* New York: New York Academy of Sciences.

LYALL, C., and J. TAIT. 2005. Shifting policy debates and the implications for gov-ernance. Pp. 1–17 in C. LYALL and J. TAIT (eds.), *New Modes of Governance, Developing an Integrated Approach to Science, Technology, Risk and the Envi-ronment.* Aldershot, England: Ashgate Publishing.

Meridian Institute. 2004. *International Dialogue on Responsible Research and Development of Nanotechnology.* Washington, DC: Meridian Institute. Available at http://meridian-nano.org/Final_Report_Responsible_Nanotech_RD_040812.pdf.

Meridian Institute. 2006. *Project on Nanotechnology for Water Filtration and Purifi-cation.* Washington, DC: Meridian Institute.

NNI. 2006. *Environmental, Health, and Safety Research Needs for Engineered Nanoscale Materials.* Arlington, Virginia: National Nanotechnology Coordina-tion Office.

OECD. 2006. *Report of the OECD Workshop on the Safety of Manufactured Nano-materials: Building Co-operation, Co-ordination and Communication.* Paris, France: Organization for Economic Cooperation and Development. Available at www.oecd.org/env/nanosafety.

PIELKE, R.A. 2002. Policy, politics and perspective. *Nature 416,* 367–368.

RADNOR, M., and J.D. STRAUSS. 2003. *Commercializing and Managing the Converging New Technologies.* Evanston, Illinois: Northwestern University.

RENN, O., and M.C. ROCO. 2006. Nanotechnology and the need for risk governance. *Journal of Nanoparticle Research 8*(2), 153–191.

ROCO, M.C. 2005. The emergence and policy implications of converging new tech-nologies integrated from the nanoscale. *Journal of Nanoparticle Research 7*(2-3),129–143.

ROCO, M.C., and W.S. BAINBRIDGE, eds. 2001. *Societal Implications of Nanoscience and Nanotechnology.* Dordrecht, Netherlands: Kluwer.

ROCO, M.C., and W.S. BAINBRIDGE, eds. 2003. *Converging Technologies for Improving Human Performance.* Dordrecht, Netherlands: Kluwer.

ROCO, M.C., and W.S. BAINBRIDGE, eds. 2006. *Nanotechnology: Societal Implications.* 2 volumes. Berlin: Springer.

ROCO, M.C., and C.D. MONTEMAGNO, eds. 2004. *The Coevolution of Human Potential and Converging Technologies*. New York: New York Academy of Sciences.

ROCO, M.C., S. WILLIAMS, and P. ALIVISATOS. 1999. *Nanotechnology Research Directions*. Dordrecht, Netherlands: Kluwer.

SPOHRER, J.C., and D.C. ENGELBART. 2004. Converging technologies: science and business perspectives. Pp. 50–82 in M.C. ROCO and C.D. MONTEMAGNO (eds.), *The Coevolution of Human Potential and Converging Technologies*. New York: New York Academy of Sciences.

United Nations Development Programme (UNDP). 2001. *Human Development Report*. New York: Oxford University Press.

UNESCO. 2006a. The ethics and politics of nanotechnology. Paris, France: UNESCO. Available at http://unesdoc.unesco.org/images/0014/001459/145951e.pdf.

UNESCO. 2006b. Global Ethics Observatory. Paris, France: UNESCO. Available at www.unesco.org/shs/ethics/geobs.

WILSTON, J., and R. WILLIS. 2004. See-through science: why public engagement needs to move upstream. London: Demos. Available at www.demos.co.uk.

WINNER, L. 1977. *Autonomous Technology: Technics-out-of-control as a Theme in Political Thought*. Cambridge, Massachusetts: MIT Press.

World Economic Forum. 2006. *Global Risks 2006*. Geneva, Switzerland: WEF. Available at www.weforum.org.

Transformative Concepts in Scientific Convergence

WILLIAM SIMS BAINBRIDGE

National Science Foundation, Arlington, Virginia 22230, USA

ABSTRACT: **This article suggests eight high-level concepts that can promote convergence by identifying analogies across fields of science and engineering.** *Conservation*: **Many properties are conserved, through symmetries, parity laws, and feedback-regulated stabilities in complex adaptive systems.** *Indecision*: **Inconsistency, undecidability, uncertainty, chance, deterministic chaos, and similar concepts are fundamental principles in the dynamics of systems over time.** *Configuration*: **Detailed, dynamic structures of objects determine their properties, notably the unity of nature at the nanoscale.** *Interaction*: **Elements of a system influence each other, generating higher-level dynamics and other emergent phenomena.** *Variation*: **Statistical distributions of properties are caused by the combination of chance and divergent processes of interaction.** *Evolution*: **Marked by drift, natural selection, and a trend toward greater complexity, evolution exploits variation to develop new configurations that compete through interactions.** *Information*: **Scientific laws can be analyzed in terms of information content, and flow, while the doing of any science today relies heavily upon information technology.** *Cognition*: **Mental or computational process is the dynamic aspect of information, fundamental to the human practice of science.**

KEYWORDS: **conservation; indecision; configuration; interaction; variation; evolution; information; cognition**

Many factors are helping to bring scientific fields together, and to lay the basis for new technologies that draw upon multiple scientific disciplines. New tools, from atomic-force microscopes to supercomputers, help scientists in many fields do their research. Every field uses mathematics, and this universal language helps people in different fields communicate with each other. As progress becomes increasingly difficult in one field, researchers and engineers turn to adjacent fields for help. The goal of this article is to offer a set of

The views expressed in this essay do not necessarily represent the views of the National Science Foundation or the United States.

Address for reprints: William Sims Bainbridge, National Science Foundation, Arlington, VA 22230. Voice: 703-292-7470.

e-mail: wbainbri@nsf.gov

Ann. N.Y. Acad. Sci. 1093: 24–45 (2006). © 2006 New York Academy of Sciences.
doi: 10.1196/annals.1382.003

principles, or categories of concepts, which could help promote the kind of analogical, creative thinking that could advance convergence.

The principles are very high-level concepts, and they are not intended to be detailed or rigorous. Rather, each points in the general direction of a set of rigorous models, theories, processes, or formulae. I imagine that these eight could form the tablet on which to write a "theory of everything," or a design for the human future.

1. Conservation
2. Indecision
3. Configuration
4. Interaction
5. Variation
6. Evolution
7. Information
8. Cognition

CONSERVATION

Matter, energy, and possibly many other quantities are conserved: They are neither created nor destroyed, but merely transformed. Without a high degree of conservation, the universe would not persist or be stable enough for intelligent life to evolve. However, all conservation laws have limited scope. Some are only very approximate, such as the stability of crime rates in society, but none-the-less vary only within certain limits.

"Why is there something rather than nothing?" Principles of conservation answer that question by reversing it: "What suppresses chaos sufficiently to permit humans to perceive meaningful phenomena?" Without conservation, the cosmos would be a blooming, buzzing confusion. This is a version of the anthropic theory, holding that some features of the world we perceive are a selection effect (Barrow and Tipler 1986; Bainbridge 1997). Only in a universe that had these features, could complex biological organisms evolve, gain intelligence, invent science, and ask themselves why the universe possesses the features it does. Even in a conducive environment, biological evolution requires hundreds of millions of years, so the basic constituents of physical reality must hold a high degree of stability over that span of time, or there will never be any observers of any kind, let alone cosmologists.

Whatever the merits of these ideas, the primary source of conservation is the stability of natural laws and parameters at the subatomic level, and many higher-level conservation laws can be reduced to conservation in physics. But it is also possible that conservation may emerge spontaneously at higher levels of complexity, through the operation of adaptive systems.

When governments first began collecting social statistics systematically, it became apparent that rates of many kinds of human behavior were rather stable, from one year to the next, although different societies might have different characteristic rates. In an 1864 book whose title might be translated, *The Lawful Regularity of Apparently Voluntary Human Actions Seen from the Standpoint of Statistics*, Adolf Wagner demonstrated the stability of rates of marriage, crime, suicide, results of school exams, and the percentage of letters mailed that carry incorrect addresses.

Arguably, some kind of homeostatic principle operates in society, automatically adjusting rates of some individual behaviors to keep them close to optimum, as part of a self-sustaining complex adaptive system (Davis and Moore 1945; Parsons 1951; Davis 1959). Perhaps the market is responsible; if there are too few doctors, the profession will be able to demand higher pay, and this will attract more talented people to it. Or the political system may do the job; increased crime will cause greater investment in police. Across the sciences, the concept of complex adaptive systems provides one possible explanation for empirical stabilities.

Ecological thinking promotes convergence by connecting a phenomenon in one field to another in a different field. Consider the concept of *carrying capacity*. For example, the human carrying capacity of the Earth is the maximum sustainable number of people who can live on the planet (Cohen 1995). Given constant technology, this number is set by conditions of the nonhuman natural environment, including subjects studied by biologists and geologists. When parts of a system interact, the results may vary chaotically over time, such as the populations of predators and prey, such as foxes and rabbits (Maynard Smith 1982).

Psychologists note that individual people tend to have characteristic *set points* determining how happy they generally are, quite apart from what is happening in their lives. Sudden good or bad fortune will displace mood above or below this set point, but biological homeostasis will return them to their habitual level of happiness (Rowe 2001). This is related to a fundamental assumption we might call the conservation of personality, that individual human beings tend to be highly resistant to change (Wiggins 1996). This connects conservation to memory.

Following the convergence strategy, we can seek conservation principles in fields quite remote from physics and chemistry. The challenge is to discover, explain, and then to exploit all the conservation principles we can find, whenever possible benefiting from past accomplishments in one science for new achievements in another.

INDECISION

Nearly a century ago, my clergyman great-grandfather wrote to his medical–scientist son, "Don't be too dead sure in scientific work. Perhaps you do not need such caution, as you are naturally conservative, but all along the line we have reached the period of uncertainty. Dogmatism must go to the scrap heap, in all the sciences as well as in theology. Do not be ashamed of reasonable agnosticism. A world of knowledge is yet to be approached by: 'I don't know.'"[1]

This was written at the time when Einstein's ideas had just begun to circulate among intellectuals outside physics, but I prefer to consider relativity in the cognition section, below. By indecision I mean undecidability, ambiguity of perception, or inability to predict. Undecidability, inconsistency, and uncertainty are not merely minor factors that inconvenience mathematicians and physicists, but may be a fundamental necessity for existence. If symmetry is a kind of conservation, then symmetry breaking is a kind of indecision. Without some initial inhomogeneity, perhaps generated by quantum effects in the very first moment of the "Big Bang," gravity would not have been able to concentrate matter into galaxies and stars, and estimating that inhomogeneity is a current challenge for astronomers.

If all parameters of existence were always conserved, then there could be no change, no events, and no life. Yes, if the universe were already a diverse collection of objects in motion, conservation alone would allow them to interact in complex ways. But the generation of the universe in the first place, and many kinds of small-scale event throughout time, require unpredictable inputs. In physics, Heisenberg's uncertainty principle is the most familiar example, and Gödel's analysis of inconsistency and incompleteness is a prominent example in mathematics (Heisenberg, 1958; Nagel and Newman, 1958; Van Heijenoort, 1967). Words like indeterminacy and undecidability are relevant here; later we will encounter complementarity, which, however, suggests symmetry and thus conservation.

The nebulous concept of chance has played an important but ambiguous role not only in human life but also in culture. When he decisively crossed the Rubicon, thereby invading Italy, Caesar famously announced, "Alea jacta est," or "The die is cast." The idea that human decisions are made in an aleatoric world is both profound and commonplace. The avant-garde composer, John Cage (1959), contended that aleatoric music, consisting of random noises, comes to sound melodic once one has heard enough of it. According to Swift's *Gulliver's Travels,* the scientists in the Academy of Lagado have built a great frame holding wooden blocks on which the words of their language are written. Assistants spin the blocks, and then scan the random result for meaningful phrases, which they copy into big books, thereby making discoveries in many fields, including philosophy, poetry, politics, law, mathematics, and theology. This is convergence with a vengeance, because the method words equally well for all fields.

I find especially meaningful the story of the monkeys who produced great literature by banging randomly on the keys of typewriters. The best-known fiction story based on the idea, "Inflexible Logic" by Russell Maloney (1940),

---

[1] William Folwell Bainbridge, letter to William Seaman Bainbridge, quoted in Chautauqua lecture, July 26, 1912.

was accidentally issued at the time of my birth; the owner of the monkeys was named Bainbridge, and the chief monkey was named Bill. The metaphor of the monkeys at typewriters is widely used, and is one way of expressing concepts like "learning by trial and error" or "evolution by natural selection from random variation." For example, Ute and Jeanette Hofmann (2002) have used it as an analytical concept to understand the development of Internet.

The striking thing about Maloney's story is that Bill randomly banged out Dickens' novel *Oliver Twist* without a single error, before beginning to produce the sociological works of Vilfredo Pareto in perfect Italian. Gregory Bateson (1972, p. 400) pointed out: "If we find a monkey striking a typewriter apparently at random but in fact writing meaningful prose, we shall look for restraints, either inside the monkey or inside the typewriter... Somewhere there must have been a circuit which could identify error and eliminate it." Bateson's restraints express the fact that indecision without conservation is meaningless, and he writes at length about how such concepts promote the convergence of cognitive and information sciences.

"Inflexible Logic" is not merely a personal anecdote, but an example of something important, the location of the observer in the universe. The approximately 40 Bill Bainbridges in the United States would undoubtedly feel that this story is personally relevant to them, whereas everybody else would see nothing special in it. But if the author had chosen another name, the people who by accident had the same name would feel they had somehow been singled out. Given our nature as human beings, a convergent scientific theory that explained everything about the universe except your personal location in it, would somehow feel less than complete.

CONFIGURATION

The original vision of technological convergence is based on the unity of nature at the nanoscale, where atoms assemble into complex structures. Much of the secret of life inheres in the precise structures of protein molecules.

An excellent example is the way that a configuration concept from semiconductor physics found its way into sociology through the work of Harrison White (1970), who has the distinction of possessing doctorates in both of these fields. Electrons in a semiconductor can become dislodged from their atoms—a phenomenon below the nanoscale in which an electron may temporarily become sufficiently excited to leave the outer (valence) band of electrons in the particular atom. They then may move a few steps away from their original atoms—dynamics on the nanoscale—constituting an electric current. When an electron moves in this way, it leaves behind a "hole" into which another electron may migrate, thereby leaving behind a hole where it had come from. Thus, as negative electrons move in one direction, positive holes travel the other way, and scientists working with semiconductors have found it useful to treat these holes as real objects.

Citing the 1950 book *Electrons and Holes in Semiconductors* by William Shockley, inventor of the transistor, White applied the idea to the movement of people and job openings in formal organizations that have relatively stable bureaucratic structures. For example, when the minister of a large church retires, his vacancy is likely to be filled by someone who held a position in a medium-sized church of the same denomination. This leaves a vacancy that can be filled by a minister moving up from a small congregation. The mathematics of these occupational *vacancy chains* is comparable to the math for the movement of holes in semiconductors, so this convergence between physics and sociology is far more than just a shared metaphor.

White was especially well known for his work with social networks (Moreno 1934; Boorman and White 1976; White *et al.* 1976). From the perspective of computer science, Peter J. Denning (2004, p. 15) believes that network concepts have great potential to facilitate convergence:

> Several fields are collaborating on the development of network theory, mea-
> surement, and mapping: mathematics (graph theory), sociology (networks
> of influence and communication), computing (Internet), and business (orga-
> nizational networks). This convergence has produced useful results for risk
> assessment and reduction in complex infrastructure networks, attacking and
> defending networks, protecting against network connectivity failures, operat-
> ing businesses, spreading epidemics (pathogens as well as computer viruses),
> and spreading innovation.

The density of a social network, usually measured as the fraction of possible social relationship that actually exist, is a key characteristic. But two communities with identical density may have very different configurations. In an open network, social bonds are patterned in a roughly even way, perhaps randomly, outward from any one node to reach any other node in a finite number of steps. In contrast, a closed social network consists of clumps of multiply connected elements, groups that may entirely lack connections with each other.

Book-buying behavior can illustrate the diversity of areas to which network analysis can be applied. Dr. Roco and I recently published separate essays in a collection edited by Lynn E. Foster: *Nanotechnology: Science, Innovation, and Opportunity*. I looked that book up on the online bookseller, Amazon.com, and found that people who bought this book also bought:

Understanding Nanotechnology by the editors of Scientific American

Nanotechnology For Dummies by Richard D. Booker

Nano-Hype: The Truth Behind the Nanotechnology Buzz by David M. Berube

Nanofuture: What's Next For Nanotechnology by J. Storrs Hall

Investing in Nanotechnology: Think Small, Win Big by Jack Uldrich

FIGURE 1 shows Foster's book surrounded by these five, with arrows going from Foster's book to each of the others. Then I looked up each of the five, and found what five books were linked from each of them. Only two linked back to Foster's book, but several linked to each other. Together, this second step in tracing the network added eight books to the diagram:

> *Nanotechnology: A Gentle Introduction to the Next Big Idea* by Mark A. Ratner

> *Nanotechnology: Basic Science and Emerging Technologies* by Mick Wilson

> *Engines of Creation: The Coming Era of Nanotechnology* by Eric Drexler

> *Our Molecular Future: How Nanotechnology, Robotics, Genetics and Artificial Intelligence Will Transform Our World* by Douglas Mulhall

> *The Dance of Molecules: How Nanotechnology is Changing Our Lives* by Ted Sargent

> *The Singularity Is Near: When Humans Transcend Biology* by Ray Kurzweil

> *Nanotech Fortunes: Make Yours in the Boom!* by Darrell Brookstein

> *The Investor's Guide to Nanotechnology and Micromachines* by Glenn Fishbine

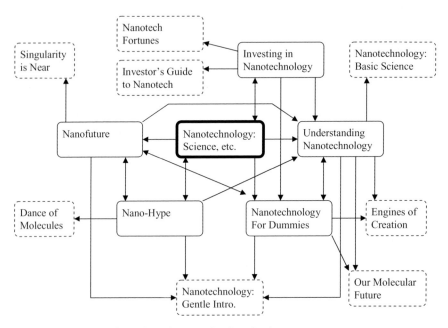

FIGURE 1. Configuration of nanotechnology books.

INTERACTION

I take the concept of interaction from social psychology, but there are analogous concepts in diverse disciplines. Elements of a system, such as individual people in a community, interact with each other in manifold ways. Two ideas especially inform our understanding of interaction: structure and emergence.

The structure of interaction in a system is a variant of configuration. Each element of the system has its own configuration, and interacts with other elements in terms of the distinctive combination of their configurations. The clearest example is probably the interaction of chemical compounds, largely determined by the structures of the molecules. Emergence refers to the appearance of larger structures on the basis of smaller or simpler one, such as in self-assembly (nanotechnology), evolution (biology), chunking (information science), or abstraction (cognitive science).

A nice illustration of interaction in computer science is the "Game of Life," devised by mathematician John Conway. Because I wanted to expand the concept, as explained below in the section about Evolution, I wrote my own program. The game space is a matrix like a huge checkerboard. In my program, it is fully 404 squares on a side, rather than 8, for a total of 163,216 squares rather than the traditional 64. FIGURE 2 shows four pictures of the area near the middle in one particular experiment. In the upper left, we see that 10 squares have been colored black, and the others are white. The "game" is a like a kind of solitaire that goes forward in a series of turn-like steps. At each step, the computer scans all 163,216 squares and follows simple rules to determine whether each of the squares should be black or white the next time. The original publication conceptualized "Life" as a biological process following three rules (Gardner, 1970, p. 120):

1. *Survivals*. Every counter with two or three neighboring counters survives for the next generation.
2. *Deaths*. Each counter with four or more neighbors dies (is removed) from overpopulation. Every counter with one neighbor or none dies from isolation.
3. *Births*. Each empty cell adjacent to exactly three neighbors—no more, no fewer—is a birth cell. A counter is placed on it at the next move.

When I run my Life program, black squares flash on the screen, as the software repeats these rules, turn after turn. Remarkably, starting with two lines of five squares, separated by one white square, leads to the double-8 picture in the lower-left corner of Figure 2 after 21 turns. The next turn produces the configuration shown in the upper-right corner. Going another turn forward gives the configuration in the lower-right corner, and one more turn gives the lower-left configuration again. These three symmetrical designs then cycle endlessly for as long as one wants to run the program.

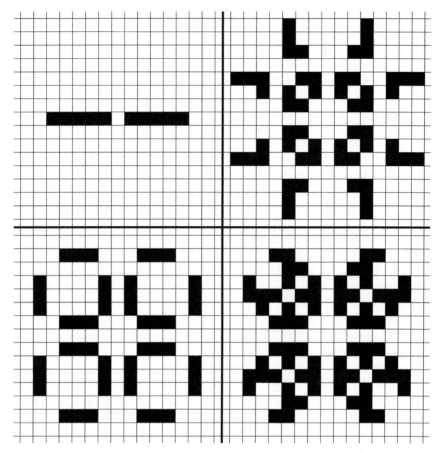

FIGURE 2. Four steps in a game of life.

Some initial configurations lead to very long sequences of diverse configurations. A different arrangement of 10 black cells leads to a complex scattering of 102 cells after 100 turns, that drops down to 56 black cells at 200 turns, and jumps up to 166 cells at 500 turns. The game pictured here starts with 10 black cells and winds up cycling through 48, 56, and 72 black cells. Depending upon the starting configuration, a great variety of results can ensue.

Conway's game is an example of a *cellular automation*, a system of cells having discrete states that change under rules that pay attention only to the cell's immediate neighborhood. It is similar to real life, in the sense that very extensive environments can arise from the local interaction of small configurations. For many decades, scientists and philosophers have debated the role that biology may play in altering the entropy in the universe (Bergson 1911), and the information content of cellular automata may vary markedly during a run

(Alavizadeh *et al.* 2006). Norman Margolus was inspired by Conway's game to argue that nature itself could be considered to be a kind of computer (2003). Stephen Wolfram (2002), creator of the Mathematica software, believes that cellular automata are the transforming tool to create a new kind of science. I would not go so far, but I agree they can offer insights about how conservation, indecision, configuration, and interaction can combine to produce complex, dynamic phenomena.

VARIATION

Although every proton is identical, physical objects containing protons differ greatly, even within species or categories. These differences can be conceptualized as different configurations of identical units, and a standard mathematical way to conceptualize variation is in terms of the probabilistic aggregation of indistinguishable events. Among the most widely used tool of statistics is the *normal distribution*, or *normal curve*, a way of conceptualizing and measuring variation (Shafer 1990).

This is not to say that the normal distribution is somehow natural or inexorable, and some of its applications have been severely criticized. For example, early research on human cognition defined *intelligence quotient* (IQ) as a child's mental age divided by chronological age, multiplied by 100. Children of various ages would take a standardized test. Then a mean score was calculated for each age, providing the norm to calculate each child's mental age. Chronological age was simply how many years old they were. For large samples, the IQs tend to follow the normal "bell shaped" distribution closely, with 68.13% of the cases falling within one standard deviation of the mean, 13.59% on either side represented by the area on the curve between one and two standard deviations, and very low tails to the curve at the extremes (e.g., Loether and McTavish 1976, p. 163). Critics became outraged, however, when standard deviations more than two below the mean were used to define separate "kinds" of mental retardation that were supposedly qualitatively different (Edgerton 1967; Mercer 1973). Even if IQ means an entirely real characteristic of the human mind, the fact that scores fit the normal curve is largely a result of the fact that items are selected for the tests, and the tests are scored, in terms of this distribution.

A common pattern of variation, across many fields, is the Zipf (1949) distribution, named after George Kingsley Zipf who believed it reflected a fundamental natural principle of least effort. Zipf's examples primarily concerned human language; for instance, an analysis of the frequency of different words in the novel *Ulysses* by James Joyce. After counting how many times a word was used (its frequency), the words were ranked in terms of their frequencies, assigning the number 1 to the most common word, 2 to the second-most common word, and so on. Zipf postulated that the product of each word's frequency by its rank was approximately constant, across all words, both common and rare alike. Like the normal curve, Zipf's distribution can be used as an analytical tool, rather than assuming it must apply in all circumstances. I will illustrate this using our first Converging Technologies publication, "Converging technologies for improving human performance: Integrating from the nanoscale" (Roco and Bainbridge 2002).

Not counting abbreviations, proper nouns, and foreign terms, the article contains 1869 different words, with duplications totaling 8462 words. Search engines tend to classify text documents not in terms of their most common words, but in terms of words that appear significantly more often than they do in other documents. For present purposes, however, a brief examination of frequent words is revealing. The six most common words in the article are general terms having nothing to do with the topic of converging technologies: *the* (appears 492 times), *and* (491 times), *of* (378), *to* (212), *in* (176), and *a* (121). The seventh most common word is *human*, appearing 117 times. This is revealing, because it demonstrates the relevance to human beings of NBIC. The next six most common words are general: *for* (92), *be* (83), *will* (75), *new* (70), *that* (68), and *is* (63). But the inclusion of *will* and *new* in this group suggests the article is oriented toward the future. Next comes *technologies*, appearing 61 times. A total of 59 words appear at least 20 times, and in descending order of frequency the other topic-relevant words in this group are: *science, research, technology, performance, convergence, converging, brain, information, scientific, engineering, fields, technological, cognitive, education, progress, based, individual, societal, areas, development, physical, systems, improving, nanoscale, potential, fundamental,* and *tools.*

More than half of the different words, 988 to be exact, are used only once. Their average rank is 1375.5. So for these words the product of frequency by rank is $1 \times 1375.5 = 1375.5$. There are 323 words used just twice, with an average rank of 720, so $2 \times 720 = 1440$, which is not very different from 1375.5. Similar numbers result for the words used three times ($3 \times 473 = 1419$), four times ($4 \times 350.5 = 1402$), and five times ($5 \times 289.5 = 1447.5$). With the usual proviso that real-world data are always somewhat noisy, Zipf's distribution seems to fit the low-frequency end of the distribution for this article. However, as FIGURE 3, shows, it does not fit the high-frequency end. More different words have high frequencies than Zipf's distribution would expect, so the products are lower than the constant for low-frequency words. Given that the article urges a rhetorical case for combining multiple fields that are usually kept separate, repeating key technical terms from the four fields, this makes sense.

In support of his view that the underlying principle applied across many realms, Zipf also cited the example of city size. Take the populations of all the cities, towns, and villages in a major nation and arrange them in descending order of size, then graph their populations. Graphed on log–log scales, it produces an approximately straight line with negative slope. The distribution

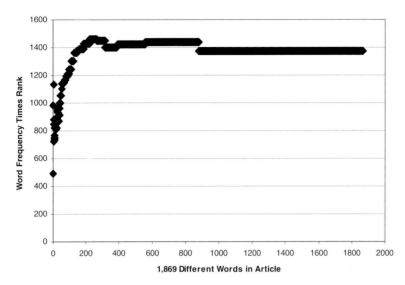

FIGURE 3. Variation of word frequencies in the first converging technologies article.

also appears to fit the sizes of corporations (Axtell 2001), the sizes of religious congregations generated from computer simulations of social interaction (Bainbridge, 2006), and nanoscale particles in magnetized ferrofluids (Skjeltorp *et al.* 2004). One would predict that Zipf's distribution also roughly fits the sizes of solid bodies in the solar system (a few planets, many moons, huge numbers of asteroids, almost infinite numbers of nanoscale dust particles) and the populations of animal species on earth (few elephants, many mice, vast swarms of gnats). There is some debate whether Zipf's discovery really reflects a meaningful natural law, or indeed what it means (Casti 1995; Belew 2000), but the distribution apparently qualifies as a pattern of variation or scaling law relevant to multiple sciences and technologies.

EVOLUTION

Natural selection from random mutation puts variation in the service of biological change (Gould 1988). Daniel Dennett (1995, p. 343) has argued that evolution by natural selection can apply outside the biological realm, following these three principles:

1. *Variation*: There is a continuing abundance of different elements.
2. *Heredity or replication*: The elements have the capacity to create copies or replicas of themselves.
3. *Differential "fitness"*: The number of copies of an element that are created in a given time varies, depending on interactions between the features of that element and features of the environment in which it persists.

For an example of how information technology can help us think about evolution beyond the biological realm, we can return to John Conway's Game of Life. We will imagine that it represents all the physical universe, with the rules representing the laws of nature. Then we will look for a higher-level selection effect, the theory that the prebiological cosmos was also subject to natural selection, in accordance with the anthropic principle, to produce a universe conducive to biology (Leslie 1982; Linde 1994). The rules for Conway's game of life can be restated:

A cell will be white on the next turn, unless:

If the cell is black then:

if it has 2 black neighbors, it will be black.

if it has 3 black neighbors, it will be black.

If the cell is white then:

if it has 3 black neighbors, it will be black.

Looking at the rules this way, one immediately wonders what happens if the rules for black cells are changed, for example like this:

A cell will be white on the next turn, unless:

If the cell is black then:

if it has 1 black neighbor, it will be black.

if it has 4 black neighbors, it will be black.

if it has 5 black neighbors, it will be black.

I wrote my program so that it could handle any combination of rules for a black cell, from always being white on the next turn to being black if there are all possible combinations of 1 through 8 black neighbors. Each combination of rules represents a different set of natural laws for the universe. Some will be more favorable for life than others. Obviously, I could add complexity for the cases when the cell is white, but I chose not to do so for this experiment. Instead, at the very center of the matrix of cells, I programmed a square of 12 cells to ignore the game's rules and be black or white entirely at random, with an equal probability. It is as if these cells were a window into another universe, from which information streams into the universe of the game. They constantly inject random configurations that may spawn flows of black cells outward from the center, analogous to the infamous Big Bang responsible for our own universe.

I then added a shell to the program, that ran through all 256 combinations of rules, and ran the game under each combination for a total of 1000 turns. Metaphorically, this compares the 256 possible universes, to see how many sets of natural laws produce "good" games of life. FIGURE 4 graphs how many black cells there were after the 1000th turn, putting the combinations in descending order of black cell population with a logarithmic vertical scale. Conway's rules, in this particular run, produce 406 black cells after 1000 turns.

Notice that about half of the 256 universes have final populations below 100, a total of 136 universes to be precise, or 53%. Another 105 universes have populations over 1000, with 93 over 10,000, 78 over 50,000, and 19 over 100,000. Conway's own rules define a universe on the "ledge" marked with an arrow in the diagram, along with a dozen other universes that had black cell populations between 302 and 450. Conway and his students selected the rules for their game such that the population would not grow without limit, but would permit patterns that had an initial propensity to grow. Perhaps all 13 of these universes have rules conducive to good life games, by Conway's definitions. The other approximately 240 universes do not. Thus, my extended version of Conway's Life is a model of the emergence of an ensemble of universes, all having somewhat different natural laws, only a small fraction of which are conducive for the evolution of life.

INFORMATION

Shannon's (1948) classic information theory (data transmission theory) emphasizes the concept of entropy, applies in cognitive science (Seow 2005), and theorists have long recognized a connection to thermodynamics. Herbert A. Simon (1996, p. 172) put the point thus:

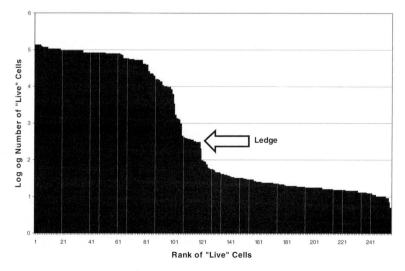

FIGURE 4. Natural selection of rule-sets for the game of life.

> Information theory explains organized complexity in terms of the reduction
> of entropy (disorder) that is achieved when systems (organisms, for example)
> absorb energy from external sources and convert it to pattern or structure.
> In information theory, energy, information, and pattern all correspond to
> negative entropy.

Physicist John Archibald Wheeler (1994) coined the slogan, "it from bit," to suggest that the primary stuff of the universe is information, rather than protons or energy. Historian David Channell (2004) predicts, "In the future, we may come to see the second law of thermodynamics (entropy) as a consequence of information theory and not the other way around." Any violation of a conservation law, or any indecision, entails the input of information.

Everybody is familiar with the vast Internet-based information infrastructure that has sprung up over the past dozen years, but I will use it briefly to illustrate one way in which it can be used to explore convergence. The National Science Foundation is organized into six scientific directorates, one education directorate, and a range of smaller offices. The Directorate for Computer and Information Science and Engineering (CISE) made 1148 research grants and other awards in the year 2005, promoting progress in information technology and related fields. The five other directorates are: Biology (BIO: 1348 awards in 2005), Engineering (ENG: 1601), Geosciences (GEO: 1364) Mathematics and Physical Sciences (MPS: 2168), and Social, Behavioral and Economic Sciences (SBE: 1065). A descriptive abstract and other information about each award is posted on the World Wide Web, accessed through an information search engine (http://www.nsf.gov/awardsearch/index.jsp). TABLE 1 shows what percentage of the abstracts from each directorate use each of the words listed.

We see that nanotechnology is largely the province of the engineering and MPS directorates, the concept of evolution is nearly as important for the geosciences as for biology, and that all the sciences make use of concepts like *information, interaction,* and *variation*. Philosophers may be disappointed to see that the word *entropy* is not widely used. Counting word usage is a rather simple approach, but to create this table, the NSF search engine did 191,268 scans of all the words in an award abstract, an information search task that would have been unthinkable a few years ago, and the information could have been accessed from anywhere in the world. Much more complex word-search methods can be used to chart the cultural distances between scientific fields, and chart changes as some fields converge.

COGNITION

One of the most controversial ideas in the original Converging Technologies report was the idea that new technologies based on cognitive science should join nanotechnology, biotechnology, and information technology as a co-equal

TABLE 1. Use of Words in NSF Award Abstracts, 2005

	BIO%	CISE%	ENG%	GEO%	MPS%	SBE%
NANO Words:						
nanotechnology	0.6	1.0	10.1	0.1	4.0	0.8
nanometer	0.1	1.0	3.8	0.6	2.9	0.0
nanosecond	0.1	0.0	0.3	0.0	0.1	0.0
nanoscience	0.1	0.4	2.6	0.2	1.9	0.4
molecule	9.0	1.7	5.9	0.7	13.5	0.2
BIO Words:						
evolution	21.1	3.8	3.1	16.9	8.3	7.4
protein	22.6	3.0	4.2	0.9	5.3	0.3
DNA	17.8	1.7	2.2	1.2	3.0	1.4
INFO Words:						
information	36.1	43.2	17.7	22.5	18.8	44.2
informatics	3.3	1.7	0.3	0.0	0.5	0.3
computer	7.2	40.2	10.6	5.0	13.6	8.4
algorithm	2.7	33.3	9.3	2.0	9.6	1.4
Internet	3.0	13.7	1.8	1.8	1.8	2.7
COGNO Words:						
cognition	1.2	4.3	0.6	0.1	0.1	12.2
neuron	4.5	0.8	0.4	0.2	0.7	0.5
intelligence	0.3	4.7	0.7	0.0	0.3	1.8
Other Words:						
structure	27.1	19.9	31.5	25.2	40.9	22.3
network	11.1	40.4	13.4	9.7	6.8	15.9
complexity	2.5	10.1	2.5	2.3	4.2	3.3
interaction	32.3	23.7	17.7	22.6	26.1	25.6
variation	22.0	19.9	17.5	24.3	23.9	28.9
entropy	0.1	0.4	0.1	0.3	1.6	0.1

field. Cognitive science is itself a convergence of multiple disciplines, including neurobiology (cognitive neuroscience), cognitive and perception psychology, aspects of linguistics, computer science (artificial intelligence), and other fields. My own discipline, sociology, has been slow to join in the cognitive science synthesis, despite the fact that many of its theories and much of its research data are cognitive in nature (DiMaggio 1997).

Many people conceptualize cognition as the epiphenomenal result of realities on the biological or chemical level, and thus logically subordinate to the seven other categories discussed here. Alternatively, traditional modes of thought, such as those associated with the great religious movements that have survived from ancient times, tend to conceptualize all existence in terms of the cognition of God. I would suggest a different perspective, considering the nature of reality inseparable from our perception of it. It would certainly be a profound error to say that reality is subjective, because this leads to magical thinking that the world conforms to our wishes. But it is also wrong to say that the physical world exists in some objective sense, independent of anyone to perceive it. There is no ground of being, analogous to the blackboard on which a divine scientist draws his equations, across which the galaxies are arrayed. Rather, existence is the concrete relationship of objects and observers, relative to each other.

Principles of relativity apply across all of the sciences. One could say that relativity is a kind of symmetry principle that could have been considered under conservation, above, or an indecision principle. Consider Einstein's (1905) statement:

> The laws by which the states of physical systems undergo change are not affected, whether these changes of state be referred to the one or the other of two systems of coordinates in uniform translatory motion.

The relationships between elements of a system are conserved, as one shifts from one system of coordinates to another, so long as the relation between the coordinate systems also remains constant. Defining north as south, and south as north, does not change the measured distance between two cities. I prefer to introduce relativity here, as an aspect of cognition, because it concerns the arbitrariness of the framework from which we conduct measurements and explain behavior. Again, this does not mean that the measurements and explanations themselves are arbitrary, nor that they conform to human desires, but that there is no single, unique model of the world.

A higher-level question that currently lacks a satisfactory answer is whether all the good models can be translated into each other through some finite system of equivalences. If the aim of science were to learn the mind of God, and God had a single conception of the universe, then it would in principle be possible for humans to discover the one, single truth. In the absence of a God, no particular model of the universe is privileged over others that match human observations equally well.

Heisenberg (1958, p. 112) has noted that Newton's work assumes a principle of relativity as well, and Newton lived two centuries before Einstein. Prior to the work of Copernicus, Kepler, Galileo, Newton, and a host of lesser-known scientists of their era, philosophers and ordinary people alike assumed that the natural framework for measuring motion was the motionless Earth, and objects tended to remain in their proper locations unless something made them move. After Newton, scientists were comfortable with the idea that all things were in motion, and that the movement of any object could be measured in terms of many different frameworks (Toulmin and Goodfield 1962).

Principles of relativity are common in the social sciences, and Peat (2002, p. 3) has noted the parallel between Einstein's theory of special relativity and cultural relativism in sociology. The principle of *cultural relativism* can be stated in several different ways: The morality or immorality of an action is relative to the standards of the particular culture from which it is judged. Judgments of right and wrong are never objective, but exist in relation to particular social groups. It would be wrong to imagine that sociological concepts of relativity derived from Einstein. For example, anthropologist Franz Boas argued as early as 1896 for the need to understand any custom in relation to the whole culture of which it is a part.

Cultural anthropologist Bronislaw Malinowski proposed the concept of *functional equivalence* in situations of cultural relativism. Two very different customs could be alternate ways of performing the same functions, just as different words could signify the same thing in different languages. At present, each field of science or engineering has to some extent its own culture, the particular concepts and terminology it uses, and a key challenge for convergenists is how to translate them into each other, or to find the larger language of which they are dialects.

CONCLUSION

We will need to consider a wide range of concepts and concept schemes for unifying science. Each conceptual system will need extensive development work, for example, exploring whether categories should be collapsed into each other or split to reflect finer distinctions. One often-fruitful approach is to develop an overarching conceptualization that connects categories into a coherent group. The eight concepts can be grouped in four pairs, as shown in TABLE 2. One concept in each pair represents order, and the other chaos. This distinction should be obvious for most of the pairs. In the case of variation, I am conceptualizing that concept in terms of a range of differences across cases, places, or dimensions, without implying that the range or distribution changes over time.

Entirely other conceptual approaches should be explored, including those that concern tactics for scientific research, rather than categorizations of phenomena. In 1955, physicist John Archibald Wheeler (1994, p. 3) was asked whether a unifying concept can be applied from one field of science and technology to another. He replied in the affirmative, listing seven principles by which we can achieve progress toward convergence:

1. The unknown is knowable.
2. Advance by trial and error.
3. Measurement and theory are inseparable.
4. Analogy gives insight.
5. New truth connects with old truth.

TABLE 2. **Reconceptualization of the category structure**

	Order	Chaos
Existence	Conservation	Indecision
Nature	Configuration	Interaction
Complexity	Variation	Evolution
Consciousness	Information	Cognition

6. Complementarity guards against contradiction.
7. Great consequences spring from lowly sources.

These principles are clear, except perhaps the sixth. Wheeler derives his principle of complementarity from the fact that we cannot simultaneously know the momentum and position of an electron, and it applies equally well to the complementary wave and particle descriptions of light. Interestingly, the popular online reference, Wikipedia, lists four fields that use the term: physics, economics, molecular biology, and system thinking. *Complementarity* in economics refers to goods that tend to be valued together, and in molecular biology the term applies to the pair of matched strands of DNA. The meaning in systems theory is almost identical to that in physics, asserting that the view of a system possessed by one observer will not be identical to the view belonging to another. Wheeler (1994, pp. 231–233) endorsed the way Niels Bohr applied complementarity to humans: Free will and determinism are equally valid but incompatible ways to explain human behavior.

In 1979, Wheeler (1994, p. 147) suggested another seven principles that could achieve a wider view of science and create new convergent technologies:

1. Discover unity
2. Create a system
3. Find economic feasibility
4. Reach harmony through intuition
5. Build a model
6. Serve as a science–technology generalist
7. Make decisions by imaginative interaction with alternative scenarios

In a way, these seven steps unite the rigor of science with the intuition of art, and Wheeler notes that those technological geniuses of the 19th century, Robert Fulton and Samuel F. B. Morse, had been artists. Metaphor without methodology is lost, but meticulousness without emotion is aimless.

Conservation, Indecision, Configuration, Interaction, Variation, Evolution, Information, and Cognition are a system of metaphors that can generate creative insights. To move forward in one domain D1, look how another domain D2 has employed one or more of these concepts, and imagine how similar thinking could be employed in D1. As a result, domains become linked and begin to merge. Through convergence, they can serve the two main goals of science effectively.

One goal of science is *knowledge*, and from knowledge comes wisdom. Science should provide all educated people with an accurate if qualitative understanding of existence and human life. This overarching principle is Wheeler's faith that the universe really is comprehensible. Now, in the middle of the history of science, expertise requires fragmentation. The end result of science should be a simple model that "comprehends" the many more complex models of subsidiary phenomena.

The second goal of science is to serve human material *welfare*, through engineering design. To achieve higher-level functionality in engineering requires concepts for integrating systems across domains and scales. That is, Converging Technologies both require and promote the unification of science. NBIC demands a set of abstract but meaningful concepts that encompass many lower-level concepts and usefully integrate diverse fields. Other candidate concepts should be explored, as well, and my eight are merely a first start. Transformative concepts offer wisdom as well as power, if we can find the correct and effective way of thinking.

REFERENCES

ALAVIZADEH, A., J. CURRY, C. KELLEHER, C. LEWISTON, A. RESNICK, E. SOLIS, and Y. BAR-YAM. 2006. Information theoretic and complexity considerations in four classes of cellular automata *NECSI One-Week Intensive Course in Complex Systems*. New England Complex Systems Institute, web.mit.edu/eps/Public/NECSI/NECSI_CA.pdf

AXTELL, R.L. 2001. Zipf distribution of U.S. firm sizes. *Science 293*, 1818–1820.

BAINBRIDGE, W.S. 1997. The Omicron Point: sociological application of the anthropic theory. Pp. 91–101 in R.A. Eve, S. Horsfall, and M.E. Lee (eds.), *Chaos and Complexity in Sociology*. Thousand Oaks, California: Sage Publications.

BAINBRIDGE, W.S. 2006. *God from the Machine*. Walnut Grove, California: AltaMira.

BARROW, J.D., and F.J. TIPLER. 1986. *The Anthropic Cosmological Principle*. New York: Oxford University Press.

BATESON, G. 1972. *Steps to an Ecology of Mind*. New York: Ballantine.

BELEW, R.K. 2000. *Finding Out About*. New York: Cambridge University Press.

BERGSON, H. 1911. *Creative Evolution*. New York: Henry Holt and Company.

BOAS, F. 1896. The limitations of the comparative method of anthropology. *Science* n.s. *4*, 901–908.

BOORMAN, S.A., and H.C. WHITE. 1976. Social structure from multiple networks. II. role structures. *American Journal of Sociology 81*(6), 1384–1446.

CAGE, J. 1959. *Indeterminacy*. Folkways Records FT 3704.

CASTI, J.L. 1995. Bell curves and monkey languages. *Complexity 1*(1), 12–15.

CHANNELL, D.F. 2004. The computer at Nature's core. *Wired 12*(2), http://wired-vig.wired.com/wired/archive/12.02/view.html?pg=2.

COHEN, J.E. 1995. *How Many People Can the Earth Support?* New York: W. W. Norton.

DAVIS, K. 1959. The myth of functional analysis as a special method in sociology and anthropology. *American Sociological Review 24*, 757–772.

DAVIS, K., and W. MOORE. 1945. Some principles of stratification. *American Sociological Review 10*, 242–249.

DENNETT, D.C. 1995. *Darwin's Dangerous Idea*. New York: Simon and Schuster.

DENNING, P.J. 2004. Network laws. *Communications of the ACM 47*(11), 15–20.

DIMAGGIO, P. 1997. Culture and cognition. *Annual Review of Sociology 23*, 263–287.

EDGERTON, R.B. 1967. *The Cloak of Competence*. Berkeley: University of California Press.

EINSTEIN, A. 1905. On the electrodynamics of moving bodies. Pp. 35–65 in H.A. Lorentz, A. Einstein, H. Minkowski, and H. Weyl (eds.), *The Principle of Relativity*. London: Methuen [1923].

GARDNER, M. 1970. The fantastic combinations of John Conway's new solitaire game "Life." *Scientific American 223*(October), 120–123.

GOULD, S.J. 1988. Trends as changes in variance. *Journal of Paleontology 62*(3), 319–329.

HEISENBERG, W. 1958. *Physics and Philosophy*. New York: Harper and Row.

HOFFMANN, U., and J. HOFMANN. 2002. Monkeys, typewriters and network: the internet in the light of the theory of accidental excellence. Schriftenreihe der Abteilung "Organisation und Technikgenese" des Forschungsschwerpunkts Technik-Arbeit-Umwelt am Wissenschaftszentrum Berlin für Sozialforschung http://skylla.wz-berlin.de/pdf/2002/ii02-101.pdf

LESLIE, J. 1982. Anthropic principle, world ensemble, design. *American Philosophical Quarterly 19*(2), 141–151.

LINDE, A. 1994. The self-reproducing inflationary universe. *Scientific American 271*(November), 48–55.

LOETHER, H.J., and D.G. MCTAVISH. 1976. *Descriptive and Inferential Statistics*. Boston: Allyn and Bacon.

MALONEY, R. 1956. Inflexible logic. Pp. 2262–2267 in J.R. Newman (ed.), *The World of Mathematics*. New York: Simon and Schuster [1940].

MARGOLUS, N. 2003. Looking at nature as a computer. *International Journal of Theoretical Physics 42*(2), 309–327.

MAYNARD SMITH, J. 1982. *Evolution and the Theory of Games*. New York: Cambridge University Press.

MERCER, J.R. 1973. *Labeling the Mentally Retarded*. Berkeley: University of California Press.

MORENO, J.L. 1934. *Who Shall Survive?* Washington, DC: Nervous and Mental Disease Publishing Company.

NAGEL, E., and J.R. NEWMAN. 1958. *Gödel's Proof*. New York: New York University Press.

PARSONS, T. 1951. *The Social System*. New York: Free Press.

PEAT, F.D. 2002. *From Certainty to Uncertainty*. Washington, DC: Joseph Henry Press.

ROCO, M.C., and W.S. BAINBRIDGE. 2002. Converging technologies for improving human performance: integrating from the nanoscale. *Journal of Nanoparticle Research 4*(4), 281–295.

ROWE, D.C. 2001. Do people make environments or do environments make people. Pp. 62–74 in A.R. Damasio, A. Harrington, J. Kagan, B.S. McEwen, H. Moss, and R. Shaikh (eds.), *Unity of Knowledge*, Vol. 935. New York: Annals of the New York Academy of Sciences.

SEOW, S.C. 2005. Information theoretical models of HCI: a comparison of the Hick-Hyman Law and Fitts' Law. *Human-Computer Interaction 20*, 315–352.

SHAFER, G. 1990. The unity and diversity of probability. *Statistical Science 5*(4), 435–444.

SHANNON, C.E. 1948. A mathematical theory of communication. *Bell System Technical Journal 27*, 379–423, 623–656.

SHOCKLEY, W. 1950. *Electrons and Holes in Semiconductors, with Applications to Transistor Electronics*. New York: Van Nostrand.

SIMON, H.A. 1996. *The Sciences of the Artificial*. Cambridge, Massachusetts: MIT Press.

SKJELTORP, A.T., K.L. KRISTIANSEN, G. HELGESEN, R. TOUSSAINT, E.G. FLEKKOY, and J. CERNAK. 2004. Self-assembly and dynamics of magnetic holes. Pp. 165–179 in A.T. Skjeltorp and A.V. Belushkin (eds.), *Forces, Growth and Form in Soft Condensed Matter*. Dordrecht, the Netherlands: Kluwer.

TOULMIN, S., and J. GOODFIELD. 1962. *The Fabric of the Heavens*. New York: Harper.

VAN HEIJENOORT, J., ed. 1967. *From Frege to Gödel*. Cambridge: Harvard University Press.

WAGNER, A.H.G. 1864. *Die Gesetzmaessigkeit in den Scheinbar Willkuerlichen Menschlichen Handlungen vom Standpunkte der Statistik*. Hamburg: Boyes und Geisler.

WHEELER, J.A. 1994. *At Home in the Universe*. Woodbury, New York: American Institute of Physics.

WHITE, H.C. 1970. *Chains of Opportunity*. Cambridge, Massachusetts: Harvard University Press.

WHITE, H.C., S.A. BOORMAN, and R.L. BREIGER. 1976. Social structure from multiple networks. I. blockmodels of roles and positions. *American Journal of Sociology* *81*(4), 730–780.

WIGGINS, J.S., ed. 1996. *The Five-Factor Model of Personality*. New York, NY: Guilford.

WOLFRAM, S. 2002. *A New Kind of Science*. Champaign, Illinois: Wolfram Media.

ZIPF, G.K. 1949. *Human Behavior and the Principle of Least Effort*. Cambridge, Massachusetts: Addison-Wesley.

Wilson and the Unification of Science

ULLICA SEGERSTRALE

Illinois Institute of Technology, Chicago, Illinois 60616, USA

ABSTRACT: This article analyzes the thought and intellectual contribution of Edward O. Wilson, among the most prominent and influential
convergenists. It concentrates on the deep ambition going as a bright
thread through Wilson's whole scientific output: the unification of science and knowledge. It traces the background of this ambition in Wilson's personal history and follows its various articulations throughout
his career.

KEYWORDS: consilience; convergence; sociobiology

WILSON'S UNIFICATION PROGRAM

Edward O. Wilson is our best example of a living scientist who has explored
the implications of unification while contributing to its accomplishment—
across the biological and cognitive fields but with implications for all scientific convergence. Nominally an entomologist, he has written or coauthored a
number of books about insects, and of course ants, his favorite species. But
he was also influential in creating the broad convergent field of sociobiology
and is the well-known author of a number of books, most of which are written
in a language that reaches both the specialist and the general public: *Sociobiology*, *On Human Nature*, *Biophilia*, *Promethean Fire*, *The Diversity of Life*,
The Future of Life, and *Consilience* that explicitly urges convergence of all the
sciences.

His goals are both scientific and extra-scientific. In fact, for Wilson the
unification of science is part of what I have elsewhere called his larger
moral-cum-scientific agenda (Segerstrale 2000). Understanding this agenda
and its background, the basic elements of Wilson's scientific methodology and
metaphysics—such things as the nature of scientific explanation, and the nature of human and animal societies—as well as his particular heuristic choices,
will go a long way toward understanding Wilson's unification program. This
will also help us account for some of the criticisms that have come his way.

Address for correspondence: Ullica Segerstrale, Professor and Chair, Department of Social Sciences,
Illinois Institute of Technology, 3301 S. Dearborn Ave., Suite 116, Chicago, IL 60616. Voice: 312-567-
5128; fax: 312-567-6821.
e-mail: segerstrale@iit.edu

Ann. N.Y. Acad. Sci. 1093: 46–73 (2006). © 2006 New York Academy of Sciences.
doi: 10.1196/annals.1382.004

Wilson's unification program is a complex one. It has many different components and it has evolved over a time span of almost 40 years, as can be traced in Wilson's many popular books and articles. Perhaps the program itself is best described as Wilson over time trying to tackle the idea of unification from a number of different angles as new scientific tools become available to him and as he develops his overall research agenda. As the academic and cultural context changes, different aspects of the program get emphasized. Meanwhile, at any specific point, the unification program is presented as the solution to larger intellectual or social problems.

Wilson had at least three different objectives in promoting the unification of science and knowledge. The first is what might be called a general unification wish. This is a personality feature and intellectual drive that Wilson shares with many other academics: the desire to produce order out of chaos. In Wilson's case, he does it through mathematical modeling of seemingly intractable fields and through the provision of unifying concepts. This unification wish is more modest, directing itself to specific scientific areas, "messy fields" in need of "cleaning up." This is most apparent before the advent of *Sociobiology* in 1975.

The second ambition is already directed toward the specific goal of unifying the natural and social sciences, that grand, often elusive, academic goal attempted by many before Wilson, both scientists and philosophers. This is also one of the goals explicitly stated in *Sociobiology*, although a goal that Wilson was not able to seriously deal with—in explicit form at least—before *Consilience* in 1998. The reason for this was largely the raging sociobiology controversy, where critics interpreted any attempt to discuss human nature and human future as support for a conservative political agenda (Segerstrale 2000).

The third objective is his attempt to capture also the moral realm and render it under scientific and material control. Such a project partly entails taking away the monopoly on ethics from the philosophers—this he starts already in *Sociobiology*—while providing a scientific bulwark against "the theologians" and their seemingly arbitrary values. This objective reflects Wilson's ambition to ground human values on a solid scientific—read "evolutionary"—basis.

SUPERORGANISM AND CYBERNETICS

After completing his undergraduate work and a MS in biology at the University of Alabama, Wilson came as a graduate student to Harvard in the early 1950s, and became a member of the Harvard faculty in 1958. During his doctoral studies in biology, Wilson had been socialized to the holistic "superorganism" concept, and as a Junior member of the prestigious Society of Fellows—an elite intellectual society at Harvard University—he was to meet it again in different forms (Brinton 1959). This meant that Wilson during a crucial period in his scientific career came to absorb what Ghiselin (1974,

p. 224) has called the "crypto-vitalist" spirit prevalent at Harvard during this time.

Wilson was a "second generation" student of W. M. Wheeler, the eminent Harvard entomologist and champion of the superorganism concept. Wheeler (1928a, 1928b), who was a socialist and inspired by Kropotkin, was interested in the cooperation and division of labor in insect societies. This was something that interested Wilson as well. Indeed, insect societies have traditionally represented a natural opportunity for researchers who wanted to pursue their scientific interests working on topics with perceived moral or political implications.

Wheeler, as it so happened, was a close friend of L. J. Henderson, the extremely influential founder of the Society of Fellows. Henderson, originally a biochemist, had become fascinated with the idea of applying the concept of physiological homeostasis to the study of human societies. With the help of ideas from the Italian sociologist Vilfredo Pareto, whom Wheeler and Henderson had "discovered" and introduced to an American audience, Henderson further developed the ideas of homeostasis and equilibrium (Parsons, 1953; Heyl 1968; Homans 1984). Henderson's influence was enormous. Not only did his ideas come to strongly affect the new sociological paradigms developed by such Junior Fellows as Talcott Parsons and George Homans, but also he passed on "his conception of scientific method, social science methodology, and specifically of the place of equilibrium" to a whole generation of Harvard students (Russett 1966, p.117).

Wilson, then, absorbed two sets of concepts at more or less the same time: the superorganismic approach to the division of labor in insect societies (from Wheeler, indirectly) and the notion of social equilibrium (from Henderson, indirectly). But there was a third "hidden curriculum" conveyed by the informal weekly dinner discussions in the Society of Fellows. And this was the view that it was through an equilibrium model that a larger intellectual goal of Henderson's could be achieved—making sociology a branch of natural science (Russett 1966, pp. 111, 117). It seems therefore that it is basically Henderson's scientific program that we can see reflected in Wilson's evolving agenda, too: the old dream of unity among all of science.

Wilson later abandoned the superorganismic conception of the division of labor. But there is no indication that Wilson seriously gave up the metaphysical notion of the superorganism. At the very beginning of *Sociobiology*, for instance, he explicitly recognized the importance of "holistic" studies in his discussion of emergent properties. In fact, it was precisely for the study of such emergent properties that Wilson (1975, p.7) suggested the introduction of a "new holism."

This "new holism" can be regarded as a translation of the old superorganism metaphor into a new language. What was the nature of this new language and where did it come from? Donna Haraway (1981–1982) has argued that the language of sociobiology was an example of a larger reformulation of science that took place after the Second World War, using the new principles of communication technology developed during the war. What was taking place was a "cybernetic translation."

In the case of sociobiology this translation happened in two steps. The first step was taken by T.C. Schneirla, the leader of the school of comparative psychology, who took initiative to bring about the demise of the superorganism concept in physiology. Comparative psychology was a field characterized by a strong physiological outlook and preference for explanation in terms of proximate rather than ultimate factors. Later Wilson, looking for a way of dealing with hierarchical concepts, found and picked up Schneirla's "cybernetic translation," but shifted the focus of explanation of behavior to evolutionary factors instead (e.g., Schneirla 1971).

Ghiselin (1974, p. 227) thought it odd that Wilson (1971a, p. 64) praised comparative psychologists like Schneirla for their reductionist approach while completely ignoring the differences in basic philosophy between their field and his own. True, there was rivalry between comparative psychology and ethology at the time for dominance in behavioral biology. However, there is no real mystery here, if one assumes that Wilson was primarily interested in heuristics. In general Wilson tended to use any new tool that seemed useful for his theory building efforts. Ultimately, Wilson's scientific efforts were to serve his moral interests, in his life-long combined moral-cum-scientific agenda.

Haraway traces the beginning of Wilson's interest in communication to his own pathbreaking studies of chemical communication through pheromones after the mid–1950s, and especially to his studies of the accuracy of the "mass response" in regard to food. Wilson had found that the behavior in both ants and honey bees was "near the optimum level of accuracy of mass response" (Wilson 1962).

Haraway described Wilson's new interest in the new type of biology and new type of cybernetic explanation as follows:

> For Wilson, concepts like superorganism were archaic verbal play, not explanation. Explanation in the new biology was the fruit of an experimental, quantitative program that dis-assembled and re-assembled *in vitro* the biological system at hand into different sorts of natural-technical objects. These objects were pre-eminently code-structures and control elements. Animal behavior was in this respect no different from molecular biology—and both drew from technological communications systems theories in enforcing such an experimental, quantitative program. Other kinds of explanations just no longer "counted" (Haraway 1981–1982).

Wilson himself corroborates this interpretation in his *The Insect Societies*. There he prophetically states in his last chapter:

> In time all the piecemeal analyses will permit the reconstruction of the full system *in vitro*. In this case an *in vitro* reconstruction would mean the full explanation of social behavior by means of integrative mechanisms experimentally demonstrated and the proof of that explanation by the artificial

induction of the complete repertory of social responses on the part of the
isolated members of insect colonies (Wilson 1971a, p. 319).

SOCIOBIOLOGY AS A UNIFYING SCIENTIFIC DISCIPLINE

Wilson's program for a general theory of sociobiology, was formulated already in *The Insect Societies*:

> The principal goal of a general theory of sociobiology should be an ability to
> predict features of social organization from a knowledge of these population
> parameters combined with information on the behavioral constraints imposed
> by the genetic constitution of the species. It will be a chief task of evolution-
> ary ecology in turn to derive the population parameters from a knowledge
> of the evolutionary history of the species and of the environment in which
> the most recent portion of that history has unfolded (Wilson 1971b, p. 401).

Sociobiology as a project, however, was much bigger than his integrative
work on insects, and involved Wilson venturing into the field of vertebrates
where he was not a specialist. But Wilson was led by his strong vision for a
unified science of sociobiology:

> Biologists have always been intrigued by comparisons between societies of
> invertebrates, especially insect societies, and those of vertebrates. They have
> dreamed of identifying the common properties of such disparate units in a
> way that would provide insight in all aspects of social evolution, including
> that of man. The goal can be expressed as follows: when the same parameters
> and quantitative theory are used to analyze both termite colonies and a troop
> of rhesus macaques, we will have a unified science of sociobiology (Wilson
> 1975, p. 4).

Moreover, Wilson was convinced that he would be able to handle this challenge. The reason was his earlier experiences in what he saw as similar situations. In 1981 he characterized both his earlier task in biogeography and
the new one in sociobiology as "visionary enterprises." Biogeography was
"terribly messy"; it was a "major unformed field, full of curious fragments of
information, just like the social sciences today, it had no structure like population genetics. . ." Wilson felt the challenge and urge to go into this field and
provide it with structure. His collaboration with MacArthur was excellent—
Wilson knew the detailed facts and MacArthur was a sophisticated modeler.
And when this field was structured, it was only natural for Wilson to be on the
lookout for other "messy fields." (This, in fact, would be a taste preference
throughout his career.)

Indeed, Wilson saw himself as the only member of a small 1960s group of
radical young evolutionists who had remained the true "keeper of the flame"
in regard to the group's mission to create something new. Other members
of this small group were among others Richard Levins, Robert MacArthur,
and L. B. Slobodkin (Wilson, interview). The overall situation in evolutionary

biology at this time was, according to Wilson (1975, p. 64), one of stagnation. What unified these young biologists was among others a "holistic" interest in evolutionary ecology, that is, the actual evolutionary history of a species in a changing environment. At the end of the 1960s, most of the group members, Lewontin (1968), Levins (1968), and MacArthur and Wilson (1967) had contributed to the development of the new theory (Wilson 1971b).

Wilson certainly continued with this kind of effort. He was convinced that the Modern Synthesis had opened up promising new avenues for evolutionary biology. At the time the whole idea of treating social behavior as undergoing evolution, just like morphological traits, was new to science. In *Sociobiology* Wilson (1975, p. 4) boldly stated at the outset: "This book makes an attempt to codify sociobiology into a branch of evolutionary biology and particularly of modern population biology."

This would also mean a reorganization of the map of scientific disciplines. According to Wilson, with the advent of sociobiology, ethology, and comparative psychology were no longer the central, unifying fields of behavioral biology: "Both are destined to be cannibalized by neurophysiology and sensory physiology from one and sociobiology and behavioral ecology from the other" (Wilson 1975, p. 6). In this version of sociobiology, Wilson's goal was to make sociobiology a total quantitative and predictive discipline:

> The ultimate goal is a stoichiometry of social evolution. When perfected, the stoichiometry will consist of an interlocking set of models that permit the quantitative prediction of the qualities of social organization—group size, age composition, and mode of organization, including communication, division of labor, and time budgets–from a knowledge of the prime movers of social evolution (Wilson 1975, p. 63).

The "prime movers" here were phylogenetic inertia (resistance to change) and ecological pressure. In such militant formulations, Wilson tries to put sociobiology on the map, asserting himself in relation to already existing disciplines. But Wilson also employed more general formulations in this book, starting with his basic definition of sociobiology as "the scientific study of the biological basis of all social behavior, including man."

Here Wilson was operating in a different type of unifying mode, with a much broader aim. This was Wilson demonstrating to his zoological colleagues at large that a common field actually existed, and that common problems could now be analyzed in a new light. By writing his book (and corresponding with a great number of vertebrate zoologists in the process), Wilson in fact created, or codified, the very field of "sociobiology"—a feat recognized by the Animal Behavior Society, which in 1989 rated *Sociobiology* the most important book on animal behavior of all time. Also in naming the field "sociobiology," Wilson saw himself as following the tradition established by John Paul Scott, who had coined the term to refer to "the interdisciplinary science which lies between the fields of biology (particularly ecology and physiology) and psychology and sociology."

In synthesizing *Sociobiology*, Wilson very much remained in the naturalist tradition. In fact, large parts of Wilson's big tome read like an ethology textbook, with rich detail on animal behavior, and full with illustrations. After all, *Sociobiology* was a coffee table book: Wilson wanted to convey to a larger public a new way of looking at behavior. Wilson's sociobiology, then, was at the same time a more specific scientific program, employing a particular explanatory tools and an umbrella discipline encompassing a wide range of studies of social behavior.

Looking back at *Sociobiology*, there is no doubt that it had great impact—above all as a comprehensive, comparative view of the genetic foundations of social behavior, and as a breaker of the prevailing taboo on biological explanations of humans. Many probably believe that Wilson's 1975 book was based on gene selectionism and the general game-theoretical approach that was to later characterize sociobiology. But that was true of Dawkins and his *The Selfish Gene* (1976), not Wilson. Wilson in fact did not accept a gene-selectionist approach, nor did he work within a game-theoretical explanatory framework. Unlike Dawkins, Wilson also insisted on the reality and importance of group selection. Wilson's was a different, more comprehensive synthesis, whose theory building aimed at capturing the full richness of nature. Dawkins, on the other hand, was aiming for a clear explication of the common logic behind the new theoretical contributions by Bill Hamilton, George Williams, Robert Trivers, John Maynard Smith, and others, using "the gene's eye view" as his conceptual tool (cf. Segerstrale 2006).

HUMAN NATURE AND HUMAN CULTURE

In 1971 Wilson did not appear too keen on including humans in his general scheme for sociobiology. The comparisons he stressed were rather the ones between insects and vertebrates. The remoteness in phylogenetic origin between these two groups was important for the development of a general theory. Wilson even used such formulations as "(i)f we exclude man, with his unique language and revolutionary capacity for cultural transmission. . ." (Wilson 1971b, p. 402).

What was it that made Wilson later shift his standpoint to include also humans in his synthesis? It is clear that this question must have preoccupied Wilson, considering his "heritage" from Wheeler and Henderson, but he also knew that there were formidable theoretical obstacles to the application of principles of population genetics to man. It appears that he was working on a solution around the same time as he published *The Insect Societies*. In 1969 Wilson was invited to a huge Smithsonian symposium, Man and Beast, dealing with the relationship between ethology and the human sciences and the potential contributions that biology could make to contemporary urban problems. Konrad Lorenz' recently published *On Aggression* (1966) had particularly stirred the hope that biologists might have something to contribute. (Read in the right spirit, Lorenz could be seen as an impassioned appeal to humankind to explore its own nature and find ways to prevent a dangerous arms race.)

As Wilson himself indicated some two decades later at the follow-up conference Man and Beast Revisited, the 1969 conference "was an early milestone in the development of sociobiology," in that it brought together scholars from different fields and showed that a common language was possible (Wilson 1991a). At this conference himself Wilson acted as a strongly liberally minded biologist. He took issue with people like Robert Ardrey (1966) and others who wished to emphasize competition as a driving force of evolution. He also spoke against a vision of innate aggressiveness in animals and against aggression as a ubiquitous trait. His main point was that aggression was probably an adaptive trait, and also in man. Whatever our Stone Age nature may have been like, Wilson argued, there had been ample time for us to have changed our nature over and over again. Citing a number of animal studies that showed that evolution could be speeded up; he said he believed that, for humans, a significant change could happen in as little as 10 generations or 200–300 years.

But Wilson's particular "scientific liberal" stance also meant that he also took issue with the other extreme in regard to humans: the overemphasis on culture. According to Wilson, it was "much too early to attempt to make a judgment on the matter, as Dobzhansky . . . has done with the following statement: 'Culture is not inherited through genes, it is acquired by learning from other human beings . . . In a sense, human genes have surrendered their primacy in human evolution to an entirely new, nonbiological or superorganic agent, culture. However, it should not be forgotten that this agent is entirely dependent on the human genotype.' Obviously human genes have surrendered a great deal, but perhaps they have kept a little of their old heritability and responsiveness to selection. This amount should be measured, because it is crucial to the planning of future society" (Wilson 1971c, p. 208).

The big theme at the conference was "Can man cope?" Lorenz and others had presented a gloomy situation of technology (in the form of weaponry) and other cultural innovations outrunning humans' capacity to adapt. Culture was progressing faster than humans were evolving. But Wilson maintained a relative optimism in the face of the situation of mankind: human evolution might in principle be speeded up so as to match the progress of cultural evolution. He believed in "significant alteration in, say, emotional and intellectual traits within no more than ten generations—or about three hundred years" (Wilson 1971c, p. 207). He concluded: "Man therefore has the genetic capacity to track some of the dominant features of particular cultures. Whether he does so—and to what degree—remains an open question."

In many ways, the basic agenda for *Sociobiology* and other later works was set out in this early paper, at least in regard to Wilson's long-range plan for mankind. Indeed, Wilson appears already in 1969 as something of a gene–culture interactionist. At the same time, Wilson was surely not an evolutionary psychologist (to use a current term), because he objected to the idea of a once and for all formed human nature. "Man makes himself genetically" was Wilson's provocative-sounding slogan at the conference, in clear opposition to both a biological determinist and a culturist view.

Wilson wanted to further establish his contrarian-sounding claim that aggression was not an innate trait by undertaking a broad comparative analysis across species. Such an analysis would show that aggression as a trait varied widely, and that it required particular ecological and other conditions for its expression. This again would have to be argued in the context of a general overview of variation in animal social behaviors, all of which would be seen as subject to adaptation by natural selection. For that Wilson would need empirical studies of different species' social behavior in different ecologies. (Wilson had already started an inventory in his own paper, largely of variation of aggression in insects, which he also presented in his paper.) He also needed a theory, which made it plausible that social behavior was, in fact, adaptive. And he needed more evidence of "nice" rather than "nasty" social behaviors.

Luckily, at the same Washington conference was also John Crook, the acknowledged leader in comparative ecological studies of social behavior (Crook 1971). This meant that Wilson here got a head start in regard to one of his ambitions with his project on sociobiology: to demonstrate the adaptiveness of social behavior in animals. (Ironically, this would later become one of the many things that the opponents of sociobiology would criticize him for.) Moreover, at this conference was Lionel Tiger with his "human biogram" (Tiger and Fox 1971) and also young Bill Hamilton, who a few years earlier had published his seminal paper on the evolution of social behavior, in which he had especially outlined how it was possible for altruism to evolve and spread as a social trait (Hamilton 1964). "It was all there," said a colleague of Wilson's, who later saw clear traces of this Washington event in *Sociobiology*.

BIOLOGIZING THE SOCIAL SCIENCES

The most ambitious part of *Sociobiology* was to include also sociology and the other social sciences and the humanities in the Modern Synthesis (Wilson 1975, p. 4). This unification of the social and natural sciences can be seen as a bid for an even larger synthesis. Wilson hoped that the scientific explanations of sociobiology would soon be able to replace the unscientific ones of the social sciences and ethics. He described this so that from a macroscopic natural history point of view "the humanities and social sciences shrink to specialized branches of biology" (p. 547). One of the functions of sociobiology would be to reformulate the foundations of the social sciences so that this would be possible (p. 4). For Wilson, that meant making the social sciences more predictive.

This was clearly a tall order. A major obstacle in the case of predicting human behavior was the free will of individuals. Wilson concluded that detailed histories of human individuals could not be predicted, and in this sense there was indeed free will. But he continued:

> And yet our behavior is partially determined in a second and weaker sense. If the categories of behavior are made broad enough, events can be predicted with confidence... (T)he human being will speak and conduct a wide range of activities characteristic of the human species. Moreover, the statistical properties of populations of individuals can be specified... (Entomologists have produced detailed characterizations of the average flight patterns of honeybees to flowers).

> To a lesser extent and still unknown degree the statistical behavior of human societies might be predicted, given a sufficient knowledge of human nature, the histories of the societies, and their physical environment...(C)ultures are not superorganisms that evolve by their own dynamics. Rather, cultural change is the statistical product of the separate behavioral responses of large numbers of human beings who cope as best they can with social existence (1978, pp. 77–78).

Thus, it was through statistics that Wilson believed that he would be able to attain his goal of making sociology a predictive, and therefore "real" science. This had consequences for Wilson's conception of societies. In order to make predictive statements based on the new "hard" science branch of evolutionary biology, population genetics, societies had to be conceived of as populations. In this way they could be subjected to the statistical apparatus of population biology. In principle, both biological and cultural inheritance could be analyzed in analogous fashion as based on traits (Wilson 1975, p. 14; 1978, p. 33).

The question he did not discuss, however, was whether it was correct to regard a culture or a society as "the summed actions of thousands or millions of poorly understood individual human beings" (Wilson 1978, p. 207). For Wilson, however, there was no doubt, as he dismissed Durkheim and holistic conceptions of society as mistaken. The clue to Wilson's thinking about individual and society is to be found in the individualistic and utilitarian thinker J. S. Mill, whom Wilson quotes in one of his mid 1970s articles:

> If laws of social phenomena, empirically generalized from history, can, when once suggested, be affiliated to the known laws of human nature; if the direction taken by the developments and the changes of human society can be seen to be such as the properties of man and of his dwelling-place made antecedently probable, the empirical generalizations are raised into positive laws, and sociology becomes a science (Mill quoted in Wilson 1977).

Is this a methodological position or does Wilson's choice reflect a belief about the world? It appears that he really believes in the primacy of the individual in relation to society. This can be seen from various discussions of human individuals' capacity for social contracts in *On Human Nature*, and from his statement that he knows what societies really are ("I have seen so many societies around the world," interview). (Moreover, Wilson's view of human individuality is based on the biological contrast he makes between mammals and insects, for example, 1978, p. 199). So, while Wilson is an ontological holist in regard to insect societies—although a methodological reductionist in modeling them—in relation to human societies, Wilson is both an ontological and methodological reductionist.

WILSON'S MORAL AGENDA

But even before Wilson in *Sociobiology* announced his wish to unite the social and natural sciences, he had made another programmatic statement. On the very first page of the book he argues that ethical philosophers need to take into account the evolved nature of our minds:

> The biologist, who is concerned with questions of physiology and evolutionary history, realizes that self-knowledge is constrained and shaped by the emotional control centers in the hypothalamus and limbic system of the brain. These centers flood our consciousness with all the emotions—hate, love, guilt, fear, and others—that are consulted by ethical philosophers who wish to intuit the standards of good and evil. What, we are then compelled to ask, made the hypothalamus and limbic system? They evolved by natural selection. That simple biological statement must be pursued to explain ethics and ethical philosophers, if not epistemology and epistemologists, at all depths (Wilson 1975, p. 3).

Also, Wilson on the same page made altruism into the central problem of sociobiology. This was an expression of his life-long moral-cum-scientific agenda, driving him to pursue problems that were at the same time epistemologically and ethically challenging. But, in addition, Wilson had an idiosyncratic moral problem—a hangup, if you will—which motivated him to find ever more creative solutions. Basically, he was looking for a way to prove that scientific materialism was superior to religion.

Wilson's life-long moral agenda is perhaps most clearly spelled out in *On Human Nature* (1978). There he explains that he wants to provide a solution to what he sees as the pervasive and erroneous religious domination of current social life, including the scientifically advanced United States (pp. 141–142, 170). The moral code invoked by "the theologians" is arbitrary and causes needless guilt and suffering among the population. Meanwhile, this code, written in total ignorance of biology, is taken seriously, and there is no sign of the hoped-for retreat of organized religion in the era of science, especially not in the United States. "Men, it appears, would rather believe than know" (p. 170).

Where does this kind of militant attitude to religion derive from? Here we have to go back to the deeply religious environment of Wilson's childhood and adolescence. Wilson was raised in Alabama as a fundamentalist Southern Baptist. At the age of 15 years he went through a conversion experience at a revival meeting and was "born again" by being baptized (interview in 1981, cf. Wilson 1994). He had a sense of religious awe, but, as he later explained it, this was "more of a blind emotional acceptance. . .a rite of transition. . .a special form of allegiance to the tribe in front of the shaman" (interview). Then at the age of 17 years he left the church and became a free thinker. He had become disappointed with the "theater" and "fraudulent activity" of the church. He had also found evolution: "I had discovered that what I most loved on the planet, which was life on the planet, made sense only in terms of evolution and the idea of natural selection, and that this was a far more interesting, richer and more powerful explanation than the teachings of the New Testament."

Analyzing religion from a sociobiological perspective would yield a double benefit. It would be a great challenge for theoretical development in his field to tackle "the most complex and powerful force in the human mind." But more importantly, an explanation of religion in terms of evolutionary biology would give scientific materialism the final victory over religion: "If religion. . . can be systematically analyzed and explained as a product of the brain's evolution, its power as an external source of morality will be gone forever" (Wilson 1978, p. 201).

Throughout *On Human Nature*, Wilson grappled with God in different ways. On the basis of at least one scientific principle God would already be excluded as superfluous, he ventured: "The scientist's devotion to parsimony in explanation excludes the divine spirit and other extraneous agents" (1978, p. 192). Still, Wilson conceded that "God remains a viable hypothesis as the prime mover, however undefinable and untestable that conception may be" (1978, p. 205). But science would be triumphant in the end: "[T]he final decisive edge enjoyed by scientific naturalism will come from its capacity to explain traditional religion, its chief competitor, as a fully material phenomenon" (1978, p. 192).

One way in which Wilson saw a possibility to outcompete religion had to do with the revelation of the future. The future would be revealed when sociobiology would be able to establish an evolutionary trajectory for mankind. Science would substitute divine prophecy. But here he needed the social sciences, and in their present form they were not usable. Human nature would have to be factored in. Historians tried to find laws of history, but their views of human nature had no scientific basis:

> "The invisible hand remained invisible, the summed actions of thousands of millions of poorly understood individual human beings was not to be computed. Now there is reason to entertain the view that the culture of each society travels along one or the other of a set of evolutionary trajectories whose full array is constrained by the genetic rules of human nature. . . As our knowledge of human nature grows and we start to elect a system of values on a more objective basis, and our minds at last align with our hearts, the set of trajectories will narrow still more. . . As the social sciences mature into predictive

disciplines, the permissible trajectories will not only diminish in number but our descendants will be able to sight farther along them" (1978, p. 207)

In a surprise reference to the Bible, Wilson presented sociobiology as the answer of science to God's challenge to Job (38:18): "Have you comprehended the vast expanses of the world? Come, tell me all this if you know." "Yes, we do know and we have told," said Wilson (1978, p. 202). With the help of sociobiology, science would be able to substitute not only divine prophecy but also fulfill one of the great dreams of social theorists.

It was important for Wilson's larger moral goal to ensure that there was no way for an independent moral reality to exist—a world of not biologically grounded, and therefore arbitrary, moral values postulated by theologians, ethical philosophers, and others. Wilson formulated his basic dilemma as follows:

> But to the extent that principles are chosen by knowledge and reason remote from biology, they can at least in principle be non-Darwinian. This leads us ineluctably back to the second great spiritual dilemma. The philosophical question of interest that it generates is the following: Can the cultural evolution of higher ethical values gain a direction and momentum of its own and completely replace genetic revolution? I think not. The genes hold culture on a leash. The leash is very long, but inevitably values will be constrained in accordance with their effects on the human gene pool. The brain is a product of evolution. Human behavior—like the deepest capacities for emotional response which drive and guide it—is the circuitous technique by which human genetic material has been and will be kept intact. Morality has no other demonstrable ultimate function (Wilson 1978, p. 167).

In other words, Wilson's suggestion of genes holding culture on a leash was not a wish to support a conservative social order—as alleged by his critics in the sociobiology controversy—but rather to demonstrate the ultimate adaptive function of morality. Unlike many other sociobiologists, and even if he considered this a theoretical possibility, Wilson could not really "afford" to leave the cultural realm as a separate one. Materialism had to be guaranteed. But in 1978 Wilson also admitted that "the evolutionary epic" was itself a piece of mythology rather than a definite truth: "The evolutionary epic is mythology in the sense that the laws it adduces here and now are believed but can never be definitely proved to form a cause-and-effect continuum from physics to the social sciences, from this world to all other worlds in the visible universe and backward through time to the beginning of the universe" (Wilson 1978, p. 192).

WILSON AND THE SYNTHETIC GOD

So, Wilson had tried to rebut traditional religion, "explain it away," or put culture on a leash. But God still remained a viable hypothesis. Now, how would one go about testing God as a hypothesis? At a Star Island symposium in 1979

Wilson suggested that this could be done through the "creation of varieties of synthetic biological gods" (Wilson 1980, p. 427):

> This . . . could be accomplished by models of brain action, utilizing computer simulations and working progressively away from the cellular mechanisms of human cognition. One would then test, in the sociobiological mode, whether the peculiarities of the human perception match the exigencies of the particular environment in which the evolution of the human brain is inferred to have taken place. If such matching does exist, then the mind harbors a species god, which can be parsimoniously explained as a biological adaptation instead of an independent, transbiological force. The species god is perhaps more potent than a tribal god but unlikely to be the reflection of a universal deity (Wilson 1980, p. 427).

In other words, Wilson would again attempt an *in vitro* reconstruction, just as he had suggested earlier in the case of insect societies. He would be matching a model to reality. The ultimate refutation of God as a hypothesis would be the creation of a synthetic god.

In the meantime Wilson continued his search for loopholes for God: "Another possible refugium of divine influence was in the deep recesses of the mind" (Wilson 1980, p. 425). But there were ways of coping with this, too.

> For their part, the materialists are convinced that . . .(e)very nuance of mental action will prove not only to have a physical basis, but also to represent idiosyncratic adaptations to the special circumstances in which the brain evolved. When these Darwinian isomorphisms include also what has hitherto been explained as divine revelation, the biological god will disappear and the concept of a personal deity will revert to the category of blind faith (Wilson 1980, p. 426).

Speaking for "the materialists," Wilson told the Star Island symposium that this was how the biological god in the future would disappear. But was it really necessary to think like Wilson if one was a materialist? And did he himself really believe that "every nuance of mental action will prove . . . to have a physical basis?" Yes, was the answer I got in my interview with him in 1981. Wilson explained that he saw himself as an "expansionist," that is, someone who saw no limits to science. Here he followed Loren Graham (1980):

> I just believe, to put it as simply as possible, that science should be able to go in a relatively few decades to the point of producing a humanoid robot which would walk through that door. The first robot would think and talk like a Southern Baptist minister, and the second robot would talk like John Rawls. In other words, somehow I believe that we can reconstitute, recreate, the most mysterious features of human mental activity. That's an article of faith but it has to do with expansionism. That's expansionism! (Wilson, interview).[3]

Not surprisingly, such a conception was criticized by a number of philosophers at the time. Stuart Hampshire (1978) formulated a particularly detailed criticism, which Wilson himself in interview recognized as "very serious," charging that Wilson wants to be a materialist but really is an interactionist, who separates our physical functioning from our mental functioning while trying to understand the relationship between the two.

But also Wilson's Harvard Medical School colleague Bernard Davis, an ardent defender of sociobiology ever since the beginning considered his friend's view in this respect exaggerated. Even if neurophysiology could make enormous progress, this did not mean that we would be able to infer the *content* of a thought from knowledge of the underlying mechanisms (Davis 1980, and interview). Also Dawkins, whom critics often coupled together with Wilson stated quite early on that he did not believe we could get to content and meaning with artificial intelligence. He had used "robot" in his *The Selfish Gene*, but that was meant in a metaphorical way (Dawkins 1982, p. 14)

The people that Wilson here identified with were apparently the artificial intelligence people at MIT. Ironically, at the time, many scientists close to these cognitive studies considered a determination of the actual content of thought so far off as to be practically impossible. Thus, both Noam Chomsky and Walter Rosenblith of MIT were quite skeptical when I interviewed them as to the promises of these cognitive scientists, and thought their claims exaggerated. According to them, recently also other scientists who earlier were highly optimistic had turned pessimistic when it came to the near future for cognitive studies.

But Wilson was a scientific optimist, and his scientific optimism for cognitive science and his moral long-term goal went hand in hand. Through making every "nuance" of mental activity accounted for on a physical basis, he hoped to finally make sure that no bit of meaning escaped from his leash. It now becomes easier to understand the occasional overstatements on the part of Wilson: these derived not at all from a conservative wish to support the status quo (as his political critics claimed), but rather from a desire to prove the superiority of evolution to "the theologians."

INTEGRATING THE MIND

The obvious next step for Wilson would be to somehow scientifically account for the "deep recesses of the mind." This was to become part of his ambition in his next book *Genes, Mind, and Culture*, the result of a scientific collaboration with Charles Lumsden, a postdoctoral student trained in theoretical physics. Lumsden had originally come to Wilson's lab to model ants, not humans, but the project was changed when it turned out that he was interested in cognitive studies. Somebody able to model his insights from *On Human Nature* was exactly what Wilson now needed. Also, he was used to working with mathematically talented collaborators (he had modeled biogeography with MacArthur and caste in the Hymenoptera with George Oster) (Oster and Wilson 1978).

The scientific task at hand was to put the sociobiological reasoning about humans in explicit mathematical form. In this way Wilson and Lumsden tried to meet head-on a criticism often made of *Sociobiology*, that population genetics was not the right tool for explaining cultural differences. This kind of critique potentially undermined Wilson's whole attempt to bring human behavior into the Neo-Darwinian Synthesis. One of the fiercest critics was his Harvard colleague Richard Lewontin (1976), who doubted that any "multiplier effect" could have created the world's cultural diversity in just a few thousand years on the basis of modest genetic variation.

In *Genes, Mind, and Culture*, Lumsden and Wilson now argued that even small genetic differences and changes could explode up into significant cultural differences and changes; there could be feedback, from cultural change to genetic change. Ideas of this type in *Sociobiology* and in *On Human Nature* had been vulnerable to criticism since they had not been backed up mathematically. The new book would now demonstrate mathematically how Wilson's earlier reasoning in fact held up and how the "multiplier effect" worked. Human sociobiology would finally be put on a firm quantitative basis.

Interestingly, in my interview with him, Wilson presented *Genes, Mind, and Culture* as an entirely *new* idea about sociobiology, quite different from earlier views. This was also spelled out in the book itself:

> In evaluating the peculiarities of human behavior, they [sociobiologists and ethologists] tend to speak of patterns of behavior having a human-specific genetic basis, hence of genes that prescribe behavior. When learning is treated at all, it is viewed largely as a process by which packets of information that encode explicit behaviors leap between generations and colonize the brain— in the same way as pathogens invade hosts.

> For mankind at least, these postulates are radically incorrect. Behavior is not explicit in the genes, and mind cannot be treated as a mere replica of behavioral traits. In this book we propose a very different view in which the genes prescribe a set of biological processes, which we call epigenetic rules, that direct the assembly of the mind. This assembly is context dependent, with the epigenetic rules feeding on information derived from culture and physical environment... [C]ulture is the translation of the epigenetic rules into mass patterns of mental activity and behavior...Genes are indeed linked to culture, but in a deep and subtle manner (Lumsden and Wilson 1981, p. 2).

It is possible that Wilson earlier entertained several coexisting views, or was in transition himself between an "older" and a "newer" type of sociobiology, while finally with *Genes, Mind, and Culture* committing himself more fully to the idea of gene–culture coevolution. But it seems to me that a rough idea of gene–culture coevolution was there from the very beginning, showing up already in 1969 in his presentation at the Man and Beast conference.

With this new book, Wilson had found a way to answer his earlier critics. He had demonstrated that it was indeed possible to derive also patterns of cultural diversity from what he called "biological ground rules." At the same time, he was one step closer to his ambition to integrate the social and natural sciences. After all, he had now shown mathematically how evolutionary biology could be made relevant to central concerns of the social sciences.

Genes, Mind, and Culture was the mathematical demonstration of how it was possible, after all, for the genes to hold culture on a leash: "The epigenetic rules will... tend to channel cognitive development toward certain culturgens as opposed to others. We refer to this relation informally as the 'leash principle' in order to make it metaphorically more vivid: genetic natural selection operates in such a way as to keep culture on a leash" (Lumsden and Wilson 1981, p. 13).

But there was that old connection to Wilson's moral agenda. If we substitute culture with religion (as Wilson tended to do in *On Human Nature*), then Wilson with this new book had now finally scientifically shown that religion could be kept on a leash. He was now closer to satisfying his deep urge to supersede traditional theology by a view based on materialism and evolution. And since his new models took into account also the human mind, he was now reaching into that possible last refugium of God with the help of quantitative science. In my interview with him at the time, Wilson was quite excited: "We produced the first theory! We are the only game in town! We are the only ones who have a theory which takes what is known about cognitive psychology, development, and so on, and ties this together in a series of models and conceptual schemes."

There were, however, criticisms of this coevolutionary modeling attempt. A typical critique was of the reductionist assumptions of the models. Culture, for instance, was defined as a "sum of mental constructs and behaviors, including the construction and employment of artifacts" (Lumsden and Wilson, p. 3). This of course went quite against holistic or symbolical conceptions of culture and society. Indeed, Lewontin, far from being appeased by Wilson's modeling attempt, was dismayed at his now trying to embrace the social sciences with reductionism and statistics (Lewontin 1981). (Lewontin had a holistic view of society and long-standing skepticism about statistics in social sciences.) The anthropologist Edmund Leach wrote an ironical review in *Nature* (Leach 1981). And fellow biologist John Maynard Smith, after scrutinizing the mathematics for several months, concluded that it did not really support the book's verbal arguments in a strong way, although it showed that under rather special assumptions the coevolutionary feedback loop could work (Maynard Smith and Warren 1982). (Maynard Smith was one of the very few who actually checked the math.) The basic idea of a coevolutionary feedback loop that included the mind was an interesting one to many researchers at the time, but the Wilson and Lumsden models as such were not picked up and used by others—probably they were not seen as practical enough. Perhaps the best way of regarding *Genes, Mind, and Culture* is to see it as a demonstration that this kind of thinking could be mathematically formulated at all. Such a demonstration could serve multiple purposes for Wilson.

THE SEAMLESS WEB

In his 1998 book *Consilience*, Wilson borrowed the 19th century scientist William Whewell's original notion, giving it a new connotation. Whewell had used the term "consilience" (literally "jumping together") to describe a particular phenomenon in science: the support of an explanation within one scientific field by the explanation of a quite different set of phenomena in another field. This kind of support across fields typically gives scientists added faith in their theories.

But for Wilson, consilience meant more than the conjunction of explanations from different scientific fields. It meant the unity of knowledge, a quest that Wilson traced back to the Enlightenment. (Indeed, the publication of *Consilience* was accompanied by his article "Resuming the Enlightenment Quest"). The Enlightenment's ideal, Wilson noted, was to render the world understandable with the help of universal science, and this applied to man and society, too. But later this ideal was abandoned, and the social sciences and humanities were seen as possessing different categories of truth and autonomous ways of knowing. They were not regarded as amenable to scientific analysis (Wilson 1998b).

This was all going to change, Wilson assured his readers. Unity of knowledge could again be achieved, through a new field of inquiry, "a new foundational discipline of the social sciences and humanities." This new field of research would involve the "broad and largely unexplored terrain of phenomena bound up with the material origins and functions of the human brain" (Wilson 1998b).

Wilson hoped to unite "the disparate facts of the disciplines by consilience, the perception of a seamless web of causes and effects" (Wilson 1998a). The problem was how to find an explanation that would span the existing gap between the natural sciences and the liberal arts, between nature and culture. But Wilson believed that he had found the answer in the idea of gene–culture coevolution, and particularly the epigenetic rules. These were the tools needed for making sense of the world as a "seamless web of cause and effect."

Wilson compared his approach to logical positivism, the famous earlier attempt to unify science. Consilience was clearly superior. The logical positivists were philosophers and saw objective truth as a philosophical problem. They did not know how the brain worked, which was why they could not "track material phenomena of the outer world through the labyrinth of causal processes in the inner mental world, and thus precisely map outer phenomena onto the inner material phenomena of conscious activity" (Wilson 1998b, p. 27). But the problem Wilson argued, was an empirical one, "solvable only by a continuing investigation of the physical basis of the mind itself. In time, like so many searches of the past, it will be transformed into the description of a material process" (p. 27). We see here that Wilson never gave up his idea of truth as direct correspondence or model building. He was firmly convinced that subjective meaning could be derived from an objective description of a physical process. (Recall for instance his notion about a synthetic god.)

For Wilson, as an idea, consilience was both intellectually and emotionally satisfying while providing the needed direction for solving urgent problems. In his book he identified three main advantages:

First, consilience corresponds to our basic human quest: "The assumptions … about a lawful material world, the intrinsic unity of knowledge, and the potential of indefinite human progress are the ones we take most readily into our hearts, suffer without, and find maximally rewarding through intellectual advance" (Wilson 1998a, p. 8).

Second, consilience will solve the tension between the two cultures. The way to proceed is to "view the boundary between the scientific and literary cultures … as a mostly unexplored terrain awaiting cooperative entry from both sides" (Wilson 1998a, p. 126). In other words, for Wilson, the boundary is simply a research problem:

> *What, in final analysis, joins the deep, mostly genetic history of the species as a whole to the more recent cultural histories of its far-flung societies? That, in my opinion, is the nub of the relationship between the two cultures.* It can be stated as a problem to be solved, the central problem of the social sciences and the humanities, and simultaneously one of the great remaining problems of the natural sciences (Wilson 1998a, p. 126, italics added).

Third, there are practical and pedagogical reasons for advocating consilience. The problems facing the world are not part of either social science or natural science, they are part of both. We need a core curriculum in colleges and universities that takes into account the cause-and-effect connections among the great branches of learning: "not metaphor. . . .but material cause-and-effect" (Wilson 1998a, pp. 269–270). The gaps in knowledge that look particularly promising for consilient exploration are "the final unification of physics, the reconstruction of living cells, the assembly of ecosystems, the coevolution of genes and culture, the physical basis of mind, and the deep origins of ethics and religion" (p. 268).

How did Wilson think that the arts could be included in his grand unification project? His answer was interesting. The arts are also pursuing truth. After all, they "embrace not only all physically possible worlds but also all conceivable worlds innately interesting and congenial to the nervous system and thus, in the uniquely human sense, true" (Wilson 1998a, p. 268). Even the seemingly tricky problem of meaning could be resolved: "What we call meaning is the linkage among the neural networks created by the spreading excitation that enlarges imagery and engages emotion" (p. 115).

At the center of the unification project were the epigenetic rules, Wilson's new unification tool. For Wilson, as science was progressing, there would be ever new evidence accumulating on such things as the universality of color terms, the genetic control of medical conditions affecting behavior, or the biologically constrained nature of esthetic preferences, Wilson believed. (This was the type of evidence earlier offered in *Genes, Mind, and Culture*). And for him, this represented steadily accumulating evidence for the unity between the natural and social sciences. (This is also why a lecture called "Uniting the Natural and Social Sciences" was mostly an expose of new data of this kind).

For Wilson, this was all so clear. Consilience was a beautiful, total, synthetic vision of the interconnectedness of the world, organic and nonorganic, nature and culture, material and spiritual, practical and moral. The epigenetic rules, which biased our perceptions in a particular human way, constituted the crucial link between the subjective world and objective reality. In his book, Wilson in his eloquent style tried to convey his vision in different ways to different audiences (even including the creationists). Could people not see? For Wilson, with his youthful experiences in evangelist exultation, it was quite possible to transport himself into a futuristic vision of total consilience. It was a type of "kingdom come" that he described for his readers. He wanted them to convert.

In more sober scientific moments in the book, though, Wilson was quite willing to cautiously assess the project and its potential reception. Here he freely admitted that some pieces of his big scenario relied on assumptions that looked very similar to belief. This oscillating writing style was idiosyncratic of E. O. Wilson and actually already clearly identifiable in the first and last chapters of *Sociobiology*. (Not surprisingly, it was these chapters that later were to become subject to major, hostile misinterpretation by Wilson's political critics.)

UNIFICATION AND ITS DISCONTENTS

Wilson clearly struck a chord with the general public and apparently many educators, judging from the popularity of *Consilience* on amazon.com and college campuses. Were these readers willing to follow Wilson all the way, or were they excited about the many diverse pieces of scientific information that Wilson was bringing up and intricately tying together? Or both? Others were not so easily convinced. The philosopher Richard Rorty objected that the examples of epigenetic rules that Wilson cited were simply not persuasive enough. He did not doubt that these kinds of rules existed, he wrote, but to go all the way from these to unity of all knowledge would take a large leap of faith. More importantly, Rorty pointed out that it was unclear how knowledge of science would be helpful for solving moral or political problems. Unlike Wilson, Rorty (1998) believed in a natural (and useful) division of labor between the natural sciences and the humanities, in which the former helped us achieve a goal, and the latter helped us decide what the goal should be.

Jerry Fodor (1998), a specialist on cognitive science, echoed some of Rorty's objections. Also he wondered why Wilson would assume that a view of the unity of explanation should entail the view of a unity of reality, too. After all, there was a difference between epistemology and metaphysics. Fodor also questioned Wilson's belief that the success of the natural sciences was connected to their unity. According to him, different natural sciences had typically explained science in their own different "dialects," not in the language of basic physics. If anything, rather than unification, the natural sciences showed a proliferation of new disciplines. Finally, he protested against Wilson's assumption that everything would have to be reducible to physics (e.g., Wilson, 1998a, p. 266). A position of scientific realism was quite compatible with a view of reality as made up of different levels of organization.

More devastating was Fodor's verdict on Wilson's reliance on cognitive neuroscience. According to Fodor, cognitive neuroscience, the attempt to model how the brain implements the mind, was, if anything, a good example of science's *failure* to unify vertically—despite heroic efforts and great expenditure. And this was the very discipline that Wilson was betting his consilience project on! It seemed to Fodor that Wilson had "swallowed whole" the recent brain science literature, a genre that he himself classified as "associationism with engineering jargon." He noted that in *Consilience* Wilson had described memory as involving nodes, linkages, and resonance of circuits. Meaning, again, was created in the form of linked concepts simultaneously experienced. Fodor thought it odd that Wilson was so impressed with evidence of the type "disturbance of particular circuits of the human brain often produces bizarre results." For Fodor, such things clearly paled in comparison with the really big contributions to the field—Turing's computational theory of thought, Chomsky's discovery of the mathematical structure of language—neither of which had anything to do with neurological research.

CONNECTING SCIENCE AND VALUES

Wilson had a rather special view of what the Enlightenment quest was all about. For him it appeared to be primarily about the unity of knowledge—not about such things as universal standards for truth, justice, and morals, or about reason in science and human affairs. Indeed, Rorty questioned Wilson's equation of the Enlightenment project with the unity of all branches of learning. According to him, it was quite possible to be devoted to the Enlightenment vision of human rights and social justice without knowing anything about, say, the workings of the brain.

Wilson's special interpretation can be further highlighted by comparing his view with that of the German social theorist Jurgen Habermas, a long-time promoter of the Enlightenment ideal. From the beginning Habermas' fear has been that the "lifeworld" of norms and values will get "colonized" by the objectifying logic of science and technology (see e.g., Habermas 1970, 1979, 1984). This concern, in turn, derives exactly from Habermas' different interpretation of the essence of the Enlightenment quest as the vision of a rational society. A rational society is a society whose goals and values are freely settled on in a process of rational discourse. Because for Habermas science is unproblematically progressive and truth-generating; his concern is with protecting the more vulnerable world of norms and values, and the social conditions for rational discourse. So, for Habermas, the means–end rationality involved in science and technology, and the "practical reason" involved in social discourse are fundamentally different, but complementary, types of rationality.

Wilson's interest in the unity of all realms of learning—over and above the specific Enlightenment quests of each of these separately—might be called a hyper-Enlightenment quest. In this respect, Wilson is different from "regular" scientists, philosophers, and others, who might be described as pursuing "ordinary" Enlightenment quests. In fact, in the first chapter of *Consilience* Wilson himself contrasts two types of thought, the "Ionian" and the "Icarian" mode. The first one is the quest for knowledge and truth over belief. The other refers to the story of Icarus, who perished when he flew toward the sun. Wilson himself can be seen as oscillating between these two modes, depending on whether he acts as an objectivist scientist or a visionary. Speaking as a scientist, he vehemently defends the objectivity of science, criticizing his scientific opponents as ideologically biased. Speaking as a visionary with concern for the future of Man and the world, he operates in his "evangelist" or advocacy mode, where he freely embraces values (and some would argue, ideology). No wonder some readers have felt there is a double message (Todorov 1998). Not even Wilson's close colleagues always know what to think.

Meanwhile the unity of science, pursued at a more modest level, is clearly something that many of Wilson's colleagues would agree that there should exist. There needs to be some kind of coherence, consistency, or compatibility of explanations at different levels in science, so that explanations at one level would not be contradictory to explanations at another level (see for instance the discussion by Cosmides and Tooby 1992). But this does not mean that they would necessarily be willing to take the next step. Still, this will sort itself out. Because in science truth is not revealed, but lies in the hands of the scientific community. The success of an idea depends on the extent to which other scientists are willing to follow in Wilson's footsteps, one of Wilson's colleagues noted, operating in a relentlessly Ionian mode (cf. Gross 1998).

For a "regular" scientist Wilsonian consilience does require an unusual set of commitments: a belief that the unity of the world entails the unity of explanation, a belief that explanation can only mean explanation in the language of physics, a belief in the identity of brain and mind, explanation and understanding, and finally, a sense of a deep connection between a knowledge of evolutionary biology and human values.

But Wilson appears as an indomitable optimist. Quite early in *Consilience* he pulled the rug from under his critics by declaring himself "guilty, guilty, guilty" to all kinds of possible epistemological crimes—"conflation, simplism, ontological reductionism, scientism, and other sins." At the same time however, he diminished their import by classifying them as the objections of "a few professional philosophers" to his unification project (p. 11). He insisted that his project was at least worth a try.

One source of particular tension between Wilson and many potential allies has to do with his persistent reluctance to leave the world of values alone. Wilson has from the very beginning been interested not only in examining human nature and human values, but also in *prescribing* values for humankind. Already in *Sociobiology* he suggested that "a genetically accurate and hence completely fair code of ethics" must wait for further contributions of evolutionary sociobiology (op. cit., p. 575). He also mused that "[a] science of sociobiology, if coupled with neurophysiology, might transform the insights of ancient religions into a precise account of the evolutionary origins of ethics and hence explain the reasons why we make certain moral choices instead of others at particular times" (Wilson 1975, p. 129).

In *On Human Nature*, again, he argued that "The principal task of human biology is to identify and to measure the constraints that influence the decisions of ethical philosophers and everyone else, and to infer their significance through neurophysiological and phylogenetic reconstructions of the mind. . . . In the process, it will fashion a biology of ethics, which will make possible the selection of a more deeply understood and enduring code of moral values" (Wilson 1978, p. 196).

Of course, he has recognized this himself—facts and values may just not link up as neatly as he would wish. In his own allusion to the Icarus story in this book, he said he saw his consilience as an admittedly vaulting ambition. He recognized that the whole idea of consilience could be wrong, but believed that we would find out "in a few decades" if his view was correct (Wilson 1998a, p. 268).

CONSILIENCE AND RECONCILIATION

There was an additional side to consilience. Wilson also presented it as a metaphysical worldview, a belief "shared by only a few scientists and philosophers" (Wilson 1998a, p. 9). Seeing consilience as a metaphysical project meant that it could serve as both science and belief at the same time. Here we had, then, yet another meaning of "consilience"—a reconciliation between science and religion. Indeed, in *Consilience* Wilson even tried to reach his potentially most reluctant audience—the creationists. He declared himself empathetic to the feelings of this group—"and conciliatory"—bringing up his own background education as a Southern Baptist (p. 129). Consilience, in other words, was Wilson's total answer to the needs of mankind, including its spiritual needs.

Consilience was the work of Wilson that brought together all his ambitions, epistemological, ethical, and metaphysical, relevant both to mankind and life on

Earth as a whole. It was the synthesis of syntheses. At the same time Wilson here reintroduced his original wish from *Sociobiology*: his grand vision of unifying the social and natural sciences, nature and culture, bringing also Man into the Neo-Darwinian synthesis.

Wilson never gave up sociobiology as an idea, but after *Genes, Mind, and Culture* he found additional routes to plead for his vision. With the biophilia idea (the human need for nature, published as *Biophilia* in 1984) and his later campaigns for saving the rainforest and warning about the extinction of life on Earth, Wilson was in fact also arguing for the idea of a biologically grounded human nature. This idea of a deep connection between man and nature struck a chord with academics and the general public, and by the time of publication of the *Diversity of Life* (1992) Wilson was definitely on his way toward ungluing the "bad sociobiologist" label pinned on by his critics, transforming himself into an indisputably "good" protector of the environment.

Over a quarter century, different parts of his complex message, presented in different books in different forms, were capable of being digested by different constituencies. Over this time, Wilson himself did not change, but the cultural climate did. It became gradually more receptive to the idea of a genetically underpinned basic human nature—that very vision, which was so much re-sisted during the early stages of the sociobiology debate, and which still in the mid 1980s triggered a book with the title *Not in Our Genes* (Lewontin *et al.* 1984).

With *Consilience*, Wilson sketched a new all-encompassing scientific pro-gram with evolutionary biology as the core discipline. In the middle of the 20th century, the epoch-making scientific breakthrough had happened in molecular biology with Watson and Crick, DNA, and the Central Dogma. There had been a time when molecular biology had threatened to drive older naturalistic fields totally out of business. Wilson had picked up the fight early on with his syn-thetic and quantitative efforts in *Sociobiology*. At the end of the century Wilson gave us his response to that challenge. He was offering the world of science nothing less than a new and total Central Dogma, this time with evolution, not molecular biology, at its center.

At the same time Wilson had now fulfilled his deepest metaphysical ambi-tion: he had found a way to reach into those "inner crevices of the mind" where he in 1980 admitted that God may still be dwelling. He had secured through "a seamless web of cause and effect" the absence of any refugium for this god. No external values could any longer seep in, the only values were those coming from the "species god."

Wilson had already taken care of morality by explaining it as one among many epigenetic rules (Ruse and Wilson 1985) and in *Consilience* he was now finally able to pack religion, too, away. Religion was not only a product of our naturally myth-making brain (as he had argued already in *On Human Nature*), but it was also nothing but an adaptation! Submission to a superior being—religious behavior—was just an extension of a well-known biological survival strategy. At the same time Wilson in *Consilience* continued his plea from *On Human Nature*: since our brains are anyway programmed for myth-making, let us adopt the evolutionary epic, the best myth we have.

After Wilson abandoned his faith as a Southern Baptist at the age of 17 years, all of his life has involved some kind of reckoning with religion with the help of his new adopted paradigm, evolution. It is not too much to say that it was the need to resolve the tension between science and religion that was the driving force behind his larger synthetic quest beginning around the age of 40 years. This took different forms: an attempt to demonstrate that humans possessed positive adaptive traits (as a protest against the negativistic 1960s ethological writers), the wish to keep culture (in the form of religion) on a leash, the demonstration that morality was a species-specific adaptive trait, and so on. An important ingredient in this was also Wilson's emphasis on human emotions as making up a central part of our species nature, something that would probably inform our choices also when it came to future technological possibilities of engineering our own genome. Emotions, as it were, would keep reason on a leash.

Meanwhile his quest was infused with the energy and beauty of the evangelist preachings of his childhood, his love for life on Earth, and the inspiration coming from Wheeler's insect society superorganism, a model for a combined scientific and moral agenda. It went through a period of "new holism" and a number of more specialized projects, such as sociobiology and the defense of biodiversity, only to be reunited in a big would-be cosmic synthesis. But from here it was back again, to a revisit to his initial inspirations: the superorganism, and "the Creation." In 2006, Wilson published books on both these topics.

In fact, Wilson's relative militancy in pitting science against religion in *On Human Nature* and at the Star Island Symposium later abated in favor of more of a reconciliation between the two. Wilson has always operated on a number of fronts. One strategy has even been to try to convince "the theologians" that they need to take into account what we currently know about human nature, not operate with an "Iron Age" model (Wilson 1991b).

What many of the political critics did not understand back in the time of the sociobiology controversy was that Wilson represented an older tradition in biology, one that naturally and explicitly combined science with values. Among other more recent representatives for this tradition were Konrad Lorenz, C. H. Waddington, and Vero Wynne-Edwards. Still another way of classifying Wilson, however, is as one of the great scientific-cum-metaphysical "cosmic" synthesizers, similar to someone like Ernst Haeckel or Teilhard de Chardin (cf. Holton 1978). Wilson's synthetic work was never really about any "mere" unification of academic fields. His various efforts were always part of a much bigger project, whose aim was ultimately to provide a total explanation of the world and what it meant to be human.

REFERENCES

ARDREY, R. 1966. *The Territorial Imperative*. London: Collins.

BRINTON, C. 1959. *The Society of Fellows*. Cambridge, MA: Harvard University Press.

COSMIDES, L., and J. TOOBY. 1992. Cognitive adaptations for social exchange. Pp. 163–228 in J. Barkow, L. Cosmides, and J. Tooby (eds.), *The Adapted Mind*. New York: Oxford University Press.

CROOK, J. 1971. Sources of cooperation in animals and man. Pp. 235–260 in J.F. Eisenberg and W.S. Dillon (eds.), *Man and Beast*. Washington, DC: Smithsonian Institution.

DAVIS, B.D. 1980. The importance of human individuality for sociobiology. *Zygon 15*, 275–293.

DAWKINS, R. 1976. *The Selfish Gene*. Oxford and New York: Oxford University Press.

DAWKINS, R. 1982. *The Extended Phenotype*. Oxford and New York: Oxford University Press.

ECCLES, J. 1980. *The Human Psyche*. The Gifford Lectures, University of Edinburgh, 1978-79. Berlin: Springer Verlag.

FODOR, J. 1998. Look! (Review of E. O. Wilson's *Consilience*). *London Review of Books* 29 October, 3, 6.

GHISELIN, M.T. 1974. *The Economy of Nature and the Evolution of Sex*. Berkeley: University of California Press.

GRAHAM, L.R. 1980. *Between Science and Values*. New York: Columbia University Press.

GROSS, P., 1998. The Icarian impulse. *The Wilson Quarterly* Winter:39–49.

HABERMAS, J. 1970. *Toward a Rational Society*. Boston: Beacon Press.

HABERMAS, J. 1979. *Communication and the Evolution of Society*. Boston: Beacon Press.

HABERMAS, J. 1984. *The Theory of Communicative Action. Volume I: Reason and the Rationalization of Society*. Boston, MA: Beacon Press.

HAMILTON, W.D. 1964. The genetical theory of social behavior. I and II. *Journal of Theoretical Biology 7*, 1–16; 17–32.

HAMPSHIRE, S. 1978. The illusion of sociobiology. *The New York Review of Books*, October 12, 64–69.

HARAWAY, D. 1981–1982. The high cost of information in post-World War II evolutionary biology: ergonomics, semiotics, and the sociobiology of communication systems. *The Philosophical Forum 13* (2–3), 244–278.

HEYL, B.S. 1968. The Harvard "Pareto Circle." *Journal of the History of the Behavioral Sciences 4*, 316–334.

HOLTON, G. 1978. The new synthesis? Pp. 75–97 in M.S. Gregory, A. Silvers, and D. Sutch (eds.), *Sociobiology and Human Nature*. San Francisco: Jossey Bass.

HOMANS, G.C. 1984. *Coming to My Senses: The Autobiography of a Sociologist*. New Brunswick, New Jersey: Transaction.

LEVINS, R. 1968. *Evolution in Changing Environments*. Princeton, NJ: Princeton University Press.

LEACH, E. 1981. Biology and social science. Wedding or rape? *Nature 291*, 267–268.

LEWONTIN, R.C., ed. 1968. *Population Biology and Evolution*. Syracuse, NY: Syracuse University Press.

LEWONTIN, R.C. 1976. Interview. *The Harvard Gazette*, January 16.

LEWONTIN, R.C. 1981. Sleight of hand. *The Sciences* July–August:23–26.
LEWONTIN, R.C., S. ROSE, and L.J. KAMIN. 1984. *Not in Our Genes: Biology, Ideology, and Human Nature*. New York: Pantheon Books.
LORENZ, K. 1966. *On Aggression*. London: Methuen.
LUMSDEN, C.L., and E.O. WILSON. 1981. *Genes, Mind and Culture: The Coevolutionary Process*. Cambridge, Massachusetts: Harvard University Press.
LUMSDEN, C.L., and E.O. WILSON. 1983. *Promethean Fire*. Cambridge, Massachusetts: Harvard University Press.
MACARTHUR, R.H., and E.O. WILSON. 1967. *The Theory of Island Biogeography*. Princeton: Princeton University Press.
MAYNARD SMITH, J., and N. WARREN. 1982. Models of cultural and genetic change. *Evolution 36*, 620–627.
OSTER, G.F., and WILSON, E.O. 1978. *Caste and Ecology in the Social Insects*. Princeton: Princeton University Press.
PARSONS, T. 1953. Some comments on the state of the general theory of action. *American Sociological Review 18*(6), 618–631.
RORTY, R. 1998. Against unity. *Wilson Quarterly 22* (Winter), 28–38.
RUSE, M., and E.O. WILSON. 1985. The evolution of ethics. *New Scientist* 17 October: 50–53.
RUSSETT, C.E. 1966. *The Concept of Equilibrium in American Social Thought*. New Haven, Connecticut: Yale University Press.
SCHNEIRLA, T.C. 1971. *Army Ants: A Study in Social Organization*. San Francisco: W. H. Freeman.
SEGERSTRALE, U. 2000. *Defenders of the Truth: The Battle for Science in the Sociobiology Debate and Beyond*. New York: Oxford University Press.
SEGERSTRALE, U. 2006 "An Eye on the Core—Dawkins and Sociobiology." Pp. 75–97 in A. Grafen, and M. Ridley (eds.), *Richard Dawkins – How A Scientist Changed the Way We Think*. New York: Oxford University Press.
TIGER, L., and R. FOX. 1971. *The Imperial Animal*. New York: Holt, Rinehart, Winston.
TODOROV, T. 1998. The surrender to nature. *New Republic* April 27:29–33.
WHEELER, W.M. 1928a. *Emergent Evolution and the Development of Societies*. New York: W.W. Norton.
WHEELER, W.M. 1928b. *The Social Insects, their Origin and Evolution*. New York: Harcourt, Brace.
WILSON, E.O. 1962. Chemical communication among workers of the fire ant, Solenopsis Saevissima. *Animal Behavior 10*, 134–164.
WILSON, E.O. 1971a. *The Insect Societies*. Cambridge, Massachusetts: Harvard University Press.
WILSON, E.O. 1971b. The prospects for a unified sociobiology. *American Scientist 59*, 400–403.
WILSON, E.O. 1971c. Competitive and aggressive behavior. Pp. 181–217 in J.F. Eisenberg, and W.S. Dillon (eds.), *Man and Beast: Comparative Social Behavior*. Washington, DC: Smithsonian Institution Press.
WILSON, E.O. 1975. *Sociobiology: The New Synthesis*. Cambridge, Massachusetts: Harvard University Press.
WILSON, E.O. 1977. Biology and the social sciences. *Daedalus 106* (4), 127–140.
WILSON, E.O. 1978. *On Human Nature*. New York: Bantam Books.
WILSON, E.O. 1980. The relation of science to theology. *Zygon 15*, 425–434.
WILSON, E.O. 1984. *Biophilia*. Cambridge, Massachusetts: Harvard University Press.

WILSON, E.O. 1991a. Sociobiology and the test of time. Pp. 77–80 in M.H. Robinson, and L. Tiger (eds.), *Man and Beast Revisited*. Washington, DC: Smithsonian Institution Press.

WILSON, E.O. 1991b. Scientific humanism and religion. *Free Inquiry 11*(2), 20–23.

WILSON, E.O. 1992. *The Diversity of Life*. Cambridge, Massachusetts: Belknap Press/ Harvard University Press.

WILSON, E.O. 1994. *Naturalist*. Cambridge, Massachusetts: Island Press.

WILSON, E.O. 1998a. *Consilience: The Unity of Knowledge*. New York: Alfred Knopf.

WILSON, E.O. 1998b. Resuming the Enlightenment quest. *The Wilson Quarterly* Winter: 16–27.

WILSON, E.O. 2000. *The Future of Life*. New York: Knopf.

Converging Technologies in Higher Education

Paradigm for the "New" Liberal Arts?

ROBERT T. BALMER

Union College, Schenectady, New York 12308, USA

ABSTRACT: This article discusses the historic relationship between the practical arts (technology) and the mental (liberal) arts, suggesting that Converging Technologies is a new higher education paradigm that integrates the arts, humanities, and sciences with modern technology. It explains that the paradigm really includes all fields in higher education from philosophy to art to music to modern languages and beyond. To implement a transformation of this magnitude, it is necessary to understand the psychology of change in academia. Union College in Schenectady, New York, implemented a Converging Technologies Educational Paradigm in five steps: (1) create a compelling vision, (2) communicate the vision, (3) empower the faculty, (4) create short-term successes, and (5) institutionalize the results. This case study of Union College demonstrates it is possible to build a pillar of educational excellence based on Converging Technologies.

KEYWORDS: engineering education; academia; implementing change; paradigm shift; 21st century

INTRODUCTION

Technological advances often occur at the interfaces of conventional fields. Analog and digital computer technology grew out of the intersection of mathematics and electrical engineering; mechatronics (i.e., robotics) grew from the intersections of mechanical, electrical, and computer engineering; nanotechnology from the confluence of physics, chemistry, and engineering, and so on. The phrase "Converging Technologies" is used to describe the process wherein unrelated fields of technology intersect (or "converge") to produce new and often unexpected technologies and associated fields of study. In recent years, such technologies have been evolving rapidly, far outpacing the

Address for correspondence: Robert T. Balmer, 11711 N. Vega Ave., Mequon, WI 53097. Voice: 262-643-4025; fax: 518-388-6789.
e-mail: balmerr@union.edu

Ann. N.Y. Acad. Sci. 1093: 74–83 (2006). © 2006 New York Academy of Sciences.
doi: 10.1196/annals.1382.005

multigenerational time frame typically required for change to occur in higher education.

In her article on "Liberal Arts for a New Millennium," Joyce Baldwin (2000) opens with the question: "In an era when technology is changing everything, does the definition of 'an educated person' still include a background in the liberal arts?" This volatile introduction challenges the definition of liberal arts. Baldwin concludes that "we urgently need a new set of guidelines, a new paradigm, to shape the direction of education for the 21st century, to prepare students not only for the marketplace but for life, enriching their experiences, broadening their horizons and inspiring them to embrace learning as a lifelong pursuit." Converging Technologies may be that new paradigm.

TRADITIONAL LIBERAL ARTS

Traditional liberal learning is generally recognized to include the arts, humanities, and the sciences. In the minds of many today there is little difference between the terms "science" and "technology," with technology often being viewed simply as applied science. However, historically these terms have very different meanings.

The meaning of the word "science" comes from the Latin verb "to know," and refers to *mental* labor. The word "technology," on the other hand, comes from the Greek word "techne," (art or craft), and refers to *manual* labor. Early technologists were presumed to use their hands and not their minds, and became the essence of the "trades."

The term "liberal" in *liberal arts* originally meant "appropriate for free men" (i.e., the gentlemen of antiquity), which was a proper education for the social elite. Only men free of financial concerns had the luxury to learn material only for the joy of learning itself. Aristotle has been quoted saying that the liberal arts "are those which tend to enjoyment, where nothing accrues of consequence beyond the activity itself."

Consequently, the liberal arts have for centuries represented the opposite of professional or vocational "training" (as opposed to "education," the distinction being an inflammatory topic in academic circles today). The servile arts were skills learned solely for the sake of doing something for remuneration. For example, teachers are trained, but philosophers are educated.

By the Middle Ages the liberal arts had solidified into seven arts, organized in two groups. The first group (trivium) contained grammar, logic, and rhetoric, and second group (quadrivium) contained advanced study in arithmetic, geometry, astronomy, and music. The trivium focused on thought and communications, resulting in the conferring of a Bachelor of Arts degree (and the status of "gentleman"). The quadrivium was more advanced in the sciences of the time and produced the Master of Arts degree.

TECHNOLOGY AND THE NEW LIBERAL ARTS

Today the trivium has become the literacy required to liberate people from a life of social servility (e.g., working in fast-food restaurants), and, with a little imagination, the modern quadrivium can be viewed as the professional, scientific, and technical disciplines. The American Society of Civil Engineers recently concluded (Report from the ASCE Task Committee on the First Professional Degree 2001) that the requisite body of specialized knowledge to practice as a professional civil engineer is best obtained through a combination of an engineering baccalaureate degree plus a master's degree (or equivalent), thus making the first *professional* degree in civil engineering the Master of Science degree. This implies that civil engineering graduates will have acquired the intellectual tools needed for logic and communications (the objectives of the trivium) plus the specialization within a disciplinary field (the objectives of the quadrivium). It also reflects the relationships between learning the unchanging fundamentals, such as a liberal education, and a changing specialized field, that is, a professional education (Schachterle 1997).

George Bugliarello, President Emeritus and former Chancellor of the Polytechnic University, has written that: "Today's conflicts between the views that the humanities hold of science and engineering and the views science and engineering hold of the humanities weaken the very core of our culture. Their cause is lack of integration in today's education among subjects that hark back to the medieval trivium and quadrivium" (Bugliarello 2003). Bugliarello feels that integration of intellectual activity is urgently needed because no field can be learned in isolation today. And in terms of societal leadership, 21st century technology is so complex and so pervasive that no one can lead effectively without understanding the practical implications of technological decisions.

The movement to a new paradigm for engineering education is already under way. The current young generation of liberal arts and engineering faculty seems more aware of the impact of technology on society, and are more accepting of new directions and collaborations, than are their senior colleagues. Additionally, both liberal arts and engineering students today are more career-oriented than in the past. Since any college that has 40% or more of its graduates in the liberal arts can call itself a "liberal arts college," hundreds of liberal arts colleges graduate thousands with degrees that match almost any job imaginable, such as journalism, business, criminal justice, and nursing (Neely 1999).

Since the mid 20th century, there has been political pressure to reduce the number of credits required for an engineering degree from around 140 to 120. A few leading colleges have programs offering an engineering BA degree with a fifth year of study required for an engineering BS degree (e.g., Dartmouth). Even the Accreditation Board for Engineering and Technology (ABET) has liberalized the requirements for program accreditation with Criteria 2000, much to the dismay of the National Council of Examiners for Engineering and Surveying who felt that perhaps the low passing rates on the Fundamentals of Engineering exam was a reflection of the new ABET criteria (NCEES 2003).

In the 1940s, only 20% of high school graduates went to college, and most went to a liberal arts institution. By the mid 1970s, only half of all baccalaureate degrees were granted in a liberal arts discipline (including science). By the end of the 20th century, 65% of high school graduates went to college and nearly 60% of the degrees granted were in a pre-professional or technical field. The number of students attending community colleges increased greatly since 1970, and now 2-year associate degree schools account for more than 40% of the college population. Given the importance of higher education in a developed society, it is very possible that by the mid 21st century a liberal arts college education will be as common as a high school education in the mid 20th century.

THE CONVERGING TECHNOLOGIES PARADIGM

What does the phrase "Converging Technologies" mean? In academia it has several inclusive meanings. First, Converging Technologies are the new and often unexpected technologies that appear at the interfaces of existing fields of study. At first blush, because of the word "Technologies," this term seems to refer only to science and engineering. However, it really includes all fields in higher education from philosophy to art to music to modern languages and beyond, because all of the traditional liberal arts involve some use of technology (e.g., the physical media used in painting and sculpture, the instrumentation and reproduction of music, and the media and transmission of language). Thus Converging Technologies focuses creative thought on new ideas that are changing the landscape of global society.

Why is it important? It is important to the future of our students and our society. Abbott and Masterman put it best: *"Students who do not understand how the new and converging technologies work, how they construct meaning, how they can be used, and how the evidence they present can be weighed and evaluated are, in contemporary cultures, considerably disadvantaged and disempowered"* (Abbott and Masterman 1997).

To implement this insight, it is necessary to understand the psychology of change in academia. Change in academia has always been difficult. Of the 66 institutions that existed continuously from 1530 to 1980, 62 were liberal arts universities (Kerr 1980). It has often been said that: "Changing a university is like moving a grave yard—you do it one faculty grave at a time!" So, how do we implement curricular change in academia? The following 10 rules were developed by Joseph Zolner, Director, Harvard Institutes for Higher Education, as a guideline for implementing change in academia (Balmer, *et al.* 2000).

1. Loss of Control—Change is exciting when it is done *by* the faculty but not when done *to* the faculty.
2. Too Much Uncertainty—Significant uncertainty can spell doom for administrators seeking to introduce new ideas into their institutions.
3. Surprise, Surprise—Some (falsely) believe that the best way to implement change is to "sneak up" on faculty and inform them of a change at the moment of implementation.
4. The "McDonalds Factor"—Familiarity breeds comfort, so build on institutional strengths faculty know, understand, and appreciate about their program, department, or institution.
5. Ripple Effects—Inevitably, changes send ripples beyond their intended impact.
6. Loss of Face—Change often implies that someone's past actions were "wrong," or at least ill-conceived.
7. Concerns About Competence—Change inevitably raises troubling questions about the faculty's ability to get a new job done.
8. More Work—One reason faculty resist change is that it often requires more work, adding new demands to an already-full agenda.
9. Past Resentments—Skeletons in administrative or departmental closets can easily impede change.
10. Sometimes the Threat is Real—Sometimes a threat posed by change is a legitimate source of concern and reason to embrace the status quo.

Union College in Schenectady, New York, offers an instructive case study of how to implement a Converging Technologies Educational Paradigm. The college used Zolner's 10 rules to identify the following five steps to lead change in academia:

Step 1: Create a Compelling Vision

> After discussion with various faculty groups we concluded that technology is now growing at the interfaces of traditional academic fields. Then it became obvious that to achieve our education goals we needed to break down the communication and territorial barriers between departments. The convergence of traditional fields to create new fields of study was clearly an aspect of the 21st century, so we decided to call our new educational paradigm "Converging Technologies."

Step 2: Communicate the Vision

> We made numerous presentations to faculty (who were at first skeptical), to administration (including trustees), to alumni groups, and to students, describing our vision and the meaning of the phrase "Converging Technologies." We also brought local leaders onboard to lend credibility to the paradigm. Alumni and industrial leaders innately knew the meaning and importance of the phrase "Converging Technologies" because they had been dealing with its impact for several years. We also put articles in newspapers, alumni

magazines, and Union College catalogs and brochures touting the values of a 21st century Converging Technologies education.

Step 3: Empower the Faculty

We established Converging Technologies faculty working committees to discuss curricula revision, course development, industrial support, faculty loading, and so forth. We then held off-campus faculty planning retreats with speakers from industry that reinforced the Converging Technologies vision. Faculty participation was recognized with released time to develop new courses or modify existing courses, and faculty seeking external funds in Converging Technologies areas were supported. Finally, we encouraged and supported faculty to develop new Converging Technologies academic majors, minors, and areas of concentration.

Step 4: Create Short Term Successes

We regularly announced the development of new Converging Technologies courses as well as Converging Technologies material added to existing courses to the faculty, administration, and student body. We successfully solicited industry and government sponsored Converging Technologies research and student projects. We attended College curriculum committee meetings to support the approval of Converging Technologies majors, minors, and areas of concentration. Finally, we began to advertise for and hire new faculty with interdisciplinary backgrounds and research interests.

Step 5: Institutionalize the Results

We gained considerable administrative support with our short term successes. That made it easier to solicit trustees and influential alumni to support institutionalizing Converging Technologies programs. We also worked with our development office to establish alumni funded Converging Technologies Centers and Chairs with endowments. By advertising Converging Technologies courses and programs on the Union College web site, in the College catalog, and adding Converging Technologies as one of the pillars of excellence of the College, we broadcast our commitment to this new higher education paradigm.

A PILLAR OF EXCELLENCE

The Converging Technologies initiative began at Union College in the spring of 2001, and after just 4 years it had been fully institutionalized (cf. http://www.union.edu/CT). It is now recognized and accepted across campus as one of the distinguishing features of Union, one of its pillars of excellence. In each of the following interdisciplinary areas, students benefit from the close collaboration between and within engineering and the liberal arts that Converging Technologies fosters at Union.

The minor in *Bioengineering* has been designed for engineering, science, and nonscience majors alike. Any student with an interest in interdisciplinary fields emerging at the intersection of the biology, computer science, and engineering may choose this minor. Students participate in a multidisciplinary core course in bioengineering in addition to developing content knowledge and process skills in biology, engineering, or a related science outside their major field.

The *Digital Arts* program is an interdisciplinary endeavor between the Visual Arts and Computer Science. In addition to new faculty and courses, a computer lab has been created that comprises the latest computer graphics hardware and software.

The *Environmental Studies* program is designed for students with a strong interest in understanding and solving environmental problems. The program allows students the opportunity to explore areas of environmental policy, environmental science, and environmental engineering.

Entrepreneurship provides a natural linkage between engineering and the liberal arts, and teaches a mindset among students that it is alright to pursue their passion. The Economics Department now offers a course on "The Mind of the Entrepreneur." This course gives students three perspectives: economic barriers to the entrepreneur; the entrepreneur as a creator of demand; and entrepreneurial thinking. Underlying the course is the traditional economic paradigm of resource allocation in a market economy.

Mechatronics is a design philosophy that encourages engineers to integrate precision mechanical engineering, digital and analog electronics, control theory, and computer engineering in the design of intelligent products, systems, and processes. The mechatronics approach shortens design cycles, lowers costs, and produces elegant solutions to design problems that cannot easily be solved by staying within the bounds of the traditional engineering disciplines.

Nanotechnology is the new frontier of science and engineering that is most likely to change the way almost everything is designed and made. Union College's effort to strengthen its undergraduate program in Nanotechnology was recently recognized by the National Science Foundation with a grant in its Nanotechnology in Undergraduate Education (NUE) program. Many believe that controlling of the arrangements of atoms and molecules will result in a new technological revolution.

The new *Neuroscience* major is designed for students with interests that intersect the fields of Biology and Psychology. This major consists of two tracks: the Bioscience track and the Cognitive track. The bioscience track focuses on the biological basis of neural development, function, and plasticity. The cognitive track provides students with an understanding of how neural networks and brain mechanisms give rise to specific mental processes and behavior.

Pervasive Computing is a family of technologies that allows mobile or diffuses access to networks and especially to the Internet. Its influence on many facets of our lives is increasingly significant as innovations in technology prompt modifications in ways people communicate and live. Students interested in the social and ethical aspects of computing combine courses in Computer Science with Philosophy. Typical new courses in this field include: Cyberfeminism, Technology and Human Values, and The Self in Cyberspace.

The *Science, Medicine and Technology in Culture* program has both a major and a minor. Science and engineering students can explore the social context of their professions by means of a minor, and humanities and social sciences students can include the social consequences of science and engineering in their education.

Union College also allows students to create their own major, called an Organizing Theme. With the philosophy of expanding understanding by lowering barriers, Converging Technologies presents opportunities to put together ideas from multiple disciplines, and focus them on one unifying theme.

CONVERGING TECHNOLOGIES AND ACADEMIC RESEARCH

While Union College is primarily an undergraduate institution, since 2001 we have noticed a significant increase in student research (cf. www.union.edu/About/CT/Support/). Current Converging Technologies area research includes:

1. *Music and Engineering:* Forging new links between music and engineering is natural for Electrical Engineering Professor Palma Catravas, who performed solo with the Baltimore Symphony Orchestra when she was 12 and completed a double degree in electrical engineering and piano performance as an undergraduate.
2. *Chemistry and Engineering:* The aerogel project began in 2002 with a senior student interested in the properties of aerogels (extremely low density solids). They have very interesting thermal insulating properties; work well as the basis for a catalyst or sensors because of their enormous surface area per volume, and also have interesting electrical properties. This led faculty from the Chemistry and Mechanical Engineering to discover substantial overlaps in their research interests, and resulted in an NSF grant to establish an aerogel fabrication laboratory.
3. *Digital Mapping of Historic Cordoba Spain:* With funding from the Keck Foundation, Union developed several mini-terms abroad with the express goal of bringing engineering and liberal arts students together. Recently, students conducted a digital mapping project of Cordoba Spain. While in Cordoba, student teams were assigned different periods of Cordoba history, and were charged with creating different map layers and the reference materials to link to the map. The project is online at: doc.union.edu/Spain/Project
• *Equidistant Letter Sequences in Homer's Iliad:* In a joint project between Classics and Computer Science two students searched for the presence

of encrypted messages in Homer's Iliad. After searching for equidistant letter sequences (ELS) in the Iliad they concluded ELS behavior appears to be present but were uncertain of its significance.

- *Modeling the Tomb of a Qing Emperor:* Two students received funding from our East Asian Studies Program Freeman Foundation grant to travel with Professor Nixi Cura in the Visual Arts Department to China, where they visited an 18th century burial tomb from the Qing dynasty. When they returned they produced a computer-generated three-dimensional rendering of the tomb, including a fly-through, and pan-and-zoom camera views. The project is online at: http://cs.union.edu/SeniorProjectPage-2004/

- *Bioinformatics:* A Java program was developed that automates a database search process for sequences of amino acids from many proteins. The software allows the user to examine multiple sequences and to adjust sequence lengths. Once the computer results are obtained, laboratory tests are performed and these results are then entered into a database that can be queried to find results that might be useful to biologists.

CONCLUSION

As FIGURE 1 shows, the Converging Technologies innovations at Union College achieved wide scope. To date, in the area of curriculum development, we have created over 30 New Converging Technologies courses, created

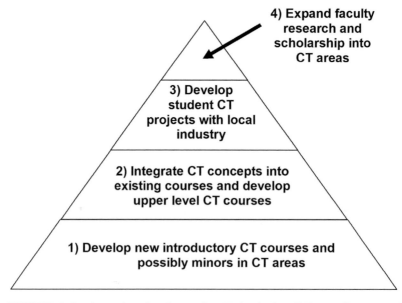

FIGURE 1. Implementing the Converging Technologies (CT) paradigm at Union College.

new Converging Technologies majors and minors, and integrated Converging Technologies topics into numerous existing courses. Importantly, we established a Converging Technologies microscopy laboratory containing AFM, STM, SEM, and NMR equipment and a new "Center for Bioengineering and Computational Biology" funded by the Howard Hughes Medical Institute (http://bioengineering.union.edu/). The college appointed a full-time CT Director and a full-time Converging Technologies Laboratory Technician. We also obtained funding to renovate an existing building as a "Converging Technologies Center." To provide guidance and oversight, we created an external Converging Technologies Advisory Board composed of influential alumni. In all these efforts, we received full support and encouragement from the Board of Trustees.

Converging Technologies represents a paradigm shift in problem solving in all academic fields. Converging Technologies innovations are impacting social and cultural values more rapidly than any single technology in recent history, and have created a need for a new approach to undergraduate and graduate education. To implement the necessary curricula changes it is important to gain the support of faculty and administration to develop postmodern programs that provide graduates with the necessary skills to become independent learners and leaders in the 21st century.

REFERENCES

ABBOTT, C., and L. MASTERMAN. 1997. Media Literacy, Information Technology and the Teaching of English. *The Centre for Literacy: Working Papers on Literacy 2*, Quebec, Canada, online at http://www.centreforliteracy.qc.ca/Publications/paper2/medialit.htm

AMERICAN SOCIETY OF CIVIL ENGINEERS. 2001. Engineering the future of civil engineering. *Report from the ASCE Task Committee on the First Professional Degree*, online at http://www.asce.org/pdf/tcfpd-complete.pdf

BALDWIN, J. 2000. Liberal arts for a new millennium. *Carnegie Reporter 1*(1), online at http://www.carnegie.org/reporter/01/liberal_arts/index.html

BALMER, R.T., TRAVER, C., and WILLIAMS, G., eds. 2000. *Proceedings of the Workshop on Implementing Curricular Change in Engineering Education*, Union College.

BUGLIARELLO, G. 2003. A new trivium and quadrivium. *Bulletin of Science, Technology and Society 23*(2), 106–113.

KERR, C. 1980. Three thousand futures: the next twenty years for higher education. *Carnegie Council for Policy Studies in Higher Education*. San Francisco: Jossey-Bass.

NCEES. 2003. Minutes of the Meeting of the Professional Engineering Committee of the Board held August 7.

NEELY, P. 1999. The threats to liberal arts colleges. *Daedalus, the Journal of the American Academy of Arts and Sciences 128*(1), 27–46, online at http://www.collegenews.org/prebuilt/daedalus/neely_article.pdf

SCHACHTERLE, L. 1997. A liberal education for the 2000's. *Proceedings of the ASEE/IEEE Frontiers in Education Conference*, online at http://fie.engrng.pitt.edu/fie97/

Biomimetic Nanotechnology

OSAMU TAKAI

EcoTopia Science Institute, Nagoya University, Nagoya 464-8603, Japan

ABSTRACT: *Biomimetic materials processing* (BMMP) is defined as the design and synthesis of new functional materials by refining knowledge and understanding of related biological products, structures, functions, and processes. By using BMMP, we can make a new nanotechnology, which is named "biomimetic nanotechnology." This is based on lessons from nature, becomes important for industries from the viewpoint of its applications, and closely relates to "converging technologies." The concept and applications of this biomimetic nanotechnology are described in this article.

KEYWORDS: anotechnology; self-assembled monolayers; SAMs; biomimetic materials processing; BMMP

BIOMIMETIC NANOTECHNOLOGY

Living organisms produce a wide variety of materials at room temperature and atmospheric pressure. Moreover, each material produced plays a key role in each function in biological systems. *Biomimetic materials processing* (BMMP) is defined as the design and synthesis of new functional materials by refining knowledge and understanding of related biological products, structures, functions, and processes. Hence BMMP is not a simple imitation of biological materials processes, but is advanced materials processing for bionics, electronics, photonics, mechanics, magnetics, medicine, and so on. BMMP, therefore, is closely related to nanotechnology and we can make a new nanotechnology by using BMMP. We name this nanotechnology "biomimetic nanotechnology," which is based on lessons from nature. This also relates closely to converging technologies.

BMMP AND BIOMIMETIC NANOTECHNOLOGY

By means of BMMP we can prepare "biomimetic materials" or more widely "bioinspired materials." For example, advanced ceramics can be synthesized by using BMMP on the basis of biomineralization. Living organisms use reactions

Address for correspondence: Osamu Takai, EcoTopia Science Institute, Nagoya University, Furo-cho, Chikusa-ku, Nagoya 464-8603, Japan. Voice: +81-52-789-3259; fax: +81-52-789-3260.
e-mail: takai@plasma.numse.nagoya-u.ac.jp

Ann. N.Y. Acad. Sci. 1093: 84–97 (2006). © 2006 New York Academy of Sciences.
doi: 10.1196/annals.1382.006

in solutions for the synthesis of bioceramics. We can, however, use reactions in gases and plasmas as well as solutions. Then the dry processing (including plasma processing) plays an important role in BMMP in conjunction with wet processing. Generally speaking, unique features of materials processing in biological systems are: preferential proceeding of reactions with time and space and highly developed organization of fine structures and forms.

Biological materials processing is actually performed by self-organization of molecular assemblies, and molecular recognition at interfacial reaction sites. Therefore, we introduce techniques of self-assembling and interfacial molecular recognition into BMMP. The functions on the basis of forms also play an important role in living organisms. "Form" and "function" are keywords in BMMP.

Our conceptual approach is as follows. The distinctive characteristics of biological processes are normal temperature and pressure, liquid phase reaction, high selectivity and anisotropy, and self-assembly. Biological materials are characterized as composites at the molecular or cluster level (organic–organic or organic–inorganic), heterogeneous systems, and minute structures. Biomimetic materials processing follows some combination of process–mimetic and function–mimetic approaches. Its final goals are to create functional materials using harmless substances under normal temperature and pressure, and to develop materials functionalities through the control of properties and form at the nanoscale.

We are studying "how form is created" and "what functionalities form has." This requires analysis of elementary processes, development of analytical systems, and establishment of the principles for biomimetic process designing. Form can be created by self-assembly under two very different sets of conditions. In the liquid phase, reactions occur on an organic interface in a manner analogous to biological processes. In the vapor phase, cluster accumulation occurs with vacuum evaporation under incident angle control. The functionalities include optical and electronic materials, biocompatible materials, and many applications at boundaries between electronic and biological fields.

Crystal growth at an organic-inorganic interface is an especially key element in BMMP. Preparation of such an organic interface with controlled chemical functionalities is critical. Then we use organosilane self-assembled monolayers (SAMs) for the preparation of surfaces with controlled chemical properties including reactivity, hydrophobicity, and isoelectric point, and with controlled nanostructures. Toward this direction, we are studying micropatterned and nanopatterned SAMs and their applications. After we prepare the suitable place for some reaction by this patterning, we can create a new functional material on the limited place by using selective crystal growth. We are using many types of biomimetic surfaces prepared by various techniques.

Elucidation of structures of organized molecular systems formed at solid–liquid interfaces is important to understand and design BMMP. Therefore atomic force microscopy (AFM), which has the ability to detect intermolecular interactions and surface potentials at very high spatial resolution, is applied to identify surface-confined molecules of interest. We have developed AFM systems for measuring multipoint force spectroscopy and electronic surface properties.

We have explored various techniques for creation of space with "form" and molecular recognition functionality related to biomimetic nanotechnology. For example, thin film growth with molecular recognition can involve induction of growth, control of form, micro-nano-structured growth, and preferential cell growth. For spatial resolution measurements of molecular recognition we use scanning probe microscopy (SPM) and computer simulation. Potential applications of functional biomimetic surfaces include ultra water repellency, lubricating ultra-thin films, biomedical polymers, electrochromic thin films (such as windows that change color depending on an electric current) and molecular memory. Medical applications include tissue engineering, medical materials, and clinical testing. Biomimetic materials can be used as insulators in metal oxide semiconductor gates, sensor components, and for molecular selection.

WATER-REPELLANT SURFACES IMITATING LOTUS LEAVES

Wettability control at water–solid interfaces from ultra hydrophilicity to ultra hydrophobicity is important both in basic research and in industrial applications (Hozumi and Takai 1996, 1997, 1998; Onda *et al.* 1996; Hozumi *et al.* 1997; Tadanaga *et al.* 1997; Takai *et al.* 1997a, 1997b; Miwa *et al.* 2000; Wu *et al.* 2002a, 2002b, 2003a, 2003b, 2004; Teshima *et al.* 2003, 2004, 2005a, 2005b). Recently, high water repellency or high hydrophobicity is required for glass, ceramics, semiconductors, plastics, paper, and metals in various industrial fields. Moreover, the addition of high transparency to high water-repellency is necessary in many industrial applications. When the contact angle of a water droplet is more than about 150 degrees, we can say that this state is ultra water-repellency.

Leaves of the lotus plant show ultra water-repellency because of the precisely controlled roughness of their surfaces. This is known as the "lotus effect." A water droplet on a lotus leaf can move smoothly, indicating ultra water-repellency. Now we can use environmental scanning electron microscopes (ESEM) where we can introduce a gas at a pressure of up to 2000 pascals and observe a surface in low vacuum without a conducting layer on a sample. We put a piece of the lotus leaf at the sample holder in the ESEM chamber, introduce the water vapor at about 600 pascals, and reduce the sample temperature to less than around 10°C. Then we can observe water droplets condensed on the leaf surface. FIGURE 1 shows the ESEM photo of the water droplets on the lotus leaf. The sizes of the droplets are 1–200 μm and their shapes are almost spherical. The water repellency is very high and independent of the size of the water droplet.

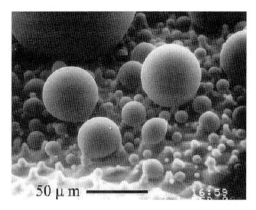

FIGURE 1. ESEM photo of water droplets on a lotus leaf.

The surface of the lotus leaf was observed by field-emission scanning electron microscope (FESEM) after coating with platinum. The FESEM photos are given in FIGURE 2. The small prongs are formed on the leaf, and these prongs have much smaller prongs. These smaller prongs show a nanotube-like form. This surface has a fractal-like structure to increase the surface area and roughness. This geometrical factor is important for the ultra water-repellency combined with the surface chemical-like wax to reduce the surface energy. The combination of the geometrical factor and the chemical component to reduce the surface energy is essential to obtain the ultra water-repellency. The lotus leaves give us the hint to obtain it.

Ultra water-repellent silicon oxide films have been synthesized similarly by plasma-enhanced chemical vapor deposition (CVD) using organosilicon compounds, for example, trimethylmethoxysilane (TMMOS) and fluoro-alkyl silanes (FASs), as raw materials. These film surfaces are biomimetic surfaces of lotus leaves. Furthermore, we can prepare transparent ultra water-repellent

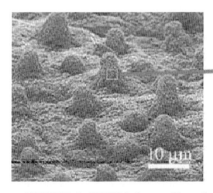

FIGURE 2. FESEM photos of lotus leaf surfaces.

(a) Glass Substrate   (b) PMMA Substrate

FIGURE 3. Water droplets on coated glass and polymethylmethacrylate.

films by controlling the surface roughness precisely. Again, the shapes of water droplets are almost spherical, independent of their sizes. The surface of the ultra water-repellent silicon oxide film lacks the prongs, which lotus leaves have, but has some controlled roughness.

Transparency is an additional significant function that lotus leaves do not have. The photos of the water droplets are shown in FIGURE 3 for the glass substrate (*a*) and the polymethylmethacrylate (PMMA) substrate (*b*), coated by transparent ultra water-repellent silicon oxide films. Measured by AFM, the root mean square roughness for the ultra water-repellent film is 86 nm, whereas that of the highly water-repellent film is 11 nm. The precise control of the surface morphology is most important to obtain the transparent ultra water-repellent films.

Ultra water-repellent coatings would be very important for such industrial fields as antifreezing materials, automotive parts, beverage and food containers, building materials, communication devices, electronic devices and sensors, marine equipment, medical materials, optical parts, packaging materials, precision machine parts, snow repelling materials, textiles, and transport pipes. Therefore the concept of BMMP becomes important in industrial fields.

Three-Dimensional Cell Cultures Using Ultra Water-Repellent Surfaces

At the present time, studies on "tissue engineering" are developing rapidly. This field of engineering concerns the formation of transplantable tissues and organs by the culture multiplication of cells taken from patients or their relatives. Tissue engineering is the key in regenerative medical techniques and plays a requisite role in the cure for intractable diseases. In this field, one of the main subjects is growing cells in three dimensions, and forming tissues. For this reason, the development of the method of forming clumps of cells, or

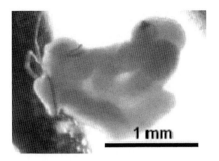 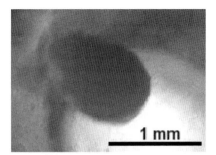

After 7 days   After 30 days

FIGURE 4. Human mesenchymal stem cells cultured on an ultra-hydrophobic surface.

three-dimensional cultures of cells, becomes important as a preliminary step toward the formation of tissues.

Several methods for three-dimensional culture are under study, such as using polymer materials or zero gravity in space. However, these methods have problems, such as the development of detoxification processes of toxic substances produced in the production of polymers, the development of special equipment, and the high cost. Thus, we have devised a three-dimensional cell culture method by using the ultra water-repellent surfaces.

Our research shows clearly that cell culture in three dimensions is possible in a culture-medium liquid with a spherical shape, using the characteristic that a water droplet becomes spherical on an ultra-hydrophobic surface. Hence simple three-dimensional cell culture templates have been developed by using ultra water-repellent coatings for culturing cartilage cells, embryo-stem (ES) cells, and other types. It is expected that the cell in a culture solution will adjust to the form of the culture solution, and will be differentiated in three dimensions by using the characteristic of the ultra-hydrophobic surface on which a water droplet becomes like a perfect sphere. If a cell culture liquid is actually dropped on a cell culture dish coated by the ultra-hydrophobic film, the culture solution droplet does indeed form a nearly perfect sphere.

Three-dimensional culture of human mesenchymal stem (hMS) cells was carried out by using sphere-like droplets. FIGURE 4 shows the results of the culture after 7 and 30 days. The growth of the cells could be checked, and after 30 days the cells were suggested to be differentiated into the cartilage cells.

Moreover, three-dimensional culture of the ES cells of mouse can be performed by using this technique. FIGURE 5 shows the results of the culture after 1, 2, 3, and 7 days. The ES cells grow densely from day to day and show beating. Thus ultra water-repellent surfaces can be used as three-dimensional cell culture templates.

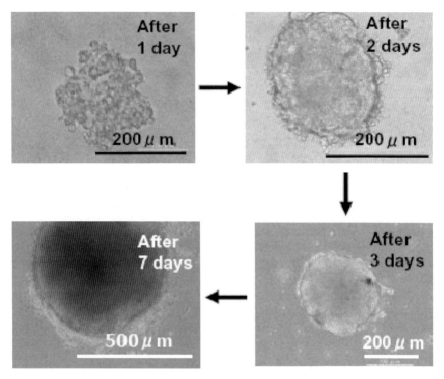

FIGURE 5. ES cells cultured on an ultra-hydrophobic surface.

Application of Patterns to Site-Selective Cell Cultures

By irradiation of vacuum ultraviolet (VUV) light on the ultra-hydrophobic film surface, methyl groups or fluoroalkyl groups are changed into hydroxyl groups or carboxyl groups, and it becomes possible to change an ultra-hydrophobic surface into an ultra-hydrophilic state.

A xenon excimer lamp with a wavelength of 172 nm can be used as a source of VUV light. Ultra-hydrophobic/ultra-hydrophilic micro/nano patterns can be formed by performing this irradiation through a photomask. FIGURE 6 shows an array of 25 μm water droplets on the ultra-hydrophobic/ultra-hydrophilic pattern, taken by ESEM. The water droplets condense only on the hydrophilic areas. By this method, a micro/nano array of water droplets can be formed, and it can be applied to the production of microlenses, photonic crystals, cell arrays, and the like.

Specific cell cultures can be expected on the surface of the ultra-hydrophobic/ultra-hydrophilic pattern since site-selective attachment and growth of cells are performed due to the great difference in cell affinity. If the site-selective cell culture using such a surface is realized, the culture of

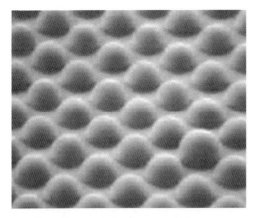

FIGURE 6. ESEM photo of a water droplet array.

cells corresponding to the form of various organisms will be attained, and it will lead to big progress of the advanced regeneration medical field.

The site-selective culture of mouse fibroblasts (NIH-3T3) was carried out by using the surface of the ultra-hydrophobic/ultra-hydrophilic micropattern. FIGURE 7 shows the result of the culture after 3 days taken with a phase contrast microscope. The fibroblasts were observed to be growing only on the ultra-hydrophilic areas. Generally, it is believed that cells attach easily on a hydrophobic surface, and they have difficulty attaching on a hydrophilic surface. Our result demolishes this established theory. One of the causes of the above phenomenon relates to the influence of the minute concavo–convex structures on the scale of several dozen to several hundred nanometers. The cells

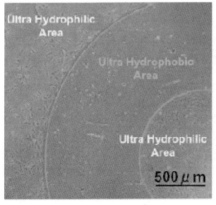
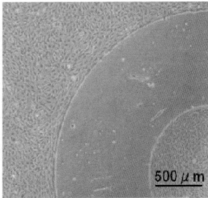

After 1 day   After 3 days

FIGURE 7. A fibroblast culture on a micropattern.

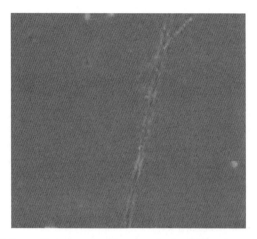

FIGURE 8. Culture of a human capillary on a hydrophilic area.

recognize not only a surface's chemical nature but also minute concavo–convex structures. The detailed causes must be determined in future research.

We have experimented with culturing fibroblast cells in an array on the ultra-hydrophobic/ultra-hydrophilic micropattern. The cells are cultured only on the hydrophilic areas and the site-selectivity is very good. This technique is applicable to such important tasks as the screening of new drugs and the detection of cancer.

By using this technique, it is possible to culture normal human umbilical vein endothelia (HUVE) cells to form capillaries. FIGURE 8 depicts a 20-μm diameter capillary cultured on a patterned surface. Only on the ultra-hydrophilic area does the capillary grow tubularly. This implies that the minute blood vessel will be reproduced by the micro/nano patterning technique.

SAMs AND THEIR APPLICATIONS

SAM is a single layer of organic molecules prepared by means of self-assembly on a substrate in a liquid or gas phase (Ulman 1996; Hozumi *et al.* 1999, 2001; Sugimura *et al.* 2000, 2001, 2002a, 2002b; Hayashi *et al.* 2001, 2002a, 2002b, 2002c; Saito *et al.* 2001, 2002a, 2002b, 2004a, 2004b, 2005). When a suitable combination of a substrate material and organic molecules is selected, and the substrate is located into a solution or vapor, which contains the organic molecules, the molecules are chemically adsorbed onto the substrate surface through the chemical reaction of the molecules with the substrate material. Using the CVD method, the adsorbed molecules gather closely due to interactions among molecules under a certain condition during the chemisorption process, and a monolayer with highly oriented molecules is formed on the substrate surface. As the monolayer formation is completed, the growth of the layer is stopped automatically, because the molecule-covered surface runs out of reaction site and the adsorption reaction does not continue. Such an ultra-thin organic film is called SAM due to spontaneous assembling of organic molecules. A two-dimensional arrangement in SAMs is formed in a process where the whole system is approaching an equilibrium. This means that SAMs are close to a thermodynamically stable state.

Terminated functional groups located at the tops of organic molecules chemisorbed onto a substrate surface cover over the surface. It is, therefore, possible to design and control physical and chemical properties of the surface by the selection of terminated functional groups. For example, it is possible to add surface reactivity by choosing amino, epoxy, or vinyl groups, or to reduce surface energy by selecting alkyl or fluoroalkyl groups.

Organosilane SAMs have especially high stability because they are immobilized at substrates through siloxane bonding, a kind of covalent bonding, and neighboring molecules are bonded together through a siloxane network. Therefore organosilane SAMs are much superior to other SAMs in mechanical strength and chemical stability with the largest possibility of practical uses for surface modification and surface functionalization. We are using SAMs as resists or templates for etching, selective area growth of metals and semiconductors, water-droplet arrays, selective immobilization of nanoparticles and nanocolloids, selective immobilization of organic molecules, bioarrays, molecular memories, and molecular recognition sites. Moreover, the fabrication of molecular devices is possible by immobilizing functional molecules, such as DNA and proteins, selectively at fine structured SAMs, which have reactive terminated groups like amino, carboxyl, and chlorine groups. We can create many types of nanostructures and crystal growth based on lessons from nature by means of the SAM techniques.

Micro/Nano Pattering of SAMs

Lithography, or patterning, is an indispensable technology in micro/nano fabrication processes for semiconductor integrated circuits, sensors, displays, macro/nano machines, bio devices, and cell cultures. In photolithography, a photosensitive organic polymer thin film called *photoresist* is coated onto a substrate, and a photomask pattern is transferred to the resist by exposure through the photomask. As the degree of integration in integrated circuits increases from year to year, development of lithography technology is required, in which more precise patterning and transferring are possible.

The SAMs are applicable to lithography with high resolution. The thicknesses of SAMs are 1–2 nm, depending on the length of molecules composed. Moreover, the SAMs consist of molecules of the same kind, and there is no variation in molecular mass in SAMs, which is different from the case with polymer films. Therefore SAMs are highly promising as high-resolution resists. Uniform coating of SAMs is also possible onto substrates with three-dimensional complex shapes, fine-structured substrates, and inner surfaces of tubes.

From the viewpoint of environmental issues, conventional lithographic processes discharge liquid wastes, such as developing solutions and resist-removal ones, however, the SAM lithographic process does not produce liquid waste. The consumption of raw materials used in the process is extremely small because of the thickness of 1–2 nm. The raw material of 2 μL is enough to coat the area of 1 m^2. The use of SAMs is superior to the conventional resist process in solving environmental and resources problems. In addition, the use of SAMs leads to better productivity due to the self-stopping process from a standpoint of industrial applications.

We are investigating lithographic techniques using SAMs by employing VUV light, electron and ion beams, and SPM. Notably, the methods using VUV light and SPM are carried out under atmospheric pressure or in low vacuum, which makes their industrial applications advantageous on the cost front. The wide range of pattering from a single nanometer to several hundred microns becomes possible by the combination of VUV lithography and SPM. After patterning the SAMs, we can use the patterned SAMs for micro/nano fabrication. Given all these possibilities, the usefulness of SAMs is extremely high.

We are using micro/nano patterned SAMs as templates for micro/nano synthesis and assembling. Patterned SAMs are useful for etching, wiring, selective area growth of metals and semiconductors, water droplet arrays, molecular arrays, DNA arrays, protein arrays, cell arrays, selective immobilization of nanoparticles and nanocolloids, selective immobilization of organic molecules, and molecular memory. The SAMs have wide potential applications to the preparation of advanced functional materials and surfaces.

Molecular Memory Using SAMs

Nanoprobe electrochemistry plays an important role in nanotechnology. Recently, we have discovered chemical reversibility between the aminoterminated surface on an organosilane SAM and the nitrosoterminated one via the nanoprobe electrochemical technique. By using this chemical reversibility we can make a surface potential memory. An amino-terminated SAM is prepared from p-aminophenyl-trimethoxysilane through CVD. Surface potential is measured by Kelvin force microscopy (KFM), and surface potential imaging is obtained by this measurement. In positive applied bias voltages, the surface potentials of the scanned area are dramatically shifted to negative surface potentials against that of Au-tip. Scanning the area with positive applied bias voltage leads to a positive shift in the surface potential. Moreover, the surface potential can be recovered even after multiple repetitions of scanning with positive and negative applied bias voltages. Finally, the surface potential memory is successfully demonstrated, based on this surface potential reversibility. By using this memory principle, one molecule can work as one memory site, and we can make an ultra-high-density memory. To realize this memory it is necessary to improve the high integration of dot-patterns, stability, life-time, writing and erasing speeds.

CONCLUSION

"Biomimetic nanotechnology" relates to "Converging Technologies" closely and includes nano-bio-info-cogno ("NBIC") provinces. "Lessons from nature" will be tremendously important for science and technology in the 21st century.

We have developed a technique to prepare ultra water-repellent thin films on any material at almost room temperature, modeled after lotus leaves, and a patterning technique for these films. The micro/nano patterns of ultra-hydrophobic/ultra-hydrophilic areas are made by the VUV irradiation through a photomask. The three-dimensional cell cultures and the site-selective cell cultures are achieved by using the surfaces and patterns. These cell culture techniques are applicable to tissue engineering.

We have also developed the technique using SAMs for micro/nano fabrication and assembling as a basis for biomimetic nanotechnology. The micro/nano patterned SAMs are applicable to many fields. "Biomimetic nanotechnology" will play an important role for our future life.

REFERENCES

HAYASHI, K., H. SUGIMURA, and O. TAKAI. 2002c. Force microscopy contrasts due to adhesion force difference between organosilane self-assembled monolayers. *Applied Surface Science 188,* 513–518.

HAYASHI, K., N. SAITO, H. SUGIMURA, and O. TAKAI. 2001. Frictional properties of organosilane self-assembled monolayer in vacuum. *Japanese Journal of Applied Physics 40,* 4344–4348.

HAYASHI, K., N. SAITO, H. SUGIMURA, O. TAKAI, and N. NAKAGIRI. 2002a. Regulation of the surface potential of silicon substrates in micrometer scale with organosilane self-assembled monolayers. *Langmuir 18,* 7469–7472.

HAYASHI, K., N. SAITO, H. SUGIMURA, O. TAKAI, and N. NAKAGIRI. 2002b. Surface potential contrasts between silicon surfaces covered and uncovered with an organosilane self-assembled monolayer. *Ultramicroscopy 91,* 151–156.

HOZUMI, A., and O. TAKAI. 1996. Effect of hydrolysis groups in fluoro-alkyl silanes on water repellency of transparent two-layer hard coatings. *Applied Surface Science 103,* 431–441.

HOZUMI, A., and O. TAKAI. 1997. Preparation of ultra-repellent films by microwave plasma-enhanced CVD. *Thin Solid Films 303,* 222–225.

HOZUMI, A., and O. TAKAI. 1998. Preparation of silicon oxide films having a water-repellent layer by multiple-step microwave plasma-enhanced chemical vapor deposition. *Thin Solid Films 334,* 54–59.

HOZUMI, A., K. USHIYAMA, H. SUGIMURA, and O. TAKAI. 1999. Fluoroalkylsilane monolayers formed by chemical vapor surface modification on hydroxylated oxide surfaces. *Langmuir 15,* 7600–7604.

HOZUMI, A., T. KONDO, I. KAJITA, H. SEKOGUCHI, N. SUGIMOTO, and O. TAKAI. 1997. Effects of methyl and perfluoro-alkyl groups on water repellency of silicon oxide films prepared by microwave plasma-enhanced chemical vapor deposition. *Japanese Journal of Applied Physics 36,* 4959–4963.

HOZUMI, A., K. USHIYAMA, H. SUGIMURA, Y. YOKOGAWA, T. KAMEYAMA, and O. TAKAI. 2001. Amino-terminated self-assembled monolayer on a SiO_2 surface formed by chemical vapor deposition. *Journal of Vacuum Science and Technology A19,* 1812–1815.

MIWA, M., A. NAKAJIMA, A. FUJISHIMA, K. HASHIMOTO, and T. WATANABE. 2000. Effects of the surface roughness on sliding angles of water droplets on superhydrophobic surfaces. *Langmuir 16,* 5754–5760.

ONDA, T., S. SHIBUICHI, N. SATOH, and K. TSUJII. 1996. Super-water-repellent fractal surfaces. *Langmuir 12,* 2125–2127.

SAITO, N., J. HIEDA, and O. TAKAI. 2004a. Fabrication of a built-in patterned metal microstructure on a polymer substrate using a microstructured organic monolayer template. *Electrochemical and Solid State Letters 7,* C140–C141.

SAITO, N., K. HAYASHI, H. SUGIMURA, and O. TAKAI. 2001. Surface potentials of patterned organosilane self-assembled monolayers acquired by kelvin probe force microscopy and ab initio molecular calculation. *Chemical Physics Letters 349,* 172–177.

SAITO, N., K. HAYASHI, H. SUGIMURA, and O. TAKAI. 2002a. The decomposition mechanism of p-chloromethylphenyltrimethoxysiloxane self-assembled monolayers on vacuum ultraviolet irradiation. *Journal of Materials Chemistry 12,* 2684–2687.

SAITO, N., K. HAYASHI, H. SIGIMURA, O. TAKAI, and N. NAKAGIRI. 2002b. Surface potential images of self-assembled monolayers patterned by organosilanes: ab initio molecular orbital calculations. *Surface and Interface Analysis 34,* 601–604.

SAITO, N., S.H. LEE, T. ISHIZAKI, J. HIEDA, H. SUGIMURA, and O. TAKAI. 2005. Surface-potential reversibility of an amino-terminated self-assembled monolayer based on nanoprobe chemistry. *Journal of Physical Chemistry B109,* 11602–11605.

SAITO, N., S.H. LEE, N. MAEDA, R. OHTA, H. SUGIMURA, and O. TAKAI. 2004b. Exploration of the chemical bonding forms of alkoxy-type organic monolayers directly attached to silicon. *Journal of Vacuum Science and Technology A22,* 1925–1927.

SUGIMURA, H., T. HANJI, K. HAYASHI, and O. TAKAI. 2002a. Surface potential nanopatterning combining alkyl and fluoroalkylsilane self-assembled monolayers fabricated via scanning probe lithography. *Advanced Materials 14,* 524–526.

SUGIMURA, H., K. USHIYAMA, A. HOZUMI, and O. TAKAI. 2000. Micropatterning of alkyl- and fluoroalkylsilane self-assembled monolayers using vacuum ultraviolet light. *Langmuir 16,* 885–888.

SUGIMURA, H., K. HAYASHI, N. SAITO, N. NAKAGIRI, and O. TAKAI. 2002b. Surface potential microscopy for organized molecular systems. *Applied Surface Science 188,* 403–410.

SUGIMURA, H., K. HAYASHI, N. SAITO, O. TAKAI, and N. NAKAGIRI. 2001. Kelvin probe force microscopy images of microstructured organosilane self-assembled monolayers. *Japanese Journal of Applied Physics 40,* 4373–4377.

TADANAGA, K., N. KATATA, and T. MINAMI. 1997. Formation process of super-water-repellent Al_2O_3 coating films with high transparency by the sol-gel method. *Journal of American Ceramics Society 80,* 3213–3216.

TAKAI, O., A. HOZUMI, and N. SUGIMOTO. 1997b. Coating of transparent water-repellent thin films by plasma-enhanced CVD. *Journal of Non-Crystalline Solids 218,* 280–285.

TAKAI, O., A. HOZUMI, Y. INOUE, and T. KOMORI. 1997a. Application of MO calculation to plasma-enhanced CVD using organosilicon compounds. *Bulletin of Materials Science 20,* 817–822.

TESHIMA, K., H. SUGIMURA, Y. INOUE, O. TAKAI, and A. TAKANO. 2003. Ultra-water-repellent poly(ethylene terephthalate) substrates. *Langmuir 19,* 10624–10627.

TESHIMA, K., H. SUGIMURA, Y. INOUE, O. TAKAI, and A. TAKANO. 2004. Wettability of poly(ethylene terephthalate) substrates modified by a two-step plasma process: ultra water-repellent surface fabrication. *Chemical Vapor Deposition 10,* 295–297.

TESHIMA, K., H. SUGIMURA, Y. INOUE, O. TAKAI, and A. TAKANO. 2005a. Transparent ultra water-repellent poly(ethylene terephthalate) substrates fabricated by oxygen plasma treatment and subsequent hydrophobic coating. *Applied Surface Science 244,* 619–622.

TESHIMA, K., H. SUGIMURA, A. TAKANO, Y. INOUE, and O. TAKAI. 2005b. Ultrahydrophobic/ultrahydrophilic micropatterning on a polymeric substrate. *Chemical Vapor Deposition 11,* 347–349.

ULMAN, A. 1996. Formation and structure of self-assembled monolayers. *Chemical Reviews 96,* 1533–1554.

WU, Y.Y., H. SUGIMURA, Y. INOUE, and O. TAKAI. 2002b. Thin films with nanotextures for transparent and ultra water-repellent coatings produced from trimethylmethoxysilane by microwave plasma CVD. *Chemical Vapor Deposition 8,* 47–50.

WU, Y.Y., H. SUGIMURA, Y. INOUE, and O. TAKAI. 2003b. Preparation of hard and ultra water-repellent silicon oxide films by microwave plasma-enhanced CVD at low substrate temperatures. *Thin Solid Films 435,* 161–164.

WU, Y.Y., M. KURODA, H. SUGIMURA, Y. INOUE, and O. TAKAI. 2003a. Nanotextures fabricated by microwave plasma CVD: application to ultra water-repellent surface. *Surface and Coatings Technology 174,* 867–871.

WU, Y.Y., M. BEKKE, Y. INOUE, H. SUGIMURA, H. KITAGUCHI, C.S. LIU, and O. TAKAI. 2004. Mechanical durability of ultra-water-repellent thin film by microwave plasma-enhanced CVD. *Thin Solid Films 457,* 122–127.

WU, Y.Y., Y. INOUE, H. SUGIMURA, O. TAKAI, H. KATO, S. MURAI, and H. ODA. 2002a. Characteristics of ultra water-repellent thin films prepared by combined process of microwave plasma-enhanced CVD and oxygen-plasma treatment. *Thin Solid Films 407,* 45–49.

Signal-Transducing Proteins for Nanoelectronics

FABIO PICHIERRI

COE Laboratory, Tohoku University, IMRAM, 2-1-1 Katahira, Aoba-ku, Sendai 980-8577, Japan

ABSTRACT: This aim of this article is to provide novel paradigms for 21st century nanoelectronics by taking inspiration from the biology of signal transduction events where Nature has solved many complex problems, particularly those concerned with signal integration and amplification.

KEYWORDS: bioelectronics; biological signal transduction; proteins; macrodipole; quantum biochemistry

THE NANOELECTRONICS REVOLUTION

If the last part of the 20th century will be remembered for the extraordinary advances in information technology (IT) or IT revolution (desktop PC, supercomputers, Internet, etc.), the beginning of the 21st century will be certainly associated with the advent of nanotechnology. But what does the term nanotechnology mean? In simple words, nanotechnology covers all the scientific and technological aspects that are connected to the design and manufacture of nanometer scale devices. Nanoelectronics is the subarea of nanotechnology that is specifically concerned with the development of electronic devices and their components (Goser *et al.* 2004). From a certain perspective, nanoelectronics appears to be the logical continuation of the IT revolution.

So far, two approaches have been employed toward the miniaturization of electronic components: top-down and bottom-up approach. The aim of the former approach is that of reducing the size of (already) small objects whereas that of the latter is to build devices by assembling together either atoms or molecules. The former approach is generally accomplished with the aid of photolithographic techniques whereas the latter employs either scanning probe methods (Wiesendanger 1994) to manipulate atoms or the principles of supramolecular chemistry (Lehn 1995) to achieve the self-assembly of molecules. The birth of molecular electronics is associated with a seminal research paper written by Aviram and Ratner in 1974 (Aviram and Ratner 1974).

Address for correspondence: Fabio Pichierri, COE Laboratory, Tohoku University, IMRAM, 2-1-1 Katahira, Aoba-ku, Sendai 980-8577, Japan. Voice/fax: +81-22-217-5110.
e-mail: fabio@tagen.tohoku.ac.jp

Ann. N.Y. Acad. Sci. 1093: 98–107 (2006). © 2006 New York Academy of Sciences.
doi: 10.1196/annals.1382.007

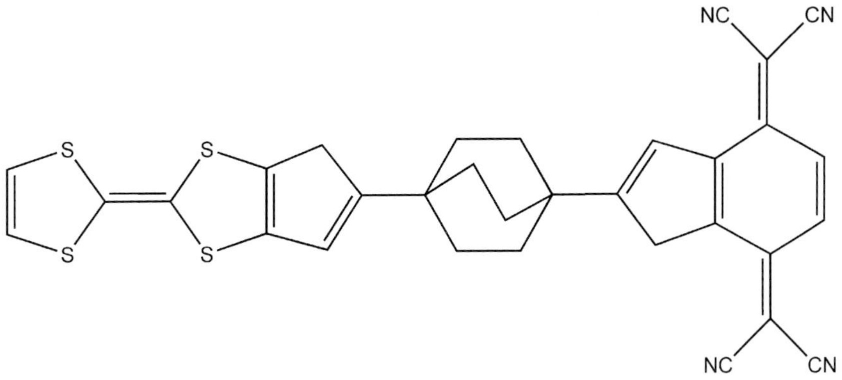

FIGURE 1. Aviram–Ratner molecular rectifier.

These authors made the original theoretical proposal that a single molecule possessing a donor–spacer–acceptor structure would behave as a diode when placed between two electrodes. The structure of this molecular rectifier is shown in FIGURE 1. Up until now, several molecular-scale devices have been synthesized by research chemists: molecular wires, switches, logic gates, etc. (Joachim *et al.* 2000). Also biological molecules, such as proteins (e.g., azurin) and DNA, are potential candidates for nanoelectronic devices owing to their complex architectures as well as for their participation in a variety of complex molecular processes (e.g., electron transfer, photosynthesis, etc.) that occur in Nature (Nicolini 1996).

Whether the molecular computers of the next generation will be made of synthetic or biological molecules is yet unknown. However, what is clear right now is that not only the size of the components but their functionality too matters. In other words, molecular components must work in concert and, hence, necessitate to be interconnected with one another while maintaining their own individuality (integration of components and signals). Furthermore, the interaction of a nanoscale device with the surrounding macroscopic world requires that the signals be amplified (signal amplification) so as to increase the signal-to-noise ratio. Fortunately for us, Nature has already solved many of these complex problems as seen in the biology of signal transduction.

BIOLOGICAL SIGNAL TRANSDUCTION

Biological signal transduction investigates how an extracellular signal is transduced into an intracellular biological effect (Eyster 1998). Simply put, a signal transduction process is activated through the interaction of a hormone (generally a polypeptide) with its target receptor located on the cell's surface. As schematically shown in FIGURE 2, ligand-receptor binding activates a

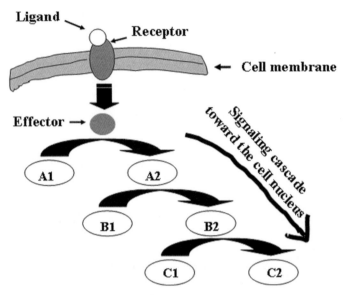

FIGURE 2. Signaling cascade inside the cell.

series of intracellular processes, such as receptor dimerization, phosphorylation of amino acid residues in proteins, and conformational changes of protein
domains, which initiate a signaling cascade inside the cell. Three types of
membrane-bound receptors have been characterized so far (Helmreich, 2001;
Gomperts *et al.* 2002):

1. G-protein-linked receptors
2. Enzyme-linked receptors
3. Ion channels

Let us briefly explain the different characteristics of each membrane-bound
receptor. G-protein receptors are seven-pass transmembrane proteins that are
being activated upon ligand binding. A conformational change of the receptor
favors the interaction with an intracellular linker/transducer G-protein, which
subsequently dissociates to interact with an effector enzyme. The signaling
cascade is then started by the effector enzyme in the active (ON) state. When
the effector enzyme becomes inactive (OFF state) the signaling cascade is
interrupted thus halting the transmission of the signal.

Enzyme-linked receptors are somewhat simpler than G-protein-linked receptors since their catalytic domains are integrated within the receptor itself
and, hence, they do not need the assistance of additional proteins like the G-
proteins. This characteristic makes them interesting candidates for bioinspired
nanoelectronics. Signal transduction pathways involving enzyme-linked receptors also start from a ligand-binding event that takes place outside the cell

and favors receptor dimerization. This, along with a conformational change of the intracellular domain, gives rise to the autophosphorylation of the receptor. The (auto)phosphorylation reaction involves the transfer of a phosphoryl group (PO_3^-) from ATP to amino acid residues, such as tyrosine or serine (Pichierri and Matsuo 2003). Intracellular proteins that recognize the phosphorylated residues can then interact with the receptor and be subsequently phosphorylated. Protein phosphorylation is a key event that starts the downstream propagation of the signal inside the cell.

Finally, ion channels are membrane proteins that facilitate the transport of charged ions across the cell's membrane. It is worth mentioning that only recently it became possible to crystallize ion channel proteins to obtain single crystals of a quality that is sufficiently good for X ray structure analysis. The 2003 Nobel Prize for Chemistry has been awarded to Roderick MacKinnon who was first to determine the atomic structure of the potassium (K^+) channel (MacKinnon 2004).

NATURE'S SOLUTION TO COMPLEX PROBLEMS

As mentioned above, Nature has already solved two extremely complex problems, namely those of signal integration and signal amplification, and implemented the corresponding processes in cell biology. The process of *signal integration* is schematically shown in FIGURE 3 (left). Here two membrane-linked surface receptors, R1 and R2, are independently activated by their associated ligands, L1 and L2, respectively. Two signaling cascades converge

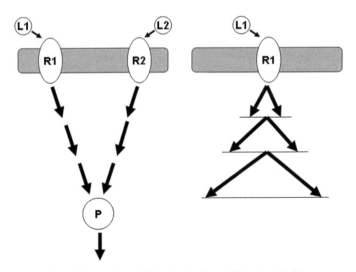

FIGURE 3. Signal integration (left) and signal amplification (right) processes.

toward a common target, the protein (P), which integrates the signal and prop-
agates it downstream inside the cell. The second important process for signal
transduction biology is that of *signal amplification* shown in FIGURE 3 (right).
Here ligand binding to a membrane-linked surface receptor activates the signaling cascade inside the cell. The signal is then amplified at every one step.

As an interesting example of biological signal amplification process we
mention that occurring in the visual transduction cascade where the activation of one Rhodopsin molecule produces the hydrolysis of 10^5 cyclic GMP
molecules at the end of the catalytic cascade (Alberts *et al.* 2002). This means
that the signal is amplified 10^5 times! Let us notice that the above processes
of signal integration and signal amplification do require the concerted participation of a large number of specialized enzymes and substrates. Enzymes that
participate in a specific signal transduction pathway are being synthesized by
the cell itself while many of the substrates are either transported across the cell
membrane or synthesized *in situ*.

SIGNAL-TRANSDUCING PROTEINS: THE SH2 DOMAIN

The SH2 domain is one of the most important recognition domains for
phosphorylated peptides, such as those carrying a phosphotyrosine residue. Its
structure is composed of a central anti-parallel β-sheet flanked by two α-helices
to form the so-called α/β/α motif shown in FIGURE 4. High affinity binding of
phosphopeptides is achieved through the insertion of a phosphotyrosine head
into a binding pocket located at one of the two α/β interfaces. This one is a
key event in the signal transduction pathways originated from the receptors of
the tyrosine kinase family.

I have selected the crystal structure of the SH2 domain of p56lck tyrosine
kinase since it has been recently determined at atomic resolution (1.0 Å) (Tong
et al. 1996). The atomic coordinates of this protein domain have been deposited
in the Protein Data Bank (PDB) under the reference code 1LKK. The protein
has been crystallized at pH 6.5 in complex with a short phosphopeptide, de-
noted to as pYEEI (pY = phosphotyrosine, E = glutamate, I = isoleucine),
which is bound to it through eight hydrogen bonds and three salt bridges. A
network made of six hydrogen bonds involves the phosphotyrosine (pY) moi-
ety that interacts with the side-chains of two arginine residues and two serine
residues.

Electronic structure calculations were performed so as to assess the magnitude of the interaction energy of the protein–ligand complex, the effect of
the ligand on the charges of the amino acid side-chains of the protein, and the
topology of the molecular orbitals (Pichierri 2004). This type of calculations
can also provide an estimate of the permanent dipole moment of the protein,
which can be regarded as a measure of the polarization of electronic charge in
a molecule. The magnitude of the dipole moment calculated with this method

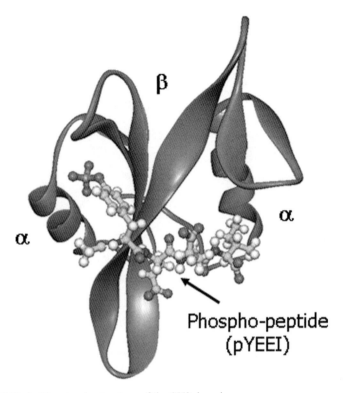

FIGURE 4. The atomic structure of the SH2 domain.

has been validated for α-chymotrypsin (Pichierri 2003), a protein that has been subjected to several experimental studies.

FIGURE 5 shows the most interesting result obtained from the quantum mechanical calculations on the SH2 domain. The calculations indicate that, upon binding, the dipole moment vector of the protein changes its orientation by rotating about 150 degrees around the axis parallel to that of one α-helix. The magnitude of the dipole moment decreases only slightly, namely from 136 to 110 Debye. These results, albeit theoretical, represent the first proof of the existence of sizeable quantum mechanical effects that appear in a specific signal transduction event (Pichierri 2004). In the next paragraph I will discuss how this biomolecular switch could be implemented in the construction of protein-based nanoelectronic devices.

PROTEIN-BASED DEVICES FOR NANOELECTRONICS

Probably, the most ambitious goal would be that of implementing a full-signal transduction pathway so as to achieve either signal integration or signal

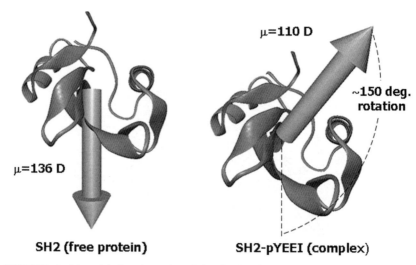

FIGURE 5. Ligand-induced rotation of the dipole moment of the SH2 domain.

amplification (FIG. 3). This implies the possibility of employing whole cells so as to perform a novel form of computing termed cellular computing (Amos 2004). Working with large ensembles of cells, however, might be quite difficult since little or no external control can be exerted on the ongoing intracellular signal transduction processes. Furthermore, since signal transduction pathways are directed from the outside to the inside of cells, the problem of how to extract the processed signal might be not so trivial to solve. A simplified and more pragmatic approach to adopt here is that of isolating one or a few elements of a signal transduction pathway whereby sizeable quantum mechanical effects are known to operate. Above we have seen how the change in the direction of the dipole moment upon peptide binding may act as a molecular-scale switch or a two-state (On/Off) system (FIG. 5). It is worth noticing that the term switch is commonly employed by biologists to indicate those protein–ligand complexes that are found in the bound–unbound state. Not all the known protein–ligand complexes, however, are likely to produce the sizeable quantum mechanical effect that is observed for the SH2 domain.

A further extension of the single biomolecular switch is that of building an array of dipoles so as to achieve signal amplification by means of vector addition. This could be done by attaching the protein on a metallic surface, such as that of gold, which can form stable covalent bonds with the thiol groups (-SH) of cysteine residues. The resulting supramolecular device might be sensible enough to interact with an external probe or electronic circuit, as shown in FIGURE 6. The protein array displayed in FIGURE 6 might be useful for the development of protein-based chips that could be employed in the nanoelectronic devices of the 21st century. Protein-based chips have already been constructed

_n_ SH2 + _n_ Peptide ⟶ _n_ (SH2:Peptide)

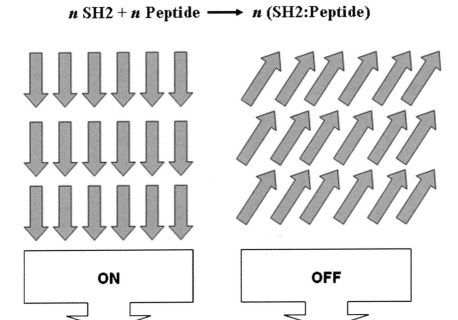

FIGURE 6. Array of SH2 dipoles subject to a concerted rotation induced by ligand binding.

and employed to perform immunoassays for medical diagnostics (Kojima *et al.* 2003).

Another example of protein-based device is shown in FIGURE 7. Here a single protein is employed as the sensing element of a biosensor (Buerk 1995). The protein is coupled to a transduction element that has the ability to detect any change in the electronic structure or molecular conformation of the protein upon ligand binding. A nano-biosensor based on these principles could be implanted permanently inside the body and thus being employed in detecting the concentration of specific molecules in biological fluids for an entire life span. A typical example of Nanodevice could be the nanoscale version of Clark's electrode (Clark *et al.* 1953) for the real-time monitoring of oxygen concentration in the blood.

SUMMARY

Nature through evolution has solved several complex problems, such as those concerned with signal integration and amplification, which are now emerging in many branches of nanotechnology. In this article I took inspiration from the biology of signal transduction events and discussed possible scenarios on

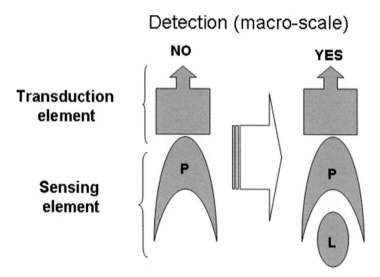

FIGURE 7. A simplified scheme showing the working principle of a biosensor.

how to use a specific protein, the SH2 domain of tyrosine kinases, to manufacture protein-based nanoelectronic devices. Additional issues that need to be seriously addressed in the development of any molecular-based computer or device are those related to both the thermodynamic and structural stabilities of the (bio)molecular components. The convergence of different scientific disciplines (chemistry, physics, biology, medicine) with engineering will hopefully help to overcome many technological obstacles that today are encountered by researchers working in the field of nanotechnology.

ACKNOWLEDGMENTS

I thank Fujitsu Ltd. (Tokyo) for providing the MOPAC2002 software package necessary to carry out the electronic structure calculations on the SH2 domain and to Dr. J.J.P. Stewart for his technical assistance with the software and useful suggestions. The research presented herein is sponsored by the 21st century COE project "Giant Molecules and Complex Systems" of MEXT hosted at Tohoku University.

REFERENCES

ALBERTS, B., A. JOHNSON, J. LEWIS, M. RAFF, K. ROBERTS, and P. WALTER. 2002. *Molecular Biology of the Cell* 4th ed. New York: Garland Science.
AMOS, M. 2004. *Cellular Computing*. Oxford: Oxford University Press.

AVIRAM, A., and M.A. RATNER. 1974. Molecular rectifiers. *Chemical Physics Letters* 29, 277–283.

BUERK, D.G. 1995. *Biosensors*. New York: CRC Press.

CLARK, L.C., R. WOLF, D. GRANGER, and Z. TAYLOR. 1953. Continuous recording of blood-oxygen tensions by polarography. *Journal of Applied Physiology 6*, 189–193.

EYSTER, K.M. 1998. Introduction to signal transduction: a primer for untangling the web of intracellular messengers. *Biochemical Pharmacology 55*, 1927–1938.

GOMPERTS, B.D., I.M. KRAMER, and P.E.R. TATHAM. 2002. *Signal Transduction*. London: Elsevier Academic Press.

GOSER, K., P. GLOSEKOTTER, and J. DIENSTUHL. 2004. *Nanoelectronics and Nanosystems*. Berlin: Springer-Verlag.

HELMREICH, E.J.M. 2001. *The Biochemistry of Cell Signaling*. New York: Oxford University Press.

JOACHIM, C., J.K. GIMZEWSKI, and A. AVIRAM. 2000. Electronics using hybrid – molecular and mono-molecular devices. *Nature 408*, 541–548.

KOJIMA, K., A. HIRATSUKA, H. SUZUKI, K. YANO, K. IKEBUKURO, and I. KARUBE. 2003. Electrochemical protein chip with arrayed immunosensors with antibodies immobilized in a plasma-polymerized film. *Analytical Chemistry 75*, 1116–1122.

LEHN, J.M. 1995. *Supramolecular Chemistry: Concepts and Perspectives*. New York: Wiley-VCH.

MACKINNON, R. 2004. Potassium channels and the atomic basis of selective ion conduction (Nobel Lecture). *Angewandte Chemie International Edition 43*, 4265–4277.

NICOLINI, C. 1996. *Molecular Bioelectronics*. Singapore: World Scientific.

PICHIERRI, F. 2003. Computation of the permanent dipole moment of α-chymotrypsin from linear-scaling semiempirical quantum mechanical methods. *Journal of Molecular Structure (Theochem) 664–665*, 197–205.

PICHIERRI, F. 2004. A quantum mechanical study on phosphotyrosyl peptide binding to the SH2 domain of p56lck tyrosine kinase with insights into the biochemistry of intracellular signal transduction events. *Biophysical Chemistry 109*, 295–304.

PICHIERRI, F., and Y. MATSUO. 2003. Mechanism of tyrosine phosphorylation catalyzed by the insulin receptor tyrosine kinase: a semiempirical PM3 study. *Journal of Molecular Structure (Theochem) 622*, 257–267.

TONG, L., T.C. WARREN, J. KING, J. BETAGERI, S. ROSE, and S. KAKES. 1996. Crystal structures of the human p56lck SH2 domain in complex with two short phosphotyrosyl peptides at 1.0 Å and 1.8 Å resolution. *Journal of Molecular Biology 256*, 601–610.

WIESENDANGER, R. 1994. *Scanning Probe Microscopy and Spectroscopy: Methods and Applications*. Cambridge: Cambridge University Press.

The Case for Nanogeoscience

MICHAEL F. HOCHELLA, JR.

Department of Geosciences, Virginia Polytechnic Institute and State University, Virginia Tech, Blacksburg, Virginia 24061, USA

ABSTRACT: In the last 200 years, geoscience has been about the convergence of sciences and technologies, particularly from the fields of chemistry and physics, while adding techniques, observations, and reasoning that seem to be wholly "geologic" in origin and nature. However, more recently, geoscience has also become an actively participating domain of at least three of the four major "NBIC" (nano-bio-info-cogno) enterprises, namely nanoscience and technology, modern molecular biology, and information technologies. This article will emphasize perhaps the least obvious of these connections, the "nano" aspects of the geosciences, and also adds a few aspects of the influence of modern molecular biology. There is no question that these new convergences are beginning to change the way geoscientists think about Earth, with critical applications in many areas of modern environmental science.

KEYWORDS: geoscience; nanogeoscience; nanoscience; nanotechnology; environmental science

INTRODUCTION

Geoscience, in the broadest sense the science of the nonliving, solid Earth, as well as the hydrosphere (the water envelope that surrounds our planet) and the atmosphere, has always been a field populated by far fewer scientists than the "fundamental" fields of science, namely mathematics, physics, and chemistry. Even biology, while not a fundamental science but roughly the same age as geoscience (the modern versions of both of these sciences date back to just over 200 years ago), has dramatically more practitioners. Nobel Prizes are not given in geoscience. Few people have ever heard of the most famous geoscientists of all time, for example, James Hutton, the father of modern geology, Victor Goldschmidt, friend of Albert Einstein, and the father of modern geochemistry, or Claire Patterson, the discoverer of the age of the Earth at 4.55 billion years. Yet these geoscientists, and countless others, have allowed us to understand our only home in the universe. They have answered questions that are at the core of human curiosity, like where this planet came from and

Address for correspondence: Michael F. Hochella, Jr., Department of Geosciences, 4044 Derring Hall, Virginia Tech, Blacksburg, VA 24061. Voice: 540-231-6227; fax: 540-231-3386.
e-mail: hochella@vt.edu

Ann. N.Y. Acad. Sci. 1093: 108–122 (2006). © 2006 New York Academy of Sciences.
doi: 10.1196/annals.1382.008

how it has evolved through eons of time. Geoscientists have answered questions of enormous practical significance, such as how we can find, recover, and use the Earth's nonliving riches, how we can understand and best avoid its wrath (from volcanic activity to flooding to earthquakes), and where the Earth might be going in the future (most recently made famous by the notion of human-promoted global climate change). In terms of sustaining the Earth, which means keeping the planet's life support systems functional without going into significant or long-term decline, geoscience and bioscience, working together, are the key components.

Given the history and influence of geoscience, it is not surprising that it is a science of confluence. Although modern geoscience can claim scientific methods that seem to be uniquely its own, the influence of physics, creating the distinct subfield of geophysics, and chemistry, creating the distinct subfield of geochemistry, are unmistakable and vital. Advanced and complex mathematics and computational science are key to both, but particularly geophysics, and in addition, atmospheric science. Advances and discoveries in all of the geoscience fields combined have tremendous influence on everything from determining where fossil fuels and metallic raw materials are coming from now, and where they will come from in the future, to understanding the mode and degree of the spread of toxins from anthropogenic pollution sources as well as the behavior and supply of our most important natural resource, water, to the state of our ultraviolet radiation protective blanket, ozone in the lower troposphere. And the list goes on and on.

Very recently, especially in the last 10 to 20 years, other sciences have begun to infiltrate the geosciences with enormous (some would say breathtaking) positive potential. These fields are nanoscience and molecular biology. Ultimately, although their influence will not rival the overall and timeless influence of physics and chemistry (just because these two are truly the fundamental scientific base of nearly all sciences, including geoscience), they are definitely becoming highly influential, and it is the opinion of this author and many others that they will be the root of several geoscience breakthroughs with global consequences in the future.

Nanoscience and Nanotechnology in General

Except possibly for the current revolution in biology and the health-related sciences, the revolution that we are presently witnessing in nanoscience and nanotechnology, and its coupling to advanced molecular chemistry, probably holds the greatest potential in shaping the world of the future. This point has been well justified and documented (e.g., Roco 1999; Lowndes 2000; Roco *et al.* 2000). Governments and industries worldwide have clearly recognized this situation, especially over the last decade, and they are investing billions of dollars in a concerted effort to capitalize on nanotechnology both in the near and long term. It will be very interesting to see how the Earth sciences and geochemistry in particular will ride this rapidly cresting wave.

Nanoscience, nanotechnology, and advanced molecular chemistry are relatively new and rapidly expanding fields that are providing revolutions in all sciences and engineering fields on the scale of what genomics and proteomics have done in recent years for the biological sciences and biotechnology. Nanoscience is based on the fact that properties of materials change as a function of the physical dimension of those materials, and nanotechnology takes advantage of this by applying selected property modifications of this nature to some beneficial endeavor. The prefix "nano" is used because the property dependence on physical size is generally observed close to the nanoscale, somewhere around 1 to 50 or 100 nm. The size at which changes are observed depends on the specific material and the property in question. Properties change in these confined spaces because the electronic structure (i.e., the distribution of electron energies) of the material is modified here in the gray area between the bulk and atomistic/molecular realms, or equivalently between the continuum and strictly quantum domains.

The Special Role that Mineralogy Plays

The geoscience subfield of mineralogy is typically and strongly entangled with nanogeoscience. The first point to emphasize is that some scientific historians consider mineralogy to be the base science, or root science, of the geosciences as a whole, and specifically, that geology grew out of mineralogy from the 17th through 19th centuries (e.g., Laudan 1994). One also needs to realize that early on, the contribution of the "science" of mineralogy was not so much about Earth understanding, but Earth survivability for our predecessors. When it comes to ancient hominids, one of the earliest and greatest inventions was making fire on demand. Hominids with these skills enjoyed a greatly expanded range of livable climates, as well as the first source of nonsolar light, the ability to cook, and defense–offense capabilities. Fire on demand was achieved, at least in part, by using minerals (for example, flint and pyrite) that when struck together produced a spark.

No one knows when early peoples first learned to make fire on demand; estimates range from 1.5 million to 500,000 years ago. The oldest commonly accepted evidence is associated with Homo erectus populations and dates from 500,000 years ago at the site of Zhoukoudian, China (e.g., Klein 1989). Though anthropologists cannot date the appearance of a mineral-based fire striker, they can say with certainty that by some 40,000 to 50,000 years ago, in the Paleolithic period on the present-day Eurasian continent, Homo sapiens were expert fire starters and almost certainly used mineral fire strikers. The first human use of metals, all of which are obtained from minerals, started only about 15,000 years ago with the utilization of gold and copper. The invention of mixing (alloying) tin and copper to make a much tougher metal, bronze, was another monumental achievement that had enormous influences. The beginning of a more modern scientific mineralogy waited until the middle of the 16th century. At that time, Georgius Agricola, the German scholar and physician with a keen interest in minerals and mining, may have also been one of the first environmental geoscientists, writing "When the ores are washed, the water which has been used poisons the brooks and streams and either destroys the fish or drives them away." He was unquestionably, and astutely, describing a very serious environmental problem known as acid mine drainage that persists even today.

Much more recently, Australian/English physicist W.L. Bragg, in 1913, determined the atomic structure of the mineral halite (sodium chloride or table salt), and in doing so, measured the size of the repeating unit of atoms that make it crystalline. Using X ray diffraction, the length of one edge of the cubic "unit cell" was determined to be precisely 0.564 nm, essentially the first nanoscale measurement in history. Young Bragg won the Nobel Prize for this in 1915, along with his father, W. H. Bragg. (To this day, W. L. Bragg remains the youngest Nobel recipient in the history of the prize. He was only 25 years old at the time.)

Presently, the geoscience foundational science of mineralogy, despite its remarkable history, has become mature. Naturally, it is difficult to study deep Earth minerals in the mantle and core, so our knowledge is largely limited to the Earth's crust. Well over 4000 minerals have been described and studied to date, but fewer and fewer minerals are discovered as time passes, and these, although highly interesting, are exceedingly rare. The rapidly developing fields of nanomineralogy, as well as mineral–microbe interaction, are a big part of the future of this subfield. Both topics have global environmental consequences, and both topics are massively broad with only minor development to date. They may generate new foundational subdisciplines in all of the geosciences.

A MATTER OF SCALE, AND WHY NANO AND GEO CAN WORK TOGETHER

At first glance, nano and Earth seem about as far apart as one can imagine. *Nanogeoscience* seems to be a word connecting opposites. More specifically, a nanometer relative to a meter is the same as a marble relative to the size of this planet. We might as well be talking about nanoastrophysics, or nanoastronomy, sounding even more unmatched. In fact, to a growing number of Earth scientists, the term *nanogeoscience* makes perfect sense. To gain perspective, one can consider the scale of natural phenomena in terms of powers of ten greater or less than one meter.

At the small end of the universe, fundamental particles, such as electrons and quarks, are smaller than 10^{-18} m (the smallest dimension that can be currently measured), and they may approach 10^{-30} m in size according to some variants of string theory. A hydrogen atom is just over 10^{-10} m or one-tenth of a nanometer in diameter. The scale of the Earth itself (10^7 m) is a full 17 orders of magnitude larger than one of the hydrogen atoms in its oceans. Two more orders of magnitude define the 10^9 m diameter of the sun. The Milky Way galaxy is nearly 10^{21} m in diameter, and the most distant observed galaxy is on the order of 10^{26} meters away. Interestingly, a meter or the scale of a human being is near the middle of this range of sizes.

The scale of the Earth sciences, or geosciences, fits neatly within the universal scale, and actually only covers about a third of it. A crystallization nucleus of the common mineral calcite ranges between 10^{-9} and 10^{-8} m, and then a bacterial cell measures roughly 10^{-6} m. The living world has become an integral part of the geosciences, and therefore is included in the Earth science scale. An inorganic quartz crystal can be as small as a living bacterium. Quartz, the most common of all minerals in the Earth's crust, varies tremendously in size, over many orders or magnitude, from below 10^{-6} m to, rarely, many meters, as do many minerals. An open pit mine can range between 10^2 and 10^3 m, whereas the Red Sea is 10^5 m wide and 10^6 m long.

The nanoscale is generally considered to be from 1 to 100 nm, or 10^{-9} to 10^{-7} m. Within the dimensional scale of the universe, and even within the dimensional domain of the geosciences, the nanometer niche seems inconspicuous, and perhaps even inconsequential. Yet, we are finding out that such is not the case.

How the Small Can Drive Big Systems

On Earth and even in the cosmos, it is often the case that a microphenomena affects or fully dictates a macroevent. Perhaps this is even the most exciting part of science, when macrosystem behavior can be explained by microsystem mechanics, all this across an unimaginable number of dimensional orders. A spectacular example of this in the field of astrophysics involves the formation of a neutron star. These stars are believed to form in remnants of supernovae with masses about 8 to 30 times that of our own sun. With pressures so high that any more would result in a black hole, proton–electron collisions result in neutrons, the opposite of β-radioactive decay, giving the neutron star its name and its major building blocks. Neutron stars can pack the mass of our sun into an area equivalent to an average sized city, and these stars also generate the highest magnetic fields known in the universe, up to 100 trillion times greater than the Earth's magnetic field. Their ultimate collapse can result in another supernova, resulting in gases spread over light years (one light year is on the order of 10^{16} m). Therefore, the reverse β-decay reaction, described at the scale of nuclear reactions (10^{-15} m or so), results in astronomical phenomena seen over light years of distance, 30 orders of magnitude greater in dimensional space.

Given this example, and remembering that the overall scale of the Earth sciences covers much less than 20 orders of magnitude in dimensional space, perhaps nanogeoscience no longer seems like a term which is out of character by any means. There are in fact many examples on Earth of small-scale phenomena whose consequences, or direct effects, in fact drive large-scale processes and are important and/or observed over very large scales. Although the conditions and resulting consequences are not as extreme as can be found elsewhere in the cosmos (the neutron star example given above is a great example of a cosmic extreme), these more "subtle" stories are vital to our understanding and use of, and survivability on, this planet. In many cases, these stories form the baseline portions of the tale of our very existence on our blue lifeboat in space.

A great example on Earth of this kind of thinking, of small driving big, is to have a look at a very unusual substance, water. We live on a water planet. The great majority of the surface of the Earth (between 70 and 75%) is covered with water. Ninety-seven percent of the Earth's near-surface water is in the oceans. Only 2% of this water is tied up in ice in the form of glaciers and the polar ice caps (that percentage is dropping due to global warming), less than 1% is groundwater, less than 0.02% is in lakes and inland seas, and about 0.001% is in rivers, the atmosphere, and in all living things combined! Deeper in the planet, it is not clear how much water is tied up in the Earth's mantle, but one needs to carefully consider it because the mantle makes up about 80% of the volume of Earth. Small amounts of water, or its "parts" like hydroxyl, exist in mantle minerals. If we assume that water exists in these mantle minerals at an average level of just 300 parts per million, or 0.03%, we suddenly have enough water to fill another ocean!

With all this water, and because it is absolutely essential to life as we know it, the chemical and physical properties of this deceptively simple substance has always been of interest to scientists. And it turns out, perhaps not surprisingly, that water and ice are rather deviant in their behavior. H_2O is an odd-shaped molecule, resulting in highly interesting electrical, mechanical, and chemical properties. I will just emphasize one unusual property here, one that we are all familiar with, but probably one that we never realized would radically alter life if it were not this way. Therefore, this becomes a very important micro-driving macro-story. For the vast majority of liquids, when they freeze, the molecules that make up the liquid pack more tightly together. The frozen liquid becomes more dense relative to the liquid. When water freezes to ice, the opposite happens. Ice is about 9% less dense than water and floats on its surface. If this were not so, the Earth would be a very different place. Rivers and lakes would freeze from the bottom up, killing the vast majority of organisms because they cannot survive freezing. Just from this chemical peculiarity, and remembering that life first evolved in water, we have found something that must have affected the evolution of life on the planet, surely in fundamentally, Earth-changing ways.

WHAT EXACTLY DOES NANO HAVE TO DO
WITH EARTH SYSTEMS?

Nanomaterials can be manufactured, but they are also naturally occurring. In fact, nanomaterials are essentially ubiquitous in nature (e.g., Banfield and Navrotsky 2001; Hochella 2002). Many have been known for several decades, and more are being discovered all the time, but the scientific emphasis has now shifted to that of measuring, understanding, and ultimately predicting the property changes from the bulk to nanodomains (Hochella and Madden 2005). Certainly, Earth scientists are also beginning to use nanoscience to develop nanotechnology that should play important roles in Earth sustainability issues of the future.

Numerous examples of nanogeoscience involve the "critical zone" of the Earth. The critical zone, as defined in a 2001 National Research Council book entitled "Basic Research Opportunities in Earth Science" (Jordon 2001), is the place where the land meets the fluid envelopes of the Earth, that is, the hydrosphere and atmosphere. It is the place where we live, and it is the place that provides us with fresh water, agriculture, and many vital natural resources, such as timber and most mineral deposits. Considering all the geo- and bioaspects of this zone, it is probably the most heterogeneous and complex portion of the entire Earth, yet understanding it relatively well is certainly important in intelligently sustaining this planet for human habitation.

Water–Rock–Bacteria Nanoscience

Although by no means developed, nearly all aspects (both geo- and bioprocesses) of weathering, soil, and water–rock interaction science are inexorably linked to nanoscience. Within the Earth's near-surface, materials that are broken down, as well as materials that are produced, are often in the nanoscale regime. Further, as organic molecules, simple and complex, as well as bacteria and all flora and fauna in soils and rocks interact with the mineral components present, nanodimensions and nanoscale processes are the order of the day. If one does not know what is going on at this scale (and generally we do not), one can by no means have the complete picture of these exceptionally complex systems.

The biggest scientific problem is that one needs to know how things work at this small and awkward scale in the first place. The reason that one needs to know this is because processes that occur at the micron and larger dimensions simply do not scale down to the nanoscale. Within the nanoscale, as we have mentioned above, entirely different processes are possible, processes found nowhere else in the dimensional scale of the Earth.

One of the most important interactions in the weathering environment and in soils is mineral–bacteria association. The bacteria, typically in the micron-size range, with dynamic membranes of physiological suites of organic molecules, interact with surfaces of any one of thousands of minerals, each with their own compositions, surface atomic structures, and microtopographies. This interaction takes place over nanometers of distance as their surfaces approach one another, are in contact, and separate. All of these interaction forces, between fully viable bacteria and various mineral surfaces in aqueous (water) solution, were first measured quantitatively using a variation of atomic force microscopy, a technique that we call biological force microscopy, or BFM (Lower *et al.* 2000, 2001, 2005).

FIGURE 1 is a rendition of a BFM. A single living cell (the short rod in the image with rounded terminations), or groups of cells, are attached to the cantilever of an atomic force microscope (the triangular wafer to which the cell is attached in the image). The cantilever can be precisely raised or lowered with Angstrom resolution. As the cell begins to interact with the surface, the cantilever will bend in response, and this movement is monitored via the laser bouncing off the back of the cantilever as shown.

The type of data obtained from the BFM is shown in FIGURE 2 (from Lower *et al.* 2000) as a force-distance plot. The distance (in nanometers, nm) is between the two surfaces being tested, and the force (in nanoNewtons, nN) is that between the two surfaces at some distance. A positive force on the vertical scale is repulsive, and a negative force is attractive. In this example, the two traces near zero force that show positive (repulsive) force at small separation distances were collected as the mineral and bacterium surfaces approached each other. The trace showing negative (attractive) force was recorded after the two surfaces had been in contact, and were being pulled apart; such a pull-off signature occurs when biomolecules on the outer cell membrane have bonded to the mineral surface, and upon mineral–bacterium separation, are stretching and breaking free, molecule by molecule.

FIGURE 1. A BFM.

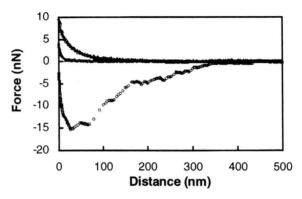

FIGURE 2. A force-distance plot of data from a BFM.

Measurements of this type speak to the heart of nanoscience, insofar as the observer is looking at nanoNewtons of force over nanometers of distance. As a bacterial cell and a mineral surface are brought closer together, the confined water layer in between is subject to the same attributes discussed just above, influencing and influenced by the macromolecular outer cell envelope of the bacterium and the mineral surface itself. Certainly, we have now been able to measure distinct and significant differences in the forces of interaction as a function of changes in the mineral surface, the intervening solution, and the bacterial surface (both in terms of different species and different growth conditions). It is easy to see how this aspect of nanoscience will have applications to bacterial transport and contamination in groundwater aquifers (aquifers are subsurface rock or sediment layers through which water is stored and moves), subsurface *in situ* bioremediation, the use of wastewater for irrigation or for groundwater recharge, and many other issues pertaining to mineral–microbe interaction.

A specific example of understanding bacteria transport using nanoscience has recently been published (Cail and Hochella 2005). The BFM technique described above was used in this study to measure forces and distances of interaction between the bacterium *Enterococcus faecalis* and silica glass. *E. faecalis* (previously *Streptococcus faecalis*) is a common soil and groundwater microorganism for which there has been much investigation and research. Silica glass plates were used not only because of their simplicity of form and chemistry, but also because the surface properties and characteristics of this glass are similar to quartz surfaces. In this case the glass surfaces were used to simulate quartz grains in, for example, a sandstone aquifer where these grains, cemented together to form a hard rock, allow the passage of subsurface water. Water resources like these are tapped by wells worldwide and used for human consumption. In the research of Cail and Hochella, nanodistance and nanoforce measurements, made in water of various pHs (acidities) and ionic strengths (background salt concentrations), were used to calculate the sticking efficiencies between *E. faecalis* and the silica glass surfaces. Sticking efficiency is defined as the fraction of particles colliding with a surface that becomes attached to that surface. Accurate predictions of sticking efficiency are vital to successfully modeling particle transport in natural sediments. Filtration theory was then used to predict the bacterium travel distance in a sandstone aquifer.

The results showed that nanoforces over nanodistances play the vital role between micron-sized particles (in this case bacteria, 1000 times larger than a nanometer) and large mineral grains forming an aquifer in the subsurface. The measurements and calculations at a water pH of 5 (a typical, slightly acidic pH) showed that when the ionic strength is relatively high, the transport distance of *E. faecalis* in the simulated sandstone aquifer is very small, on the order of millimeters. However, at the same pH, but an ionic strength just 10 times lower, the nanoforce interaction between the cells and surfaces is modified significantly, and the calculated distance of transport is very long, on the order of many kilometers. If this bacterium was a pathogen (a disease-producing organism), such transport distance variation would be critical information. In this case, the difference between pathogens trapped harmlessly deep in the subsurface, versus pathogens easily transported through aquifers to water wells, for example, are the nano interactions between cells and minerals deep underground. This is an excellent example of how nanophenomena can play the key role in large-scale, macro-processes.

Metal Transport Nanoscience

Metal transport in the environment is often of great environmental concern, whether related to radioactive waste disposal, acid mine drainage, industrial pollution, or any number of other scenarios. Metal mobility ultimately depends on (1) the chemical reactivity of the metal in question as dictated by bonding characteristics and interactions, and (2) the part of the environment through which transport occurs (soil, groundwater, surface water, atmosphere, etc.). Brown (2001) and Selim and Sparks (2001) provide interesting perspectives on several aspects of these issues. A fundamental question that can be easily overlooked is simply whether the metal in question is moving as aqueous complexes, as part of a precipitate, or as sorbed complexes on particles. It is often assumed that if the metal in question passes a submicron filter (typically in the 0.2–0.5 μm range, i.e., 200–500 nm), then that metal is considered to be an aqueous species. In these cases, investigators simply have no better way to handle what is obviously missing from this approach. That is, metals can in fact, and presumably often are, transported within or on nanoparticles, not as aqueous species. In the future, as we learn to better deal with the nanoscale in terms of observation, analysis, and modeling, this assumption will be less and less necessary.

One example where this is already the case is in the Clark Fork River Superfund Site, Montana, the largest Superfund site in the United States. Here, mining since the 1860s has contaminated over 1600 km^2 of land with lead, arsenic, zinc, and copper. In many areas, even zink and copper are over the toxic threshold of most flora and fauna. All these metals are distributed among millions of cubic meters of mine tailings that have moved down the Clark Fork River drainage over the last one and a half centuries. Until recently, it was not completely clear how the metals were tied up in these highly weathered tailings, having also over time mixed with local soils and stream sediments. Therefore, metal transport mechanisms and bioavailability were difficult to fully assess. Now, analytical transmission electron microscopy (TEM) has been used to give a detailed picture of where the metals are within these complex materials (Hochella *et al.* 2005a, 2005b). Perhaps not surprisingly, most of the toxic metal is tied up in or on nanoparticles. One of the nanophases present, ferrihydrite (a poorly crystalline hydrous iron oxide), is well known for prolific metal uptake in contaminated sediments. A new nanophase was also discovered, one that is apparently far more reactive than even ferrihydrite at heavy metal uptake. It is a secondary manganese oxide mineral that is probably very similar to the mineral vernadite (nominally $MnO_2 \cdot nH_2O$, a poorly crystalline sheet manganate). It is likely that the ferrihydrite surfaces catalyzed aqueous manganese oxidation that resulted in the verdnadite-like phase (Hochella *et al.* 2005a). The extraordinary heavy-metal sorptive capability of the vernadite-like phase makes it a promising candidate as a reactive medium in permeable barriers that are used in environmental remediation.

Nanogeoscience's Relevance to the Atmosphere

Minerals in the atmosphere, in the form of dust, have not been studied nearly as much as minerals on the continents and in the oceans. Yet minerals make up a small but highly significant part of the atmosphere, and several reviews have appeared, which nicely explain why this is the case (Buseck *et al.* 2000; Pósfai and Molnár 2000; Anastasio and Martin 2001). Although most of us have seen pictures of vast amounts of mineral dust emanating from volcanic eruptions, with massive dust plumes rising high into the atmosphere, wind-blown dust from arid and semi-arid lands, which cover 30% of the Earth's terrestrial surface, as well as from agricultural land contributes far more to the flux that enters the atmosphere each year. The amount of this land-born mineral dust in the Earth's atmosphere at any one time is large, usually estimated to be in the neighborhood of 2000 Tg per year (1 Tg = 10^{12} grams). This far exceeds the dust from biological debris. The other main source of mineral dust in the atmosphere originates from the surface of the ocean, where sea spray evaporates and crystallizes into halite (NaCl) and various hydrous sulfates.

The other interesting thing about minerals in the atmosphere is that they can travel tremendous distances. Mineral grains larger than 75 μm have been reported more than 10,000 km away from their source region. Major wind storms in the Sahara can result in dust transportation within the troposphere (the lower 15 km of the atmosphere) all the way to North and South America. Huge wind currents from Tibetan windstorms in Asia have taken mineral dust over the north Pacific, North America, and eventually to Greenland in a journey of tens of thousands of kilometers.

But what does this have to do with nanoscience? Mineral dust particles larger than 10 μm in size tend to settle back out of the air stream relatively quickly. Minerals that can travel high in the troposphere great distances tend to be much less than 10 μm in their largest dimension. In fact, in many atmospheric mineral dust samples collected over the years, the average particle size that has been found, based on mass, is between 2 and 5 μm. However, the most common particle size, based on number, is submicron and more typically 0.1 μm, which is 100 nm. There is a significant proportion of particles below this in size, well down into the nanometer range of dimension.

As more dust enters the atmosphere due to the consequences of human activity (from direct effects, such as clearing of land and desertification, versus indirect effects, such as global warming), it becomes more important to understand the effects of mineral dust on the gaseous composition of the atmosphere, cloud formation conditions, and global-mean radiative forcing (i.e., heating or cooling effects). Although we understand these processes in principal, many important details are not known. For example, because the optics of minerals are complex, and because there are so many mineral types in the atmosphere over such a large size range, it is not known whether the overall effect of atmospheric mineral dust contributes to warming or cooling the planet. This will require more knowledge of the mineral types, sizes, and distributions around the globe, as well as their light sorption and scattering characteristics. Further, the surface chemistry and reactivity of these mineral dust particles will dictate their interaction with atmospheric gases, which results in cloud formation characteristics and atmospheric gas compositions. How cloud types and gaseous atmospheric composition will change in the presence of more mineral nanoparticles is not known.

On a more local level, nanoparticles in the atmosphere have the potential to carry undesirable materials, such as toxic heavy metals. For example, Utsunomiya et al. (2004) collected airborne particles over Detroit, Michigan (USA), and they found many nanoparticles, ranging down in size to just a few nanometers, that contained metals regulated by federal agencies in many countries due to their toxicity, including arsenic, chromium, lead, and selenium. Particles of this type have inflammatory potential in lung tissue, and the chemical toxicity of these particles may be particularly high due to their size and reactivity.

WHERE IS NANOGEOSCIENCE GOING IN THE FUTURE?

In the geosciences, nanoscience is growing rapidly. FIGURE 3 shows the exponential rise of peer-reviewed nano-related publications in the geosciences literature since 1990. Nanoscience has started to be applied to mineral–bacteria interaction, environmental geochemistry (including toxic metal transport and retention in the environment), atmospheric chemistry, soil science, and rock weathering as described above. But this is only the beginning.

The future directions of nanoscience in the geosciences will include a determination of the identity, distribution, and unusual chemical properties of nanosized particles and/or films in the oceans, on the continents, and in the atmosphere, and how they drive Earth processes in unexpected ways. Further, nanotechnology will be the key to developing the next generation of Earth and environmental sensing systems. Both nanoscience and nanotechnology will provide new directions in contaminant remediation research and development, as well as other areas important to Earth sustainability issues. Finally, advanced molecular chemistry will be an integral part in all things nano, as the fields are often inseparable.

Although geochemists and mineralogists have just begun to measure property changes as a function of size in the nanoregime, we anticipate that this property variability is essentially universal, and that large deviations from bulk properties should be expected in particle sizes less than a few tens of nanometers. Aggregation should not affect these property changes, as long as the particles remain discrete. There are a number of attributes of nanoparticles

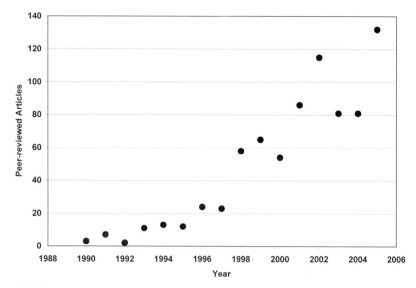

FIGURE 3. Nano-related publications in the geosciences literature.

that may result in characteristic changes that deviate from the bulk, including electronic structure modification (distribution and population of electronic states), surface site variation, defect densities and distributions, and surface and edge nanotopography.

Nanoscience and technology are central keys to the next great revolution in the Earth sciences. Nanoscale particles, films, and confined fluids are ubiquitous in nature (on the continents and especially throughout the critical zone, and in the atmosphere and oceans). Although they are everywhere, we do not understand them very well, even from a fundamental physical chemistry point-of-view. However, it is becoming more common to observe their deviant behavior (relative to the same material at a larger scale) in laboratory and field studies in both biologically and abiotically dominated systems. Because of the minute sizes involved, the interface to bulk ratios are extremely large in these nanoscale components of bulk systems, and therefore interfaces become even more important than usual. It is imperative that we provide an effective vehicle to scientifically pursue interface interactions in the nanoregime of Earth systems. Critical insight into local, regional, and even global phenomena await our understanding of processes that are relevant at the smallest scales of Earth science studies.

Nanogeoscience is in a relatively early stage of development. Therefore, large gaps in our knowledge of this area exist, making the next few years an exciting time of new realizations, discovery, and change.

ACKNOWLEDGMENTS

The writing of this article was supported by current funding from the National Science Foundation through grant DGE-0504196, and the Department of Energy through grant DE-FG02-06ER15786.

REFERENCES

ANASTASIO, C., AND S.T. MARTIN. 2001. Atmospheric nanoparticles. Nanoparticles and the Environment. *Reviews in Mineralogy and Geochemistry 44*, 293–349. Washington, DC: Mineralogical Society of America.

BANFIELD, J.F., and A. NAVROTSKY, eds. 2001. Nanoparticles and the environment. *Reviews in Mineralogy and Geochemistry 44*. Washington, DC: Mineralogical Society of America.

BROWN, G.E., JR. 2001. How minerals react with water. *Science 294*, 67–70.

BUSECK, P.R., D.J. JACOB, M. PÓSFAI, J. LI, and J.R. ANDERSON. 2000. Minerals in the air: an environmental perspective. *International Geology Review 42*, 577–593.

CAIL, T.L., and M.F. HOCHELLA, JR. 2005. The effects of solution chemistry on the sticking efficiencies of viable *Enterococcus faecalis*: an atomic force microcopy and modeling study. *Geochimica et Cosmochimica Acta 69*, 2959–2969.

HOCHELLA, M.F., JR. 2002. Nanoscience and technology: the next revolution in the Earth sciences. *Earth and Planetary Science Letters 203*, 593–605.

HOCHELLA, M.F., JR., and A. MADDEN. 2005. Earth's nanocompartment for toxic metals. *Elements 1*, 191–195.

HOCHELLA, M.F., JR., T. KASAMA, A. PUTNIS, C. PUTNIS, and J.N. MOORE. 2005a. Environmentally important, poorly crystalline Fe/Mn hydrous oxides: ferrihydrite and a vernadite-like mineral from a massive acid mine drainage system. *American Mineralogist 90*, 718–724.

HOCHELLA, M.F., JR., J.N. MOORE, C. PUTNIS, A. PUTNIS, T. KASAMA, and D.D. EBERL. 2005b. Direct observation of toxic metal-mineral association from a massive acid mine drainage system: implications for metal transport and bioavailability. *Geochemica et Cosmochimica Acta 69*, 1651–1663.

JORDON, T.H. 2001. *Basic Research Opportunities in Earth Science.* Washington, DC: National Academy Press.

KLEIN, R.G. 1989. *The Human Career: Human Biological and Cultural Origins.* Chicago: University of Chicago Press.

LAUDAN, R. 1994. *From Mineralogy to Geology: The Foundations of a Science, 1650-1830.* Chicago: University of Chicago Press.

LOWER, B.H., M.F. HOCHELLA, JR., and S.K. LOWER. 2005. Putative mineral-specific proteins synthesized by a metal reducing bacterium. *American Journal of Science 305*, 687–710.

LOWER, S., M.F. HOCHELLA, JR., and T.J. BEVERIDGE. 2001. Bacterial recognition of mineral surfaces: nanoscale interactions between Shewanella and α–FeOOH. *Science 292*, 1360–1363.

LOWER, S., C. TADANIER, and M.F. HOCHELLA, JR. 2000. Measuring interfacial and adhesion forces between bacteria and mineral surfaces with bacterial force microscopy. *Geochimica et Cosmochimica Acta 64*, 3133–3139.

LOWNDES, D.H., ed. 2000. *Nanoscale Science, Engineering and Technology Research Directions.* Oak Ridge: Oak Ridge National Laboratory.

PÓSFAI, M., and A. MOLNÁR. 2000. Aerosol particles in the troposphere: a mineralogical introduction. Pp. 197–252 in D.J. Vaughan and R.A. Wogelius (eds.), *Environmental Mineralogy.* Budapest: Eötvös University Press.

ROCO, M.C., ed. 1999. *Nanotechnology: Shaping the World Atom by Atom.* Washington, DC: National Science and Technology Council, The Interagency Working Group on Nanoscience, Engineering, and Technology.

ROCO, M.C., S. WILLIAMS, and P. ALIVISATOS, eds. 2000. *Nanotechnology Research Directions: IWGN Workshop Report.* Norwell: Kluwer Academic Publishers.

SELIM, H.M., and D.L. SPARKS, eds. 2001. *Heavy Metals Release in Soils.* New York: Lewis Publishers.

UTSUNOMIYA, S., K.A. JENSEN, G.J. KEELER, and R.C. EWING. 2004. Direct identification of trace metals in fine and ultrafine particles in the Detroit urban atmosphere. *Environmental Science & Technology 38*, 2289–2297.

Path to Bio-Nano-Information Fusion

JIA MING CHEN AND CHIH-MING HO

University of California, Los Angeles, California 90095, USA

ABSTRACT: This article will discuss the challenges in a new convergent discipline created by the fusion of biotechnology, nanotechnology, and information technology. To illustrate the research challenges, we will begin with an introduction to the nanometer-scale environment in which biology resides, and point out the many important behaviors of matters at that scale. Then we will describe an ideal model system, the cell, for bio-nano-information fusion. Our efforts in advancing this field at the Institute of Cell Mimetic Space Exploration (CMISE) will be introduced here as an example to move toward achieving this goal.

KEYWORDS: biotechnology; informatics; microfluidics; nanotechnology

PATH TO BIO-NANO-INFORMATION FUSION

The convergence between nanotechnology and biotechnology attracts much public attention because this fusion can potentially revolutionize our understanding and practice of medicine, a topic dear to the hearts of everyone. Nanotechnology, first described by Richard Feynman in 1959 (Feynman 1959), represents a discipline that intentionally engineers structures with sizes at the nanometer-scale and leverages unique properties manifested only in this small scale. Biotechnology is the field that develops techniques to manipulate biomolecules from cells, DNA, and proteins. Given the inherent nanoscale of biomolecules and the unique functional properties they display, it is inevitable that nanotechnology will spur the advancements of disease diagnoses and drug developments. The synergetic effort has already begun to provide unprecedented tools for medical doctors and scientists to examine the human body. Not surprisingly, the complexity of the human body far exceeds any engineered devices. Furthermore, processing the information flows from macromolecules through cells, organs, and to the human body is beyond the current capability but absolutely needs to be done. The challenge lies in how to coherently fuse these three fields: nanotechnology, biotechnology, and informatics, into a single domain of knowledge that can attain the potential of revolutionizing the understanding and practice of medicine (Ho *et al.* 2006).

Address for correspondence: Chih-Ming Ho, Mechanical and Aerospace Engineering Department, School of Engineering and Applied Science, Engineering IV, Room 38-137J, 420 Westwood Plaza, Los Angeles, CA 90095-1597. Voice: 310-825-9993; fax: 310-206-2302.
e-mail: chihming@ucla.edu

Ann. N.Y. Acad. Sci. 1093: 123–142 (2006). © 2006 New York Academy of Sciences.
doi: 10.1196/annals.1382.009

CONVERGENCE OF SCIENCES AT SMALL SCALES

The length scale on which scientists and engineers perform their crafts with control is becoming incredibly microscopic. Over the past 50 years, tremendous progress has been made to enable engineers and scientists from many different fields to access the nanoscopic world with ever more precise control. The invisibly tiny particles of matter like atoms, molecules, DNA, and proteins are no longer abstract concepts conjured by scientists to explain our physical world. Researchers can image these small particles, position them in desired patterns, or use them as key structural elements in the fabrication of nano/micro machines.

Electron microscopy can image individual atoms that form the lattices of a crystal or visualize the structure of an individual protein frozen in its natural cellular environment. In 1989, physicists at Bell Laboratory arranged 35 individual xenon atoms to spell its parent company's three-letter logo, IBM (Eigler and Schweizer 1990). The sharpest needle known in the form of the cylindrical-shaped carbon nanotubes (Iijima 1991) is being touted as an enabling component for many innovations.

In chemistry, one can now monitor the chemical reaction of a single molecule, as well as design molecules to self-assemble into an ultra-thin monolayer on surfaces. In biology, not only can researchers image the helical DNA molecule that carries life's genetic code, but they can also transcribe the entire genetic map of a human and modify the genetic codes. In the technological frontier, electronic engineers routinely print and correctly wire 275 million transistors onto a surface area smaller than a U.S. stamp in order to produce a microprocessor (e.g., the IBM Power5). To put this in perspective by an analogy, printing 275 million alphabetic characters (the same font size of this writing) will require approximately 100 volumes of a 500 page-textbook, or about two bookshelves full of papers written front and back.

When the working length scale of research reached nanometers, many scientific disciplines converged. A key reason lies within the fact that the important elements studied by traditionally different fields become the same at this scale. For example, the interdisciplinary field of molecular electronics spawned from researchers with very different domains of expertise, each trying to understand and use the electronic properties of molecules at the nanometer scale. In the early 1900s, physicists were interested in applying quantum mechanics to more complex systems with multiple atoms, such as the molecule. The community developed the molecular orbital theory, Hund-Mulliken Theory (Mulliken 1927), of electrons inside a molecule for electron density calculations. Soon after, chemists were learning to synthesize molecules with desirable functions. They designed and synthesized variations of molecules that contained electron acceptor and donor sites, resulting in molecules with electron transport properties similar to the well-established transistors in semiconductor electronics (Aviram and Ratner 1974).

Meanwhile, semiconductor engineers are seeking an alternative transistor design to replace the silicon-based metal-on-silicon (MOS) before the ubiquitous silicon electronics reaches its physical limit of advancement, as reflected in The International Technology Roadmap for Semiconductors.[a] They are collaborating with chemists and physicists to fabricate novel electronics devices based on self-assembled monolayers of artificially designed molecules, where the currents transverse through molecular orbitals instead of conduction bands, thus establishing the field of molecular electronics. Molecular electronics is only one example of a field of convergence where multiple disciplines each initially used their own tools to explore the properties of electron transport in individual molecules but later found synergy that lead to innovation. At the nanometer scale, the element being studied is shared by many diverse fields, and this commonality is driving significant convergence of traditionally separated scientific disciplines.

FORCES AND MOTIONS AT THE NANOMETER SCALE

Before we delve into the technical challenges of interfacing bio-nano-information fusion, it would be instructive to describe the uncommon world where the nanometer-scale functional molecules, the building blocks in the fusion research, perform their functions. These biological functions are mostly carried out by the forming or breaking of chemical bonds. Force is a key player in making the reactions happen. The motion of these molecules carry information from one location to another in the biological system, and is another key factor in accomplishing biological functions.

The nanoscale world where functional molecules live would look unfamiliar and downright strange to most of us. The first noticeable difference is the fact that the force of gravity, which governs our daily activities, is negligible. The van der Waals (dispersion) force, one among several kinds of unfamiliar forces, becomes prominent in the nanoscale. Its attractive force component, in the order of piconewtons, is significant over a distances of 100 μm, but has a decaying binding energy potential inversely proportional to the sixth power of separation. Its repulsive component has a much shorter range and stiffens with the twelfth power of distance. The thermal energy, kT, of a molecule moving at room temperature (k is the Boltzmann constant and T at room temperature is 300 K) is about 4×10^{-21} J (26 meV). This energy is comparable to the van der Waals binding potential of typical nanometer particles. Consequently, the van der Waals force brings nano-objects together, but the nano-objects frequently split apart because of thermal excitation, unless they become entangled by other stronger forces (dipole–dipole interaction, hydrophobic interaction, ionic bond are the most common, with force strength approximately 10 times, 100 times,

---

[a] www.itrs.net

and 1000 times of van der Waals, respectively). Another very important force consideration that determines the proximity of biomolecules is this: most biomolecules have residual surface charges (usually negative), which generates an electrostatic field that determines their interactions among each other as well as the aqueous environment (i.e., highly dependent on ionic concentration and the resulting boundary layer effect). *Holding or releasing nanometer scale objects together or apart in a controlled manner is a significant challenge in nanotechnology applications.*

The concept of up or down is irrelevant in the nanoworld, but isotropy, the measure of asymmetry, such as the difference found near surface and the bulk volume, is useful. This nanoworld of biological molecules is densely embedded in water molecules (1 g/cm^3 or 33 water molecules in 1 nm^3 of volume; note that at room temperature water molecules continuously form clusters that create local density fluctuations). Movement in the nanoworld would feel extremely viscous like a fish swimming in molasses, because the Reynolds Number is proportional to a swimmer's size (the smaller the Reynolds Number in the medium, the higher the viscous effect). Nevertheless everything is moving, randomly bombarding each other and knocking each other off its course at an interaction rate on the order of 10^{12} times per second (slower near proteins: Lu *et al.* 2004). The consequence is that maintaining the direction of a trajectory is not difficult, but practically impossible without some kind of built-in tethering support mechanisms. The microtubules in the skeletal structure of cells or the myosin filaments of the muscle cells are examples of such tethering supports. *Controlling the direction or trajectory of nanometer scale object for achieving guided movement or transport is a challenge.*

A reasonably useful image that sketches the motion observed in the nanoworld is zigzag movements, i.e. the Brownian motion. The diffusive transport due to this random motion is very slow. For instance, a sucrose molecule (about 1 nm in length) has a diffusion coefficient of 5×10^{-6} cm^2/s in water at room temperature (Jones 2004), which means it takes an hour to move 1 μm along the chemical gradient direction from its original source. Larger biomolecules have even slower diffusion coefficients. Obviously alternative transportation mechanism, other than diffusion, must be used for delivery (i.e., nutrients and other essential macromolecules) inside a nano system. *Transporting or delivering a collection of molecules (e.g., chemical mixing or drug delivery) in a timely manner is a challenge in the nanometer scale.*

The three challenges for researchers to precisely manipulate functional molecules in the nanoworld (mentioned above in italics) are obviously nontrivial and are in need of innovative solutions.

A successful example of an organism that met all the challenges mentioned above is the cell. The biological cell is a magnificent self-organized system. The cell's activities are carried out by biomolecules, such as the millions of proteins with sizes ranging from 1 to 20 nm. The cell's ability to robustly coordinate the immense number of nanometer scale machineries contained in its fluidic capsule is awe inspiring. With this ability to control activities at the nanometer scale, the cell self-organizes into an independent living unit at the size of only a few micrometers. The key attribute that makes it a complete system is its comprehensive set of capacities to: sense (monitor its *biological* surroundings and responses), decide (process incoming signals and trigger an optimal response through *information* processes), and actuate (modify its *nanometer-scale* environment to a more suitable one for survival). These sophisticated functions are a result of the movements and reactions of the molecular machines governed by a complex information-processing network. The cell's responses to the internal and external stimulations through organized molecular activities make it an ideal model system for bio-nano-information fusion research.

CORE TECHNOLOGIES FOR STUDYING BIO-NANO-INFORMATION-FUSED SYSTEMS

A collection of core technologies needs to be developed for analyzing and manipulating nano subjects and integrated into an engineering system which can be applied to learn, mimic, and control the biological cellular system. Researchers must first be able to see at the scale of biomolecules, ideally without disturbing the viability or normal metabolism of the cell. It is also essential that the researchers have the ability to control the environment and stimuli exposed to the cell. This ability includes the manipulation of the fluid carrying the biological specimens at a smaller scale comparable to the size of individual cell and biomolecules. Once the fluidic environment has been mastered, tools must be provided to manipulate the cells and biomolecules living within the fluid. These can be electrostatic manipulation techniques, such as dielectrophoresis (DEP), or optical based, such as optical laser tweezers. Also, instruments capable of monitoring cellular behavior nondestructively are essential. These elemental tools, once developed, need to be integrated to form specific system platforms that can meet the stringent requirements for studying cellular system. The following sections will provide examples of these core technologies developed at the Institute for Cell Mimetic Space Exploration (CMISE).

Optical Nanoscopes

The ability to visualize the objects being studied is the first step toward much progress in science and technology. The advents of the optical microscope, electronic microscope, scanning tunneling microscope, and atomic force microscope (AFM) each opened a new chapter in scientific discoveries. In the world of biomolecules, our ability to see objects inside living cells is very limited. Currently, visualization of biological activities relies on variations of microscopes, confocal microscopy, X-ray crystallography, environmental scanning electron microscope (SEM), cryoelectron transmission electron microscopy (cryo TEM), and AFM. The optical microscopy techniques are severely constrained in spatial resolution (in practice, limited to approximately 200 nm resolution) due to the diffraction limit. Although single isolated events in the nanometer resolution can be monitored using techniques such as fluorophore, two or more simultaneous events cannot be spatially resolved below the optical diffraction limit. Electron microscopy techniques can provide subnanometer resolution, but they require the sample be placed in a vacuum, which rules out the possibility of studying a live biological unit. The ideal instrument to visualize nanoscale molecular activity would provide real-time imaging of live cells similar to optical microscopy and have the spatial resolution of an electron microscope.

Innovative optical visualization solutions for the nanometer scale are being developed using the concept of *superlens*, a technique that uses plasmonic resonances from a thin slab of material to enhance and compensate the evanescent loss of the imaging electromagnetic wave. Researchers in the Zhang group at the University of California, Berkeley, demonstrated this optical technique, showing that it can image with spatial resolution below 60 nm, more than six times below the optical diffraction limit of the 365 nm light source (Fang *et al*. 2005).[b] Superlens is capable of producing sub-diffraction limit images because it is designed to better recover the evanescent waves of the source image via the excitation of surface plasmons on a thin film lens placed in proximity (although much further than the typical optical evanescent decay length). The condition for a superlens requires that a proper thickness of the thin film lens, which would induce surface plasmon resonance for a given source wavelength, as well as a match between the lens' permittivity (wavelength dependent) equal in magnitude and opposite in sign to that of the adjacent media.

The researchers in Zhang's group demonstrated a superlens system using a silver film. FIGURE 1 summarizes their experimental results. Image A shows the AFM recording of the original image with line width of 40 nm. B shows the image captured by the superlens, with line width measured at 89 nm. C shows the image using a control without the superlens, showing a line width of 321 nm, which is near the expected diffraction limit of the 365 nm source.

Microfluidics Systems

Microfluidics is a backbone technology for bionano research. Living organisms sustain their lives in fluid. The quintessential fluidic processes include moving, stopping, and mixing of fluids as well as separating and concentrating

[b] http://www.me.berkeley.edu/faculty/zhang/

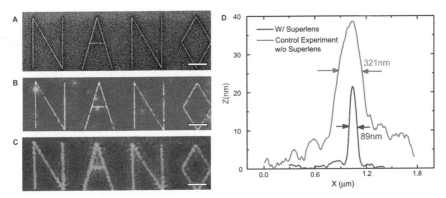

FIGURE 1. Testing the silver superlens (Data also presented in *Science* 2005;308: 534–537).

embedded particles. Strong surface molecular effects and high viscous dissipation are the main challenges for handling fluids in micron-size biochemical reactors. CMISE researchers have extensively studied the rich nano/microfluidic phenomena for 15 years, since the dawn of the microfluidics field. We examined the interactions of fluid and surface molecules.[c] Various surface property controls have been developed for optimizing the biochemical processing (Lan *et al.* 2005; Luo *et al.* 2005).[d] Actuation schemes, including electrokinetic, hydrodynamic, or magnetic forces, have been developed for controlling fluidic processes in micro/nano bioreactors as well (Ho and Tai 1998; Wong *et al.* 2004b).

A unique, digital microfluidic system to control and manipulate biological fluids using chip technology has been developed by the Kim group's micromanufacturing laboratory at UCLA.[e] The design and operation of this microfluidic device are droplets based. The nanoliter droplets are moved by unbalanced surface tension force generated by a grid of electrodes along a surface the size of a stamp. Using this digital microfluidic platform, most if not all of the manual labor steps, such as pipetting, liquid transfer, and manipulation, can be automated. Any standard biochemical protocols can therefore be replaced by multiple aliquot droplets merging and splitting in a specified sequence determined by a computer algorithm. A complete microfluidic chip with all the necessary electronic controllers to accomplish this is only approximately the size of a palm pilot.

The digital microfluidics is based on the principle of controlling surface tensions of a liquid droplet on an insulated electrode by an applied electric potential (Moon *et al.* 2002; Cho *et al.* 2003). The surface tension is proportional

[c] http://ho.seas.ucla.edu/ and http://mems.caltech.edu/index.htm
[d] http://www.seas.ucla.edu/ms/faculty1/dunn.html
[e] http://cjmems.seas.ucla.edu/

to the second power of the electrical potential. The potential gradient along the electrode generates an unbalanced surface force, which moves the droplets. Because the force generation is capacitive, the system consumes very little power and only a battery is required, making it very compact and portable. Without the need for pumps and valves, this system of fluidic manipulation is robust and simple to use. The fluid processing protocol is easily programmable and can be modified at any given time. The key challenge of the digital fluidic device is that the surface tension force generated by the applied voltage is diminished by high concentrations of charged molecules. New techniques, such as using surface molecular property control or carrier fluids, are being developed to overcome this challenge and are showing promise.[f] This technology platform is also being tested for space flight at the Reed group at Texas A&M University using small satellite launches.[g]

Manipulating Biological Particles in Fluids

The next consideration in working with biological systems at the nanometer scale is to handle the small biological particles (cells, biomolecules, small tissues, etc.) embedded in fluid. The ability to manipulate biological cells and micrometer-scale particles plays an important role in many biological and colloidal science applications. Developing this capability is significantly more challenging because, as late as a decade ago, there were no macroscale tools that could manipulate a single cell or few biomolecules directly, aside from containing them in small aliquots of liquid medium. The recent progress with micromachined mechanical tweezers (Lu et al. 2005), AFM, laser optical tweezers, and electrokinetic forces have made this manipulation capability more accessible. Nevertheless, each of these methods is far from able to bring two biological particles together in a simple manner.

Micromachined mechanical tweezers is the miniaturized version of normal tweezers. Being micrometer scaled, their size is typically comparable to cells (a couple of microns), and therefore they can physically pick and manipulate a single cell (Lu et al. 2005).

Laser optical tweezers form by focusing a beam of coherent laser light (Ashkin 1970). The sharp gradient of optical energy from the focusing creates a strong potential well that confines a biological particle tightly at a single spot. The trapped particle follows the movement of the beam and is released when the laser beam disappears, offering a flexible tool for manipulation of individual microparticle. An operational problem of the laser optical tweezers is the high intensity it requires, which usually is powerful enough to chemically

---

[f] http://www.chem.ucla.edu/dept/Organic/garrell.html
[g] http://aggiesat.org/

damage the biological molecule being confined in the optical beam. Laser optical tweezers can damage cells and the functions of most enzymes if the exposure time is not very short.

The AFM (Binnig *et al.* 1986) is a nanoscale version of the micromachined mechanical tweezers, using a single sharp tip (usually below 100 nm) instead of a pair of tweezers to pick, deposit, and manipulate large molecules, such as DNA and antibodies. In this case, it is possible to pick a small subject, but release of the captured particle is a significant challenge due to the adhesive effect of van der Waals force. Another dilemma known as "fat fingers" (Smalley 2001) is a more obvious problem, simply stating that the tool is much larger than the biological particles, even for the AFM tip, as biomolecules are often smaller.

Electrokinetic forces are commonly used to manipulate biomolecules in fluid. Among them, DEP force is a popular one due to the fact that it can provide either attractive or repulsive forces (Wong *et al.* 2004a). The DEP force results from the interaction of the induced dipoles in particles subjected to a nonuniform electric field. Generally speaking, electrokinetic forces and other mechanisms provide flexible design of the electrical potential field. DEP force, however, is effective only in low ionic concentration fluid, because ions smear out the nonuniform potential field.

The Wu group at the University of California, Berkeley, recently uses light to create an "Optoelectronic Tweezers" system, an optical image-driven DEP technique that permits high-resolution patterning of nonuniform electric fields on a photoconductive surface for manipulating microscale particles, such as individual live cells (Chiou *et al.* 2005).[h] The optical power used in this method is 100,000 times less intense than laser optical tweezers, and therefore shows almost no negative impact on biological functions. Furthermore, the much less expensive incoherent light sources, such as light emitting diodes (LED) and mercury lamps, can be used. Combining an LED source and a digital micromirror spatial light modulator to pattern the optical images in real-time, the team has demonstrated that they can manipulate individual live cells simply on a computer screen, or use the computer algorithm to simultaneously control the positioning of over 15,000 particles in a 1 mm^2 area.

FIGURE 2 shows a result that uses computer vision technology to automatically rearrange an array of microparticles simultaneously. This figure illustrates how the Optoelectronic Tweezer system uses computer microvision-based techniques to automatically draw square light patterns around microbeads (10 to 20 mm diameters) and then executes the commands to shuffle the particles into a predetermined design without manual intervention.

These optoelectronic tweezers use optical images to create high-resolution virtual electrodes for the parallel manipulation of a large number of single

[h] http://www.eecs.berkeley.edu/~wu

FIGURE 2. Demonstration of an optoelectronic tweezer system (Image provided by Ming Wu at UC Berkeley).

particles. The liquid containing biological particles of interest is sandwiched between an upper transparent electrode and a lower photoconductive surface consisting of multiple featureless layers of common semiconductor films. A voltage bias (10V AC) is applied across the two surfaces sandwiched the fluid and the photoconductive layers. Patterned optical illumination on the photoconductive layer reduces the impedance of the layer and therefore forms a virtual electrode pattern, which generates a DEP force. Because of the photoconductive gain, the minimum optical intensity required to turn on a virtual electrode is $10\,\text{nW}\,\mu\text{m}^{-2}$, or a power intensity that is approximately 100,000 times lower than that of laser optical tweezers. This significantly reduces the specification requirement of the light source to cost-effective incoherent sources, such as the commonly available mercury lamps or LED. Because incoherent sources are not strictly point sources like lasers, the optoelectronic techniques can generate forces over a large area at a given time. We can then simultaneously manipulate many micron size particles spread in that region.

An interesting application that the Wu group has demonstrated is the selective separation of living cells from a sample containing both live and dead cells. The dead cells were discriminated by the optoelectronic technique because their cell membranes' permeability is significantly different from that of live cells, after losing the functions that normally maintain a differential ionic concentration across the living membrane. FIGURE 3 shows the result of one experiment in which the optical image of the letters "UCLA" is used to attract live cells (fluorescently tagged) from a random distribution of both live and dead cells in solution.

Monitoring the Behavior of a Single Cell in Real-Time

The cell is a micron scale system containing millions of molecules to maintain internal operations and to communicate with the external environment. Technological tools that deal with individual cells will necessarily

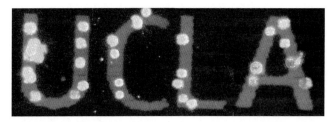

FIGURE 3. An optoelectronic tweezers experiment with live cells (Image provided by Ming Wu at UC Berkeley).

require the capability to detect nanoscale molecules and to monitor the internal functional status of single cells.

Members of CMISE have placed an AFM on top of a cell and measured the time-resolved displacement of the cell membrane. An almost monotone frequency was detected (Pelling *et al*. 2004; Gimzewski *et al*. 2005).[i] A cell is a thin wall structure containing millions of macromolecules suspended in liquid and supported by a microtubular network. The detected vibrations represent cellular system response to intrinsic or external perturbations. These signals are similar to the sound from a stethoscope and indicate the overall physiological state of a cell.

FIGURE 4 illustrates the experimental design for using AFM to study single living *Saccharomyces cerevisiae* (Baker's yeast) suspended in yeast extract, peptone, and dextrose (YPD) medium and trapped by a polycarbonate filter. On the left, a schematic of the AFM is superimposed on an actual AFM image of a living cell. The optical image of the AFM measuring the cells in a petri dish is also shown on the bottom right. The cells are at the end of the log phase when they are mostly stationary and not dividing rapidly. The AFM is used to image as well as placed in contact with the cell to measure the natural motion of its membrane. The nanomechanical motion of the cells is examined in a constant temperature at a range between 22°C and 30°C, inside an acoustically isolated environment.

The most intriguing result, shown at the upper right in FIGURE 4, reveals that living yeast cells exhibit local temperature-dependent, periodic oscillation at characteristic frequencies in the audio range (0.8 to 1.6 KHz). An extensive series of control experiments was performed to exclude any contribution of possible artifacts from the AFM instrumentation. The oscillation amplitudes are observed to range from 1 to 7 nm, averaging around 3 nm. The oscillation frequencies for different cells across different fresh samples are within 5% of each other at a given experimental condition. If the cells are exposed to a metabolic inhibitor, this periodic motion of the cell membranes ceases. There is a strong temperature-dependent frequency shift, with frequency increasing at

---

[i] http://www.chem.ucla.edu/dept/Faculty/gimzewski/ and http://www.teitell-lab.com/

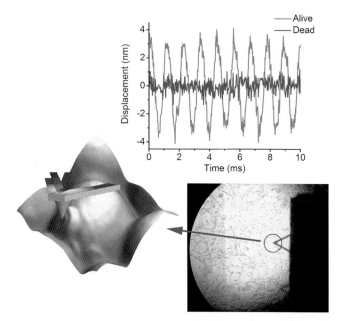

FIGURE 4. AFM of a living yeast cell (Image provided by J. Gimzewski at UCLA).

higher temperature, suggesting a source of motion that is related to its biological energy state. Analyzing the temperature dependency of the oscillation motion yields an activation energy of about 58 kJ/mol, which is consistent with the cell's metabolism involving molecular motors, such as kinesin, dynein, and myosin. The force magnitude of the motions observed, approximately 10 nN, suggests that it is the resultant of a concerted nanomechanical activity within the cell.

Cells produce metabolites, usually small molecules, from their metabolism (Fung *et al*. 2005).[j] Monitoring these metabolites correlates the metabolic activities of the cell, providing information about the cell's physiological status without damaging the cell. For example, astronauts are exposed to extraordinary amounts of radiation while in space and their cells' metabolism is affected. As a consequence, the concentration of the metabolite nitric oxide (NO) will increase. Because the cell-to-cell interactions significantly increase the complexity in interpreting the changes in the metabolite concentration, modulating the effect of NO increase by negative feedback of hormone secretions, single cell monitoring is more useful for the continuous monitoring of metabolic changes of the cells, as the McCabe group has shown.[k]

---

[j] http://www.seas.ucla.edu/~liaoj/, http://www.genetics.ucla.edu/labs/sabatti/home/, http://www.ics.uci.edu/~emj/

[k] http://www.mcip.ucla.edu/mcipfacultyindiv.php?FacultyKey=1339

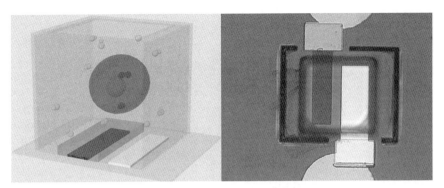

FIGURE 5. Schematic and image of a well for a single cell (Image provided by Scott Miserendino at CalTech).

Tai's group at the California Institute of Technology is developing microwell arrays for monitoring single cell metabolism.[l] The microwells are equipped with electrochemical detectors that would monitor metabolite secretion from the cell, particularly of NO. Electrochemical detection is ideal for small-volume low-concentration monitoring of electrochemically active analytes, providing specificity as well as sensitivity. Under practical conditions, 0.1 µM detection level is expected, while 0.1 nM can be achieved using vertical carbon nanotubes (Miserendino *et al.* 2006). Combined with microfluidics, the Tai group will move and culture single cells in each of these microwells that are integrated with electrochemical sensors. FIGURE 5 shows a schematic of the device design and an image of a single well. Arrays of individual cells and their metabolite output can be monitored to analyze cell responses to environmental exposure, such as radiation.

Another method of monitoring responses of the cell is the ionic channel activities in the cell membrane. To this end, the Judy group at UCLA is developing a microfabricated planar patch-clamp system integrated with microfluidic components for automated fluidic handling and cell attachment.[m]

The patch-clamp technique, developed in the 1970s (Neher and Sakmann 1976), provides a unique method to measure minuscule ionic current signals of one or many individual ion channels embedded across the cell membrane. The traditional patch-clamp technique is very manually intensive, requiring the heating and pulling of a pipette to form a smooth tip with a diameter of approximately 1 µm. The smooth tip clamps a patch of cell membranes containing one or more ion channels. The ionic current flowing from the pipette tip through the ion channels into the intracellular fluid can be recorded by highly sensitive electronics. These ionic currents generated from the gating of ion-channels control many cellular processes, and therefore indicate the

[l] http://mems.caltech.edu/
[m] http://www.judylab.org/

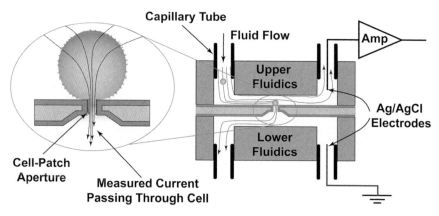

FIGURE 6. Schematic of a planar patch-clamp dose-response measurement system (*JMEMS* 2006;15: 214–222).

activations of important cellular signaling pathways. Unfortunately, the process of fabricating the pipette tip and making patch clamps is cumbersome and low in reliability. The long time involved in preparing a patch clamp with a pipette tip makes recording large numbers of cell responses a significant challenge. On the other hand, recording cell responses from many cells would be particularly interesting to pharmaceutical companies who are testing the cell electrophysiological responses to drug simulation, such as in neurons, cardiac myocytes, and pancreatic beta cells.

The microfabricated patch-clamp system being developed by researchers, such as those in the Judy group, holds the promise of the parallel processing of many cells, automated microfluidic handling, and compatibility with the gold standard of biological analysis, optical microscopy (Matthews and Judy 2006). The Judy group designed a planar patch-clamp system (in contrast to pipette tip) with a silicon-dioxide patch aperture and integrated polydimethylsiloxane (PDMS) microfluidics. FIGURE 6 illustrates their system and its designed operation. The microfluidics design provides the automated fluid control required to load the cells for clamping and enables rapid fluid exchange, important for maintaining cell viability and injecting drug candidate stimulations. The other necessary components integrated in this system include the Ag/AgCl electrodes as well as good optical access, making it compatible with standard optical microscopy.

With the current system, there are multiple fluidic ports for cell injection and fluid exchange, the fluidic channels are designed for 7 to 10 μm cells, the diameters of cell-patch sites are 500 nm to 2.5 μm, and a cell patch-clamp/sealing technique that achieve above 1 GigaOhm resistance (a value that is required in patch-clamp technique to properly measure current across ion channels). Conceptually, the cell is injected through one port and the microfluidics is used to clamp the cell at the patch site. Selected chemical stimulations can be injected through other available fluid exchange ports, and the ionic currents across the cell membrane are monitored through the integrated electrodes. The Judy group is using this system to automate the patch-clamp recording of single-cell dose-response of drugs in several cell lines including the transfected human embryonic kidney (HEK 293) line and the Chinese hamster ovary (CHO) line.

Integrating Technologies to Develop Application-Specific Systems

The fusion of biotechnology, nanotechnology, and informatics is most useful when applied to specific problems where innovative solutions can be provided through leveraging varieties of technologies. We provide two projects as examples where researchers from different fields applied their biotechnology and nanotechnology to meet the challenges in biology and medicine.

The most common primary malignant liver cancer, hepatocellular carcinoma, rarely affects affluent countries, such as the United States (less than 1% of all cancers in United States). However, in some parts of the world, it is a major health problem, responsible for up to half of all cancer cases. If detected early, surgical removal of the small tumor offers a cure. However, if the tumor grows to a size that involves both liver lobes, the survival rate is low. There exist methods to screen high-risk individuals for the primary liver cancer before it comes deadly, but most of which require sophisticated and expensive procedures, such as ultrasound imaging of the abdomen or detecting the blood tumor marker (alpha-fetoprotein) in well-equipped diagnostic laboratories. The widespread utility of these screening methods is limited because of their costs, making their availability impractical in third world countries where the disease is most prevalent.

In collaboration with the UCLA Jonsson Comprehensive Cancer Center (JCCC),[n] the CMISE institute started a project to develop an early liver cancer screening system that offers the possibility of using it in third world countries. The goal is to establish an automated molecular sensing system for the detection of the tumor marker, alpha-fetoprotein. The sample preparation and the biomarker sensing processes will be carried out in a disposable chip of the engineering system and would be automated with little or no assistance needed from trained medical personnel.

The CMISE–JCCC project leverages three matured laboratory technologies (in the Uittenbogaart group,[o] Kim group,[p] and Ho group[q] at UCLA) to meet these challenges: an assay technique selective to alpha-fetoprotein using a modified enzyme-linked immunosorbent assay (ELISA) protocol, the digital

---

[n] http://www.cancer.mednet.ucla.edu/
[o] http://www.cancer.mednet.ucla.edu/institution/personnel?personnel_id=45687
[p] http://cjmems.seas.ucla.edu/
[q] http://ho.seas.ucla.edu/

microfluidic platform for automated sample preparation, and a fluorescence-based optical system with single molecule detection capability (Wang *et al.* 2005). The key technical challenges to overcome in this project include (*a*) modifying the technologies to be compatible with each other for complete system integration, and (*b*) compensating for the loss of efficiency from the requirement of compatibility. Currently, the researchers are enhancing the protein identification selectivity in the modified ELISA, improving the ability to electrically manipulate fluids with high biomolecule concentration, and increasing the detection sensitivity level. Selectivity, concentration levels, and sensitivity have reached theoretical specifications. Also, the feasibility of integrating the fundamental steps of the assay protocol and microfluidic system as well as the optical detection platform has been demonstrated. Future work will include full integration and a successful discrimination of alpha-fetoprotein from whole blood samples.

Proteomics, which follows the revolutionary progress of genomics, will require similar high-throughput data collection instrumentation available to genomics to attain similar breakthroughs of that field. Collecting and processing large amounts of data for extracting useful information and understanding the biological phenomenon are additional tasks to the development of effective analytical technologies. The current standard methods in proteomics rely on the pairing of analytical separation, such as 2D gel electrophoresis and mass spectrometry (MS). One such technology platform, the matrix-assisted laser desorption/ionization–mass spectrometer (MALDI-MS) has become the "work horse" of this emerging field. FIGURE 7 illustrates the typical processing steps for MALDI-MS. The MALDI-MS is an appealing candidate for the high-throughput instrument that is required for a breakthrough in proteomics. The current hurdles in high-throughput lie with the time-consuming manual pipetting steps to mix the sample with the required matrix on a surface that can be delivered to the MS injection inlet. High-end MALDI-MS systems use robotics for these tasks, making the cost of such systems prohibitively high for most proteomics laboratories. If the robots can be replaced by an inexpensive automation device, a high-throughput MALDI-MS can be affordable to nearly all proteomics researchers, potentially propelling an abrupt advancement in this field.

A project that leverages the digital microfluidics technology from the Kim group[r] and the surface chemistry expertise of the Garrell group[s] at UCLA was initiated to provide a solution to this challenge. The focus of the project is to demonstrate that the automated solution handling technique is compatible with the MALDI-MS for all fluid sample preparation steps. The research team succeeded in demonstrating an inline sample preparation

[r] http://cjmems.seas.ucla.edu/
[s] www.chem.ucla.edu/dept/Organic/garrell.html

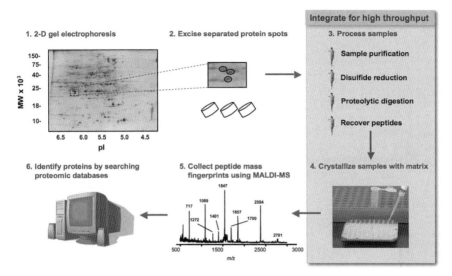

FIGURE 7. The steps of a traditional MALDI-MS (Image provided by Robin Garrell at UCLA).

technique for MALDI-MS based on the digital fluidics technology platform, providing an inexpensive automation system that can eliminate the time-limiting manual processes. The key steps for which they demonstrated successful automation include (*a*) purification of the protein digests, a key determining step for the signal-to-noise ratio of the resulting mass spectrum, and (*b*) co-crystallization of the sample and matrix, the final step before the laser injection of specimen into the MS. In the purification process, the research team compared results using a novel digital microfluidics technology platform, called Electrowetting–on–dielectric (EWOD), with a commercial pipetting protocol. The comparison of the MS spectra of myoglobin is shown in FIGURE 8. The EWOD results show new peaks at higher mass, as well as more separations between peaks (improved peak identification) in general.

The comparison illustrates that the digital microfluidics platform outperforms the commercial product in the signal-to-noise ratio, number of peptides identified, and percentage of the sequence coverage. We believe the performance advantage of the new method lies in the fact that no desorption and elution of the purified analytes is required. The desorption/elution step of the commercial method is inefficient for recovering larger, more hydrophobic peptides tightly bound to the commercial C_{18} column, whereas the digital fluidic platform can go directly into the co-crystallization step on the same surface and enable direct injection of specimen into the MS.

Commercial Preparation Product   **EWOD**

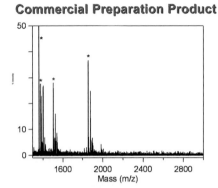 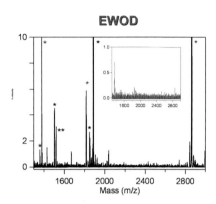

FIGURE 8. Spectra of myoglobin by a commercial pipette preparation protocol versus EWOD. Data are taken with assistance by the Joseph A. Loo group at UCLA and also presented in *Anal. Chem.* 2005;77:534–540.

CONCLUSIONS

Researchers in biosciences, nanotechnologies, and informatics are developing quintessential tools to answer questions in biology and medicine. The inventions meet the extraordinary challenges found in the nanoworld, providing innovative techniques to image nondestructively with nanometer precision, manipulate quantities at the molecular scale, and manage the fluidic environment in which biomolecules reside. These tools also enable arrays for the parallel control of millions of biological specimen with the same precision, a feat that any living cell demonstrates: self-organization by the coordination of millions of biomolecules that carries specific function and information within its capsule.

At CMISE, our members have developed a suite of unique nanotechnology based tools for studying the biomolecules that function in the nanoworld of biological systems, such as a cell. We are in the process of integrating these tools in to an engineering system, a smart petri dish, which will be able to sense the biological environment, to process the information and to actuate and modify the biological system under study. Arrays of bioreactors containing single cells can be used to study stochastic expression of single cells. The information and signal exchange of individual cells that can be measured in these new studies were previously hidden because of the averaging effect in population-based measurements. These massive arrays can generate sufficient data to map the information network and pathways found in cells and organized tissue structures. The coordinated activities of the cell arrays will provide the awe-inspiring capabilities of organized tissues, organs, and every other complex cellular structure. These future research efforts will be our path to bio-nano-information fusion, which will lead to a better understanding of the life sciences and the enrichment of human life.

ACKNOWLEDGMENTS

The authors would like to express their gratitude to the students/post-docs and faculty members of CMISE. Their ingenious ideas, hard work, and congenial working demeanors make the challenging research a fun experience. This work is supported by a NASA URETI program (Contract number NCC 2-1364).

REFERENCES

ASHKIN, A. 1970. Acceleration and trapping of particles by radiation pressure. *Physical Review Letters 24*, 156–159.

AVIRAM, A., and M.A. RATNER. 1974. Molecular rectifiers. *Chemical Physics Letters 29*, 277–283.

BINNIG, G., C.F. QUATE, and C.H. GERBER. 1986. Atomic force microscope. *Physical Review Letters 56*, 930–934.

CHIOU, P.Y., A.T. OHTA, and M.C. WU. 2005. Massively parallel manipulation of single cells and microparticles using optical images. *Nature 436*, 370–372.

CHO, S.K., H. MOON, and C.J. KIM. 2003. Creating, transporting, cutting, and merging liquid droplets by electrowetting-based actuation for digital microfluidic circuits. *Journal of Microelectromechanical Systems 12*, 70–80.

EIGLER, D.M., and E.K. SCHWEIZER. 1990. Positioning single atoms with a scanning tunnelling microscope. *Nature 344*, 524–526.

FANG, N., H. LEE, C. SUN, and X. ZHANG. 2005. Sub–diffraction-limited optical imaging with a silver superlens. *Science 308*, 534–537.

FEYNMAN, R.P. 1959. There's plenty of room at the bottom: an invitation to enter a new field of physics. Available at http://www.zyvex.com/nanotech/feynman.html.

FUNG, E., W.W. WONG, J.K. SUEN, T. BULTER, S.-G. LEE, and J.C. LIAO. 2005. A synthetic gene-metabolic oscillator. *Nature 435*, 118–122.

GIMZEWSKI, J.K., J. REED, M.A. TEITELL, and P.G. MALAN. 2005. Immunological biosensors. Pp. 265–280 in D. Wild (ed.), *The Immunoassay Handbook*. London, UK: Elsevier.

HO, C.M., and Y.C. TAI. 1998. Micro-electro-mechanical-systems and fluid flows. *Annual Review of Fluid Mechanics 30*, 579–612.

HO, D., D. GARCIA, and C.M. HO. 2006. Nanomanufacturing and characterization modalities for bio-nano-informatics systems. *Journal of Nanoscience and Nanotechnology 6*, 875–891.

IIJIMA, S. 1991. Helical microtubules of graphitic carbon. *Nature 354*, 56–58.

JONES, R.A.L. 2004. *Soft Machines: Nanotechnology and Life*. Oxford, UK: Oxford University Press.

LAN, E., B. DUNN, and J.I. ZINK. 2005. Nanostructured systems for biological materials. Pp. 53–80 in T.V. Dinh (ed.), *Protein Nanotechnology: Protocols, Instrumentation, and Applications*. Totowa, NJ: Humana.

LU, W., J. KIM, W. QIU, and D. ZHONG. 2004. Femtosecond studies of tryptophan solvation: correlation function and water dynamics at lipid surfaces. *Chemical Physics Letters 388*, 120–126.

LU, Y., Z. AN, and C.J. KIM. 2005. A microhand: modeling, manufacturing, and demonstration. Pp. 650–653 in *Proceedings of IEEE Micro Electro Mechanical Systems*

2005, January 30-February 3, Miami, Florida. New York: Institute of Electrical and Electronics Engineers.

LUO, T.J., R. SOONG, E. LAN, B. DUNN, and C. MONTEMAGNO. 2005. Photo-induced proton gradients and ATP biosynthesis produced by vesicles encapsulated in a silica matrix. *Nature Materials 4*(3), 220–224.

MATTHEWS, B. and J.W. JUDY. 2006. Design and fabrication of a micromachined planar patch-clamp substrate with integrated microfluidics for single-cell measurements. *IEEE/ASME Journal of Microelectromechanical Systems 15*, 214–222.

MISERENDINO, S., J. YOO, A. CASSELL, and Y.-C. TAI. 2006. Electrochemical characterization of parylene-embedded carbon nanotube nanoelectrode arrays. *Nanotechnology 17*, S23–S28.

MOON, H., S.K. CHO, R.L. GARRELL, and C.J. KIM. 2002. Low voltage electrowetting-on-dielectric. *Journal of Applied Physics 92*, 4080–4087.

MULLIKEN, R.S. 1927. Electronic states and band spectrum structure in diatomic molecules. *Physical Review 29*, 637–649.

NEHER, E., and B. SAKMANN. 1976. Single-channel currents recorded from membrane of denervated frog muscle fibres. *Nature 260*, 799–801.

PELLING, A.E., S. SADAF, E.B. GRALLA, J.S. VALENTINE, and J.K. GIMZEWSKI. 2004. Local nanomechanical motion of the cell wall of *Saccharomyces cerevisiae*. *Science. 305*, 1147–1150.

SMALLEY, R.E. 2001. Of chemistry, love and nanobots. *Scientific American 285*, 76–77.

WANG, T.-H., Y. PENG, C. CHEN, P.K. WONG, and C.M. HO. 2005. Single-molecule tracing on a fluidic microchip for quantitative detection of low-abundance nucleic acids. *Journal of the American Chemical Society 127*, 5354–5359.

WONG, P.K., C.-Y. CHEN, T.-H. WANG, and C.-M. HO. 2004a. Electrokinetic bioprocessor for concentrating cells and molecules. *Analytical Chemistry 76*, 6908–6914.

WONG, P.K., T.-H. WANG, J.H. DEVAL, and C.-M. HO. 2004b. Electrokinetics in micro devices for biotechnology applications. *IEEE/ASME Transactions on Mechatronics 9*, 366–376.

Three Levels of Neuroelectronic Interfacing

Silicon Chips with Ion Channels, Nerve Cells, and Brain Tissue

PETER FROMHERZ

Department of Membrane and Neurophysics, Max Planck Institute for Biochemistry, Martinsried/Munich, Germany

ABSTRACT: We consider the direct electrical interfacing of semiconductor chips with individual nerve cells and brain tissue. At first, the structure of the cell-chip contact is studied. Then we characterize the electrical coupling of ion channels—the electrical elements of nerve cells—with transistors and capacitors in silicon chips. On that basis it is possible to implement signal transmission between microelectronics and the microionics of nerve cells in both directions. Simple hybrid neuroelectronic systems are assembled with neuron pairs and with small neuronal networks. Finally, the interfacing with capacitors and transistors is extended to brain tissue cultured on silicon chips. The application of highly integrated silicon chips allows an imaging of neuronal activity with high spatiotemporal resolution. The goal of the work is an integration of neuronal network dynamics with digital electronics on a microscopic level with respect to experiments in brain research, medical prosthetics, and information technology.

KEYWORDS: ion channels; microionics; neuroelectronic hybrids; neuronal dynamics; semiconductor chips; transistors

INTRODUCTION

Both computers and brains work electrically. However, their charge carriers are different—electrons in solid silicon and ions in liquid water. It is an intellectual and technological challenge to join these different systems directly on the level of electronic and ionic signals. Already in the 18th century, Luigi Galvani established the electrical coupling of inorganic solids and excitable living tissue. Today, after 50 years of dramatic developments in semiconductor

Address for correspondence: Peter Fromherz, Max Planck Institute for Biochemistry, Am Klopferspitz 18, D-82152 Martinsried/Munich, Germany.
e-mail: fromherz@biochem.mpg.de

Ann. N.Y. Acad. Sci. 1093: 143–160 (2006). © 2006 New York Academy of Sciences.
doi: 10.1196/annals.1382.011

microtechnology and cellular neurobiology, we may envisage a multisite integration of microionics and microelectronics with numerous nerve cells and microelectronic devices (Fromherz 1985, 1996, 2005).

Usually, the coupling of electronic signals and of the ionic signals in neurons is achieved with perfectly unpolarized solid/water contacts such as Ag/AgCl electrodes where ionic and electronic currents are transformed by an electrochemical reaction. That approach is not well suited for iono-electronic interfacing on a microscopic scale with thousands of contact sites. Semiconductor chips must be shielded from corrosion in water. Efficient interfacing must be implemented with polarized solid/water contacts without ionic or electronic current. The communication between microionics and microelectronics is achieved by displacement currents across an insulating oxide.

In the present article, we consider step by step the physicochemical mechanism of bioelectronic interfacing on the scale of nanometers, micrometers, and millimeters. We start with the contact between an individual nerve cell and a silicon chip. Then we study the interfacing of the fundamental devices of the brain—ion channels—and fundamental devices of computers—capacitors and transistors. On that basis, we consider the interfacing of nerve cells with capacitors and transistors and the assembly of simple bioelectronic hybrids with two nerve cells and simple neuronal networks. Finally, we address problems with respect to the electronic interfacing of brain tissue.

CELL-CHIP CONTACT

A simple hybrid with a nerve cell from rat brain and a transistor in silicon is depicted in FIGURE 1 (Voelker and Fromherz 2005). The cell is surrounded

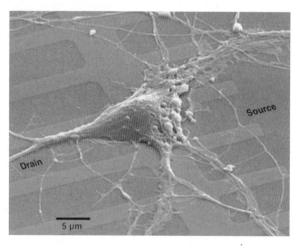

FIGURE 1. Nerve cell from rat brain on silicon chip.

by a membrane with an electrically insulating core of lipid. That lipid bilayer (thickness about 5 nanometers) separates the bath with 150 mM sodium chloride from the cytoplasm with about 150 mM potassium chloride. The silicon is coated with thermally grown silicon dioxide (thickness 10 nanometers) that suppresses electrochemical processes that lead to a corrosion of silicon and to a damage of the cells.

The basic problem with respect to an electrical interaction of cell and chip is the structure of the contact between lipid bilayer and oxide. The crucial questions are: (*a*) What is the distance? (*b*) What is the electrical resistance? They are answered by optical experiments.

Distance

Silicon reflects light such that standing modes of the electromagnetic field are formed in front of its surface. We take advantage of that effect to measure the distance of cells and silicon using fluorescent dye molecules as antennas (Lambacher and Fromherz 2002). We fabricate silicon chips with microscopic oxide terraces (size 2.5 μm × 2.5 μm, step height about 20 nanometers), culture cells in electrolyte and label the lipid bilayer with a fluorescent dye. The terraces of defined height together with the unknown distance between chip and cell bring the membrane into different positions in the standing modes. As a consequence, the absorption and the emission of light by the dye are modulated. A micrograph of an astrocyte from rat brain on a silicon chip is shown in FIGURE 2A (Braun and Fromherz 2001). The scale bar measures 10 μm.

When we evaluate the intensities with an electromagnetic theory, we find that there is a cleft between the oxide and the lipid bilayer. Results for HEK293 cells on chips coated with fibronection reveal that the distance is around 70 nanometers, independent of the electrical resistivity of the bath (Gleixner and Fromherz 2006).

That separation is caused by proteins in the membrane (glycocalix) and on the chip (fibronectin). It is an interesting task to reduce that distance by physical and chemical modifications of the chip and by genetic modifications of the membrane, without impairing the viability of the cells.

Resistance

The electrical coupling of chip and cell depends on the electrical resistance of the 70-nanometer layer between the oxide and the lipid bilayer. To measure that resistance, we apply an alternating voltage to the chip. The resistance and the capacitances of oxide and membrane determine the voltage across the attached membrane. We detect the phase shift of the alternating voltage by a fluorescent dye with a molecular Stark effect that relies on a sensitivity of light absorption and light emission to the electrical field across the membrane.

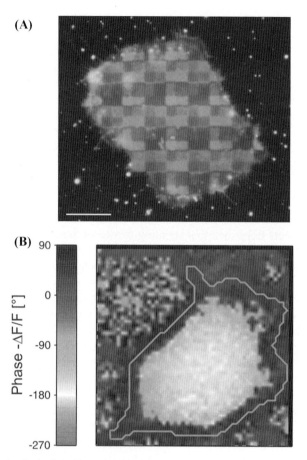

FIGURE 2. Optical probing of cell-chip contact.

A phase map of the relative change of fluorescence intensity at a frequency of 50 kHz is shown in FIGURE 2B for a HEK293 cell on fibronectin (Gleixner and Fromherz 2006). Within the area of cell adhesion, the phase is rather smooth between $-90°C$ and $-180°C$. When we evaluate the phase map in terms of an electrical model, we can determine the electrical resistance of the layer between chip and cell—given the capacitances of oxide and membrane. In normal culture medium, the sheet resistance is around 10 MΩ. When we enhance the resistivity of the bath, the sheet resistance is proportionally enhanced.

When we combine the results of the resistance measurement and of the distance measurement, we find that the 70-nanometer cleft between cell and chip is filled with electrolyte from the surrounding bath. That conductive sheet between oxide and membrane prevents an effective interaction of chip and cell by direct electrical polarization. We must find a different coupling mechanism between ionics and electronics.

ION-ELECTRON COUPLING

The electrical elements of nerve cells are voltage-gated ion channels. These molecules are embedded in the lipid bilayer of the membrane. They can be in an open and in a closed state. When they are open, they selectively transmit ionic current through the membrane—Na^+ inward current or K^+ outward current. The opening and closing of the channels are connected with a displacement of electrical charge across the membrane. As a consequence, opening and closing are controlled by the voltage across the membrane.

The electrical communication between semiconductors and cells relies on an interaction of the ion channels with the chip. Two devices are used in silicon chips, an electrolyte/oxide/silicon capacitor for activation of ion channels and an electrolyte/oxide/silicon field-effect transistor for detecting open channels (Voelker and Fromherz 2005; Wallrapp and Fromherz 2006). The interaction of channels and chips is determined by the electrical nature of the contact—the insulating oxide, the thin layer of electrolyte, and the insulating lipid bilayer (Ulbrich and Fromherz 2005; Schmidtner and Fromherz 2006).

Ion Channels and Capacitors

We test the electrical signaling from chip to cell with HEK293 cells that are transfected with the gene of the potassium channel Kv1.3. The cells are cultured on an electrolyte/oxide/silicon capacitor. A falling voltage ramp is applied to the capacitor. A displacement current flows across the oxide and leads to an ohmic current along the resistance of the cell-chip contact. The resulting negative extracellular voltage opens the channels in the attached membrane (Ulbrich and Fromherz 2005). To achieve a sufficient displacement current and a sufficient extracellular voltage, we isolate the chip with a thin layer of titanium dioxide that has a high dielectric constant. The experiment shows that we are able to control the ionic current in the cell by an electronic signal in the semiconductor with a current-voltage-current mechanism: The displacement current across the oxide is transformed to an extracellular voltage between oxide and membrane that induces an ion current through the membrane.

Ion Channels and Transistors

We test the signaling from cell to chip with HEK293 cells that are transfected with the gene of the sodium channel Nav1.4 (Schmidtner and Fromherz 2006). The cells are cultured on a chip with electrolyte/oxide/silicon field-effect transistors. When positive voltages are applied to a cell, a transient inward current is observed through the membrane as expected for Na^+ channels. Simultaneously, a transient transistor signal appears. A quantitative evaluation shows that the transistor voltage is proportional to the membrane current as controlled by the resistance of the cell-chip contact. We are able to control the electronic current in the semiconductor by an ionic signal in the cell again by a current-voltage-current mechanism: The ionic current through the membrane is transformed to an extracellular voltage between oxide and membrane that controls the electron current in the semiconductor.

NERVE CELL ON SEMICONDUCTOR

The first step toward an integration of neuronal dynamics and digital electronics is an interfacing of individual nerve cells and silicon microstructures. We consider the excitation of nerve cells by capacitors and the recording of neuronal activity by transistors. A crucial issue with respect to capacitor stimulation and transistor recording is the contribution of the cell membrane that is attached to the chip as well as of the upper free membrane that is in contact to the bath.

When a rising or falling voltage ramp is applied to a capacitor, the extracellular voltage between chip and cell polarizes the attached membrane as well as the upper membrane. Ion channels may be affected in both domains. Of course, the induced voltages across attached and free membrane have an opposite direction. On the other hand, when a nerve cell is excited, ion currents through the attached as well as through the upper free membrane lead to a changing intracellular voltage change. The total current through the attached membrane with an ionic and a capacitive component gives rise to a voltage on the transistor. The capacitive part results from the changing intracellular voltage and depends on the ionic current through the upper free membrane.

Capacitor Stimulation

We dissociate individual nerve cells from the ganglia of pond snails and attach them to an electrolyte/oxide/silicon capacitor as shown in FIGURE 3 (Schoen and Fromherz, 2006). Rising as well as falling voltage ramps are applied to the capacitor. A circular area of the chip is insulated by a thin layer of hafnium dioxide. The intracellular voltage is recorded with an impaled micropipette.

A rising voltage ramp leads to a displacement current into the chip-cell junction and a positive extracellular voltage between chip and cell. There are voltage drops across the attached and upper membrane such that the attached membrane is hyperpolarized and the upper free membrane is depolarized. Ion channels are activated in the upper membrane, and an action potential is elicited there when the voltage ramp is above a certain threshold. A rather high slope of the ramp is required because most of the extracellular voltage between chip

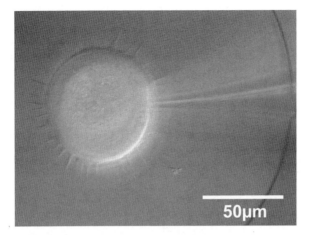

FIGURE 3. Stimulation experiment with an individual nerve cell.

and cell drops across the attached membrane with its small area and its small capacitance.

A falling voltage ramp leads to a negative extracellular voltage between chip and cell. In that case the attached membrane is depolarized. In a first step, ion channels are activated there, and in a second step the resulting inward Na^+ current depolarizes the whole cell membrane such that an action potential is elicited. The effect disappears for strong stimulation when an outward K^+ current is activated that suppresses the depolarization of the cell.

Transistor Recording

Dissociated nerve cells from the leech ganglia are placed on the open gates of electrolyte-oxide-silicon field-effect transistors. They are impaled with a micropipette electrode for stimulation and for recording of the intracellular voltage. Calibrated transistors detect the transient extracellular voltage between cell and chip. Three records are shown in FIGURE 4 (Schätzthauer and Fromherz 1998). The upper row of graphs shows the intracellular voltage, and the lower row shows extracellular voltage measured with a transistor.

In the first record, the extracellular voltage resembles the first derivative of the intracellular voltage. In the second record, the extracellular voltage resembles the waveform of the intracellular voltage. In the third example, the transistor signal shows a peak in the rising phase of the intracellular voltage and a trough in its falling phase. The different signals reflect a different contribution of ionic currents and of capacitive current through the attached cell membrane. The A-type signal is determined by the capacitive current that results from the dynamics of intracellular voltage as determined by the ionic currents of the

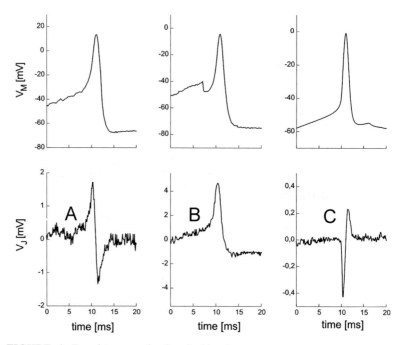

FIGURE 4. Transistor records of excited leech neurons.

upper free membrane. The B-type signal is due to ohmic leak current that is driven by the intracellular voltage. The C-type record indicates a dominance of ionic currents with a sharp Na^+ inward current and a delayed K^+ outward current.

The different types of neuronal recordings may be attributed to an inhomogeneous distribution of the ionic conductances in the attached and free part of the cell membrane and to different positions of the nerve cell on the transistor. That hypothesis can be tested when neuronal excitation is not probed with a single transistor, but with a closely packed array of transistors. Such an array is fabricated by complementary metal oxide semiconductor (CMOS) technology. FIGURE 5 shows cultured snail neurons on the surface of a CMOS chip with 16,384 sensor transistors on 1 mm^2 (Lambacher *et al.* 2004). When a selected nerve cell is excited with a micropipette, a set of transistors beneath the cell is able to map the extracellular voltages in the cell-chip contact. The transistor array allows a mapping of extracellular voltage beneath individual nerve cells with a resolution of 8 μm. These experiments are able to demonstrate that different kinds of signals, such as shown in FIGURE 4, appear at different positions of the same nerve cell. The interfacing of cell and chip depends on structural details of the attached cell.

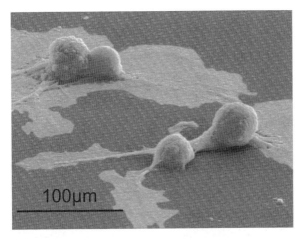

FIGURE 5. Nerve cells on multi-transistor array (MTA).

Noise

We observe that the amplitude of transistor records for nerve cells from leeches and snails is far larger than for nerve cells from rats. The reason is not a different biophysical mechanism of coupling but a different size of cell: The current through the attached membrane is proportional to the size of the cell whereas the effective resistance of the contact scales logarithmically with the contact area. As a consequence, the extracellular signals of small mammalian neurons are in the range of 100 microvolts. They can be detected only with transistors that have a particularly low noise.

It is important to note, however, that there exists a thermodynamic limit with respect to the reduction of noise in extracellular recording. The overall noise of transistor recording is due to an intrinsic noise and to the thermal noise that arises from the electrical resistance of the cell-chip contact (Voelker and Fromherz 2006). The intrinsic noise of the transistor follows a 1/f relation at low frequencies. The noise of cell adhesion is constant up to high frequencies and overcomes the transistor noise above 2 kHz. An improvement of the transistor is not meaningful for measurements at high frequencies where the noise of cell adhesion dominates.

ELEMENTARY NEUROELECTRONIC HYBRIDS

In a first step to assemble neuroelectronic hybrids, we couple pairs of nerve cells to a chip with two different pathways as illustrated in FIGURE 6. The upper diagram shows schematically how cellular neuroprosthesis is implemented by a signaling "neuron-silicon-silicon-neuron" where the activity of a neuron is

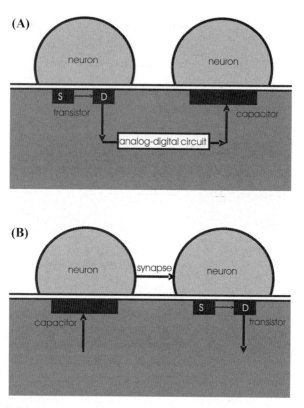

FIGURE 6. Elementary hybrid neuroelectronic devices.

recorded with a transistor and where the signal is processed on the chip and used for capacitor stimulation of a second neuron. In the lower diagram, a neuronal memory element is obtained with a signaling "silicon-neuron-neuron-silicon" where a capacitively stimulated neuron couples to a second neuron through a chemical synapse and where the postsynaptic response is detected with a transistor.

Cellular Neuroprosthesis

A hybrid system with the pathway neuron-silicon-silicon-neuron is depicted in FIGURE 7A (Bonifazi and Fromherz 2002). Two snail neurons are attached to a silicon chip with two-way contacts that consist of a transistor and a capacitor. An input neuron (left) is on a transistor with source (S), drain (D), and gate area (G), and an output neuron (right) is on the two wings of a capacitive stimulation area (CSt). Transistor and capacitor are connected by an electronic circuit on the chip. The two nerve cells have no direct contact to each other.

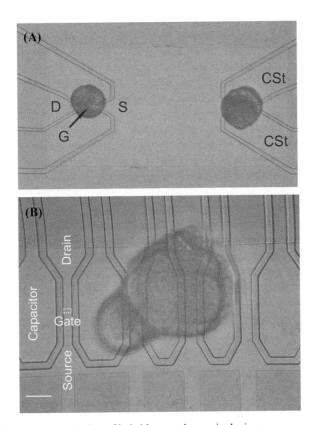

FIGURE 7. Implementation of hybrid neuroelectronic devices.

The overall function of the hybrid is as follows: The spontaneous activity of the first neuron is recorded by a transistor. The transistor record of an action potential is identified on the chip. A digital signal triggers a delay line and a burst of voltage pulses that is applied to a capacitor. Neuronal activity in a second neuron is elicited by capacitive coupling. As a result, the second neuron fires in strict correlation to the first neuron without neuronal connection. A crucial problem is cross-talk from capacitor to transistor on the chip such that artifacts of the transistor record must be eliminated on the chip.

Neuronal Memory on Chip

A hybrid system with the pathway silicon-neuron-neuron-silicon is shown in FIGURE 7B (Kaul *et al.* 2004). Two identified snail neurons VD4 and LPeD1 are attached to an array of capacitors and transistors such that they form a soma–soma contact with a chemical synapse. The presynaptic nerve cell VD4 is stimulated from a capacitor, the signal activates the chemical synapse and the postsynaptic excitation of the LPeD1 cell is recorded with a transistor. It is important that the synaptic signal transfer can be induced by the chip: In a first test, there may be no postsynaptic activity if the synaptic coupling is weak. When we apply a series of capacitive presynaptic stimuli the synaptic strength is enhanced. A second test reveals a postsynaptic action potential that is recorded by the transistor. Thus, the two-neuron hybrid implements a neuronal memory on chip.

NEURONAL NETWORKS ON CHIP

Complex neuronal networks rely on: (*a*) a mapping between sets of neurons and (*b*) an enhanced synaptic strength by correlated presynaptic and postsynaptic activity (Hebbian learning). An experimental study of network dynamics requires: (*a*) neuronal maps with a defined topology of the synaptic connections, and (*b*) a noninvasive supervision of all neurons to induce learning and to observe the performance of the network. To achieve these goals we must control outgrowth and synapse formation, and we must fabricate silicon chips with arrays of closely packed two-way contacts.

Immobilized Neurons

Neuronal networks can be obtained in cell culture from nerve cells that are dissociated from the brain of snails and rats. During outgrowth, however, the cell bodies are displaced on the chip such that the junctions with transistors and capacitors are disrupted. To overcome that problem, picket fences of organic polymers are fabricated on the chip and the neuronal cell bodies are mounted as shown in FIGURE 8A (Zeck and Fromherz 2001). The cell bodies are perfectly kept on the two-way contacts made of capacitors and transistors, even after culturing them for several days. A selected neuron is excited by a capacitor, a postsynaptic action potential is elicited through electrical synapses and the signal is recorded with a transistor.

Topographical Guidance

It is well known that the outgrowth of neurons can be controlled by chemical patterns. However, that kind of guidance is not stable as strong mechanical forces tend to induce a shortening of neurites that grow in bends or around corners. Topographical guidance by grooves may overcome that problem. An example is shown in FIGURE 8B (Merz and Fromherz 2005). Using an organic polymer, wells, and connecting grooves are fabricated on a chip with 16 two-way contacts of capacitors and transistors. After placing snail neurons into the

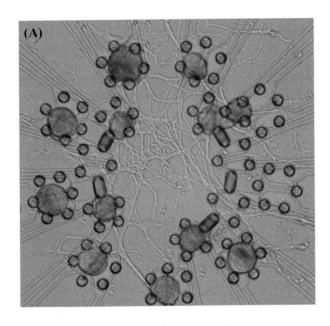

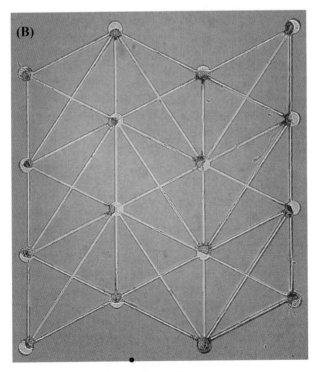

FIGURE 8. Neuronal networks on silicon chips.

wells, their outgrowth is guided by the grooves such that electrical synapses are formed. In principle, it is possible to create defined neuronal networks that are supervised from a chip. However, at present the yield of the overall assembly of the hybrids is too low to implement complex systems.

Random Nets on CMOS Chips

The problem of displaced neurons is overcome when an array of closely packed capacitors and transistors is used, such that a displaced neuron finds itself on one or more two-contact sites, wherever it is on the chip. Of course, the defined control of network geometry is sacrificed in such systems. However, when the changing geometry is continuously monitored by the CMOS chip, we may perform experiments with complex patterns of stimulation that induce a spatially distributed neuronal memory on chip.

BRAIN TISSUE ON CHIPS

Culturing of defined neuronal networks is avoided when we use neuronal networks that are provided by brains. Brain tissues with a planar structure of the networks are required to attain an efficient interfacing with a planar chip. Organotypic brain slices are particularly promising because they are only a few cell layers thick and conserve major neuronal connections when properly cut. Compared to the culture of dissociated cells, however, there are new problems when we want to interface individual nerve cells in a tissue: (a) We cannot take it for granted that individual nerve cells are attached to capacitors and transistors with a distance of 70 nanometers. (b) There are so many neuronal cell bodies embedded in glia cells and in a web of dendrites and axons, that we do not know which cell is coupled to a particular capacitor and transistor. An important task in the near future will be to investigate the structural and electrical features of the tissue-chip contact with the same optical methods that are used for cultured cells.

In a first approach, we attempt to achieve an electrical interfacing of organotypic brain slices on the level of neuronal groups, that is, to stimulate a small area of presynaptic brain tissue with a capacitor and to detect the average postsynaptic activity in another small area of tissue with a transistor. Voltage ramps at a capacitor give rise to an extracellular voltage above the capacitor that is sufficient to elicit action potentials in a set of neurons. The coherent activity of several neurons activates nerve cells at a certain distance in the cultured slice where synchronous synaptic activity leads to an extracellular voltage that is recorded with a transistor.

Two-way Interfacing

We culture a transverse slice of rat hippocampus on a chip with an array of large capacitors and an array of large transistors (Hutzler and Fromherz 2004). The capacitors are in the CA3 region whereas the transistors are in the CA1 region of the hippocampus. These two areas are connected by axons (Schaffer collateral). When the CA3 region is stimulated, excitatory synapses in the CA1 regions are activated. In a typical capacitor-neuron-neuron-transistor experiment, falling voltage steps of different height are applied to a capacitor in the region of cell bodies of CA3 (stratum pyramidale). With a certain delay, we observe negative extracellular voltages with a transistor in the dendritic region of CA1 (stratum radiatum). A postsynaptic signal appears only above a certain threshold of the capacitive stimulus. That threshold refers to the minimum extracellular voltage that is required to stimulate neurons above the center of the capacitor. An enhanced stimulus leads to an expansion of the area where the extracellular voltage is above threshold. More presynaptic neurons are excited and as a result, more postsynaptic neurons are activated such that the amplitude of the postsynaptic signal increases.

Mapping with CMOS Chip

Interfacing of brain tissue with cellular resolution requires not only a knowledge and control of the cell-chip contacts, but also a high density of capacitors and transistors. In a first approach, the mapping of postsynaptic activity is achieved on the level of neuronal groups using a CMOS chip with 16,384 sensor transistors on 1 mm^2 (Hutzler et al. 2006).

A chip is covered by an organotypic hippocampus slice where the transistor array covers the CA3 region as illustrated in FIGURE 9A. A tungsten microelectrode was used to stimulate axons that enter the CA3 region (mossy fibers). Looking at the distribution of extracellular voltage 5 ms after stimulation, we saw a negative signal in stratum radiatum (dendrites) and a positive signal in stratum pyramidale (cell bodies) as shown in FIGURE 9B. The propagating action potential in the axons activate synapses in the dendritic region where current flows into the cells such that a negative extracellular voltage is created. Compensating outward current leads to positive voltage in the region of the cell bodies. The CMOS chip provides a time resolved map of activity with a resolution of 2 kHz that can be viewed as a movie.

The experiments with small arrays of large capacitors and large transistors as well as with the multi-transistor array (MTA) of a CMOS chip are first steps toward a complete interfacing of brain tissue on the level of individual neurons. Given the known features of hippocampus, we can envisage far reaching experiments on an associative neuronal memory integrated with a semiconductor chip.

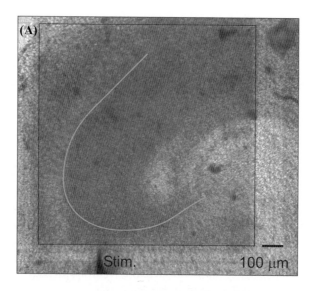

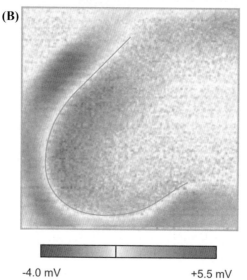

-4.0 mV   +5.5 mV

FIGURE 9. Functional mapping of brain slice by MTA recording.

SUMMARY AND OUTLOOK

At present, basic problems on the electrical interfacing of individual nerve cells and semiconductor chips are solved—the structure of the cell-chip contact and the interfacing of transistors and capacitors with recombinant ion channels and with nerve cells. Important progress is due to the development of capacitors with high dielectric constant and of transistors with low noise. With respect to hybrid systems of neuronal networks and digital microelectronics, we are in an elementary stage. Two directions may be considered: (*a*) Small defined networks of neurons from invertebrates and mammals are created with defined topology and with learning synapses. (*b*) Large neuronal nets are grown on closely packed arrays of two-way contacts fabricated by CMOS technology. With respect to the interfacing of brain slices, stimulation and recording is established on the level of neuronal groups, and high-resolution mapping is achieved with CMOS transistors. A development of large arrays of two-way contacts will allow us to implement neuronal network dynamics—such as associative memory under digital control. Of course, visionary dreams of bio-electronic neurocomputers and microelectronic neuroprostheses are unavoidable and exciting. However, they should not obscure the numerous practical problems.

REFERENCES

BONIFAZI, P., and P. FROMHERZ. 2002. Silicon chip for electronic communication between nerve cells by noninvasive interfacing and analog-digital processing. *Advanced Materials 14*, 1190–1193.

BRAUN, D., and P. FROMHERZ. 2001. Fast voltage transients in capacitive silicon-to-cell stimulation observed with a luminescent molecular electronic probe. *Physical Review Letters 86*, 2905–2908.

FROMHERZ, P. 1985. Brain on line? The feasibility of a neuron-silicon junction. In E. Neumann and R. Winkler-Oswatitsch (eds.), *20th Klosters-Winterseminar Molecules, Memory and Information*. Available online at http://www.biochem.mpg.de/mnphys/publications/85fro/85fro.pdf

FROMHERZ, P. 1996. Interfacing neurons and silicon by electrical induction. *Berichte der Bunsengesellschaft 100*, 1093–1102.

FROMHERZ, P. 2005. The Neuron-Semiconductor Interface. Pp. 339–394 in I. Willner and E. Katz (eds.), *Bioelectronics*. Weinheim, Germany: Wiley-VCH.

GLEIXNER, R., and P. FROMHERZ. 2006. The extracellular electrical resistivity in cell adhesion. *Biophysical Journal 90*, 2600–2611.

HUTZLER, M., and P. FROMHERZ. 2004. Silicon chip with capacitors and transistors for interfacing organotypic brain slice of rat hippocampus. *European Journal of Neuroscience 19*, 2231–2238.

HUTZLER, M., A. LAMBACHER, B. EVERSMANN, M. JENKNER, R. THEWES, and P. FROMHERZ. 2006. High-resolution multi-transistor array recording of electrical field potentials in cultured brain slices. *Journal of Neurophysiology 96*, 1638–1645.

KAUL, R.A., N.I. SYED, and P. FROMHERZ. 2004. Neuron-semiconductor chip with chemical synapse between identified neurons. *Physical Review Letters 92*, No. 038102, pp. 1–4.

LAMBACHER, A., and P. FROMHERZ. 2002. Luminescence of dye molecules on oxidized silicon and fluorescence interference contrast microscopy of biomembranes. *Journal of the Optical Society of America B 19*, 1435–1453.

LAMBACHER, A., M. JENKNER, M. MERZ, B. EVERSMANN, R.A. KAUL, F. HOFMANN, R. THEWES, and P. FROMHERZ. 2004. Electrical imaging of neuronal activity by multi-transistor-array (MTA) recording at 7.8 μm resolution. *Applied Physics A* **79**, 1607–1611.

MERZ, M., and P. FROMHERZ. 2005. Silicon chip interfaced with geometrically defined net of snail neurons. *Advanced Functional Materials* **15**, 739–744.

SCHÄTZTHAUER, R., and P. FROMHERZ. 1998. Neuron-silicon junction with voltage-gated ionic currents. *European Journal of Neuroscience* **10**, 1956–1962.

SCHMIDTNER, M., and P. FROMHERZ. 2006. Functional Na^+ channels in cell adhesion probed by transistor recording. *Biophysical Journal* **90**, 183–189.

SCHOEN, I., and P. FROMHERZ. 2006. The mechanism of extracellular stimulation of nerve cells on an electrolyte–oxide–semiconductor capacitor. *Biophysical Journal* doi: 10.1529/biophysj106.094763 (2006).

ULBRICH, M., and P. FROMHERZ. 2005. Opening of K^+ channels by capacitive stimulation from silicon chip. *Applied Physics A* **81**, 887–891.

VOELKER, M., and P. FROMHERZ. 2005. Signal transmission from individual mammalian nerve cell to field-effect transistor. *Small* **1**, 206–210

VOELKER, M., and P. FROMHERZ. 2006. Nyquist noise of cell adhesion detected in a neuron-silicon transistor. *Physical Review Letters* **96**, No. 228102, pp. 1–4.

WALLRAPP, F., and P. FROMHERZ. 2006. TiO_2 and HfO_2 in electrolyte-oxide-silicon configuration for applications in bioelectronics. *Journal of Applied Physics* **99**, No. 114103, pp. 1–10.

ZECK, G., and P. FROMHERZ. 2001. Noninvasive neuroelectronic interfacing with synaptically connected snail neurons immobilized on a semiconductor chip. *Proceedings of the National Academy of Sciences* **98**, 10457–10462.

Designing Highly Flexible and Usable Cyberinfrastructures for Convergence

BRUCE W. HERR, WEIXIA HUANG, SHASHIKANT PENUMARTHY, AND KATY BÖRNER

School of Library and Information Science, Indiana University, Bloomington, Indiana 47405, USA[1]

ABSTRACT: This article presents the results of a 7-year-long quest into the development of a "dream tool" for our research in information science and scientometrics and more recently, network science. The results are two cyberinfrastructures (CI): The *Cyberinfrastructure for Information Visualization* and the *Network Workbench* that enjoy a growing national and interdisciplinary user community. Both CIs use the cyberinfrastructure shell (CIShell) software specification, which defines interfaces between data sets and algorithms/services and provides a means to bundle them into powerful tools and (Web) services. In fact, CIShell might be our major contribution to progress in convergence. Just as Wikipedia is an "empty shell" that empowers lay persons to share text, a CIShell implementation is an "empty shell" that empowers user communities to plug-and-play, share, compare and combine data sets, algorithms, and compute resources across national and disciplinary boundaries. It is argued here that CIs will not only transform the way science is conducted but also will play a major role in the diffusion of expertise, data sets, algorithms, and technologies across multiple disciplines and business sectors leading to a more integrative science.

KEYWORDS: cyberinfrastructure; OSGi; plug-in; data models; analysis; network science; scientometrics; usability; flexibility; extensibility

INTRODUCTION

Fifty years back in time, few scientists used computers to conduct their research. Today, science without computation is unthinkable in almost all areas of science. Innovation and progress in most areas of science require access

Address for correspondence: Katy Börner, Indiana University, SLIS, 1320 East Tenth Street, Bloomington, IN 47405. Voice: 812-855-3256; fax: 812-855-6166.

e-mail: katy@indiana.edu

[1] This material is based upon work supported in part by the 21st Century Fund and the National Science Foundation under Grant No. IIS-0238261 and IIS-0513650. Any opinions, findings, and conclusions, or recommendations expressed in this material are those of the author(s) and do not necessarily reflect the views of the National Science Foundation.

Ann. N.Y. Acad. Sci. 1093: 161–179 (2006). © 2006 New York Academy of Sciences.
doi: 10.1196/annals.1382.013

to advanced computational, collaborative, data acquisition, and management services available to researchers through high-performance networks. These environments have been termed *cyberinfrastructures* (CI) by a National Science Foundation (NSF) blue-ribbon committee lead by Daniel Atkins (Atkins *et al.* 2003). Today, some CIs provide access to thousands of interlinked experts, services, federated data sets, and compute resources. They have reached a complexity that is hard if not impossible to specify, implement, and manage in a top-down fashion. Also, most content providers and users of these CIs are not computer scientists. They are biologists, physicists, social scientists, information scientists, and others with deep knowledge about data and algorithms and a deep interest to save lives, secure important technical infrastructures, and discover universal laws.

Scientists today use commercial packages, such as Microsoft Excel, SPSS (http://www.spss.com), Matlab (http://www.mathworks.com), Adobe Photoshop, etc., to analyze and model their diverse data sets and to visualize research results. These tools come with easy to use, menu-driven interfaces through which a set of standard features can be used. Data and file sharing are easy if collaborators use the very same tools and versions. However, it is not trivial to add your own or any other algorithm without major modifications. It is impossible to get a "customized filling" of the tools with exactly those algorithms that are needed by a user or user group.

In response to this need, a growing number of grass roots efforts aim to create data and software libraries, application programming interfaces (APIs), and repositories that help disseminate the best algorithms. In many cases, algorithms are made available as open source so that the concrete implementation can be examined and improved if necessary. Sample efforts are R (Ihaka and Gentleman 1996), StOCNet (Huisman and Duijn 2003), Jung (O'Madadhain *et al.* 2003), and Prefuse (Heer *et al.* 2005). However, the mentioned packages come as APIs or require scripting of code. None of them supports the easy, wizard-based integration of new algorithms and data sets by developers or provides a menu driven, easy to use interface for the application user.

Grid computing (Berman *et al.* 2003) aims to address the computational needs of "big science" problems, such as protein folding, financial modeling, earthquake simulation, or climate/weather modeling. It follows a service-oriented architecture and provides hardware and software services and infrastructure for secure and uniform access to heterogeneous resources (e.g., different platforms, hardware/software architectures, and programming languages), located in different places belonging to different administrative domains linked on a network using open standards. It also supports the composition of applications and services, workflow design, scheduling, and execution management. Using grid computing today is challenging. To fully take advantage of the grid, one's code must be (re)written to run in parallel on a cluster of potentially very different operating systems and environments, which appears to be a major challenge for most people who are not computer scientists. Further, access to the grid is usually through command line interfaces or customized portals optimized for the needs of specific communities. Finally, while grid computing is a powerful approach to "big science" computations, many applications can be served well without parallel computing and distributed databases. The time and effort required to make an application grid-able is considerable and only justifiable if grid resources and functionality are truly needed.

In sum, there is a gap between algorithm developers and application designers and application users. Many algorithm developers are searching for easy ways to quickly disseminate their work. Many researchers and educators are in need of good algorithms but are not equipped with the mathematical sophistication and programming knowledge required to benefit from code descriptions in research papers, implemented APIs, or advanced CIs. In many cases, users are not only interested in a single algorithm but they want tools similar to MS Excel, SPSS, Matlab, or Photoshop but with the option to customize and extend them according to their needs.

The cyber infrastructure shell (CIShell) specification aims to serve the needs of all three user groups: algorithm developers, application designers, and application users. Building on the open services gateway initiative (OSGi) specification, it supports the easy, wizard-driven plug-and-play of existing and new algorithms and data sets that are implemented as services. Data, algorithms, and additional CIShell services, such as graphical user interfaces (GUIs), schedulers, and logging services can be combined and deployed as a stand-alone tool, (Web) service, or peer-to-peer service, among others. The core CIShell implementation can be "filled" with high performance services or the data sets and services needed in a classroom setting. Hence, CIShell creates a bridge between algorithm developers, application developers, and their users.

The remainder of this article is organized as follows: First, the needs of the user groups CIShell aims to serve are detailed. Second, the inner workings of CIShell are described on an abstract level. Third, how CIShell is used by the three different user groups is explained. Fourth, diverse reference implementations are introduced. Finally, the article concludes with a discussion and an outlook of future work.

WHAT USERS WANT

Today, it is not only computer scientists who develop and create novel data sets and algorithms but also biologists, physicists, and social scientists among others. In many cases, the data sets and algorithms are used almost exclusively by the person, lab, or project that created them. Some are distributed via private web pages. Consequently, many algorithms are implemented and reimplemented countless times—a true waste of lifetime and resources. Given the effort it takes to implement a set of algorithms, comparisons of novel with existing algorithms are rare. Some algorithms are made available in compiled form or as source code. These efforts are truly appreciated by the community and lead to higher citation counts of related papers. However, there is no way to get an overview of all existing data sets and algorithms. To make things worse, data sets come in diverse formats and algorithms are implemented in very different languages and with diverse input and output formats. The diffusion of high quality data sets and novel algorithms would greatly benefit from a means to easily integrate and use existing data sets and algorithms.

There is also a need for the design of tools that provide access to exactly those data sets and algorithms that are needed by a researcher, group, or community. Commercially available tools often provide menu-driven interfaces, remote services, or scripting engines. They have workflow support, scheduling support, etc. Users will expect this from customized tools.

Analyzing and making sense of data sets frequently involves multiple steps, such as sampling, cleaning, analyzing, and sometimes visualizing for means of communication. For means of illustration, FIGURE 1 shows the diverse data sets (given in italics and underlined) and processing steps involved in a scientometric study (Mane and Börner 2004) aiming at the identification of the topic coverage of a document data set. The analysis starts with a list of documents—one document per line. This list is parsed and a term-document matrix is generated in which each cell entry states how often a certain term occurred in a certain document. The resulting term-document matrix is used to identify the top 50 most frequent terms. Next, the co-occurrence similarity of those top 50 terms is calculated. The more often two terms occur together in the same document, that is, in the same line of the original list of all documents, the

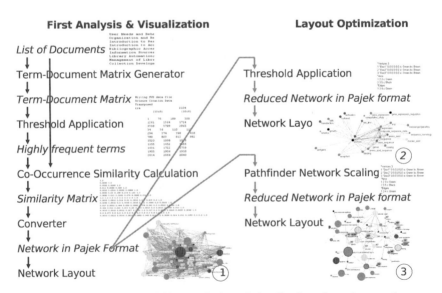

FIGURE 1. Sample acquisition, analysis, and visualization of a topic network.

higher their similarity. The similarity matrix is then converted into a list of nodes and edges that can be read by the Pajek network layout tool (Batagelj and Mrvar 1998). Unfortunately, the generated layout labeled with (1) is not very readable as almost all terms co-occur with each other in at least one of the many documents. Layout optimization is needed. In a first attempt, a threshold was applied to eliminate links below a certain similarity. However, this strategy disintegrates the network into one larger subgraph labeled (2) and many unconnected nodes. In a second attempt, Pathfinder Network Scaling (Schvaneveldt 1990) is applied to ensure that all 50 nodes stay connected yet a more readable layout is achieved, see visualization labeled with (3).

Most analyses in scientometrics and other fields of science require many more processing steps (Börner *et al.* 2003, 2007). Commonly, the output of one processing step is not compatible with the input of the next step. Tools and algorithms applied in one and the same study might be implemented in different programming languages and might only run on certain operating systems making data transfer across and the switch between platforms necessary. Many analyses are highly iterative. It is only after the entire sequence of processing steps is completed that data errors or layout optimization needs become visible. Some algorithms have a high computational complexity and have to be scheduled.

Taken together, researchers involved in data analysis, modeling, and visualization would highly benefit from a specification/application that supports the plug-and-play of algorithms written in different languages. Algorithm interface standards or converters are needed to accommodate different input and output formats. Ideally, users can select existing and generated data sets, algorithms, and existing tools via a GUI that also provides logging, scheduling, and other services.

CISHELL DESIGN

The CIShell is an open source, community-driven specification for the integration and utilization of data sets, algorithms, tools, and computing resources. The CIShell specification, API, and related documentation are available at http://cishell.org. The specification and all its reference implementations are open sourced under the Apache 2.0 license.

CIShell builds upon the OSGi specification, as described later. By leveraging OSGi, we gain access to a large amount of industry standard code and know-how that would take years to reinvent/implement. Each application—be it a stand-alone application, a scripting engine, a remote server-client, or a peer-to-peer architecture—resembles an ecology of services. FIGURE 2 depicts how CIShell applications can be deployed as distributed data and algorithm repositories, stand-alone applications, peer-to-peer architectures, and server-client architectures.

Data-Algorithm Repositories

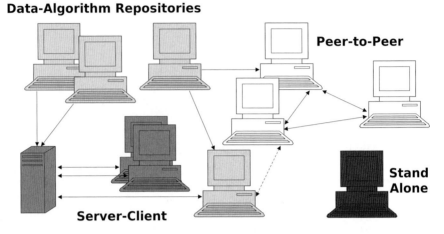

FIGURE 2. Deployment options for CIShell applications.

OSGi Specification

The OSGi specification (http://www.osgi.org) defines a standardized, component-oriented computing environment for networked services. It has been successfully used in industry from high-end servers to embedded mobile devices for 7 years. OSGi alliance members include IBM, Sun, Intel, Oracle, Motorola, NEC, and many others. OSGi is widely adopted in the open source realm, especially since Eclipse 3.0 has adopted OSGi R4 as its plug-in model. Adopting the OSGi R4 specification and technology as the underlying foundation of CIShell has many advantages.

First, the OSGi specifications define and implement an elegant, complete, and dynamic component model, which fully supports the basic functionalities of the CIShell plug-in architecture. Its class-loading model is based on top of Java but adds modularization. While Java typically uses a single class path for all the classes and resources, the OSGi-loading module layer adds private classes for a module as well as controlled linking between modules. It is also responsible for handling multiple versions of the same classes—old and new applications can execute within the same virtual machine. The dynamic installing, starting, stopping, updating, and uninstalling of bundles is well defined in the OSGi specification and adopted by all CIShell bundles. OSGi also specifies and implements a service registry that takes care of the communication and collaboration among bundles. The service registry also supports the sharing of services between bundles. Note that services can appear and disappear or be updated at any moment in time.

Second, the CIShell specification and its applications can take advantage of a large number of OSGi services that have been defined and implemented on top of the OSGi specification. These services include logging, preferences, http services (for running servlets), XML parsing, framework layering, declarative services, and many more. These services have been developed and can be obtained from several different vendors with different optimizations.

Third, given that the OSGi specification has component-oriented architecture and each service is defined abstractly and is independently implemented by different vendors, any CIShell application can choose a subset of services as needed and has no restriction to depend on the implementations of any particular vendor. Finally, by using OSGi, all CIShell algorithms become services that can be used in any OSGi-based system.

CIShell Specification

CIShell is an open source specification for the integration and utilization of datasets, algorithms, and computing resources. FIGURE 3 shows its highly modular and decentralized system architecture. It comprises a set of OSGi bundles (left) that upon start-up instantiate a set of OSGI services (right). An OSGi bundle is a plug-in, a collection of code that can be plugged and played as needed. The CIShell specification API itself is a bundle. It does not register any OSGi services but provides interfaces for data set/algorithm services, basic services, and application services.

The bundles are prioritized upon start of the application. The bundles with the highest priority are started first followed by bundles of second, third, etc. priority. Each bundle has a manifest file with a dependency list that states what packages, package versions, and other bundles it needs to run.

Each bundle can register zero or more services. The resulting set of OSGi services can be divided into data/algorithm services, basic services, application

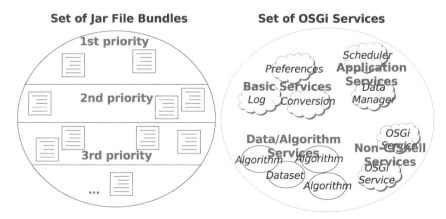

FIGURE 3. CIShell implementation.

FIGURE 4. Input and output of data set and algorithm services.

services, and non-CIShell-specific services. A data set or algorithm that is written to adhere to the CIShell specification can be used in a wide variety of applications.

Data set services do not take any input data but serve data. *Algorithm services* typically take in user-provided parameters, data, and a context for getting basic services. They commonly return data after being executed. FIGURE 4 compares both service types. However, there are exceptions; modeling algorithms do not read in data, visualization algorithms do not write out data, and depending on how integrated a toolkit is, entire toolkits integrated as algorithms may not read in or write out data.

There are several *basic services* that an algorithm service can use. These services allow an algorithm to log information, get and set configuration options, create simple user interfaces for data input, and convert data to different formats. Access to these services is made available through the context passed to the algorithm. An algorithm that uses basic services exclusively and does not create its own GUI can be run remotely.

To shorten development time by application writers, several additional services have been specified in the CIShell specification. These *application services* help to manage data that algorithms create or to schedule algorithm execution time. More services will be available in later revisions of the specification.

USING CISHELL

CIShell creates a division of labor that allows algorithm writers to concentrate on writing algorithms, data set providers on providing data, application developers on creating applications, and researchers and practitioners on using the resulting applications to advance science and technology. CIShell aims to make each of these user groups as productive as possible by providing data set and algorithm integration templates and application solutions to developers and easy to use interfaces to users, as in FIGURE 5.

Data Set/Algorithm Providers: How to Integrate Data Sets and Algorithms

Researchers and practitioners interested to widely distribute their data sets and algorithms using CIShell need to produce OSGi bundles that can be run

Dataset/Algorithm Developers   **Application Users**

CIShell Algorithm Integration Templates   *IVC Interface*

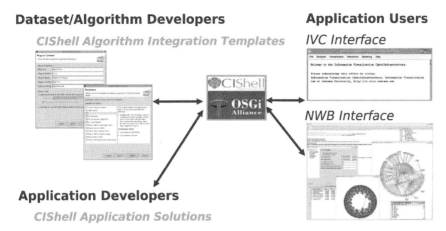

NWB Interface

Application Developers

CIShell Application Solutions

FIGURE 5. CIShell support for different kinds of users.

in any OSGi or CIShell application. To be a service in the OSGi framework, a bundle must provide three things: properties of the service (a set of key/value pairs), one or more interfaces, and an instantiated implementation of the interface(s). The service properties are very important as they are used to query the OSGi service registry for relevant algorithms, to learn where to place them in a menu, and to capture what meta-data should be shown to the user. Diverse templates are available for integrating data sets, non-Java-based algorithms (usually in the form of executables), and Java-based algorithms. Using these templates, developers can quickly produce OSGi bundles from existing data sets and code. A wizard-driven process guides the developer though a series of forms that lets them upload their data set/code and enter properties, such as its name, type, any input parameters, type of input and output data for algorithms, reference to any scholarly publications, etc. The information is then used to generate the code and documentation for a project that is used to build the jar bundle for distribution. Using this jar file, the data set–algorithm can now be run within any CIShell application.

Data sets and algorithms can also be integrated manually providing more control over how they interrelate to other services.

Application Tool Developers: How to Develop Applications

Application developers can leverage the OSGi and CIShell specification to compose a rich variety of custom applications. There are no specific templates set up for application development since the range of applications is huge. Instead, we provide well-documented CIShell reference implementations to teach application development in an exemplar-driven way. Existing OSGi implementations are another valuable source of inspiration and technical guidance.

Application developers will need to have a good understanding of OSGi in addition to the algorithm specification defined by CIShell. However, they greatly benefit from the modularity and flexibility that OSGi provides. They will not have to worry about exactly how an algorithm is implemented nor how to integrate diverse data sets and algorithms into one application. Instead, they can focus on how to design novel applications that best serve the needs of their users.

To create an application from scratch, one usually starts with a base solution that provides the OSGi framework implementation, the CIShell specification, and an implementation of the defined CIShell services. From there, an application developer can use the OSGi and CIShell specification to create an application that uses the pool of algorithm services made available in a novel way. A forthcoming technical paper on the CIShell specification and existing implementations provides details on how this is done (Herr 2007).

Alternatively, a user can take a CIShell Base Solution (OSGi plus CIShell specification and services), a set of algorithms and data sets that were either developed in house or downloaded, and a rebranded version of the CIShell reference GUI to create an application that best fits a community. This approach was taken to implement the *Information Visualization Cyberinfrastructure* (IVC) and the *Network Workbench* (NWB). Both offer a menu-driven, branded interface that provides access to different sets of algorithms and data sets, a community web page, and individual documentation on how to use them. The IVC provides access to information visualization data sets and algorithms, whereas the NWB serves a considerably larger network science community. Using one base solution to implement two very different CIs has saved us enormous amounts of time and effort in terms of design, implementation, and maintenance of the CIs.

Application Users: How to Use Applications Built Using CIShell

Researchers, educators, and practitioners are the main beneficiaries of the "empty shell" approach to the sharing of data sets, algorithms, and computing resources.

Users of CIShell applications can easily customize the "filling" of their applications—replacing old with new, more efficient code, or keeping all versions around for comparison. They can decide to either download the filling commonly used by their respective community or exactly the data sets and algorithms they need.

The CIShell specification makes possible the design of sociotechnical infrastructures that provide easy access to any data set, algorithm, tool, or compute resource in existence. Not knowing about an existing data set or algorithm, the continuous reimplementation of the very same algorithm, or the frustration caused by incompatible file formats and algorithms that run on different platforms, etc. becomes history. The more people adhere to the CIShell specification the more data sets, algorithms, other services, and applications will be available for usage and supplied by different vendors.

REFERENCE IMPLEMENTATIONS

The CIShell *base solution* combines the Eclipse (http://www.eclipse.org) Equinox OSGi R4 reference implementation, several service bundles from the Eclipse, the CIShell specification bundle, and some reference CIShell service implementation bundles into an application that can be run. It is a bare-bones distribution that has no real interface but can be filled with other bundles to provide a user interface, algorithms, data sets, and whatever else is needed in the application to satisfy users' needs. An application does not have to use this solution to make an end user application, but it is provided as a basic solution on which application developers and other advanced users can build on.

The *client-server middleware* (an application that another application can use for added functionality) application was developed as a proof of concept to show how a remote client-server could be implemented. It uses web service technology so that a client application can connect to the remote server and use the algorithms and data sets available there. In praxis, services on the server show up as proxy services on the client. They can be executed (on the server) by an application running on the client without any special handling code. If new services are added to the server, the middleware detects them, and makes them usable in all applications running on the client. This technique will be further extended in the future to create a web front-end and a peer-to-peer middleware solution.

The *scripting application* was developed as a proof of concept to show how a scripting engine could be easily integrated into a CIShell-based system. When the bundle holding this application is started, it opens a console so that a user can enter scripting code to access the OSGi service registry, find algorithms, and use them. While not as simple as a GUI, there are many users who prefer this level of interaction. A scripting interface could also be used to create a middleware application that enables other applications to transfer and execute code. By keeping a log of all user actions as scripting code, any sequence of user actions can be saved, shared, and rerun as needed.

A *GUI application* was developed as an easy to use, menu-driven interface that can be used by itself or branded for custom end-user applications. The GUI is built using the eclipse-rich client platform (RCP), which is built on OSGi. Its look and feel benefits from lessons learned in our previous CI development efforts, though with new code and some new features. This GUI is used by the CIs discussed hereafter.

INFORMATION VISUALIZATION CYBERINFRASTRUCTURE

IVC started as a software repository project in 2000. Its goal was and is to provide access to a comprehensive set of data sets, algorithms, and computing resources but also educational materials that ease the utilization of data mining and information visualization algorithms. The project's web page is at http://iv.slis.indiana.edu.

Katy Börner, Yuezheng Zhou, and Jason Baumgartner implemented the very first algorithms (Börner and Zhou 2001). In summer 2003, Jason Baumgartner, Nihar Sheth, and Nathan J. Deckard led a project to design an XML toolkit that enables the serialization and parallelization of commonly used data analysis and visualization algorithms (Baumgartner *et al.* 2003). In summer 2004, Shashikant Penumarthy and Bruce W. Herr master-minded the IVC framework. Josh Bonner and Laura Northrup, Hardik Sheth, and Jeegar Maru were involved in the implementation of the IVC and the integration of algorithms. Maggie B. Swan and Caroline Courtney were of invaluable help for the design, proof reading, and validation of the diverse online documentations. In early 2005, James Ellis, Shashikant Penumarthy, and Bruce Herr revised the IVC to use eclipse-RCP as the underlying plug-in model and GUI. Later that year, the underlying core of the IVC was separated even further from the application resulting in the Information Visualization Cyberinfrastructure Software Framework (IVCSF). In early 2006, work was started on the successor to the IVCSF, CIShell, as described in this article.

Over the last 7 years, this effort has been supported by the School of Library and Information Science, Indiana University's High Performance Network Applications Program, a Pervasive Technology Lab Fellowship, an Academic Equipment Grant by SUN Microsystems, and an SBC (formerly Ameritech) Fellow Grant, as well NSF grants DUE-0333623 and IIS-0238261.

The major components of the IVC are databases, computing resources, software, and learning modules as shown in FIGURE 6. The CIShell specification is used to integrate diverse data sets (e.g., time series, documents, matrices, networks, geospatial data) and algorithms (e.g., preprocessing, analysis, modeling, visualization, interaction).

Since 2000, the repository/CI has been used to teach the *Information Visualization* class at Indiana University. Starting 2003, it was also used in Börner's *Data Mining and Modeling* class. Since its debut on Sourceforge.net in June 2004, it has been downloaded more than 5000 times—mostly by institutions, organizations, and companies in United States, Europe, and Asia. Other InfoVis tool(kits) exist, such as:

1. Jean-Daniel Fekete's InfoVis Toolkit (Fekete 2004)
   http://ivtk.sourceforge.net
2. Visualization Toolkit software by Kitware Inc.
   http://www.kitware.com/vtk.html

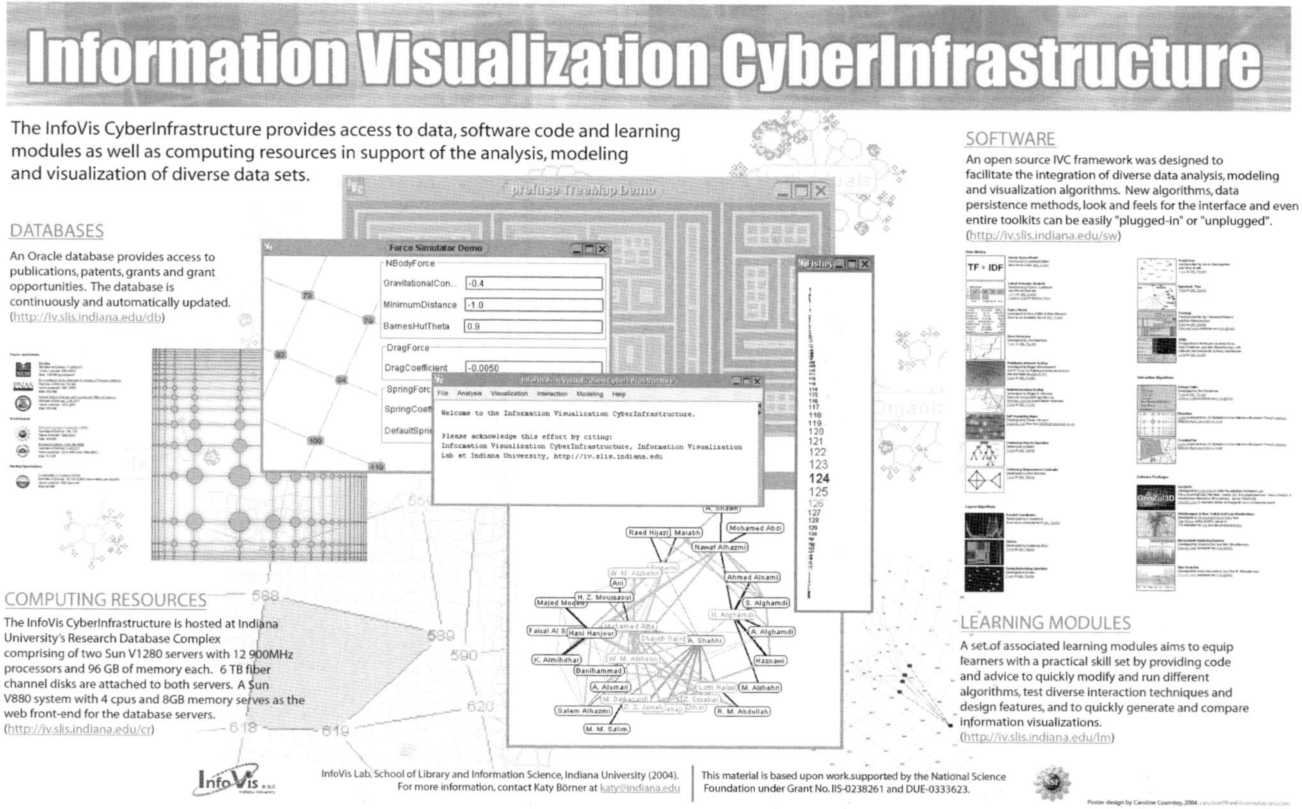

FIGURE 6. Components of the IVC.

3. the CAIDA visualization tools accessible at
   http://www.caida.org/tools
4. and the many others listed by http://vw.indiana.edu/ivsi2004/

CIShell differs from them in that it aims to ease the integration of new data sets and software algorithms by diverse noncomputer scientist developers. In the near future, there will also be a means to contribute algorithm descriptions and learning modules.

NETWORK WORKBENCH

The NWB is a network analysis, modeling, and visualization toolkit for biomedical, social science, and physics research. It is generously funded by a $1.1 million NSF award for a 3-year duration: September 2005–August 2008. Investigators are Katy Börner, Albert-Laszlo Barabási, Santiago Schnell, Alessandro Vespignani, Stanley Wasserman, and Eric Wernert. The software team is lead by Weixia (Bonnie) Huang and comprises CIShell developer Bruce Herr and algorithm developers Ben Markines, Santo Fortunato, and Cesar Hidalgo. The project's web page is at http://nwb.slis.indiana.edu.

The project will design three different applications: A NWB tool for use by network science researchers and practitioners, an educational web service that teaches biologists and others the basics of network science, and a mapping

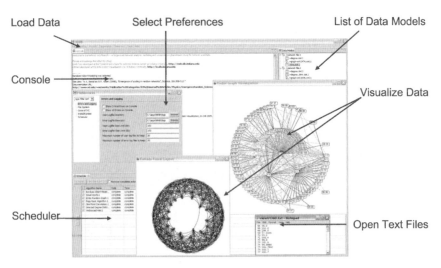

FIGURE 7. Interface of the network workbench tool.

science service that the general public can use to explore and make sense of mankind's collective scholarly knowledge.

The NWB tool uses the stand-alone CIShell GUI application and resembles the IVC. However, it has a different branding and "filling." A snapshot of the NWB tool interface is shown in FIGURE 7. Major parts are labeled.

A user can load data via the menu-driven interface or generate a network data set. She or he can analyze and visualize a data set using a wide variety of different complementary and alternative algorithms. All used data sets are listed in the right window of the interface. All user actions as well as citations for selected algorithms are printed in the console.

A generic *NWB* data format was defined to support the storage and processing of million node graphs. Using the NWB converter plug-ins, the tool can load, view, and save a network from/to a *NWB* data format file. Although the *NWB* data model is the fundamental data structure, other data models, such as the *Prefuse Graph* model and *Matrix* model, have been developed and integrated into the NWB tool.

CIShell algorithms written in diverse programming languages can be integrated and used. CIShell templates are used to integrate code written in Java, C++, or FORTRAN.

Among others, JUNG and Prefuse libraries have been integrated into the NWB as plug-ins. After converting the generated *NWB* data model into *JUNG Graph* and *Prefuse Graph* data model, NWB users can run JUNG and Prefuse graph layouts to interactively explore visualizations of their networks. NWB also supplies a plug-in that invokes the XMGrace application for plotting data analysis results.

The NWB tool has a number of unique features: It is open source, highly flexible, easily extendable, and scalable to very large networks. While some of the most powerful network tools, for example, Pajek and UCINET (Borgatti *et al.* 2002) run on Windows, the NWB tool can be compiled for multiple operating systems including Windows, Linux, Unix, and Mac OS. Another set of tools, for example, Cytoscape (Shannon *et al.* 2003) and TopNet (Yu *et al.* 2004) were designed specifically for the study of biological networks. However, we believe that the true value of network science will come from a cross-fertilization of approaches, algorithms, and technologies developed in different disciplines. Both, the NWB tool and Cytoscape use open source, plug-and-play software architectures. While Cytoscape requires all plug-ins to work with their internal data model, the NWB tool defines and uses an efficient NWB data format, but also provides support for other data formats that algorithm developers might use. GEOMI (Xu *et al.* 2006) and Tulip (Auber 2003) are both tools that support the visualization of huge graphs. GEOMI uses WilmaScope, a 3D graph visualization system. Tulip uses Open GL as the rendering engine. Both have a plug-and-play architecture, but due to sparse documentation it is very difficult for other researchers to evaluate the framework or contribute plug-ins.

DISCUSSION AND FUTURE WORK

The CIShell specification is a culmination of 7 years of toolkit development. The design has gone under several names: InfoVis Repository (IVR), IVC and specifications: IVCSF and CIShell. However, the goal is still the same, to improve the diffusion of data sets, algorithms, and applications from those that develop them to those that benefit from their usage. We have made major progress from the pre-IVR days when our programs were dispersed throughout differing operating systems and file systems and had to be run manually from the command line. Today, the CIShell specification provides a means to design highly modular, highly decoupled, very flexible, and powerful applications and infrastructures.

We are in the process of creating more reference implementations, such as a web front-end, peer-to-peer sharing, and workflow engines. The reference implementations that are already available will be extended and hardened to convert them from proof of concept to robust software applications.

A key for client–servers, web front-ends, and peer-to-peer sharing will be in a formal definition of the web service model using web services definition language (WSDL). Creation of a standard by which networked CIShell instances communicate will help these applications to easily cooperate. Furthermore, this will allow any software application (CIShell compliant or not) to be able to connect to a running CIShell instance with relative ease and security using standard web service techniques.

Another addition will apply the idea of "semantic association networks" (Börner 2006). The published papers, their authors, as well as data sets and algorithms used will all be interlinked. The linkages can then be traversed in service of superior knowledge access and management. For example, all authors who used a certain data set or algorithm can be retrieved or all algorithms that have ever been used to analyze a certain data set can be identified.

We will continue to promote and foster an atmosphere of cooperation, communication, and open access. While we will use CIShell for our own application development and usage, its value will increase with the number of people using it. We will continue to give talks and tutorials and organize workshops that introduce algorithm and application developers as well as users to CIShell and its reference implementations. The feedback and the buy-in from a growing development team and user group will be essential to the design of the best possible CIShell.

Last but not least, we would like to point out that we did benefit enormously from related efforts, such as TeraGrid (http://www.teragrid.org), R, GeoVISTA Studio (Takatsuka and Gahegan 2002), and many others. Although these systems seem to have little in common, they share the vision behind CIShell—to ease the dissemination of data sets, algorithms, and computing resources to a broad user base.

TeraGrid (http://www.teragrid.org) is an NSF-sponsored grid computing initiative that provides scientists access to massively distributed computing power and data storage for research. It supports the design of highly scalable services and computing infrastructures. However, the integration of new data sets, services, and the design of online portals is typically done by computer scientists in close collaboration with the application holders. In contrast, CIShell focuses on ease of use for algorithm/application developers and users and is mostly used for applications that do not require access to highly scalable and distributed infrastructures. However, it can be used to integrate services that support sharing of distributed data sets and services running on parallel computing resources. Note that CIShell can be interlinked with grid-based infrastructures by using the Web service protocol under development. This would make grid services available via CIShell applications or provide CIShell services, for example, data analysis, modeling, or visualization services, to grid applications.

R is a language and environment for statistical computing and graphics. It allows for addition of new packages and has a vibrant developer and user community. It is very much a text based system built around the language and integrated algorithms, but there are some externally made GUIs available. What separates R from CIShell is that R's integration methods are nontrivial and become truly difficult if code is not written in C, C++, or Fortran. CIShell supports any programming language and provides templates for data set and algorithm integration. To us, R appears to have a steeper learning curve in both using the software and integrating algorithms and packages.

GeoVISTA Studio is an open source, programming-free development environment that allows users to quickly build applications for geocomputation and geographic visualization. It uses JavaBeans to support the plug-and-play of different algorithms. A visual programming interface is employed to support the integration of new code.

To our knowledge, there exists no other effort that attempts to build an "empty shell" that supports the easy integration and utilization of data sets and code; runs on all common platforms; in a stand-alone, client-(Web)server or peer-to-peer fashion; is highly decoupled; and builds on industry standards to create a powerful, simple to use, yet highly flexible algorithm environment. It is our sincere hope that the CIShell specification will be widely adopted and used to create highly flexible and usable CIs in service of international and interdisciplinary innovation and progress.

REFERENCES

ATKINS, D.E., K.K. DROGEMEIER, S.I. FELDMAN, H. GARCIA-MOLINA, M.L. KLEIN, D.G. MESSERSCHMITT, P. MESSIAN, J.P. OSTRIKER, and M.H. WRIGHT. 2003. Revolutionizing science and engineering through cyberinfrastructure: report of the National

Science Foundation blue-ribbon advisory panel on cyberinfrastructure. Arlington, VA: National Science Foundation.

AUBER, D. 2003. Tulip: A huge graph visualisation framework. Pp. 105–126 in P. Mutzel, and M. Jünger (eds.), *Graph Drawing Softwares, Mathematics and Visualization*. Heidelberg: Springer-Verlag.

BATAGELJ, V., and A. MRVAR. 1998. Pajek – Program for large network analysis. *Connections 21*(2), 47–57.

BAUMGARTNER, J., K. BÖRNER, N.J. DECKARD, and N. SHETH. 2003. An XML Toolkit for an information visualization software repository. IEEE Information Visualization Conference, Poster Compendium. 72–73.

BERMAN, F., A.J.G. HEY, and G.C. FOX. 2003. *Grid Computing: Making The Global Infrastructure a Reality*. New York: Wiley Press.

BORGATTI, S.P., M.G. EVERETT, and L.C. FREEMAN. 2002. *UCINET for Windows: Software for Social Network Analysis*. Harvard: Analytic Technologies.

BÖRNER, K. 2006. Semantic association networks: using semantic web technology to improve scholarly knowledge and expertise management. Pp. 183–198 in V. Geroimenko and C. Chen (eds.), *Visualizing the Semantic Web*. Springer Verlag.

BÖRNER, K., and Y. ZHOU. 2001. A Software Repository for Education and Research in Information Visualization. Fifth International Conference on Information Visualisation, London, England: IEEE Press. 257–262.

BÖRNER, K., C. CHEN, and K. BOYACK. 2003. Visualizing Knowledge Domains. Pp. 179–255 in B. Cronin (ed.), *Annual Review of Information Science and Technology, Vol. 37*. Medford, NJ: Information Today, Inc./American Society for Information Science and Technology.

BÖRNER, K., S. SANYAL, and A. VESPIGNANI. 2007. Network Science. Pp. 41 in B. Cronin (ed.), *Annual Review of Information Science & Technology*. Medford, NJ: Information Today, Inc./American Society for Information Science and Technology.

FEKETE, J.-D. 2004. The Infovis Toolkit Proceedings of the 10th IEEE Symposium on Information Visualization, IEEE Press. 167–174.

HEER, J., S.K. CARD, and J.A. LANDAY. 2005. Prefuse: a toolkit for interactive information visualization. *CHI 2005-Proceedings* 421–430.

HERR, B. 2007. CIShell: Cyberinfrastructure Shell. *A Novel Algorithm Integration Framework, forthcoming*.

HUISMAN, M., and M.A.J.V. DUIJN. 2003. StOCNET: software for the statistical analysis of social networks. *Connections 25*(1), 7–26.

IHAKA, R., and R. GENTLEMAN. 1996. R: a language for data analysis and graphics. *Journal of Computational and Graphical Statistics 5*(3), 299–314.

MANE, K.K., and K. BÖRNER. 2004. Mapping topics and topic bursts in PNAS. *Proceedings of the National Academy of Sciences of the United States of America 101*(Suppl 1), 5287–5290.

O'MADADHAIN, J., D. FISHER, S. WHITE, and Y. BOEY. 2003. The JUNG (Java Universal Network/Graph) framework. *Technical Report, UC Irvine*.

SCHVANEVELDT, R.W. 1990. *Pathfinder Associative Networks: Studies in Knowledge Organization*. Norwood, NJ: Ablex Publishing.

SHANNON, P., A. MARKIEL, O. OZIER, N.S. BALIGA, J.T. WANG, D. RAMAGE, N. AMIN, B. SCHWIKOWSKI, and T. IDEKER. 2003. Cytoscape: a software environment for integrated models of biomolecular interaction networks. *Genome Research 13*, 2498–2504.

TAKATSUKA, M., and M. GAHEGAN. 2002. GeoVISTA Studio: a codeless visual programming environment for geoscientific data analysis and visualization. *The Journal of Computers and Geosciences 28*(10), 1131–1144.

XU, K., S.-H. HONG, M. FORSTER, N.S. NIKOLOV, J. HO, D. KOSCHUTZKI, A. AHMED, T. DWYER, X. FU, C. MURRAY, R. TAIB, and A. TARASSOV. 2006. GEOMI: geometry for maximum insight. Pp. 468–479 in P. Healy, and N.S. Nikolov (eds.), *Proceedings Graph Drawing*. Ireland: Limerick.

YU, H., X. ZHU, D. GREENBAUM, J. KARRO, and M. GERSTEIN. 2004. TopNet: a tool for comparing biological sub-networks, correlating protein properties with topological statistics. *Nucleic Acids Res 32*, 328–337.

The Problem of Patent Thickets in Convergent Technologies

GAVIN CLARKSON AND DAVID DeKORTE

University of Michigan, Ann Arbor, Michigan 48109-1107, USA

ABSTRACT: Patent thickets are unintentionally dense webs of overlapping intellectual property rights owned by different companies that can retard progress. This article begins with a review of existing research on patent thickets, focusing in particular on the problem of patent thickets in nanotechnology, or nanothickets. After presenting visual evidence of the presence of nanothickets using a network analytic technique, it discusses potential organizational responses to patent thickets. It then reviews the existing research on patent pools and discusses pool formation in the shadow of antitrust enforcement. Based on recent research on patent pool formation, it examines the divergent fate of two recent pools and discusses the prospects for the future formation of nanotechnology patent pools, or nanopools.

KEYWORDS: nanotechnology; patents; intellectual property

INTRODUCTION

Nanotechnology is poised to be the first major technological revolution of the 21st century, yet there is a growing concern that future innovation and commercialization will be inhibited by the explosive rate of nanotechnology patenting and the potential for the formation of patent thickets. These dense webs of overlapping intellectual property rights owned by different companies (Shapiro 2000) can present a significant barrier that must be hacked through in order to commercialize new technology. In other industries characterized by cumulative innovations and multiple blocking patents, the existence of such densely concentrated patent rights can have the perverse effect of stifling innovation rather than encouraging it. Such patent thickets are already problematic in other convergent technology areas such as biotechnology (Heller and Eisenberg 1998; Clark *et al.* 2000; Horn 2003) and information technology (Clarkson 2004).

Address for correspondence: Gavin Clarkson, Assistant Professor, University of Michigan, School of Information, School of Law, Native American Studies, 304 West Hall, 1085 S. University Ave., Ann Arbor, MI 48109-1107. Voice: 734-763-2284; fax: 734-764-2475.
e-mail: gsmc@umich.edu

Ann. N.Y. Acad. Sci. 1093: 180–200 (2006). © 2006 New York Academy of Sciences.
doi: 10.1196/annals.1382.014

Progress in the field of nanotechnology has been rapid over the past half century, with laboratories in corporations and universities researching the ability to successfully create working objects at this level. From 1985 until 2005, there were 3818 nanotech patents issued in the United States, with an additional 1777 outstanding patent applications published since 2001 (Lux 2005). This number is expected to increase exponentially as the processes required to create such technologies are further developed over the next several decades.

Nanotechnology is a quickly growing area, and has the possibility for revolutionizing a vast array of different fields and industries, including health care, electronics, pharmaceuticals, and others. According to Lux Research (2003) study, public and private companies spent $3 billion worldwide on nanotechnology. This spending only shows signs of increasing over the next several years. Given this level of spending, developing a strategy to deal with the problem of nanothickets is critical, not only to the researchers developing these new technologies but also the corporations and institutions that fund them. Without appropriate strategies, firms will be unable to capitalize on their investments, and researchers may be prevented from conducting even the most basic research because nanothickets constitute such a potentially imposing obstacle.

While nanotechnology as a scientific domain has a number of unique attributes that render it particularly susceptible to the development of patent thickets, the problem of patent thickets is not new. Over the last century and a half, organizations in technology industries attempting to advance their innovative activities have often stumbled into patent thickets (Clarkson 2004). Although the organizational responses varied widely, certain organizations have occasionally responded by constructing patent pools or organizational structures where multiple firms collectively aggregate patent rights into a package for licensing, either among themselves or to any potential licensees irrespective of membership in the pool. Such collaboration among technologically competing firms, however, has often encountered difficulty from an antitrust standpoint, even if the formation of the pool is procompetitive.

THE PROBLEM OF NANOTHICKETS

A patent does not guarantee the right to make or do anything. Instead, a patent gives the patent owner the right to exclude others from making, using, or selling anything that embodies the technology covered by the patent. When a given organization has all of the necessary patents to develop a given technology, it can proceed without intellectual property entanglements. When multiple organizations each own individual patents that are collectively necessary for a particular technology, however, their competing intellectual property rights form a "patent thicket" (Clarkson 2005).

The problem of patent thickets has recently caught the attention of much of the scientific and engineering community in a number of technological arenas (Heller and Eisenberg 1998; Merges 1999; Clark *et al.* 2000; Newberg 2000; Shapiro 2000; FTC 2002, 2003; Gilbert 2002; Glover 2002; Horn 2003; Lerner *et al.* 2003; Clarkson 2004, 2005). For example, firms in the semiconductor industry "find it all too easy to unintentionally infringe on a patent in designing a microprocessor, potentially exposing themselves to billions of dollars of liability and/or an injunction forcing them to cease production" (Shapiro 2000, p. 121). Heller and Eisenberg (1998) lament the "anticommons" in biomedical research due to the problem of patent thicketing. Particularly in the biopharmaceutical industry, patent thickets threaten the process of cumulative innovation because they act "as barriers to entry [that prevent new entrants] from using the technologies protected by such patent thickets" (Glover 2002, p. C10).

A recent FTC (2003) report notes that in certain industries the large number of issued patents makes it virtually impossible to search all the potentially relevant patents, review the claims contained in each of those patents, and evaluate the infringement risk or the need for a license. For the software industry the report cites testimony about the hold-up problems and points out "that the owner of any one of the multitude of patented technologies constituting a software program can hold up production of innovative new software" (2003, ch. 2, p. 3). For many firms, the only practical response to this problem of unintentional and sometimes unavoidable patent infringement is to file hundreds of patents each year to have something to trade during cross-licensing negotiations. In other words, the only rational response to the large number of patents in a given field may be to contribute to it.

The nanotechnology patent space experiences an even greater level of these problems because it is much more complicated than other technology areas. Because nanotechnology by definition encompasses a broad class of systems and materials, searching for nanotechnology-related publications and patents can be difficult, relative to other fields (Bawa 2004). Part of the complexity relates to the fact that nanotechnology spans a wide variety of already established fields. Because nanotechnology can be used in biomedical applications, the patent for a particular innovation may fall into the realm of biomedical patents. Likewise, a patent may be related to other such fields and classified in those fields. The present global patent classification systems are not sufficiently descriptive or designed to allow for the many unique properties that are inherent in nanotechnology innovations.

One study found that approximately 3700 patents issued between 2001 and 2003 contained one or more of several nanotechnology-related terms (Sampat 2004). These patents span 200 different US patent classes and were examined by 794 unique primary patent examiners; this last number is approximately one-quarter of the patent examiners employed by the United States Patent and Trademark Office (PTO) over this time period. As a result, a diverse group of examiners from a wide variety of backgrounds examined nanotechnology patent applications rather than examiners who could focus on nanotechnology attributes.

In order to address concerns stemming from the influx of new applications based on nanotech, the PTO announced in October 2004 that it had created a new classification for nanotechnology, Classification 977. This new classification defines nanotechnology very narrowly, however. According to the PTO, Class 977 provides for disclosures that are "(i) related to research and technology development at the atomic, molecular or macromolecular levels, in the length of scale of approximately 1–100 nanometer range in at least one dimension; and (ii) that provides a fundamental understanding of phenomena and materials at the nanoscale and to create and use structures, devices, and systems that have novel properties and functions because of their small and/or intermediate size."[1]

The creation of this new patent class did not solve the examiner problem identified by Sampat (2005), however, as a 2005 study of Class 977 by ETC Group notes that over 290 different primary patent examiners were assigned to evaluate the various Class 977 patents. This incredibly large number of examiners raises the concern that overlapping and conflicting patents could have been issued by different examiners at about the same time, with no knowledge of other such events occurring. The problem with granting such patents is obvious: if two companies with overlapping or conflicting patents unknowingly go to market with products based on these patents, it is likely that neither would have a claim superseding the other, leading to negative economic consequences to both firms. As such, the granting of those patents is in neither company's interest.

One patent examiner noted that while the creation of Class 977 is a noteworthy step, "it should be viewed as a starting point in a much larger effort to ensure that patent law develops smoothly with regard to nanotechnology." (Mouttet 2005, p. 260). Because many of the search terms used in the study by Sampat do not actually use the term "nanotechnology," it is very possible that those patents would be wholly assigned to different classifications where overlapping may occur. For example, patent thickets of overlapping patents may already be in place, given that a patent claiming a carbon nanotube would potentially conflict with similar patent applications claiming either carbonaceous cylinders or elongated cylinders. Although the recent formation of patent class 977 for Nanotechnology coupled with training for examiners in nanotechnology terminology and concepts may ameliorate the patent thicketing problem somewhat, ultimately innovators will still be forced to hack their way through these ever-burgeoning patent thickets. Because of these issues, the opportunity for collaboration and discussion between examiners on nanotechnology concerns is limited compared to other fields for which the PTO has instituted primary classification.

Related to the difficulties with classification of nanotechnology patents are the obstacles faced when searching the vast database of patents, a necessary step in both applying for patents as well as in prosecuting them. Due to the sheer

---

[1] Available at http://www.PTO.gov/go/classification/uspc977/defs977.htm

volume of material necessary to search through when conducting searches in the patent landscape, the utilization of automated techniques are necessary in order to comb through the variety of patents that have been filed. Zucker and Darby (2005) discussed one such way that nanotechnology research could be captured via NanoBank, although this proposal is more focused on the problem of overlapping research than on overlapping patents. As a result, this technique and other automated techniques are not effective when searching for "prior art" claims in nanotechnology due to the lack of a unified classification scheme for nanotech (Bawa 2004).

Another concern with the secondary nature of classifying nanotechnology in a patent application involves the possibility for applicants to author their applications so that specific nanotech terminology is omitted. Such omissions may be justified in order to prevent competitors from having access to key parts of the innovation with the expectation that the competitors would not be able to gain access to the knowledge that led to the invention.

A further problem with the new classification as a secondary classification leads directly to other problems with protections and prosecutions. The nanotech field lacks a standard terminology with which to describe the inventions in the nanotechnology sphere, leading to important difficulties in patenting these inventions (Molenda 2004). In many fields and industries, both technical and common terms are used in certain ways specific to that field in order to advance the understanding of various concepts in that field or industry. Because nanotechnology is such a relatively new field, the unique terminology has neither been established nor standardized; as a result, it may be difficult for applicants, examiners, and courts to understand the specific meanings behind the terminology used to describe these patents.

In his article on the importance of defining terminology in the nanotechnology field, Molenda (2004) discusses various notable cases in which such terminology was vital to the decision. In one court case addressing the question of terminology, the Court of Appeals for the Federal Circuit (CAFC)[2] stated that the terms in a patent claim "bear a 'heavy presumption' that they mean what they say and have the ordinary meaning that would be attributed to those words by persons skilled in the relevant art."[3] Importantly, the CAFC indicated that it should derive the "ordinary meaning" of claim terms from dictionaries, encyclopedias, and treatises.[4]

As Molenda points out, however, while the court should look to such reference sources to ascertain the meanings of the various terms used in patent applications, the definitions of the terms can vary widely. One such difference is illustrated by the variations in the definition of the word "crystal." Whereas *Webster's II New Riverside Dictionary* gives a relatively simple definition of

---

[2] The CAFC has exclusive jurisdiction over appeals involving patents.
[3] *Texas Digital Systems, Inc. vs. Telegenix, Inc.,* 308 F. 3d 1193, 1202 (2002).
[4] 308 F.3d at 1202-03.

the term, the *McGraw-Hill Encyclopedia of Science and Technology*, published the year after the *Webster* edition, provides a much more technical definition of the term.[5] The interpretation of this term would depend greatly upon which definition the court found to carry more weight within the scope of the particular patent in question. As a result, the lack of standardized technology within the field of nanotechnology could produce an element of uncertainty in patent prosecution that would not exist otherwise.

This difficulty is mitigated should the patent applicant define the terminology within the application itself. In one case involving an applicant who had included a lexicon of terminology within the application, the court looked to this lexicon in reaching an understanding of the terms in question.[6] As a result, applicants interested in the legal implications of a particular application should seek to define the terms employed in the application as clearly as possible to ensure that these terms are not misconstrued by either the patent court or competitors looking to appropriate the technology, thus avoiding unnecessary economic harm resulting from an unsuccessful patent prosecution.

The Constitutional mandate under which the PTO operates was designed to encourage innovation by inventors by providing short-term protection so that the inventor may develop the product in a reduced-competition environment. In return for this protection, the inventor agrees to make the application public so that others with interests related to the patent may improve upon the invention in the future. The field of nanotechnology is so dynamic that it presents distinctive problems. As Lemley (2005) discussed, the building blocks of so-called "enabling" technologies—computer software, hardware, the Internet, and biotechnology, among others—were left unpatented in earlier fields of invention. According to Darby and Zucker (2003), while patents are important for protecting particular biotechnology products, natural excludability provided important informal protection by slowing the dissemination of the requisite knowledge. Such is not the case in nanotechnology where firms and universities are looking to patent as much as possible as soon as possible (Lemley 2005).

IDENTIFYING NANOTHICKETS

So how has the rush to patent nanotechnology affected the patent landscape for nanotechnology? Although Clarkson's (2005) methodology for patent

---

[5] Page 169 of Webster's II New Riverside (Rev. ed. 1996) defines "crystal" as "A 3-dimensional structure made up of atoms, molecules or ions arranged in basic units that are repeated throughout the structure." McGraw-Hill Encyclopedia of Science & Technology 630 (8th edition 1997) defines "crystal" as "A solid in which the atoms or molecules are arranged periodically. ... In scientific nomenclature, the term crystal is usually short for *single crystal*, a single periodic arrangement of atoms. ... In electronics the term is usually restricted to mean a *single crystal* which is *piezoelectric*."(emphasis added).

[6] *3M Innovative Properties Co. vs. Avery Dennison Corp.,* 350 F.3d 1365 (Fed. Cir. 2003).

thicket detection is not yet fully applicable because no nanotechnology patent pools exist to evaluate, such mechanisms for mapping the patent space and identifying patent network density can still be applied because the nanotechnology patents and citations are available.

Clarkson's measure is derived from the standard network analytic measure of density. Social Network Analysis is a methodology developed by sociologists and organizational theorists to examine the social structure of groups. In this type of analysis, individuals are identified as the actors in a network, and the relationships between those actors identified are identified as ties. If the relationship from actor A to actor B can be different from the relationship from actor B to actor A, the network is referred to as a directed network (or directed graph).

While social network analysis, as a science, has been most commonly applied to describe complex dynamics in human interaction, the underlying theory and methodology is not limited to interpersonal relationships. Network analysis describes the relationships among nodes, be they people, computers, power stations, academic papers, or patents. Existing network analytic research in other areas of information sciences has concentrated on patterns of citation in literature and research (Price 1965, 1976; Redner 1998), and Newman (2000, 2001) has written extensively on the analysis of coauthorship networks within academic communities and scholarly publishing. Patents share many similar characteristics—citation practices in particular—to academic works, and that research is quite relevant. Patent space as an information network bears significant similarity to academic citation networks based on temporal limitations that specifically affect the directionality of linking vectors within a network. Similar to academic papers, a new entrant can only give citation to previous research or "prior art." Because of this linear path, patents that give rise to increased innovation can be seen as significant in creating lineages or families of technologies—possibly the seeds from which a patent thicket grows (Freeman 1979).

Previous work has demonstrated the methodological validity of using network analysis on patents. In an early study of patent networks, Podolny and Stuart (1995) developed the concept of a "technological niche" that included a focal innovation, the innovations on which the focal innovations built, the innovations that built upon the focal innovation, and the technological ties among the innovations within the niche. Using patents as the network nodes and patent citations as the network ties between nodes, they then were able to measure characteristics of innovation niches within the semiconductor industry to determine how subsequent innovations may or may not build upon the focal innovation. Those same authors used similar techniques in two subsequent articles. One article examined the evolution of technological positions among firms (Stuart and Podolny 1996), and the other examined organizational survival within technological niches (Podolny et al. 1996).

Not only did these early studies establish the methodological validity of applying network analytic techniques to patent networks in general, but much

TABLE 1. Nanoscale science and engineering keywords (Sampat 2004)

Atomistic simulation
Atomic force microscop∗
Biomotor
Molecular device
Molecular electronics
Molecular modeling
Molecular motor
Molecular sensor
Molecular simulation
Nano∗
Quantum computing
Quantum dot∗
Quantum effect∗
Scanning tunneling microscop∗
Self assembl∗
Self assembl∗

of their analysis of technological niches and competitive crowding was also based on a variation of *network density*, a fundamental network analytic concept (Marsden 1990; Wasserman and Faust 1994). As part of a study of patent thickets in electronics and medical devices, Clarkson made certain necessary modifications for the temporal constraints of patent networks. He also developed a modified density calculation for the patent space in order to examine patent thickets and calculate patent thicket densities and was able to demonstrate that patent thickets are objectively differentiable from the surrounding patent universe (Clarkson 2005).

To visualize the growing patent thicket in nanotechnology, we began by downloading front-page data for all of the patents issued since 2000 from the PTO's ftp site. We then searched the patent abstracts using the terms listed in TABLE 1 and identified 2998 nanotechnology patents issued between January 1, 2000 and December 31, 2004. Using an automated XML parser, we were able to extract the intragroup citations for the downloaded nanotechnology patents. In order to visualize the growth of the patent thicket, we utilized some of the network analytic techniques have been applied to patent spaces for purposes of visualization. Force-directed placement techniques (Fruchterman and Reingold 1991) have been used to present arrangements identifying complex information spaces (Schroeder 1999), and Clarkson (2005) previously incorporated this technique into a network analytic computational methodology for mapping patent space and visually identifying patent thickets.

To represent the temporal nature of nanothicket growth, we generated a series of graphs for each year of our data set. FIGURE 1 illustrates the relationships between patents in the nanotechnology space for the years 2000, 2002, and 2004. Each point in the figure represents one patent, and the edges denote a reference made by one patent to another in the space.

A report by Lux Research (2005) indicates that there may be multiple nanothickets, covering three separate platform technologies: dendrimers, quantum dots, and carbon nanotubes. According to their report, fullerenes and nanowires seem less crowded. Given the presence of ever increasing nanothickets covering at least three of five fundamental nanotechnology platforms, however, the logical next question would be what should firms do in response to the presence of nanothickets?

PATENT POOLS

Patent thickets are not a new phenomenon, and when the total number of owners of the conflicting intellectual property rights is small, the response to the patent thicket problem has often been to cross-license (Grindley and Teece 1997; Teece 1998, 2000). When more than two parties are involved, however, the transaction costs of cross-licensing between all of the parties can be prohibitive, and additional economic barriers exist such as hold-ups and double marginalization (Viscusi *et al.* 2000). In response to these challenges throughout the last 150 years, organizations have attempted to solve the multiparty patent thicketing problem by constructing patent pools. Usually, each firm assigns or licenses its individual intellectual property rights to a specific entity that in turn exploits the collective rights by licensing, manufacturing, or both. Different licensing arrangements are then available, depending on whether the licensee is a member of the pool and how the resulting royalties are subsequently distributed among the members of the pool.

While even the PTO has suggested patent pooling as a solution to the patent thicketing problem (Clark *et al.* 2000), the cooperative formation of patent pools by technologically competing firms has often encountered difficulty from an antitrust standpoint, even if the pool itself has procompetitive benefits. While the antitrust and intellectual property regimes were frequently in tension for most of the 20th century, with patent pooling often facing rather aggressive antitrust enforcement even in situations where the pool was procompetitive, recent developments indicate, however, that these two areas of law can be aligned so as to foster rather than stifle innovation. The 1995 *Guidelines for the Licensing of Intellectual Property* (*IP Guidelines*), jointly issued by the US Department of Justice (DOJ) and the Federal Trade Commission (FTC), formally acknowledged that collective ownership structures for intellectual assets, including patent pools, could potentially be procompetitive solutions to the patent thicket problem.

Although the revenues generated from sales of devices based in whole or in part on patent pool technologies are at least $100 billion US per year (Clarkson 2004), the patent pooling phenomenon has received few scholarly treatments, and most of those have been historical in nature. Vaughan (1925) describes patent pool formation in the late 19th and early 20th century and examines a

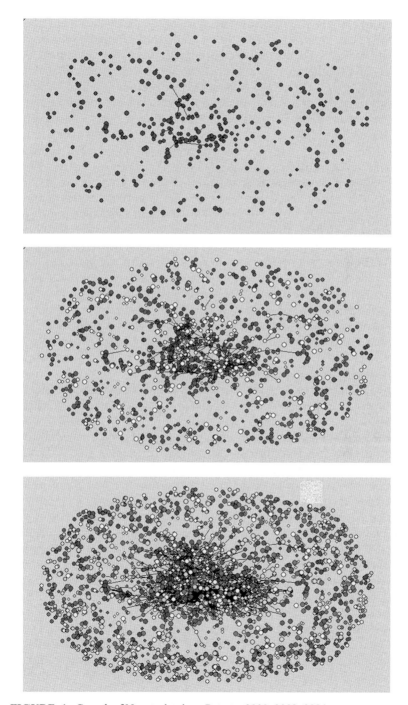

FIGURE 1. Growth of Nanotechnology Patents, 2000, 2002, 2004.

number of early pools. Three examinations of the phenomenon have been in the form of case studies. Cassady (1959) examines the formation and operation of a patent pool by Thomas Edison that aggregated all of the important patents for the early motion picture industry. Thompson (1987) describes the first patent pool, which was formed in the 19th century around intellectual property conflicts in the sewing machine industry. Bittlingmayer (1988) examines the formation of an aircraft patent pool during World War I. While many scholars have written favorably about patent pool formation (Vaughan 1925; Merges 1996, 1999; Newberg 2000), others have focused on potential competitive problems posed by patent pools (Priest 1977; Taylor 1992; Carlson 1999).

A number of economists have recently written on patent pools. Both Choi (2003) and Shapiro (2003) have examined patent pools in the context of patent litigation settlements constrained by antitrust law. In a different article specifically examining patent pools, Shapiro (2000) uses Cournot's (1838) original analysis of the "complements problem" to argue that patent pools raise welfare when patents are perfect complements and harm welfare when they are perfect substitutes. Work by Lerner and Tirole (2004) extends the analysis by examining the strategic incentives to form a pool in the presence of current and future innovations that are either substitutes for or complements to the patents in the pool. Their model allows examination of the full range between the polar cases of perfectly substitutable and perfectly complementary patents. Their paper concludes that while much research remains to be done, the construction of procompetitive pools is certainly possible. Stable pools can be formed by clearly defining patent essentialness and by scrutinizing the economic incentives provided to patent holders through pool membership versus independent licensing.

Lerner and Tirole's (2004) second paper on patent pools empirically examines the positive aspects of these arrangements, developing a set of theoretical predictions concerning the pool structure. They predict how the attributes of the pool vary with their key characteristics, such as the number of members of the pool and the rate of technical advance in the industry. They sample 63 pools established between 1895 and 2001 from the dockets of court cases, the archives of congressional hearings, and many other sources, to determine the actual structure of the pooling agreements. Their study concludes that the dynamics of management become more centralized as the pool grows larger. As pool membership increases, third-party licensing becomes more common. Such a finding is significant because restrictions on third-party licensing have historically been a trigger for antitrust scrutiny.

Gilbert (2002) reviews the antitrust treatment of patent pooling over the same time period and examines the factors that the courts identified as pertinent to the antitrust outcome. He concludes that until recently, the competitive relationship of the patents was not a major determinant of the antitrust outcome in most cases. Instead, he suggests that the courts have focused on restrictive licensing terms that affect downstream prices, although he argues that the competitive relationships between the patents should be the most important factor in assessing the procompetitiveness of a given pool.

Following Lerner *et al.*'s archival approach, Clarkson (2004) studied 101 patent pools that were at one time accused of antitrust violations by either the Antitrust Division of the DOJ, the FTC, or private antitrust actions between 1900 and 1970. The analysis indicated that a primary determinant of pool survival was an examination by the court of the existence of an underlying patent thicket. Clarkson (2005), however, notes the problems associated with a general lack of capability on the part of the antitrust regime to make an objective determination of the existence of a patent thicket, and he proposes such an objective measure based on patent thicket density.

Recent history also demonstrates the problematic nature of the antitrust regime's inability to objectively verify the existence of a patent thicket. On June 26, 1997, the DOJ issued a Business Review letter indicating that a patent pool based on MPEG-2, a technology standard for compactly representing digital video and audio signals for consumer distribution, was deemed not to be in violation of the antitrust laws of the United States. Less than a year later, however, on March 24, 1998, the FTC filed a complaint against a patent pool formed around photorefractive keratectomy (PRK), or laser eye surgery technology, and ultimately forced the pool to dissolve. Although the two pools had a number of similar characteristics, the antitrust regime gave its blessing to the MPEG pool but destroyed the PRK pool. According to Newberg (2000), the FTC litigation involving the PRK patent pool either ignored or failed to detect the underlying laser eye surgery patent thicket and did not see that the PRK pool was actually a procompetitive solution to the underlying patent thicket.

PATENT POOLS IN TWO CONVERGING TECHNOLOGIES

If patent pools in nanotechnology are to be a possible solution to nanotechnology patent thickets, they must be able to survive antitrust scrutiny. It is therefore instructive to briefly examine the divergent fates of these two recent patent pools involving the two best-established areas currently converging with nanotechnology, namely information technology and biotechnology.

The MPEG pool involves technology for digitally coded representation of moving pictures, audio, and their combination in compressed formats. The MPEG working group responsible for developing the technology standard is part of the International Telecommunication Union (ITU). Standard-setting organizations like the ITU are cognizant of the potential problem of patent thickets and have developed policies designed to prevent patent thickets from thwarting the adoption of standards-based technologies. For example, the ITU's Patent Policy provides that the holder of any known patent or any pending patent application related to any proposal made to the ITU in the process of standards-setting must submit a written statement, either waiving those patent rights or committing to negotiate licenses for those rights on a nondiscriminatory basis and on reasonable terms and conditions. Such licensing provisions are often referred to as Reasonable and Nondiscriminatory, or RAND.

Although the MPEG-1 standard was developed in 1989, the patent thicket challenges for the MPEG standards were not significantly addressed until after the release of the draft MPEG-2 standard in 1993. Given that the set of patents necessary to practice the MPEG-2 standard would come from a number of firms, the potential problem of double marginalization (Viscusi *et al.* 2000) had to be addressed in addition to the patent thicket issues,. As a result of the activities of informal meetings in 1992 and 1993 regarding intellectual property matters, a separate MPEG Intellectual Property Rights working group (MPEG IPR) was formed to specifically address issues such as: (*a*) how to identify which patent holders were willing to participate in this effort; (*b*) how to know whether they own rights necessary for implementation of MPEG-2 core technology; and (*c*) how to establish the entity's administrative structure as an ongoing effort that works with new licensees and licensers, the licensing structure, and the allocation of royalties.

Early on, the MPEG-2 community agreed on the need for an innovative way to overcome the underlying patent thicket. Otherwise, the difficulty of gaining access to a large enough body of the necessary MPEG-2 patents would jeopardize the interoperability and implementation of digital video. Since any licensing negotiations were left to the parties concerned and were performed outside of the ITU standard setting process, several of the key companies participating in the MPEG process were concerned that patent rights clearances would be an issue.

Following a series of meetings held in 1993 and 1994, the MPEG IPR working group reached a consensus about the creation and operation of the pool, and a licensing entity called MPEG LA was formed in order to administer the patent pool for virtually all of the patents essential to the MPEG-2 standard. While MPEG LA, did not have a track record of identifying essential patents, it did have a detailed written document that described the requirements for implementing the MPEG-2 standard. The *IP Guidelines* did not contain a working definition of either essentialness or patent thickets, but MPEG LA developed an objective third-party process that would prove not only the existence of a patent thicket but could also define its boundaries in terms of an objective determination of essentialness.

Another challenge facing MPEG LA was identifying the set of patents to compare against the standard. While those in the MPEG-2 process would have to abide by the RAND licensing policies required by the ITU standards bodies, it was by no means certain that essential patents would be held only by those participating in the standard setting process.

MPEG LA thus commissioned a massive study of the potentially relevant intellectual property throughout the world. While the study involved examining more than 8000 US patent abstracts, more than 1000 US patents, and more than 80 US patent prosecution histories, the prospects of getting potential pool members to submit their MPEG-relevant patents for evaluation and potential inclusion involved a certain level of uncertainty. In the laser eye surgery industry, however, the uncertainties were far more daunting.

Beginning in 1984, Dr. Charles Munnerlyn began to design an excimer laser surgical system that could be used to perform clinical surgery on the human eye without the use of scalpels or manually cutting the cornea. He partnered with a company called VISX to develop a system for the new procedure, which they called PRK. PRK showed tremendous promise for correcting nearsightedness and astigmatism. One of the primary obstacles to bringing PRK to market, however, was obtaining FDA approval. Because a PRK device would be a medical device, VISX spent tens of millions of dollars on FDA-mandated clinical trials, starting in 1987, before the FDA granted approval in 1996.

The commercialization of PRK by VISX faced another significant hurdle in the form of intellectual property issues as additional firms were developing laser refractive surgery devices, including Summit Technologies, which owned patents that potentially blocked VISX from implementing a PRK device. According to Josh Newberg, at the time a litigator at the FTC,

> With each of the firms vying for capital to finance the long lead time from prototype, through clinical trials, to FDA approval, Summit and VISX had to make educated guesses about the relative scope of each other's patent portfolios based on very limited information. The stakes were huge. If Summit was found to have a blocking position over VISX, it could exclude VISX from the marketplace altogether.[7]

In this instance the blocking situation was mutual, as VISX had patents that blocked Summit from fully implementing a PRK device, and vice versa (Newberg 2000). According to VISX CEO Mark Logan, the underlying patent thicket was suffocating both firms and "neither firm could raise any money without settling the patent issues."[8] While the patent thicket threatened to thwart the development of laser eye surgery altogether, both firms were eager to find a structure that would allow them to proceed with their FDA trials and ultimately bring a PRK device to market.

To solve their patent thicket problem, VISX and Summit formed a patent pool called Pillar Point Partners (P3) on June 3, 1992. Summit contributed 7 patents to the pool, and VISX contributed 18 patents. Collectively, these 25 patents contained more than 500 method and apparatus claims.

Having cleared the patent thicket for PRK for themselves, Summit and VISX returned to the marketplace and then competed vigorously against each other, including during the FDA clinical trial phase. Summit received FDA approval

---

[7] Interview with Josh Newberg, March 9, 2004. Professor Newberg left the FTC after the VISX litigation and is now a professor at the University of Maryland.

[8] Interview with Mark Logan, July 1, 2003.

in October of 1995, and VISX received FDA approval 5 months later. In the ensuing months, both firms expanded the PRK market as competitors, but they were soon challenged by the antitrust enforcement regime based on their cooperative effort to clear the PRK patent thicket.

ANTITRUST REVIEW

Any organization concerned about potential antitrust issues has the right to submit a proposed agreement or structure in advance to antitrust enforcement officials for evaluation. At the DOJ this process is called the Business Review Procedure.[9] The FTC has a similar procedure for issuing Advisory Opinions.[10] Preparing a request for *ex ante* antitrust review is both cumbersome and expensive, and many smaller companies do not submit such requests.

Given the troubled history of patent pools, the management of MPEG LA was justifiably concerned about antitrust scrutiny. Fortunately, however, the proposed MPEG-2 pool would be evaluated under the recently enacted provisions of the *IP Guidelines*, which explicitly acknowledge that patent pools may provide procompetitive benefits. Having crafted a structure as procompetitive as they thought possible, MPEG LA submitted its request for Business Review on April 28, 1997.[11] The DOJ issued a Business Review letter on June 26, 1997, stating that it was "not presently inclined to initiate antitrust enforcement action against the conduct"[12] proposed by MPEG LA.

The DOJ began its formal analysis of the proposed patent pool with an inquiry into the validity of the patents and their relationship to each other, stating that attempts to shield invalid or expired intellectual property rights would not withstand antitrust scrutiny. Assuming that all of the patents to be included in the pool were valid, and based on the representations of the complementary nature of those patents, the DOJ acknowledged that a package license for patents in a patent thicket "can be an efficient and pro-competitive method of disseminating those rights to would-be users."[13] In the case of MPEG, the DOJ indicated that it viewed the pool as a procompetitive aggregation of intellectual property. The DOJ's comfort with that position was enhanced by the fact that MPEG LA had used an independent expert to determine which patents were essential to comply with the MPEG-2 standard, thus objectively defining the boundaries of the underlying patent thicket.

The MPEG pool ultimately became the "gold standard" for patent pool formation, and a number of subsequent patent pools were formed following the

---

[9]   28 C.F.R. § 50.6.

[10]   16 C.F.R. § 1.1 *et sequation*

[11]   Letter from Garrard Beeney to Joel Klein, April 28, 1997.

[12]   Letter from Joel Klein, June 26, 1997, available at http://www.gov/atr/public/busreview/1170.htm

[13]   *Id.*

pattern set by MPEG. Each of those pools, however, was based on a standard. The lack of patent pool formation outside of the standards-based context may be due, in part, to the antitrust entanglements of the PRK pool, which did not have the benefit of a standard to demonstrate the existence of an underlying patent thicket.

Unlike MPEG LA, P3 did not submit its structure for antitrust review, and almost exactly two years after VISX received FDA approval to begin selling PRK devices in the United States, the FTC issued a complaint on March 24, 1998, alleging that Summit and VISX had violated the antitrust laws. The FTC's complaint contained several assumptions, however, which were core to its argument. Contrary to the assertions of VISX and Summit, the FTC disputed the existence of an underlying patent thicket. Critical to this position was the FTC's belief that the primary VISX patent was invalid, asserting that it had been obtained fraudulently by withholding relevant information from the PTO during prosecution. The FTC also implicitly assumed that VISX and Summit were no longer competing aggressively because of the existence of the P3 pool, despite the fact that the two firms were still competing with one another in the sale or lease of PRK equipment.

The FTC sought an order requiring VISX and Summit to dissolve the patent pool and prohibiting the firms from fixing the prices that doctors must pay to use the firms' PRK lasers. Faced with an aggressive and well-funded government agency, neither VISX nor Summit was in a position to put up much of a fight.

VISX and Summit settled with the FTC in August 1998, and agreed to dissolve the pool. The FTC continued to allege that the VISX patent was invalid, but VISX ultimately prevailed in a decision by an administrative law judge in June of 1999. Despite the FTC's initial allegations of fraud before the PTO, VISX was further vindicated when the PTO issued a reexamination certificate reaffirming the validity of the VISX patent in September 2000. The FTC then reopened the case and dismissed the complaint altogether in February 2001.

Could the PRK pool have been formed in such a way so as to survive antitrust scrutiny? Given the erroneous position that the FTC took on the VISX patent, the pool was likely doomed from the start. The approach taken by the FTC, however, is still subject to criticism, as many of the assumptions upon which it based its initial actions were shown to be suspect (Newberg 2000), which raises the question as to whether the FTC action was ultimately in the public interest.

Carl Shapiro (2000) raises two particularly thorny issues regarding patent thickets in analyzing the VISX and Summit result. First, if the two firms reasonably believed that their respective patent portfolios blocked each other at the time they formed the pool, was such a belief sufficient to justify the formation of a pool? How hard were they required to look into the validity of each other's patent claims before agreeing to form the P3 pool? Second, assuming that each firm believed it could work around the other's patents, would forcing them to do so ultimately benefit the consumer? Shapiro also questions the FTC's insistence that a cross-license was a superior alternative to a patent pool, as any new entrant would have to negotiate two separate licenses in order to access the necessary PRK patents.

When comparing the MPEG and PRK pools, Newberg (2000) suggests that certain differences may have been a function of their respective industries. In examining the MPEG pool, Newberg notes that the pool members are huge firms with enormous resources whose main business is not the licensing of these pooled patents, but rather, the manufacture and sale of telecommunications and consumer electronics hardware.

In contrast, Newberg points out that VISX and Summit were small start-up companies that were trying to create a completely new industry based on a technological innovation. They faced a capital-intensive technology, a long product development cycle, massive regulatory barriers, and potentially ruinous patent infringement litigation. For Summit and VISX, the laser refractive surgery business was the only business, and a single adverse patent ruling—or even the perception of vulnerability to adverse patent rulings—could dry up their capital and put them out of business (Newberg 2000, p. 28).

Newberg also justifies their license fee arrangement, noting that instead of trying to recover their capital investment by charging high machine prices, VISX and Summit presented the marketplace with a substantially lower machine acquisition cost compared to the actual cost of the machine. To make up for the lower revenues from machine sales, Newberg argues that VISX and Summit were justified in using the per-procedure fee as a kind of metering device, "the more the machines were used, the more money Summit and VISX would make in procedure fees" (Newberg 2000, p. 28). Newberg also identifies the benefit of using "the pooling arrangement to reduce the risk of [patent] litigation, while continuing to compete on machine sales, and also as a way of hedging the risk that one firm would receive FDA approval later, or perhaps not at all" (p. 28).

Although neither the DOJ nor the FTC specifically made an assessment of the existence or nonexistence of an underlying patent thicket, the DOJ was able to assume the existence of a thicket based on the procedures put forward by MPEG that were designed to evaluate the essentialness of patents submitted for pool inclusion.

Given the reliance on a standard for the determination of essentialness, the DOJ's assumption was a safe one. In the case of PRK pool, however, the FTC appears to have incorrectly assumed that no thicket existed and proceeded accordingly.

The MPEG and PRK pools were similar in many respects. They were both formed around emerging technologies in order to facilitate adoption of those technologies. They were also both formed around a collection of blocking and complementary patents. Ultimately, the MPEG patent pool appears to have survived the antitrust examination for two primary reasons. First, MPEG appears to have specifically crafted their pooling agreements in order to avoid antitrust problems using the *IP Guidelines*. Second, and certainly equally important, MPEG LA was able to develop an objective process that demonstrated the existence of a thicket coincident with the proposed pool.

NANOPOOLS AS A POSSIBLE SOLUTION
TO PATENT THICKETS

A firm with a nanotechnology patent that finds itself enmeshed in a patent thicket has a number of strategic options. It can sue anyone that it finds that may be potentially infringing its patent, but if it attempts to commercialize its patent, either it or its potential licensees face the same litigation risk from other nanotechnology patent holders. In addition, bringing a patent infringement action in court is expensive. According to the American Intellectual Property Law Association, the median cost for a patent litigation can often exceed $2 million and easily reach $4 million (AIPLA 2003). Particularly for startup firms, such costs could be prohibitive.

An alternative strategy would be for nanotechnology patent holders to form a patent pool, both clearing the nanothicket for that technology and facilitating "one-stop technology platform licensing" (Horn 2003). Such arrangements avoid the problems of double-marginalization and economic holdup by essential patent holders, and in the case of pools based on standards, have survived antitrust scrutiny.

The American National Standards Institute's Nanotechnology Standards Panel (ANSI-NSP) was established by ANSI in August 2004 in order for the major institutions with a stake in the nanotechnology industry to come together and work toward establishing a set of standards.[14] The goal of ANSI-NSP is to coordinate the agreement of such standards as nomenclature/terminology with which to communicate, as well as materials properties and measurement procedures to facilitate the commercialization of the variety of uses and applications of nanotechnology. As with the MPEG pool and similar standards-based pools such as IEE-1394 (Firewire) and DVDs, the standards document itself can provide ample guidance as to which patents are essential and thus should be included in the pool.

The standards-setting process for nanotechnology is in its infancy, however, and the prospects for the development of standards remain uncertain. Even if ANSI-NSP can develop some standards, there may be nanothickets for which

---

[14] American National Standards Institute. "About the Nanotechnology Standards Panel." Available at http://www.ansi.org/standards`activities/standards`boards`panels/nsp/overview.aspx. Accessed January 8, 2006.

standards have yet to be developed. In these areas, an alternate strategy would be needed to form a nanopool, but in the absence of a standard, extreme care should be exercised to avoid antitrust entanglements.

Nanothickets are growing, and firms will be forced to develop strategic responses. Whether nanopools are formed using standards or reference models, the nanopooling strategy provides a mechanism for clearing the nanothickets and bringing nanotechnology-based products to the marketplace.

ACKNOWLEDGMENTS

This research was supported in part by the National Science Foundation under Grant No. IIS 0425116. Research assistance was also provided by Lian Jian and Omer Kareem.

REFERENCES

AIPLA. 2003. *Report of the Economic Survey 2003.* American Intellectual Property Law Association. Washington, DC: Fetzer-Kraus, Inc.

BAWA, R. 2004. Nanotechnology patenting in the US. *Nanotechnology Law & Business Journal 1*(1), Article 5.

BITTLINGMAYER, G.L. 1988. Property rights, progress, and the Aircraft Patent Agreement. *Journal of Law and Economics 31*(1), 227–248.

CARLSON, S.C. 1999. Patent pools and the antitrust dilemma. *Yale Journal on Regulation 16*(2), 359–399.

CASSADY, R., Jr. 1959. Monopoly in motion picture production and distribution: 1908–1915. *Southern California Law Review 32*, 325–390.

CHOI, J. 2003. Patent Pools and Cross-Licensing in the Shadow of Patent Litigation. CESinfo Working Paper Series No. 1070. Available at http://ssrn.com.abstract-466062 (accessed November 17, 2006).

CLARK, J., J. PICCOLO, B. STANTON, and K. TYSON 2000. Patent pools: a solution to the problem of access in biotechnology patents? United States Patent and Trademark Office. Available at www.uspto.gov/web/offices/pac/dapp/opla/patentpool.pdf (accessed November 17, 2006).

CLARKSON, G. 2004. *Objective Identification of Patent Thickets: A Network Analytic Approach.* Harvard Business School Doctoral Thesis. Cambridge, MA: Harvard University.

CLARKSON, G. 2005. Patent informatics for patent thicket detection: a network analytic approach for measuring the density of patent space. Academy of Management Conference, Honolulu.

COURNOT, A.A. 1838. *Researches into the Mathematical Principles of the Theory of Wealth.* Tr. Nathaniel Bacon (New York: The Macmillan Co. 1897).

DARBY, M.R., and L.G. ZUCKER 2003. Grilichesian breakthroughs: inventions of methods of inventing and firm entry in nanotechnology. NBER Working Paper 9825. (National Bureau of Economic Research), available at http://www.nber.org/papers/w9825 (accessed November 17, 2006).

ETC. 2005. *Nanotech's 'Second Nature' Patents: Implications for the Global South.* ETC Group. Available at http://www.etcgroup.org/en/materials/publications. html?id=54 (accessed November 17, 2006).

FREEMAN, L.C. 1979. Centrality in social networks: conceptual clarification. *Social Networks 1*(1), 215–239.

FRUCHTERMAN, T.M.J., and E.M. REINGOLD 1991. Graph drawing by force-directed placement. *Software—Practice & Experience 21*(11), 1129–1164.

FTC. 2002. Patent pools and cross-licensing: when do they promote or harm competition? in *FTC Hearings on Competition and Intellectual Property Law and Policy in the Knowledge-Based Economy.* Washington, D.C. Federal Trade Commission.

FTC. 2003. *To Promote Innovation: The Proper Balance of Competition and Patent Law and Policy.* Washington, D.C. Federal Trade Commission.

GILBERT, R.J. 2002. *Antitrust for Patent Pools: A Century of Policy Evolution.* 2004 Stanford Technology Law Review 3.

GLOVER, G.J. 2002. Patent thickets and innovation markets reviewed. *National Law Journal 24*(56), C10.

GRINDLEY, P.C., and D.J. TEECE 1997. Managing intellectual capital: licensing and cross-licensing in semiconductors and electronics. *California Management Review 39*(2), 8–41.

HELLER, M.A., and R.S. EISENBERG 1998. Can patents deter innovation? The anticommons in biomedical research. *Science 280*(5364), 698–701.

HORN, L. 2003. Alternative approaches to IP management: one-stop technology platform licensing. *Journal Of Commercial Biotechnology 9*(2), 119–127.

LEMLEY, M.A. 2005. Patenting nanotechnology. *Stanford Law Review 58*, 601.

LERNER, J., and J. TIROLE 2004. Efficient patent pools.NBER. *American Economic Review 94*(3), 691–711.

LERNER, J., M. STROJWAS, and J. TIROLE 2003. *Cooperative Marketing Agreements Between Competitors: Evidence from Patent Pools.* Working Paper 9680 (National Bureau of Economic Research), available at http://www.nber.org/papers/w9680 (accessed November 17, 2006).

LUX. 2003. *The Nanotech Report 2003.* Lux Research Inc. New York.

LUX. 2005. *The Nanotech Intellectual Property Landscape.* Lux Research Inc. New York.

MARSDEN, P.V. 1990. Network data and measurement. *Annual Review of Sociology 16*, 435–463.

MERGES, R.P. 1996. Contracting into liability rules: intellectual property rights and collective rights organizations. *California Law Review 84*(5), 1293.

MERGES, R.P. 1999. *Institutions for Intellectual Property Transactions: The Case of Patent Pools.* Berkeley: University of California at Berkeley.

MOLENDA, J.J. 2004. The importance of defining novel terms in patenting nanotechnology inventions. *Nanotechnology Law & Business Journal 1*(1), Article 8.

MOUTTET, B. 2005. Nanotech and the U.S. patent & trademark office: the birth of a patent class. *Nanotechnology Law & Business Journal 2*(3), Article 5.

NEWBERG, J.A. 2000. Antitrust, patent pools, and the management of uncertainty. *Atlantic Law Journal 3*, 1–30.

NEWMAN, M.E.J. 2000. Who is the best connected scientist? A study of scientific coauthorship networks. Pp. 337–370 in E. Ben-Naim, H. Frauenfelder and Z. Toroczkai (eds.), *Complex Networks.* Berlin: Springer.

NEWMAN, M.E.J. 2001. The structure of scientific collaboration networks. *Proceedings of the National Academy of Sciences of the United States of America 98*, 404–409.

PODOLNY, J.M., and T.E. STUART 1995. A role-based ecology of technological change. *American Journal of Sociology 100*(5), 1224–1260.

PODOLNY, J.M., T.E. STUART, and M.T. HANNAN 1996. Networks, knowledge, and niches: competition in the worldwide semiconductor industry, 1984–1991. *American Journal of Sociology 102*(3), 659–689.

PRICE, D.d.S. 1965. Networks of scientific papers. *Science 149*(3683), 510–515.

PRICE, D.d.S. 1976. A general theory of bibliometric and other cumulative advantage processes. *Journal of the American Society for Information Science 27*, 292–306.

PRIEST, G.L. 1977. Cartels and patent licensing arrangements. *Journal of Law and Economics 20*, 309–377.

REDNER, S. 1998. How popular is your paper? An empirical study of the citation distribution. *European Physical Journal B, 4*(2), 131–134

SAMPAT, B. 2004. Examining patent examination: an analysis of examiner and applicant generated prior art. National Bureau of Economics, 2004 Summer Institute, Cambridge, MA.

SCHROEDER, M. 1999. Using singular value decomposition to visualise relations within multi-agent systems. Pp. 313–318 in *Third Annual International Conference on Autonomous Agents*. Seattle: ACM Press.

SHAPIRO, C. 2000. Navigating the patent thicket: cross licenses, patent pools, and standard-setting. *Innovation Policy and the Economy 1*, 119–150.

SHAPIRO, C. 2003. Antitrust limits to patent settlements. *Rand Journal of Economics 34*(2), 291–411.

STUART, T.E., and J.M. PODOLNY 1996. Local search and the evolution of technological capabilities. *Strategic Management Journal 17*(Special Issue: Evolutionary Perspectives on Strategy), 21–38.

TAYLOR, D.S. 1992. The sinking of the United States electronics industry within Japanese patent pools. *George Washington Journal of International Law and Economics 26*, 181–212.

TEECE, D.J. 1998. Capturing value from knowledge assets: the new economy, markets for know-how, and intangible assets. *California Management Review 40*(3), 55–79.

TEECE, D.J. 2000. *Managing Intellectual Capital*. Oxford: Oxford University Press.

THOMSON, R. 1987. Learning by selling and invention: the case of the sewing machine. *The Journal of Economic History 47*(2), 433–445.

VAUGHAN, F.L. 1925. Patent pools. Pp. 34-68 in *Economics of our Patent System*. New York: The Macmillan Company.

VISCUSI, W.K., J.M. VERNON, and J.E. HARRINGTON 2000. *Economics of Regulation And Antitrust*, 3rd ed. Cambridge, MA: MIT Press.

WASSERMAN, S., and K. FAUST 1994. *Social Network Analysis Methods And Applications*. New York: Cambridge University Press.

ZUCKER, L.G., and M.R. DARBY 2005. Socio-economic impact of nanoscale research: initial results and nanobank. NBER Working Paper No. 11181.

Converging Cognitive Enhancements

ANDERS SANDBERG[a] AND NICK BOSTROM[b]

[a]Oxford Uehiro Centre for Practical Ethics, Faculty of Philosophy, [b]Oxford Future of Humanity Institute, Faculty of Philosophy & James Martin 21st Century School, Oxford University, Oxford, OX1 1PT, United Kingdom

ABSTRACT: Cognitive enhancement, the amplification or extension of core capacities of the mind, has become a major topic in bioethics. But cognitive enhancement is a prime example of a converging technology where individual disciplines merge and issues transcend particular local discourses. This article reviews currently available methods of cognitive enhancement and their likely near-term prospects for convergence.

KEYWORDS: cognitive enhancement; cognition; intelligence; biotechnology; collective enhancement; mental training; converging technologies

CONVERGING COGNITIVE ENHANCEMENTS

There are few resources more useful than cognitive ability. While other resources are necessary or desirable, cognition enables them to be used for achieving personal goals. While there is little evidence that high intelligence causes happiness there appears to be ample evidence that low intelligence increases the risk for accidents, negative life events, and low income (Gottfredson 1997, 2004) while higher intelligence promotes health (Whalley and Deary 2001) and wealth. We also need better cognition in order to balance an increasingly complex society where information becomes more available and our actions have more far-reaching consequences (Heylighen 2002a, 2002b). There may also be an intrinsic existential value in being able to perceive, understand, and interact well with the world.

Cognitive enhancement may be defined as the amplification or extension of core capacities of the mind through improvement or augmentation of internal or external information processing systems. Cognition in turn can be defined as the processes an organism uses to organize information. This includes both the acquisition of information (perception), selecting (attention), representing (understanding), and retaining (memory) information, and using it to guide behavior (reasoning and coordination of motor outputs). Interventions to improve cognitive function may be directed at any one of these core faculties.

Address for correspondence: Anders Sandberg, Oxford Uehiro Centre for Practical Ethics, Faculty of Philosophy, Oxford University, Littlegate House, 16/17 St. Ebbe's St. Oxford, OX1 1PT. United Kingdom. Voice: +44(0)1865-286877; fax: +44(0)1865-286886.
e-mail: anders.sandberg@philosophy.ox.ac.uk

Ann. N.Y. Acad. Sci. 1093: 201–227 (2006). © 2006 New York Academy of Sciences.
doi: 10.1196/annals.1382.015

As cognitive neuroscience has advanced, the list of prospective internal, biological enhancements has steadily expanded (Farah *et al*. 2004). Yet to date, it is progress in information technology and cultural organization that has produced the most dramatic advances in our ability to process information. External hardware and software supports now routinely give human beings effective cognitive abilities that in many respects far outstrip those of our native minds, and institutions like peer review or markets.

There exists a long tradition in human–computer interaction dealing with cognitive enhancement, beginning with William Ross Ashby defining intelligence as the "power of appropriate selection," which could be technologically amplified similar to physical power (Ashby 1956). By offloading mental tasks to computers or embedding humans within a software context their cognitive functioning could be amplified (Licklider 1960). The aim was not artificial intelligence but rather amplifying human intelligence. The archetypal example of this approach is Douglas C. Engelbart's famous *Augmenting Human Intellect*, which defined the goal as:

> By 'augmenting human intellect' we mean increasing the capability of a man to approach a complex problem situation, to gain comprehension to suit his particular needs, and to derive solutions to problems. Increased capability in this respect is taken to mean a mixture of the following: more-rapid comprehension, better comprehension, the possibility of gaining a useful degree of comprehension in a situation that previously was too complex, speedier solutions, better solutions, and the possibility of finding solutions to problems that before seemed insoluble. And by 'complex situations' we include the professional problems of diplomats, executives, social scientists, life scientists, physical scientists, attorneys, designers—whether the problem situation exists for twenty minutes or twenty years. We do not speak of isolated clever tricks that help in particular situations. We refer to a way of life in an integrated domain where hunches, cut-and-try, intangibles, and the human 'feel for a situation' usefully co-exist with powerful concepts, streamlined terminology and notation, sophisticated methods, and high-powered electronic aids.

> Man's population and gross product are increasing at a considerable rate, but the *complexity* of his problems grows still faster, and the *urgency* with which solutions must be found becomes steadily greater in response to the increased rate of activity and the increasingly global nature of that activity. Augmenting man's intellect, in the sense defined above, would warrant full pursuit by an enlightened society if there could be shown a reasonable approach and some plausible benefits (Engelbart 1962).

An important insight was that it is not enough to improve just computer hardware and software, but psychological and organizational aspects have to be taken into account.

The cybernetic approach has in itself been technology independent by focusing on what is enhanced rather than the means of doing it. This unfortunately also causes disconnection from the richer social–ethical debate surrounding the other approaches, because they mostly take place within bioethics and medical ethics.

Studying cognitive enhancement solely in terms of bioethics, computer supported intelligence amplification or nanomedicine, risks missing the key commonalities. Converging technologies give a framework to approach the commonalities between different forms of human enhancement, as well as a way to contrast their differences and potential for divergence.

Criticisms of enhancements are often stated in a technology-independent form yet when analyzed from a converging technologies perspective they often show strong assumptions about a particular kind of technology. Those that are truly technology independent, even if originating within in a narrow area such as the genetics discourse, on the other hand raise relevant challenges for broad areas.

PHARMACEUTICAL BIOTECHNOLOGY

Today there exist a broad range of drugs that can affect cognition. Stimulant drugs like nicotine and caffeine are traditionally and widely used to improve cognition. In the case of nicotine a complex interaction with attention and memory occurs (Warburton 1992; Newhouse et al. 2004; Rusted et al. 2005) while caffeine reduces tiredness (Lieberman 2001; Smith et al. 2003; Tieges et al. 2004).

Lashley observed in 1917 that strychnine facilitates learning in rats (Lashley 1917). Since then several families of memory-enhancing drugs affecting different aspects of long-term memory have been discovered. They range from stimulants (Soetens et al. 1993; Lee and Ma 1995; Soetens et al. 1995), nutrients (Foster et al. 1998; Korol and Gold 1998; Winder and Borrill 1998; Meikle et al. 2005), and hormones (Gulpinar and Yegen 2004) over cholinergic agonists (Iversen 1998; Power et al. 2003; Freo et al. 2005) and the piracetam family (Mondadori 1996) to ampakines (Ingvar et al. 1997; Lynch 1998) and consolidation enhancers (Lynch 2002). The earliest drugs were mainly nonspecific stimulants and nutrients. For example, during antiquity honey water, hydromel, was used for doping purposes. Glucose is the major energy source for the brain, which relies on a continuous supply to function. Increases in availability (either due to ingestion or stress hormones) improve memory (Wenk 1989; Foster et al. 1998). Stimulants enhance either by increasing the amount of neuron activity or by releasing neuromodulators, both factors which make the synaptic change underlying learning more likely.

The growing understanding of memory allowed the development of more specific drugs. Stimulating the cholinergic system, which appears to gate attention and memory encoding, was a second step. Current interest is focused on intervening into the process of permanent encoding in the synapses, which has been elucidated to a great extent and hence has become a promising target for drug development. The goal would be drugs that not just allow the brain to learn quickly but also facilitate selective retention of the information that has been learned. It is known that the above families of drugs can improve performance in particular memory tests. It is not yet known whether they also promote useful learning in real-life situations.

Pharmacological agents might be useful not only for increasing memory retention, but also for unlearning phobias and addictions (Pitman *et al.* 2002; Ressler *et al.* 2004; Hofmann *et al.* 2006). Potentially, the combination of different pharmacological agents administered at different times could allow users a more fine-grained control of their learning processes, and perhaps even the ability to deliberately select the contents of their memory.

Even common, traditional, and unregulated herbs and spices, such as sage, can improve memory and mood through chemical effects (Kennedy *et al.* 2006). While less powerful than those of dedicated cholinesterase inhibitors, such effects illustrate that attempts to control access to cognition-enhancing substances would be problematic. Even chewing gum appears to affect memory, possibly by heightening arousal or blood sugar (Wilkinson *et al.* 2002).

Working memory can be modulated by a variety of drugs. Drugs that stimulate the dopamine system have demonstrated effects, as do cholinergic drugs (possibly through improved encoding) (Barch 2004). Modafinil has been shown to enhance working memory in healthy test subjects, especially at harder task difficulties and for lower performing subjects (Muller *et al.* 2004). (Similar findings, of greater improvements among low performers were also seen among the dopaminergic drugs, and this might be a general pattern for many cognitive enhancers.) On a larger battery of tasks, modafinil was found to increase forward and backward digit span, visual pattern recognition memory, spatial planning, and reaction time/latency on different working memory tasks (Turner *et al.* 2003). The reason might be that modafinil enhances adaptive response inhibition, making the subjects evaluate a problem more thoroughly before responding to it, thereby improving performance accuracy. The working memory effects might hence be part of a more general enhancement of executive function. A few other drugs may also improve executive function (Elliott *et al.* 1997; Kimberg *et al.* 1997; Mehta *et al.* 2000). Given that these functions are closely linked to what is commonly seen as intelligence, they may be the first step toward true intelligence-enhancing drugs.

Modafinil was originally developed as a treatment for narcolepsy, and can be used to reduce the performance decrements due to sleep loss with apparently small side effects and risk of dependency (Teitelman 2001; Myrick *et al.* 2004). The drug improved attention and working memory in sleep-deprived physicians (Gill *et al.* 2006) and aviators (Caldwell *et al.* 2000). Naps are more effective in maintaining performance than modafinil and amphetamine during long (48 h) periods of sleep deprivation than during short (24 h), but naps followed by a modafinil dose may be more efficient than either individually (Batejat and Lagarde 1999). These results, together with hormones like melatonin that can control sleep rhythms (Cardinali *et al.* 2002), suggest that drugs can help shape sleep and alertness patterns to improve task performance under demanding circumstances.

Creativity can also be affected pharmacologically. A study using alcohol demonstrated that a mild dose of alcohol could improve the results of a creative scientific process (Norlander and Gustafson 1996). The improvement only occurred when the subjects got the alcohol during the "incubation phase" of the creative process, the period when they were not actively working on the problem but presumably their unconscious might have been active. Giving alcohol in a picture-drawing task during the later verification phase did not promote creativity (Norlander and Gustafson 1997).

Creative thinking does not just include divergent and disinhibited thinking, but also requires convergent thinking to focus on the realization of the insight (Cropley 2006). Excessive divergence or lack of inhibition may be similar to the situation in attention deficit hyperactivity disorder (ADHD). Adult ADHD individuals show a profile of divergent thinking and do badly on convergent thinking and inhibition tasks (White and Shah 2006). Hence medications affecting ADHD might promote convergent thinking. Methylphenidate, the most common treatment and a potential executive function enhancer, did not appear to impair flexible thinking in ADHD individuals (Solanto and Wender 1989; Douglas *et al.* 1995). Giving L-dopa, a dopamine precursor, to healthy volunteers did not affect direct semantic priming (faster recognition of words directly semantically related to a previous word, such as "black-white") but did inhibit indirect priming (faster recognition of more semantically distant words, such as "summer-snow") (Kischka *et al.* 1996). This was interpreted by the authors of the study as dopamine inhibiting the spread of activation within the semantic network, that is, a focusing on the task.

There also exist drugs that influence how the cerebral cortex reorganizes in response to damage or training. Noradrenergic agonists, such as amphetamine, have been shown to promote faster recovery of function after a brain lesion when combined with training (Gladstone and Black 2000) and to improve learning of an artificial language (Breitenstein *et al.* 2004). A likely explanation is that higher excitability increases cortical plasticity, in turn leading to synaptic sprouting and remodeling (Stroemer *et al.* 1998; Goldstein 1999). An alternative to pharmacological increase of neuromodulation is to electrically stimulate the neuromodulatory centers that normally control plasticity through attention or reward. In monkey experiments this produced faster cortical reorganization (Kilgard and Merzenich 1998; Bao *et al.* 2001).

In general, pharmacological enhancement is possible here and now, although the improvements in ability tend to be a modest 10–20% improvement of test scores. As for all pharmacology, there are great interindividual variations. Using enhancer drugs optimally might include tests of neuromodulator levels to see where the brain setpoints are, pharmacogenomic tests to find how they are metabolized and neuropsychological tests to check what levels produce maximum performance. Such fine-tuning is expensive and cumbersome unless it can be automated.

OTHER BIOTECHNOLOGIES

Transcranial magnetic stimulation (TMS) stimulates neurons in the cerebral cortex by a changing magnetic field induced from a coil held to the head. It can increase or decrease the excitability of the cortex, thereby changing its level of plasticity (Hummel and Cohen 2005). TMS of the motor cortex that increased its excitability improved performance in a procedural learning task (Pascual-Leone *et al.* 1999). TMS in suitable areas has also been found beneficial in a motor task (Butefisch *et al.* 2004), motor learning (Nitsche *et al.* 2003), visuo-motor coordination tasks (Antal *et al.* 2004a, 2004b), working memory (Fregni *et al.* 2005), finger sequence tapping (Kobayashi *et al.* 2004), classification (Kincses *et al.* 2004), and even declarative memory consolidation during sleep (Marshall *et al.* 2004). Snyder *et al.* demonstrated how TMS inhibiting anterior brain areas could change the drawing style of normal subjects into a more concrete style and improve spell-checking abilities, presumably by reducing top-down semantic control (Snyder *et al.* 2003, 2004). While TMS appears to be highly versatile and noninvasive, there are risks of triggering epileptic seizures and the effects of long-term use are not known. Individual brain differences may necessitate much adjustment before it can be applied to a specific use.

Genetic memory enhancement has been demonstrated in rats and mice. In normal animals, during maturation expression of the NR2B subunit of the *N*-methyl-D-aspartate (NMDA) receptor is gradually replaced with expression of the NR2A subunit, something that may be linked to the lower brain plasticity in adult animals. Tsien's group (Tang *et al.* 1999) modified mice to overexpress the NR2B. The NR2B "Doogie" mice demonstrated improved memory performance, both in terms of acquisition and retention. This included unlearning of fear conditioning, which is believed to be due to the learning of a secondary memory (Falls *et al.* 1992). The modification also made the mice more sensitive to certain forms of pain, suggesting a nontrivial trade-off between two potential enhancement goals (Wei *et al.* 2001).

Increased amounts of brain growth factors (Routtenberg *et al.* 2000) and the signal transduction protein adenylyl cyclase (Wang *et al.* 2004) have also produced memory improvements. These modifications have different enhancing effects: unlearning took longer for these modified mice than for unmodified mice, while the mice in the Tsien study had faster than normal unlearning. Different memory tasks were also differently affected: the cyclase mice had enhanced recognition memory but not improved context or cue learning. A fourth study showed that mice with a deleted *cbl-b* gene had normal learning but enhanced long-term retention, presumably indicating that the gene is a negative regulator of memory (Tan *et al.* 2006). These enhancements may be due to changes in neural plasticity during the learning task itself, or that the developing modified brain develops in a way that promotes subsequent learning or retention.

The cellular machinery of memory appears to be highly conserved in evolution, making interventions demonstrated to work in animal models likely to have close counterparts in humans (Edelhoff et al. 1995; Bailey et al. 1996).

Genetic studies have also found genes in humans whose variations account for up to 5% of memory performance (de Quervain and Papassotiropoulos 2006). These include the genes for the NMDA receptor and adenylyl cyclase that were mentioned above, as well as other parts of the synaptic signal cascade. These are clear targets for enhancement.

Given these early results, it seems likely that there exist many potential genetic interventions that directly or indirectly improve aspects of memory. If it turns out that the beneficial effects of the treatments are not due to changes in development, then presumably some of the effects can be achieved by supplying the brain with the substances produced by the memory genes without resorting to genetic modification. But genetic modification would make the individual independent of an external drug supply and would guarantee that the substances end up in the right place.

On the other hand, studies of the genetics of intelligence suggests that there is a large number of genetic variations affecting individual intelligence, but each accounting for only a very small fraction (<1%) of the variance between individuals (Craig and Plomin 2006). This would indicate that genetic enhancement of intelligence through direct insertion of a few beneficial alleles is unlikely to have a big enhancing effect. It is possible, however, that some alleles that are rare in the human population could have larger effects on intelligence, either negative or positive. A possible example is the prediction that heterozygoticity for Tay-Sachs' disease should increase IQ by about 5 points (Cochran *et al.* 2006).

While human germline engineering is controversial, several years away and likely to be expensive, the genetic discoveries discussed here may be used for enhancement in other ways. Gene expression may be affected pharmacologically or even through food intake.

A notable form of chemical enhancement is pre- and perinatal enhancement through maternal nutrition. Administering choline supplementation to pregnant rats improved the performance of their pups, apparently as a result of changes in neural development in turn due to changes in gene expession (Meck *et al.* 1988; Meck and Williams 2003; Mellott *et al.* 2004). Given the ready availability of choline supplements, such prenatal enhancement, may already (inadvertently) be taking place in human populations. Supplementation of a mother's diet during late pregnancy and 3 months postpartum with long-chained fatty acids has also been demonstrated to improve cognitive performance in human children (Helland *et al.* 2003). Deliberate changes of maternal diet may hence be seen as part of the cognitive enhancement spectrum. At present, recommendations to mothers are mostly aimed at promoting a diet that avoids specific harms and deficits, but the growing emphasis on boosting "good fats" and the use of enriched infant formulas point toward enhancement.

COGNITIVE TECHNOLOGY

Education has many benefits beyond higher job status and salary. Longer education reduces the risks of substance abuse, crime, and many illnesses while improving quality of life, social connectedness, and political participation (Johnston 2004). There is also positive feedback between performance on cognitive tests, such as IQ tests and scholastic achievement, producing a 2.7 IQ point advantage per year of schooling (Winship and Korenman 1997). While education may be more of a social enhancement technology than a cognitive enhancement technology, it clearly has some potential for the latter.

Much of what we learn in school is "mental software" for managing various cognitive domains: mathematics, categories of concepts, language, and problem solving in particular subjects. This kind of mental software reduces our mental load through clever encoding, organization, or processing. Instead of memorizing arbitrarily large multiplication tables we compress the pattern of arithmetic relationships into simpler rules of multiplication, which in turn (among very ambitious students) can be organized into efficient mental calculation methods like the Trachtenberg system (Trachtenberg 2000). Such specific methods have a smaller range of applicability but can dramatically improve performance within a particular domain. They represent a form of crystallized intelligence, distinct from the fluid intelligence of general cognitive abilities and problem solving capacity (Cattell 1987). The relative ease and utility of improving crystallized intelligence and specific abilities have made them popular targets of internal and external software development. Cognitive enhancement attempts the more difficult challenge of improving fluid intelligence.

The challenge of improving education is perennial, and much hope is currently placed on using the results of neuroscience to improve education. However, so far pure neuroscience has provided few directly applicable tools (Goswami 2006). While this may change, the deep interdisciplinary divide that has to be bridged may prove a far greater challenge than most forms of technological convergence.

Pharmacological cognitive enhancements (nootropics) have physiological effects on the brain. So too do education and other conventional interventions. In fact, conventional interventions often produce more permanent neurological changes than do drugs. Learning to read alters the way language is processed in the brain (Petersson et al. 2000). Enriched rearing environments have been found to increase dendritic arborization and to produce synaptic changes, neurogenesis, and improved cognition in animals (Walsh et al. 1969; Greenough and Volkmar 1973; Diamond et al. 1975; Nilsson et al. 1999). While analogous controlled experiments cannot easily be done for human children, it is very likely that similar effects would be observed. Stimulation-seeking children, who might be seeking out and creating enriched environments for themselves, score higher on IQ tests and do better at school than less stimulation-seeking children (Raine et al. 2002). This also suggests that interventions that make exploring and learning more appealing to children, whether environmental or perhaps pharmaceutical, would have significant cognition-enhancing effects.

Enriched environments also make brains more resilient to stress and neu-rotoxins (Schneider *et al*. 2001). Reducing neurotoxins and preventing bad prenatal environments are simple and widely accepted methods of increasing cognitive function. These latter kinds of intervention might be classified as preventative or therapeutic rather than enhancing, although the distinction is blurry. For instance, an optimized intrauterine environment will not only help avoid specific pathology and deficits but is also likely to promote the growth of the developing nervous system in ways that ultimately *enhance* its core capacities.

In brains that have already been damaged, for example, by lead exposure, nootropics may alleviate some of the cognitive deficits (Zhou and Suszkiw 2004). It is not always clear whether they do this by curing the damage or by amplifying (enhancing) capacities that can compensate for the loss, or even whether the distinction is always meaningful. Comparing chronic exposure to cognition-enhancing drugs with an enriched rearing environment, one study found that both conditions improved memory performance and produced sim-ilar changes in the neural matter in rats. The improvements in the drug-treated group persisted even after cessation of treatment. The combination of drugs and enriched environment did not improve the rats' abilities beyond the im-provement provided by one of the interventions alone. This suggests that both interventions produced a more robust and plastic neural structure able to learn more efficiently.

Improving general health has cognition-enhancing effects. Many health problems act as distractors or directly impair cognition (Schillerstrom *et al*. 2005). Improving sleep, immune function, and general conditioning promotes cognitive functioning. Bouts of exercise have been shown to temporally im-prove various cognitive capacities, the size of the effect depending on the type and intensity of the exercise (Tomporowski 2003). Long-term exercise also improves cognition, possibly by a combination of increased blood supply to the brain and the release of nerve growth factors (Vaynman and Gomez-Pinilla 2005). Understanding this system may lead to new classes of nootropics, per-haps as a side effect of research into regenerative medicine.

Overall, improvements in the environment may be effective and widely ac-ceptable cognition enhancers, and conversely enhancement may help deprived individuals.

MENTAL TRAINING

Mental training and visualization techniques are widely practiced in elite sport (Feltz and Landers 1983) and rehabilitation (Jackson *et al*. 2004), with apparently good effects. Users vividly imagine themselves performing a task (running a race, going to a store), imagining every movement and how they feel again and again. A likely explanation for the efficacy of such exercises is that they activate the neural networks involved in executing a skill at the same time as the performance criteria for the task is held in close attention, optimizing neural plasticity and appropriate neural reorganization/ learning.

Even general mental activity, "working the brain muscle" can improve performance (Nyberg *et al.* 2003) and long-term health (Barnes *et al.* 2004), as can relaxation techniques to regulate the activation of the brain (Nava *et al.* 2004). It has been suggested that the Flynn-effect (Flynn 1987), a secular increase in raw intelligence test scores by 2.5 IQ points per decade in most western countries, can be attributed to increased demands of certain forms of abstract and visuospatial cognition in modern society and schooling, although improved nutrition and health status may also play a part (Neisser 1997; Blair *et al.* 2005). It appears that most of the Flynn effect does not reflect an increase in general fluid intelligence but rather a change in which specific forms of intelligence are developed.

The classic form of cognitive enhancement software is learned strategies to memorize information. Such methods have been used since antiquity with much success (Yates 1966; Patten 1990). One such classic strategy is "the method of loci." The user imagines a building, either real or imaginary, and in her imagination she walks from room to room, and places imaginary objects that evoke natural associations to the subject matter that she is memorizing. During retrieval, the user retraces her steps and the sequence of memorized information is recalled when she "sees" the objects she has placed along the route. This technique harnesses the brain's spatial navigation system to help remember objects or propositional contents. Other memory techniques makes use of rhyming or the fact that we more easily recall dramatic, colorful, or emotional scenes, which can serve as placeholders for items that are more difficult to retain, such as numbers or letters. The early memory arts were often used as a substitute for written text or to memorize speeches. Today, memory techniques tend to be used in service of everyday needs, such as remembering door codes, passwords, shopping lists, and by students who need to memorize names, dates, and terms when preparing for exams (Lorrayne 1996; Minninger 1997).

One study which compared exceptional memorizers (participants in the World Memory Championships) with normal subjects found no systematic differences in brain anatomy (Maguire *et al.* 2003). However, activity during encoding was different, likely reflecting the use of a deliberate encoding strategy. Especially areas of the brain involved in spatial representation and navigation were found to be consistently activated in the memorizers, regardless of whether the subjects were learning numbers, faces, or snowflakes. When asked about their memory strategies, nearly all memorizers reported using the method of loci.

In general it appears possible to attain very high memory performance on specific types of material using memory techniques. They work best on otherwise meaningless or unrelated information, such as sequences of numbers, but do not appear to help skilled everyday activities (Ericsson 2003).

There also exists a vast array of mental techniques alleged to boost various skills, such as creativity training, speed reading methods (Calef *et al.* 1999), and mind-maps (Buzan 1982; Farrand *et al.* 2002). It is unclear how widespread such techniques are, and good data regarding their efficacy is often lacking. Even if a technique improves performance on some task under particular conditions that does not necessarily mean that the technique is practically useful. In order for a technique to significantly benefit a person, it would have to be effectively integrated into her everyday work.

Of the mental training techniques, visualization may have the greatest potential for future development. While new memory arts can be developed the need for them is limited thanks to easily accessible external storage (the main exception may be remembering passwords). Serious studies of the efficiency of other mental techniques may be worthwhile. However, their specificity to particular tasks limits them. Methods of taking advantage of brain reorganization, possibly enhanced through nootropics and/or virtual reality training, appear to have general utility.

INFORMATION TECHNOLOGY

External hardware is of course already used for cognitive enhancement, be it pen and paper or computer software like personal organizers. This section can only scratch at the surface of the vast range of information technologies that have a cognitive enhancement function. There is practically no cognitive area where there does not exist external hardware or software amplification.

Many common pieces of software act as cognition-enhancing environments where the software helps give an overview, keep multiple items in memory, and perform routine tasks. Data mining and information visualization tools help produce overview and understanding where the perceptual system cannot handle the amount of data, while specialized tools like expert systems, symbolic math programs, decision support tools, and search agents expand specific skills and capacities.

What is new is the growing interest in creating intimate links between the external systems and the human user through better interaction. The software becomes less an external tool and more of a mediating "exoself." This can be achieved through mediation, embedding the human within an augmenting "shell," such as wearable computers (Mann 2001; Mann and Niedzviecki 2001) or virtual reality, or through smart environments, where capabilities of objects in the environment are extended. An example is the ubiquitous computing vision, in which objects would be equipped with unique identities and given ability to communicate with and to support the user (Weiser 1991). A well-designed environment can enhance proactive memory (Sellen *et al.* 1996) by deliberately bringing previous intentions to mind in the right context.

Another form of memory-enhancing exoself software is remembrance agents (Rhodes and Starner 1996), agents that act as a vastly extended associative memory. The agents have access to a database of previous information, such as a user's files, e-mail correspondence, etc., and suggest relevant documents based on the current context. Other exoself applications include additions to vision (Mann 1997), team coordination (Fan *et al.* 2005a, 2005b), face recognition (Singletary and Starner 2000), mechanical prediction (Jebara *et al.* 1997), and recording emotionally significant events (Healey and Picard 1998).

Given the availability of external memory support, from writing to wearable computers, it appears likely that the crucial form of memory demand will be the ability to link together information into usable concepts and associations rather than storage and retrieval of raw data. Storage and retrieval functions can be offloaded to a great extent from the brain, while the knowledge, strategies, and associations linking the data to skilled cognition so far cannot generally be offloaded.

Wearable computers and personal digital assistants (PDAs) are already intimate devices worn on the body, but there have been proposals for even tighter interfaces. Control of external devices through brain activity has been studied with some success for the last 40 years, although it remains a slow form of signaling (Wolpaw *et al.* 2000).

The most dramatic potential internal hardware enhancements are brain–computer interfaces. At present development is rapid both on the hardware side, where multielectrode recordings from more than 300 electrodes permanently implanted in the brain are currently state of the art, and on the software side, with computers learning to interpret the signals and commands (Carmena *et al.* 2003; Nicolelis *et al.* 2003; Shenoy *et al.* 2003). Early experiments on humans have shown that it is possible for profoundly paralyzed patients to control a computer cursor using just a single electrode (Kennedy and Bakay 1998) implanted in the brain and a 96 electrode prototype has been demonstrated (Hochberg *et al.* 2006). Prefrontal recordings enable choice selection with a bandwidth of 6.5 bits/s (Santhanam *et al.* 2006). Experiments in localized chemical release from implanted chips also suggest the possibility to use neural growth factors to promote patterned local growth and interfacing (Peterman *et al.* 2004).

Cochlear implants are already widely used, and there is ongoing research in artificial retinas (Alteheld *et al.* 2004) and functional electric stimulation for paralysis treatment (von Wild *et al.* 2002). These implants are mainly intended to ameliorate functional deficits and will hardly be attractive for healthy people in the foreseeable future. But the digital parts of the implant can in principle be connected to nearly any kind of software and external hardware (Hochberg *et al.* 2006). This would enable enhancing uses, such as access to software help, Internet, and virtual reality applications. It has been demonstrated that a healthy volunteer could control a robotic arm using tactile feedback, both in direct adjacency and remotely, as well as a wheelchair and perform simple neural communication with another implant (Warwick *et al.* 2003). Nondisabled people, however, would most likely achieve the same benefits through eyes, finger, and voice control. Neural implants are unlikely to become common enhancements until a "killer application" that cannot be achieved using external technology is found.

COLLECTIVE ENHANCEMENT

Much of human cognition is distributed across many minds and can be enhanced by developing more efficient forms of collaboration. Cooperative groups can detect deception better than individuals (Frank *et al.* 2004) and solve many problems better than equal numbers of individuals or even the best individuals (Laughlin *et al.* 2002; Kerr and Tindale 2004; Laughlin *et al.* 2006).

In general, the total ability of a group to perform a task increases with the size of the group as long as the members do not need to interact much. If they need to coordinate, the efficiency starts to drop as time has to be spent on coordination rather than work. In a densely connected group this eventually produces a situation where adding people reduces total performance. Reducing the density of the network by adding a hierarchy enables larger groups at the price of information bottlenecks. Social cognitive enhancement would act by either increasing the performance of individual group members (improving overall performance), improve their ability to coordinate (enabling larger groups), or improve the synergies generated by having multiple competencies.

This is an area ideally suited for embedding technologies that mediate group interactions. Virtual workspaces can enable improved pattern recognition (Hayne *et al.* 2003) and various forms of groupware attempts to facilitate collaboration. However, the greatest enhancements occur when very large groups can be facilitated: the World Wide Web and e-mail are among the most powerful kinds of cognitive enhancement software developed to date. Through the use of such social software, the distributed intelligence of large groups can be shared and harnessed for particular purposes (Surowiecki 2004).

Connected systems allow many people to collaborate in the construction of shared knowledge and solutions: the more individuals that connect, the more powerful the system becomes (Drexler 1991). The information is not just stored in the documents themselves but in their interrelations. When such interconnected information resources exist, automated systems, such as search engines (Kleinberg 1999), can extract a wealth of useful information from them.

Lowered coordination costs enable larger groups to work on common projects. Such groups of shared interests, such as amateur journalist "bloggers" and open source programmers, have demonstrated that they can successfully complete large projects, such as online political campaigns (Drezner and Farrell 2004), the Wikipedia encyclopedia, and the Linux operating system. Systems for online collaboration can incorporate efficient error correction (Raymond 2001; Giles 2005), enabling incremental improvement of product quality over time.

An interesting variant of knowledge aggregation is prediction markets (also known as "information markets" or "idea futures markets"). Here participants trade in predictions of future events, and the prices of these bets tend to reflect the best information available on the probability of whether the events will occur (Hanson et al. 2003). Such markets appear to be self-correcting and resilient, and have been shown to outperform alternative methods of generating probabilistic forecasts, such as opinion polls and expert panels (Hanson et al. 2006).

Social cognitive enhancement represents a convergence of not only information and cognitive technology, but sociology, management, and epistemology. In order to be successful a wide variety of factors must come together, making deliberate design hard. It may not be a coincidence that the most successful systems have been the most open, enabling many different groups to experiment and discover whether they can get it to work for their goals. We seldom notice the vast number of failed attempts because they are overshadowed by the explosive growth of successful systems.

NANOTECHNOLOGY

Nanotechnology has so far not been applied to cognitive enhancement, which is unsurprising given its early state. However, in basic neuroscience research many nanotechnology applications are in use or close to use. Fluorescent nanodots are used in neuroscience research, where they enable direct observation of biomolecule interaction (Mitchell 2001; Weng and Ren 2006). Nanostructured scaffolds are explored in tissue engineering (Silva et al. 2004) and nerve regrowth (Ellis-Behnke et al. 2006). One near future application with great promise is nanostructured neural interfaces (Cheung et al. 2002). Providing the right surface would both help improve signal quality and reliability. Nanoelectrodes may also be threaded through the capillary system, enabling low-invasive neurointerfacing (Llinas et al. 2005). At the very least nanotechnology is an enabler of neuroscience research relevant for cognitive enhancement.

Another near-term application pursued with much commercial interest is drug delivery through nanostructures (Panyam and Labhasetwar 2003; Sahoo and Labhasetwar 2003) or controlled-release microchips (Santini et al. 1999;

Grayson *et al.* 2003). This would enable precision pharmacology as well as possibly gene therapy.

It appears likely that as nanotechnology matures it will become an integral part of nearly all cognitive enhancement methods, be they light, powerful, and portable Internet interfaces or "smart drugs" that release modulators just when they are needed.

CONVERGING METHODS

As we have seen, many current applications already span disciplinary borders. Cognitive enhancement is based on the unity between the biological brain and the mind, and the unity between different kinds of information processing. Changing biological processes enables changes to the mind (and vice versa). Information processing is the same whether a brain or a computer does it. It hence lends itself well to the vision of converging technology.

Convergence enables many extensions of the current possibilities. As an example, take cortical plasticity. Currently it can be increased by attention, TMS, and drugs, such as amphetamines, in order to improve rehabilitation or learning. All three methods achieve the same goal using different means. Sustaining attention on a task requires motivation and can plausibly be improved using various forms of mental training; it has the benefit of being highly selective but requires significant effort. Current drugs are nonspecific and would increase plasticity in other cortical areas than the desired ones, besides effects on other parts of the brain. TMS is specific to a particular cortical area but requires training close in time and space to the stimulation equipment, and the task may be distributed over a large number of cortical areas.

Convergence easily suggests multiple ways these techniques can be improved. Improving TMS in terms of location specificity may be achieved by embedding micro- or nanoparticles close to the area to be modified (this may be particularly suitable for rehabilitation after neurosurgery) that augment the signal or help target it. By placing drugs within the particles they might promote nerve regrowth or dendritic sprouting, possibly triggered by external signals (Sershen and West 2002). The use of magnetic particles has already been explored to concentrate drugs to cancer tumors (Lubbe *et al.* 1996; Lubbe *et al.* 2001; Kim *et al.* 2006): the same mechanism could enable concentrating plasticity increasing drugs to the right cortical region even without surgery. More advanced particles or controlled-release microchips may able to sense local neuromodulator concentrations and regulate their drug release to amplify the selective effect of attention during training, making sure only the areas relevant to the training get affected.

On the macroscale, better sensor systems would enable improved understanding of individual brain chemistry, a prerequisite for finding the optimal combination of enhancer drugs. Wearable computing and other personal sensory devices enable the monitoring not only of body state but also behavior. This could enable personal data mining to find the individual optimum of, for example, blood glucose for different cognitive tasks by comparing it with monitored performance, and then based on measured glucose response to different meals suggest food intake that fits future scheduled demands. By pooling such individual data it would also be possible to make inferences on the general utility of different enhancer methods and the interactions between different factors. Rather than being a top-down academic study it might emerge as voluntary data sharing among users. This would represent an entirely new kind of epidemiological study. The difference is similar to the difference between the web-indices that seek to organize web sites into a predetermined subject hierarchy/ontology, and the current Web 2.0 experiments with generating "folksonomies" from locally tagged data (Shirky 2005). The challenges this form of "folk experimentation" poses in terms of data mining, scientific rigor (even if useful patterns are found the uncontrolled nature of the data may make strict interpretation hard), integrity concerns, and ownership concerns (are participants reimbursed for profitable discoveries?) are obviously great and may provide a very fruitful areas of research.

These scenarios are of course merely extrapolations at present, but demonstrate the synergistic potential of many current enhancement techniques.

DISCUSSION

Cognitive enhancement is already in widespread use, but not recognized as such. The morning coffee, the crossword, the e-mail program, and the cellphone are all part of our cognitive enhancement infrastructure. The new kinds of enhancement discussed in this article may appear unusual, futuristic, or problematic but will likely in time become as prosaic and accepted as the others.

It is easier to improve specialized abilities than general cognition. But the rewards are far greater for general cognition. It comes into play all the time, supporting many tasks—including uses we may not have thought of enhancing. Better memory may help education but it may also help remembering one's holiday memories and avoid forgetting keys. The overall societal impact of even a small increase in general cognitive function would likely be sizeable and desirable. Economic models of the loss caused by small intelligence decrements due to lead in drinking water predict significant effects of even a few points decrease (Salkever 1995; Muir and Zegarac 2001). Because the models are roughly linear for small changes, they can be inverted to estimate societal effects of improved cognition. The Salkever model estimates the increase in income due to one more IQ point to be 2.1% for men and 3.6% for women. (Herrnstein and Murray 1994) estimate that a 3% increase in overall

IQ would reduce the poverty rate by 25%, males in jail by 25%, high-school dropouts by 28%, parentless children by 20%, welfare recipients by 18%, and out-of-wedlock births by 25%.

Cognitive enhancement raises many ethical and social issues but also many practical challenges. Enhancements do have a price. In some cases it is a monetary price tag, but often it is a tradeoff between different abilities. Keeping awake using stimulants prevents the memory consolidation that would have taken place during sleep, and enhanced concentration ability may impair the ability to notice things in peripheral awareness. In some cases these tradeoffs can be predicted in terms of known biology or the evolutionary past of humans (Bostrom and Sandberg 2006), but often we will have to do an empirically based evaluation of what we individually value in a particular situation.

A major concern for all forms of enhancement is risk, both from enhancement itself and its effects (as well as its development in clinical trials). Enhancement users must decide when the benefits outweigh the potential risk, and how to estimate this on the basis of available information, personal goals, and their ways of life. These risks cannot always be accurately determined beforehand, nor may a user be able to defer to experts to judge whether the benefits are, to her, worth the risks. This poses a challenge to many current risk frameworks that are based on reducing the risk for the population at large: enhancement may be so individual and variable that it does not fit into a paternalistic framework. This challenge is further complicated because of the convergent nature of enhancement, which will bring different fields with conflicting risk concepts (e.g., medicine, education, and computing) into overlap. Developing a consistent, technology-independent risk management framework for converging technologies is an important task for the future, necessary for the eventual acceptance of general enhancement.

The reliability of research is also an issue. Many of the cognition-enhancing interventions show small effect sizes, which may necessitate very large epidemiological studies possibly exposing large groups to unforeseen risks.

One of the greatest challenges to developing effective cognitive enhancement is the current research model. Enhancers are tested within a laboratory setting for particular tasks. While this enables exact measurement and elimination of confounders, it does not test whether the enhancers aid real-life tasks and lifestyles. Ecological testing in real-life situations would be more relevant, but is far more expensive, time consuming, and hard to interpret. The "folk experimentation" scenario mentioned above might solve the first two problems but would likely worsen the third.

An interesting exception is military enhancement research, where studies in a more realistic (if still somewhat limited) setting are sometimes pursued. Civilian spin-offs from the current programs are likely, although the research ethics issues of military biomedical research are clearly nontrivial (cf. Pearn 2000; McManus et al. 2005 for a discussion of issues of captive subjects and informed consent).

A major challenge in developing human enhancement technologies is the need for interdisciplinary understanding. The problems facing "neuroeducation" and groupware have already been mentioned. While narrowly focused technical work is necessary, it may be that some of the most fruitful approaches will consist in creatively combining and applying work from multiple disciplines. Seeing cognitive enhancement as one field and as a general goal, rather than as multitude of unrelated pursuits, may enable us to spot many promising research questions and enhancement opportunities that would otherwise be overlooked.

REFERENCES

ALTEHELD, N., G. ROESSLER, M. VOBIG, and R. Walter. 2004. The retina implant new approach to a visual prosthesis. *Biomedizinische Technik 49*(4), 99–103.

ANTAL, A., M.A. NITSCHE, T.Z. KINCSES, ET AL. 2004a. Facilitation of visuo-motor learning by transcranial direct current stimulation of the motor and extrastriate visual areas in humans. *European Journal of Neuroscience 19*(10), 2888–2892.

ANTAL, A., M.A. NITSCHE, W. KRUSE, ET AL. 2004b. Direct current stimulation over V5 enhances visuomotor coordination by improving motion perception in humans. *Journal of Cognitive Neuroscience 16*(4), 521–527.

ASHBY, W.R. 1956. *Introduction to Cybernetics.* London: Chapman & Hall.

BAILEY, C.H., D. BARTSCH, and E.R. KANDEL. 1996. Toward a molecular definition of long-term memory storage. *Proceedings of the National Academy of Sciences of the United States of America 93*(24), 13445–13452.

BAO, S.W., W.T. CHAN, and M.M. MERZENICH. 2001. Cortical remodelling induced by activity of ventral tegmental dopamine neurons. *Nature 412*(6842), 79–83.

BARCH, D.M. 2004. Pharmacological manipulation of human working memory. *Psychopharmacology 174*(1), 126–135.

BARNES, D.E., I.B. TAGER, W.A. SATARIANO, and K. YAFFE. 2004. The relationship between literacy and cognition in well-educated elders. *Journals of Gerontology Series a-Biological Sciences and Medical Sciences 59*(4), 390–395.

BATEJAT, D.M., and D.P. LAGARDE. 1999. Naps and modafinil as countermeasures for the effects of sleep deprivation on cognitive performance. *Aviation Space and Environmental Medicine 70*(5), 493–498.

BLAIR, C., D. GAMSON, S. THORNE, and D. BAKER. 2005. Rising mean IQ: cognitive demand of mathematics education for young children, population exposure to formal schooling, and the neurobiology of the prefrontal cortex. *Intelligence 33*(1), 93–106.

BOSTROM, N., and A. SANDBERG. 2006. A Practical Approach to Human Enhancement. In J. Savulescu and N. Bostrom (eds.), *Enhancement of Human Beings.* Oxford: Oxford University Press, forthcoming.

BREITENSTEIN, C., S. WAILKE, S. BUSHUVEN, ET AL. 2004. D-amphetamine boosts language learning independent of its cardiovascular and motor arousing effects. *Neuropsychopharmacology 29*(9), 1704–1714.

BUTEFISCH, C.M., V. KHURANA, L. KOPYLEV, and L.G. COHEN. 2004. Enhancing encoding of a motor memory in the primary motor cortex by cortical stimulation. *Journal of Neurophysiology 91*(5), 2110–2116.

BUZAN, T. 1982. *Use Your Head*. London: BBC Books.

CALDWELL, J.A., Jr., J.L. CALDWELL, N.K. SMYTHE, 3rd, and K.K. HALL. 2000. A double-blind, placebo-controlled investigation of the efficacy of modafinil for sustaining the alertness and performance of aviators: a helicopter simulator study. *Psychopharmacology (Berlin) 150*(3), 272–282.

CALEF, T., M. PIEPER, and B. COFFEY. 1999. Comparisons of eye movements before and after a speed-reading course. *Journal of the American Optometric Association 70*(3), 171–181.

CARDINALI, D.P., L.I. BRUSCO, S.P. LLORET, and A.M. FURIO. 2002. Melatonin in sleep disorders and jet-lag. *Neuroendocrinology Letters 23*, 9–13.

CARMENA, J.M., M.A. LEBEDEV, R.E. CRIST, ET AL. 2003. Learning to control a brain-machine interface for reaching and grasping by primates. *Plos Biology 1*(2), 193–208.

CATTELL, R. 1987. *Intelligence: It's Structure, Growth, and Action*. New York: Elsevier Science.

CHEUNG, K.C., Y.-K. CHOI, T. KUBOW, and L.P. LEE. 2002. Nanostructured Electrodes for Improved Neural Recording. *Materials Research Society Spring 2002 Meeting*, San Francisco, CA. In R.P. Manginell, J.T. Borenstein, L.P. Lee, and P.J. Hesketh (eds.), *BioMEMS and Bionanotechnology MRS Proceedings*, Vol. 729, Section U4.9. Warrendale, PA: Materials Research Society.

COCHRAN, G., J. HARDY, and H. HARPENDING. 2006. Natural History of Ashkenazi Intelligence. *Journal of Biosocial Science 38*(5), 659–693.

CRAIG, I., and R. PLOMIN. 2006. Quantitative trait loci for IQ and other complex traits: single-nucleotide polymorphism genotyping using pooled DNA and microarrays. *Genes Brain and Behavior 5*, 32–37.

CROPLEY, A.J. 2006. In praise of convergent thinking. *Creativity Research Journal 18*(3), 391–404.

DE QUERVAIN, D.J.F., and A. PAPASSOTIROPOULOS. 2006. Identification of a genetic cluster influencing memory performance and hippocampal activity in humans. *Proceedings of the National Academy of Sciences of the United States of America 103*(11), 4270–4274.

DIAMOND, M.C., R.E. JOHNSON, and C.A. INGHAM. 1975. Morphological changes in young, adult and aging rat cerebral-cortex, hippocampus, and diencephalon. *Behavioral Biology 14*(2), 163–174.

DOUGLAS, V.I., R.G. BARR, J. DESILETS, and E. SHERMAN. 1995. Do high-doses of stimulants impair flexible thinking in attention-deficit hyperactivity disorder. *Journal of the American Academy of Child and Adolescent Psychiatry 34*(7), 877–885.

DREXLER, K.E. 1991. Hypertext publishing and the evolution of knowledge. *Social Intelligence 1*(2), 87–120.

DREZNER, D.W., and H. FARRELL. 2004. *The Power And Politics Of Blogs*. University of Chicago. Working paper. Available at http://www.utsc. utoronto.ca/~farrell/blogpaperfinal.pdf (accessed November 13, 2006).

EDELHOFF, S., E.C. VILLACRES, D.R. STORM, and C.M. DISTECHE. 1995. Mapping of adenylyl-cyclase genes type-I, type-Ii, type-Iii, type-Iv, type-V and type-Vi in mouse. *Mammalian Genome 6*(2), 111–113.

ELLIOTT, R., B.J. SAHAKIAN, K. MATTHEWS, ET AL. 1997. Effects of methylphenidate on spatial working memory and planning in healthy young adults. *Psychopharmacology 131*(2), 196–206.

ELLIS-BEHNKE, R.G., Y.X. LIANG, S.W. YOU, ET AL. 2006. Nano neuro knitting: peptide nanofiber scaffold for brain repair and axon regeneration with functional return of vision. *Proceedings of the National Academy of Sciences of the United States of America 103*(13), 5054–5059.

ENGELBART, D.C. 1962. *Augmenting Human Intellect: A Conceptual Framework*. Menlo Park, CA: Stanford Research Institute.

ERICSSON, A.K. 2003. Exceptional memorizers: made, not born. *Trends in Cognitive Sciences 7*(6), 233–235.

FALLS, W.A., M.J.D. MISERENDINO, and M. DAVIS. 1992. Extinction of fear-potentiated startle - blockade by infusion of an nmda antagonist into the amygdala. *Journal of Neuroscience 12*(3), 854–863.

FAN, X., S. SUN, M. MCNEESE, and J. YEN. 2005a. Extending the recognition-primed decision model to support human-agent collaboration. *AAMAS'05*. Utrecht, Netherlands.

FAN, X., S. SUN, J. YEN, ET AL. 2005b. Collaborative RPD-enabled Agents Assisting The Three-Block Challenge in C2CUT. *2005 Conference on Behavior Representation in Modeling and Simulation (BRIMS 2005)*. Universal City, CA, May 16–19.

FARAH, M.J., J. ILLES, R. COOK-DEEGAN, ET AL. 2004. Neurocognitive enhancement: what can we do and what should we do? *Nature Reviews Neuroscience 5*(5), 421–425.

FARRAND, P., F. HUSSAIN, and E. HENNESSY. 2002. The efficacy of the 'mind map' study technique. *Medical Education 36*(5), 426–431.

FELTZ, D.L., and D.M. LANDERS. 1983. The effects of mental practice on motor skill learning and performance—a meta-analysis. *Journal of Sport Psychology 5*(1), 25–57.

FLYNN, J.R. 1987. Massive IQ gains in 14 nations—what Iq tests really measure. *Psychological Bulletin 101*(2), 171–191.

FOSTER, J.K., P.G. LIDDER, and S.I. SUNRAM. 1998. Glucose and memory: fractionation of enhancement effects? *Psychopharmacology 137*(3), 259–270.

FRANK, M.G., N. PAOLANTONIO, T.H. FEELEY, and T.J. SERVOSS. 2004. Individual and small group accuracy in judging truthful and deceptive communication. *Group Decision and Negotiation 13*(1), 45–59.

FREGNI, F., P.S. BOGGIO, M. NITSCHE, ET AL. 2005. Anodal transcranial direct current stimulation of prefrontal cortex enhances working memory. *Experimental Brain Research 166*(1), 23–30.

FREO, U., E. RICCIARDI, P. PIETRINI, ET AL. 2005. Pharmacological modulation of prefrontal cortical activity during a working memory task in young and older humans: a PET study with physostigmine. *American Journal of Psychiatry 162*(11), 2061–2070.

GILES, J. 2005. Internet encyclopaedias go head to head. *Nature 438*(7070), 900–901.

GILL, M., P. HAERICH, K. WESTCOTT, K.L. GODENICK, and J.A. TUCKER. 2006. Cognitive performance following modafinil versus placebo in sleep-deprived emergency physicians: a double-blind randomized crossover study. *Academic Emergency Medicine 13*(2), 158–165.

GLADSTONE, D.J., and S.E. BLACK. 2000. Enhancing recovery after stroke with noradrenergic pharmacotherapy: a new frontier? *Canadian Journal of Neurological Sciences 27*(2), 97–105.

GOLDSTEIN, L.B. 1999. Amphetamine-facilitated poststroke recovery. *Stroke 30*(3), 696–697.

GOSWAMI, U. 2006. Neuroscience and education: from research to practice? *Nature Reviews Neuroscience 7*(5), 406–411.

GOTTFREDSON, L.S. 1997. Why g matters: the complexity of everyday life. *Intelligence* 24(1), 79–132.

GOTTFREDSON, L.S. 2004. Life, death, and intelligence. *Journal of Cognitive Education and Psychology* 4(1), 23–46.

GRAYSON, A.C.R., I.S. CHOI, B.M. TYLER, ET AL. 2003. Multi-pulse drug delivery from a resorbable polymeric microchip device. *Nature Materials* 2(11), 767–772.

GREENOUGH, W.T., and F.R. VOLKMAR. 1973. Pattern of Dendritic Branching in Occipital Cortex of Rats Reared in Complex Environments. *Experimental Neurology* 40(2), 491–504.

GULPINAR, M.A., and B.C. YEGEN. 2004. The physiology of learning and memory: role of peptides and stress. *Current Protein & Peptide Science* 5(6), 457–473.

HANSON, R., R. OPRE, and D. PORTER. 2006. Information aggregation and manipulation in an experimental market. *Journal of Economic Behavior & Organization* 60(4), 449–459.

HANSON, R., C. POLK, J. LEDYARD, and T. ISHIKIDA. 2003.. The policy analysis market: an electronic commerce application of a combinatorial information market. *ACM Conference on Electronic Commerce 2003*. New York: ACM Press.

HAYNE, S.C., C.A.P. SMITH, and D. TURK. 2003. The effectiveness of groups recognizing patterns. *International Journal of Human-Computer Studies* 59(5), 523–543.

HEALEY, J., and R.W. PICARD. 1998. StartleCam: a cybernetic wearable camera. *Second International Symposium on Wearable Computing*, Pittsburgh, PA, Washington, DC: IEEE Computer Society.

HELLAND, I.B., L. SMITH, K. SAAREM, ET AL. 2003. Maternal supplementation with very-long-chain n-3 fatty acids during pregnancy and lactation augments children's IQ at 4 years of age. *Pediatrics* 111(1), 39–44.

HERRNSTEIN, R.J., and C. MURRAY. 1994. *The Bell Curve*. New York, NY: Free Press.

HEYLIGHEN, F. 2002a. Complexity and information overload in society: why increasing efficiency leads to decreasing control. Available at http://pcp.lanl.gov/Papers/Info-Overload.pdf (accessed November 13, 2006).

HEYLIGHEN, F. 2002b. Tackling complexity and information overload : intelligence amplification, attention economy and the global brain. Available at http://pcp.lanl.gov/Papers/Info-Overload.pdf (accessed November 13, 2006).

HOCHBERG, L.R., M.D. SERRUYA, G.M. FRIEHS, ET AL. 2006. Neuronal ensemble control of prosthetic devices by a human with tetraplegia. *Nature* 442(7099), 164–171.

HOFMANN, S.G., A.E. MEURET, J.A.J. SMITS, ET AL. 2006. Augmentation of exposure therapy with D-cycloserine for social anxiety disorder. *Archives of General Psychiatry* 63(3), 298–304.

HUMMEL, F.C., and L.G. COHEN. 2005. Drivers of brain plasticity. *Current Opinion in Neurology* 18(6), 667–674.

INGVAR, M., J. AMBROSINGERSON, M. DAVIS, ET AL. 1997. Enhancement by an ampakine of memory encoding in humans. *Experimental Neurology* 146(2), 553–559.

IVERSEN, S.D. 1998. The pharmacology of memory. *Comptes Rendus De L Academie Des Sciences Serie Iii-Sciences De La Vie-Life Sciences* 321(2–3), 209–215.

JACKSON, P.L., J. DOYON, C.L. RICHARDS, and F. MALOUIN. 2004. The efficacy of combined physical and mental practice in the learning of a foot-sequence task after stroke: a case report. *Neurorehabilitation and Neural Repair* 18(2), 106–111.

JEBARA, T., C. EYSTER, J. WEAVER, T. STARNER, and A. PENTLAND. 1997. Stochasticks: augmenting the billiards experience with probabilistic vision and wearable computers. *The International Symposium on Wearable Computers*, Cambridge, MA, Washington, DC: IEEE Computer Society.

JOHNSTON, G. 2004. Healthy, wealthy and wise? A review of the wider benefits of education. *New Zealand Treasury Working Paper 04/04.* Wellington, New Zealand: The Treasury.

KENNEDY, D.O., S. PACE, C. HASKELL, ET AL. 2006. Effects of cholinesterase inhibiting sage (Salvia officinalis) on mood, anxiety and performance on a psychological stressor battery. *Neuropsychopharmacology 31*(4), 845–852.

KENNEDY, P.R., and R.A.E. BAKAY. 1998. Restoration of neural output from a paralyzed patient by a direct brain connection. *Neuroreport 9*(8), 1707–1711.

KERR, N.L., and R.S. TINDALE. 2004. Group performance and decision making. *Annual Review of Psychology 55*, 623–655

KILGARD, M.P., and M.M. MERZENICH. 1998. Cortical map reorganization enabled by nucleus basalis activity. *Science 279*(5357), 1714–1718.

KIM, J.S., T.J. YOON, B.G. KIM, ET AL. 2006. Toxicity and tissue distribution of magnetic nanoparticles in mice. *Toxicological Sciences 89*(1), 338–347.

KIMBERG, D.Y., M.D ESPOSITO, and M.J. FARAH. 1997. Effects of bromocriptine on human subjects depend on working memory capacity. *Neuroreport 8*(16), 3581–3585.

KINCSES, T.Z., A. ANTAL, M.A. NITSCHE, O. BARTFAI, and W. PAULUS. 2004. Facilitation of probabilistic classification learning by transcranial direct current stimulation of the prefrontal cortex in the human. *Neuropsychologia 42*(1), 113–117.

KISCHKA, U., T. KAMMER, S. MAIER, ET AL. 1996. Dopaminergic modulation of semantic network activation. *Neuropsychologia 34*(11), 1107–1113.

KLEINBERG, J.M. 1999. Authoritative sources in a hyperlinked environment. *Journal of the ACM 46*(5), 604–632.

KOBAYASHI, M., S. HUTCHINSON, H. THEORET, G. SCHLAUG, and A. PASCUAL-LEONE. 2004. Repetitive TMS of the motor cortex improves ipsilateral sequential simple finger movements. *Neurology 62*(1), 91–98.

KOROL, D.L., and P.E. GOLD. 1998. Glucose, memory, and aging. *American Journal of Clinical Nutrition 67*(4), 764s–771s.

LASHLEY, K.S. 1917. The effects of strychnine and caffeine upon rate of learning. *Psychobiology 1*, 141–169.

LAUGHLIN, P.R., B.L. BONNER, and A.G. MINER. 2002. Groups perform better than the best individuals on Letters-to-Numbers problems. *Organizational Behavior and Human Decision Processes 88*(2), 605–620.

LAUGHLIN, P.R., E.C. HATCH, J.S. SILVER, and L. BOH. 2006. Groups perform better than the best individuals on letters-to-numbers problems: effects of group size. *Journal of Personality and Social Psychology 90*(4), 644–651.

LEE, E.H.Y., and Y.L. MA. 1995. Amphetamine enhances memory retention and facilitates norepinephrine release from the hippocampus in rats. *Brain Research Bulletin 37*(4), 411–416.

LICKLIDER, J.C.R. 1960. Man-Computer Symbiosis. *IRE Transactions on Human Factors in Electronics HFE 1*, 4–11.

LIEBERMAN, H.R. 2001. The effects of ginseng, ephedrine, and caffeine on cognitive performance, mood and energy. *Nutrition Reviews 59*(4), 91–102.

LLINAS, R.R., K.D. WALTON, M. NAKAO, I. HUNTER, and P.A. ANQUETIL. 2005. Neurovascular central nervous recording/stimulating system: using nanotechnology probes. *Journal of Nanoparticle Research 7*(2), 111–127.

LORRAYNE, H. 1996. *Page a Minute Memory Book.* New York: Ballantine Books.

LUBBE, A.S., C. ALEXIOU, and C. BERGEMANN. 2001. Clinical applications of magnetic drug targeting. *Journal of Surgical Research 95*(2), 200–206.

LUBBE, A.S., C. BERGEMANN, H. RIESS, ET AL. 1996. Clinical experiences with magnetic drag targeting: a phase I study with 4'-epidoxorubicin in 14 patients with advanced solid tumors. *Cancer Research 56*(20), 4686–4693.

LYNCH, G. 1998. Memory and the brain: unexpected chemistries and a new pharmacology. *Neurobiology of Learning and Memory 70*(1–2), 82–100.

LYNCH, G. 2002. Memory enhancement: the search for mechanism-based drugs. *Nature Neuroscience 5*, 1035–1038.

MAGUIRE, E.A., E.R. VALENTINE, J.M. WILDING, and N. KAPUR. 2003. Routes to remembering: the brains behind superior memory. *Nature Neuroscience 6*(1), 90–95.

MANN, S. 1997. Wearable computing: a first step toward personal imaging. *Computer 30*(2), 25–31.

MANN, S. 2001. Wearable computing: toward humanistic intelligence. *IEEE Intelligent Systems 16*(3), 10–15.

MANN, S., and H. NIEDZVIECKI. 2001. *Cyborg: Digital Destiny and Human Possibility in the Age of the Wearable Computer.* Toronto, Canada: Doubleday Canada.

MARSHALL, L., M. MOLLE, M. HALLSCHMID, and J. BORN. 2004. Transcranial direct current stimulation during sleep improves declarative memory. *Journal of Neuroscience 24*(44), 9985–9992.

MCMANUS, J., S.G. MEHTA, A.R. MCCLINTON, R.A. DE LORENZO, and T.W. BASKIN. 2005. Informed consent and ethical issues in military medical research. *Academic Emergency Medicine 12*(11), 1120–1126.

MECK, W.H., and C.L. WILLIAMS. 2003. Metabolic imprinting of choline by its availability during gestation: implications for memory and attentional processing across the lifespan. *Neuroscience and Biobehavioral Reviews 27*(4), 385–399.

MECK, W.H., R.A. SMITH, and C.L. WILLIAMS. 1988. Prenatal and postnatal choline supplementation produces long-term facilitation of spatial memory. *Developmental Psychobiology 21*(4), 339–353.

MEHTA, M.A., A.M. OWEN, B.J. SAHAKIAN, ET AL. 2000. Methylphenidate enhances working memory by modulating discrete frontal and parietal lobe regions in the human brain. *Journal of Neuroscience 20*(6), RC65.

MEIKLE, A., L.M. RIBY, and B. STOLLERY. 2005. Memory processing and the glucose facilitation effect: the effects of stimulus difficulty and memory load. *Nutritional Neuroscience 8*(4), 227–232.

MELLOTT, T.J., C.L. WILLIAMS, W.H. MECK, and J.K. BLUSZTAJN. 2004. Prenatal choline supplementation advances hippocampal development and enhances MAPK and CREB activation. *FASEB Journal 18*(1), 545–547.

MINNINGER, J. 1997. *Total Recall. How to Boost Your Memory Power.* New York: MJF Books.

MITCHELL, P. 2001. Turning the spotlight on cellular imaging—advances in imaging are enabling researchers to track more accurately the localization of macromolecules in cells. *Nature Biotechnology 19*(11), 1013–1017.

MONDADORI, C. 1996. Nootropics: preclinical results in the light of clinical effects; comparison with tacrine. *Critical Reviews in Neurobiology 10*(3–4), 357–370.

MUIR, T., and M. ZEGARAC. 2001. Societal costs of exposure to toxic substances: economic and health costs of four case studies that are candidates for environmental causation. *Environmental Health Perspectives 109*, 885–903.

MULLER, U., N. STEFFENHAGEN, R. REGENTHAL, and P. BUBLAK. 2004. Effects of modafinil on working memory processes in humans. *Psychopharmacology 177*(1–2), 161–169.

MYRICK, H., R. MALCOLM, B. TAYLOR, and S. LAROWE. 2004 Modafinil: preclinical, clinical, and post-marketing surveillance—a review of abuse liability issues. *Annals of Clinical Psychiatry 16*(2), 101–109.

NAVA, E., D. LANDAU, S. BRODY, L. LINDER, and H. SCHACHINGER. 2004. Mental relaxation improves long-term incidental visual memory. *Neurobiology of Learning and Memory 81*(3), 167–171.

NEISSER, U. 1997. Rising scores on intelligence tests. *American Scientist 85*(5), 440–447.

NEWHOUSE, P.A., A. POTTER, and A. SINGH. 2004. Effects of nicotinic stimulation on cognitive performance. *Current Opinion in Pharmacology 4*(1), 36–46.

NICOLELIS, M.A.L., D. DIMITROV, J.M. CARMENA, ET AL. 2003. Chronic, multisite, multielectrode recordings in macaque monkeys. *Proceedings of the National Academy of Sciences of the United States of America 100*(19), 11041–11046.

NILSSON, M., E. PERFILIEVA, U. JOHANSSON, O. ORWAR, and P.S. ERIKSSON. 1999. Enriched environment increases neurogenesis in the adult rat dentate gyrus and improves spatial memory. *Journal of Neurobiology 39*(4), 569–578.

NITSCHE, M.A., A. SCHAUENBURG, N. LANG, ET AL. 2003. Facilitation of implicit motor learning by weak transcranial direct current stimulation of the primary motor cortex in the human. *Journal of Cognitive Neuroscience 15*(4), 619–626.

NORLANDER, T., and R. GUSTAFSON. 1996. Effects of alcohol on scientific thought during the incubation phase of the creative process. *The Journal of Creative Behavior 30*(4), 231–248.

NORLANDER, T., and R. GUSTAFSON. 1997. Effects of alcohol on picture drawing during the verification phase of the creative process. *Creativity Research Journal 10*(4), 355–362.

NYBERG, L., J. SANDBLOM, S. JONES, ET AL. 2003. Neural correlates of training-related memory improvement in adulthood and aging. *Proceedings of the National Academy of Sciences of the United States of America 100*(23), 13728–13733.

PANYAM, J., and V. LABHASETWAR. 2003. Biodegradable nanoparticles for drug and gene delivery to cells and tissue. *Advanced Drug Delivery Reviews 55*(3), 329–347.

PASCUAL-LEONE, A., F. TARAZONA, J. KEENAN, ET AL. 1999. Transcranial magnetic stimulation and neuroplasticity. *Neuropsychologia 37*(2), 207–217.

PATTEN, B.M. 1990. The history of memory arts. *Neurology 40*(2), 346–352.

PEARN, J. 2000. Medical ethics surveillance in the armed forces. *Military Medicine 165*(5), 351–354.

PETERMAN, M.C., J. NOOLANDI, M.S. BLUMENKRANZ, and H.A. FISHMAN. 2004. Localized chemical release from an artificial synapse chip. *Proceedings of the National Academy of Sciences of the United States of America 101*(27), 9951–9954.

PETERSSON, K.M., A. REIS, S. ASKELOF, ET AL. 2000. Language processing modulated by literacy: a network analysis of verbal repetition in literate and illiterate subjects. *Journal of Cognitive Neuroscience 12*(3), 364–382.

PITMAN, R.K., K.M. SANDERS, R.M. ZUSMAN, ET AL. 2002. Pilot study of secondary prevention of posttraumatic stress disorder with propranolol. *Biological Psychiatry 51*(2), 189–192.

POWER, A.E., A. VAZDARJANOVA, and J.L. MCGAUGH. 2003. Muscarinic cholinergic influences in memory consolidation. *Neurobiology of Learning and Memory 80*(3), 178–193.

RAINE, A., C. REYNOLDS, P.H. VENABLES, and S.A. MEDNICK. 2002. Stimulation seeking and intelligence: a prospective longitudinal study. *Journal of Personality and Social Psychology 82*(4), 663–674.

RAYMOND, E.S. 2001. *The Cathedral and the Bazaar.* Cambridge, MA: O'Reilly.

RESSLER, K.J., B.O. ROTHBAUM, L. TANNENBAUM, ET AL. 2004. Cognitive enhancers as adjuncts to psychotherapy—use of D-cycloserine in phobic individuals to facilitate extinction of fear. *Archives of General Psychiatry 61*(11), 1136–1144.

RHODES, B., and T. STARNER. 1996. Remembrance agent: a continuously running automated information retrieval system. *The First International Conference on The Practical Application Of Intelligent Agents and Multi Agent Technology (PAAM '96).* London (April 1996), pp. 486–495.

ROUTTENBERG, A., I. CANTALLOPS, S. ZAFFUTO, P. SERRANO, and U. NAMGUNG. 2000. Enhanced learning after genetic overexpression of a brain growth protein. *Proceedings of the National Academy of Sciences of the United States of America 97*(13), 7657–7662.

RUSTED, J.M., S. TRAWLEY, J. HEATH, G. KETTLE, and H. WALKER. 2005. Nicotine improves memory for delayed intentions. *Psychopharmacology (Berlin) 182*(3), 355–365.

SAHOO, S.K., and V. LABHASETWAR. 2003. Nanotech approaches to delivery and imaging drug. *Drug Discovery Today 8*(24), 1112–1120.

SALKEVER, D.S. 1995. Updated estimates of earnings benefits from reduced exposure of children to environmental lead. *Environmental Research 70*(1), 1–6.

SANTHANAM, G., S.I. RYU, B.M. YU, A. AFSHAR, and K.V. SHENOY. 2006. A high-performance brain-computer interface. *Nature 442*(7099), 195–198.

SANTINI, J.T., M.J. CIMA, and R. LANGER. 1999. A controlled-release microchip. *Nature 397*(6717), 335–338.

SCHILLERSTROM, J.E., M.S. HORTON, and D.R. ROYALL. 2005. The impact of medical illness on executive function. *Psychosomatics 46*(6), 508–516.

SCHNEIDER, J.S., M.H. LEE, D.W. ANDERSON, L. ZUCK, and T.I. LIDSKY. 2001. Enriched environment during development is protective against lead-induced neurotoxicity. *Brain Research 896*(1–2), 48–55.

SELLEN, A.J., G. LOUIE, J.E. HARRIS, and A.J. WILKINS. 1996. What brings intentions to mind? An in situ study of prospective memory. *Rank Xerox Research Centre Technical Report EPC-1996-104.* Cambridge, UK: Rank Xerox Research Centre.

SERSHEN, S., and J. WEST. 2002. Implantable, polymeric systems for modulated drug delivery. *Advanced Drug Delivery Reviews 54*(9), 1225–1235.

SHENOY, K.V., D. MEEKER, S.Y. CAO, ET AL. 2003. Neural prosthetic control signals from plan activity. *Neuroreport 14*(4), 591–596.

SHIRKY, C. 2005. Ontology is overrated: categories, links, and tags. Available at http://www.shirky.com/writings/ontology_overrated.html (accessed November 13, 2006).

SILVA, G.A., C. CZEISLER, K.L. NIECE, ET AL. 2004. Selective differentiation of neural progenitor cells by high-epitope density nanofibers. *Science 303*(5662), 1352–1355.

SINGLETARY, B.A., and T. STARNER. 2000. Symbiotic interfaces for wearable face recognition. *HCII2001 Workshop On Wearable Computing*, New Orleans, LA.

SMITH, A., C. BRICE, J. NASH, N. RICH, and D.J. NUTT. 2003. Caffeine and central noradrenaline: effects on mood, cognitive performance, eye movements and cardiovascular function. *Journal of Psychopharmacology 17*(3), 283–292.

SNYDER, A., T. BOSSOMAIER, and D.J. MITCHELL 2004. Concept formation: 'object' attributes dynamically inhibited from conscious awareness. *Journal of Integrative Neuroscience 3*(1), 31–46.

SNYDER, A.W., E. MULCAHY, J.L. TAYLOR, ET AL. 2003. Savant-like skills exposed in normal people by suppressing the left fronto-temporal lobe. *Journal of Integrative Neuroscience 2*(2), 149–158.

SOETENS, E., R. DHOOGE, and J.E. HUETING. 1993. Amphetamine enhances human-memory consolidation. *Neuroscience Letters 161*(1), 9–12.

SOETENS, E., S. CASAER, R. DHOOGE, and J.E. HUETING. 1995. Effect of amphetamine on long-term retention of verbal material. *Psychopharmacology 119*(2), 155–162.

SOLANTO, M.V., and E.H. WENDER. 1989. Does methylphenidate constrict cognitive-functioning. *Journal of the American Academy of Child and Adolescent Psychiatry 28*(6), 897–902.

STROEMER, R.P., T.A. KENT, and C.E. HULSEBOSCH. 1998. Enhanced neocortical neural sprouting, synaptogenesis, and behavioral recovery with D-amphetamine therapy after neocortical infarction in rats. *Stroke 29*(11), 2381–2393.

SUROWIECKI, J. 2004. *The Wisdom of Crowds: Why the Many Are Smarter Than the Few and How Collective Wisdom Shapes Business, Economies, Societies and Nations.* London: Random House.

TAN, D.P., Q.Y. LIU, N. KOSHIYA, H. GU, and D. ALKON. 2006. Enhancement of long-term memory retention and short-term synaptic plasticity in cbl-b null mice. *Proceedings of the National Academy of Sciences of the United States of America 103*(13), 5125–5130.

TANG, Y.P., E. SHIMIZU, G.R. DUBE, ET AL. 1999. Genetic enhancement of learning and memory in mice. *Nature 401*(6748), 63–69.

TEITELMAN, E. 2001. Off-label uses of modafinil *American Journal of Psychiatry 158*(8), 1341–1341.

TIEGES, Z., K. RICHARD RIDDERINKHOF, J. SNEL, and A. KOK. 2004. Caffeine strengthens action monitoring: evidence from the error-related negativity. *Brain Research. Cognitive Brain Research. 21*(1), 87–93.

TOMPOROWSKI, P.D. 2003. Effects of acute bouts of exercise on cognition. *Acta Psychologica 112*(3), 297–324.

TRACHTENBERG, J. 2000. *The Trachtenberg Speed System of Basic Mathematics.* London: Souvenir Press.

TURNER, D.C., T.W. ROBBINS, L. CLARK, ET AL. 2003. Cognitive enhancing effects of modafinil in healthy volunteers. *Psychopharmacology 165*(3), 260–269.

VAYNMAN, S., and F. GOMEZ-PINILLA. 2005. License to run: exercise impacts functional plasticity in the intact and injured central nervous system by using neurotrophins. *Neurorehabilitation and Neural Repair 19*(4), 283–295.

VON WILD, K., P. RABISCHONG, G. BRUNELLI, M. BENICHOU, and K. KRISHNAN. 2002. Computer added locomotion by implanted electrical stimulation in paraplegic patients (SUAW). *Acta Neurochirurgica Supplementum 79*, 99–104.

WALSH, R.N., O.E. BUDTZ-OLSEN, J.E. PENNY, and R.A. CUMMINS. 1969. The effects of environmental complexity on the histology of the rat hippocampus. *The Journal of Comparative Neurology 137*(3), 361–365.

WANG, H.B., G.D. FERGUSON, V.V. PINEDA, P.E. CUNDIFF, and D.R. STORM. 2004. Overexpression of type-1 adenylyl cyclase in mouse forebrain enhances recognition memory and LTP. *Nature Neuroscience 7*(6), 635–642.

WARBURTON, D.M. 1992. Nicotine as a cognitive enhancer. *Progress in Neuro-Psychopharmacology and Biological Psychiatry 16*(2), 181–191.

WARWICK, K., M. GASSON, B. HUTT, ET AL. 2003. The application of implant technology for cybernetic systems. *Archives of Neurology 60*(10), 1369–1373.

WEI, F., G.D. WANG, G.A. KERCHNER, ET AL. 2001. Genetic enhancement of inflammatory pain by forebrain NR2B overexpression. *Nature Neuroscience 4*(2), 164–169.

WEISER, M. 1991. The computer for the twenty-first century. *Scientific American 265*(3), 94–110.

WENG, J.F., and J.C. REN. 2006. Luminescent quantum dots: a very attractive and promising tool in biomedicine. *Current Medicinal Chemistry 13*(8), 897–909.

WENK, G. 1989. An hypothesis on the role of glucose in the mechanism of action of cognitive enhancers. *Psychopharmacology 99*, 431–438.

WHALLEY, L.J., and I.J. DEARY. 2001. Longitudinal cohort study of childhood IQ and survival up to age 76. *British Medical Journal 322*(7290), 819–822.

WHITE, H.A., and P. SHAH. 2006. Uninhibited imaginations: creativity in adults with attention-deficit/hyperactivity disorder. *Personality and Individual Differences 40*(6), 1121–1131.

WILKINSON, L., A. SCHOLEY, and K. WESNES. 2002. Chewing gum selectively improves aspects of memory in healthy volunteers. *Appetite 38*(3), 235–236.

WINDER, R., and J. BORRILL. 1998. Fuels for memory: the role of oxygen and glucose in memory enhancement. *Psychopharmacology 136*(4), 349–356.

WINSHIP, C., and S. KORENMAN. 1997. Does staying in school make you smarter? The effect of education on IQ in The Bell Curve. Pp. 215–234 in B. Devlin, S.E. Fienberg, and K. Roeder (eds.), *Intelligence, Genes, and Success: Scientists Respond to The Bell Curve*. New York: Springer.

WOLPAW, J.R., N. BIRBAUMER, W.J. HEETDERKS, ET AL. 2000. Brain-computer interface technology: a review of the first international meeting. *IEEE Transactions on Rehabilitation Engineering 8*(2), 164–173.

YATES, F. 1966. *The Art of Memory*. Chicago: University of Chicago Press.

ZHOU, M.F., and J.B. SUSZKIW. 2004. Nicotine attenuates spatial learning lead deficits induced in the rat by perinatal exposure. *Brain Research 999*(1), 142–147.

Affective Computing and Autism

RANA EL KALIOUBY,[a] ROSALIND PICARD,[a]
AND SIMON BARON-COHEN[b]

[a]Massachusetts Institute of Technology, Cambridge, Massachusetts 02142-1308,
USA

[b]University of Cambridge, Cambridge CB3 0FD, United Kingdom

ABSTRACT: This article highlights the overlapping and converging goals
and challenges of autism research and affective computing. We propose
that a collaboration between autism research and affective computing
could lead to several mutually beneficial outcomes—from developing
new tools to assist people with autism in understanding and operating
in the socioemotional world around them, to developing new computational models and theories that will enable technology to be modified to
provide an overall better socioemotional experience to all people who use
it. This article describes work toward this convergence at the MIT Media
Lab, and anticipates new research that might arise from the interaction
between research into autism, technology, and human socioemotional
intelligence.

KEYWORDS: autism; Asperger syndrome (AS); affective computing; affective sensors; mindreading software

AFFECTIVE COMPUTING AND AUTISM

Autism is a set of neurodevelopmental conditions characterized by social
interaction and communication difficulties, as well as unusually narrow, repetitive interests (American Psychiatric Association 1994). Autism spectrum conditions (ASC) comprise at least four subgroups: high-, medium-, and low-
functioning autism (Kanner 1943) and Asperger syndrome (AS) (Asperger
1991; Frith 1991). Individuals with AS have average or above average IQ and
no language delay. In the other three autism subgroups there is invariably some
degree of language delay, and the level of functioning is indexed by overall
IQ. Individuals diagnosed on the autistic spectrum often exhibit a "triad of
strengths": good attention to detail, deep, narrow interest, and islets of ability
(Baron-Cohen 2004). In this article we consider how such strengths could be
harnessed through the use of technologies to navigate the social world.

Address for correspondence: Rosalind W. Picard, Sc.D., FIEEE, MIT Media Laboratory, E15-448,
20 Ames Street, Cambridge, MA 02142-1308. Voice: 617-253-0611; fax: 617-253-5922.
e-mail: picard@media.mit.edu

Ann. N.Y. Acad. Sci. 1093: 228–248 (2006). © 2006 New York Academy of Sciences.
doi: 10.1196/annals.1382.016

Autism remains a behaviorally specified condition, the diagnosis relying on interviews and/or direct observations (LeCouteur *et al*. 1989; Lord *et al*. 1989, 1994, 2000). The diagnosis criteria include a "marked impairment in the use of nonverbal behaviors, such as eye-to-eye gaze, facial expression, body posture, and gestures to regulate social interaction," and rely on the clinician's judgment about the individual's ability to engage in social interactions, process social information and deal with social anxiety. Interventions, too, are mostly behavioral and are aimed at addressing the social interaction and communication difficulties in autism.

One of the central psychological themes in autism research is that of empathizing. Often characterized as the ability to "put oneself into another's shoes," empathizing is the capacity to attribute mental states, such as feelings, thoughts, and intentions to other people, and to respond to their mental states with an appropriate emotion (Mehrabian and Epstein 1972; Spiro 1993; Omdahl 1995; Eisenberg 2000; Harris 2003; Baron-Cohen and Wheelwright 2004). Empathy is a set of cognitive and affective skills we use to make sense of and navigate the social world (Davis 1983). The cognitive component of empathy, also referred to as theory of mind (Wellman 1992), mindreading (Whiten 1991; Baron-Cohen 1995), or taking the intentional stance (Dennett 1987), involves setting aside one's own current perspective, attributing mental states to the other person, and then making sense and predicting that person's behavior, given his or her experience. Mental states include emotions, cognitive states (such as beliefs), volitional states (such as intentions and desires), perceptual states (such as seeing or hearing), and attentional states (such as what the person is interested in). The affective component entails having an emotional response to the mental state of others. To be an empathic observer, your feeling must be appropriate to that of the person observed, for instance feeling compassion to another's distress.

Good empathizers also have good "people intuition" (sometimes known as folk psychology or common sense psychology). People intuition is the set of assumptions we make about the relationships between people's behavior, mental states, and situation (Wellman 1992). It is the basis for our social judgments about others, including the production and comprehension of pretence (Leslie 1987; Pratt and Bryant 1990), understanding that seeing-leads-to-knowing (Pratt and Bryant 1990), making the appearance-reality distinction, and understanding false belief (Wimmer and Perner 1983). When we empathize, we respond in ways that acknowledge feelings of others and we are sensitive to other's different beliefs and perspectives. In addition, empathizing allows us to share perceptual space with others, which is crucial for social learning, joint action, and joint attention (Baron-Cohen 1995). To make sense of a social situation, most people will naturally follow others' gaze direction. When people focus on nonsocial stimuli (e.g., background objects), as is often the case in autism, they may miss the gist in the social interaction (Klin *et al*. 2002, 2003).

Despite their interest in making friends, many individuals with autism report having difficulties empathizing in a spontaneous way during real-time social interaction and lacking people intuition. These difficulties vary with the severity of the condition, and include difficulty reading other peoples' non-verbal cues and mental states (Joseph and Tager-Flusberg 1997; Frith 2003), atypical gaze processing (Volkmar and Mayes 1991; Klin *et al*. 2002; Pelphrey *et al*. 2005), restricted emotional expression (Hill *et al*. 2004), difficulties gauging the interests of others in conversation (Fletcher *et al*. 1995; Volkmar and Klin 2000), and frequently launching into monologues about narrowly de-fined and often highly technical interests, such as railway tables or maps (Klin and Volkmar 1995).

Over the past 10 years, researchers in affective computing (Picard 1997) have begun to develop technologies that advance our understanding of or approach to affective neuroscience and autism. Affective computing has contributed to these fields in at least 4 ways: (i) designing novel sensors and machine learning algorithms that analyze multimodal channels of affective information, such as facial expressions, gaze, tone of voice, gestures, and physiology; (ii) creating new techniques to infer a person's affective or cognitive state (e.g., confu-sion, frustration, stress, interest, and boredom); (iii) developing machines that respond affectively and adaptively to a person's state; and (iv) inventing per-sonal technologies for improving awareness of affective states and its selective communication to others.

While much of the work in affective computing has been motivated by the goal of giving future robots and computational agents socioemotional skills, its researchers have also recognized that they face similar challenges to those who try to help people with autism improve such skills. Computers, like most people with autism, do not naturally have the ability to interpret socioaffective cues, such as tone of voice or facial expression. Similarly, computers do not naturally have common sense about people and the way they operate. When people or machines fail to perceive, understand, and act upon socioemotional cues, they are hindered in their ability to decide when to approach someone, when to interrupt, or when to wind down an interaction, reducing their ability to interact with others. A large part of natural learning involves reading and responding to socioemotional cues, so this deficit also interferes with the ability to learn from others. The field of affective computing aims to change the nature of technology so that it can sense, respond, and communicate this information. In so doing, the field has a lot to learn from people with autism, from progress they have made, and from the friends, families, and staff who work with these individuals. We should point out that we are *not* using autism as a metaphor, unlike the postautistic economics network (Post-Autistic Economics Network 2000) or Wegner's (1997) description of autistic algorithms. Our use of autism is restricted to the clinical definition.

A SYSTEMATIC APPROACH TO EMPATHY

So what do you do if, as in the cases of both autism and technology, empathizing is not something you naturally apply to the social world? You systemize. Systemizing is the drive to analyze and build systems and is one of the most powerful mechanisms to understand systems and predict change (Baron-Cohen, 2002). Systemizing involves sensing, pattern recognition, learning, inference, generalization, and prediction.

Persons diagnosed with ASC are extreme systemizers, showing intact or superior systemizing abilities, such as excellent attention to detail, islets of ability in topics like prime numbers, calendrical calculation, or classification of artifacts or natural kinds (Shah and Frith 1983; Jolliffe and Baron-Cohen 1997; Baron-Cohen *et al.* 2002; Baron-Cohen 2006). Many people with ASC attempt to systemize empathy, analyzing conversations and interactions, as it unfolds and for hours after it is over (Blackburn *et al.* 2000; Mixing Memory Blog 2005). For many, this is a tiring and draining exercise that makes it difficult to react in real time. As one person with an ASC put it:

> I study people almost to the point of obsession. I find some people's actions/motivations etc. extremely intriguing. Some people puzzle me. Often after I've had a conversation with someone I cannot sleep at night because I am analyzing the conversation. I rerun the whole thing, look at what went wrong and what didn't, work out what might have actually been meant by that, think about more accurate answers, etc. I also plan conversations ahead of time if I know I am going to have to talk to someone. In fact, conversations/social interactions all seem like a strategy game to me. You have to plan your moves in advance, work out all the possible ways the opponent might respond, and try and work out different courses of action for each of these. The only problem is, often in real time and life, the other person makes a move you haven't accounted for, resulting in the end of any conversation. Thus, while I spend vast amounts of time analyzing social situations, the practical side of things is still highly stressful and very hard to do successfully (Blackburn *et al.* 2000).

These first-hand accounts from people with autism stress that coping strategies are indeed needed for autism and suggest that systematic approaches to teaching empathy might be helpful. For example, recent interventions in autism providing computer-based methods of teaching emotion recognition have lead to an improvement in recognizing emotion (Golan *et al.* 2006). These accounts also illuminate the complexity of the social world and the challenges inherent in crafting a real-time intelligent response to high-speed complex and unpredictable information. There are no computational technologies that can perform feats of real-time socioemotional interaction. Today's most powerful robots perform much worse than people with autism at these challenges. Not only do they have difficulty understanding natural language, but they miss most of the socioaffective cues that can be used to decode the message. Robots also miss most of the facial and gestural cues, and cannot infer how these interact with what is said.

People with ASC who can systemize information about social situations can help researchers who are trying to build affective robots and agents, and future socioemotional technologies. For example, individuals with ASC tend to have a literal interpretation of what people say to them (Baron-Cohen 1988; Attwood

1998). Jonathan Bishop has developed a portable digital assistant (PDA) to help people with autism interpret frequently used idioms (Bishop 2003). For example, the system may explain that a comment, such as "Nice weather today," is not a statement of fact, which would be the literal interpretation, but an invitation to engage in casual conversation. The same technology can improve natural language processing in machines, helping them know how to better interpret what people say to them. These technologies need systematic ways to represent and handle social interactions, and people with autism have a unique ability to show researchers how to do this.

Systemizing empathy is an enormously challenging endeavor. For a start, the social world is a highly complex system of enormous variance (Baron-Cohen 2006). To date, there is no "code-book" available that maps a person's observed nonverbal cues to internal state and behavior. People with the same mental state may express these using different nonverbal cues, with varying intensities and durations. And people may use expressions that reflect mental states that are different from their true feelings or thoughts. Furthermore, when placed in the same situations, people may react differently. Empathizing is a highly uncertain process. We are never 100% sure of a person's mental state; instead, we infer mental states from observable behavior and contextual cues with varying degrees of certainty (Baron-Cohen 2003), and our average performance is probably far from 100%. For example, when shown face-videos, a panel of 18 people were only 54% accurate on labeling six categories of mental states, such as agreement, thinking, and confusion (el Kaliouby 2005).

Systemizing empathy is also challenging because affect is hard to measure (Picard *et al.* 2004). There are no continuous sensor systems that can reliably measure affective state. Without reliable sensors, how can we quantify exactly normal eye contact? There is a need to develop sensors, interfaces, signal processing, pattern recognition, and reasoning algorithms, for continuous tracking of a person's affective interactions. These technologies will be key in assessing an individual's specific areas of strengths and weaknesses, as well as measuring the efficacy of various interventions.

Affective computing over the past 10 years has been developing sensing and recognition technologies that, together with insights from people with ASC, may eventually facilitate systemizing the social world. In the next section we summarize several of the recent innovations that enable technology to sense affective states, and that have an obvious potential application to provide people with ASC with a direct "print out" of other's mental states. One of the biggest obstacles to empathy and mindreading that people with ASC report is that they cannot easily detect and read another's mental states—that they are largely unobservable. Affective computing highlights how such internal states are not wholly unobservable, that there are indicators that can make mental states more transparent or magnified, and that if these can be detected by technology, the human observer can make use of them.

AFFECT SENSING

The ability to sense a person's affective-cognitive state is the first step in mindreading. Despite many advances in brain imaging, there is not yet any technology that can read your innermost thoughts and feelings and communicate this to another. However, there are a growing number of portable sensors that can capture various physical manifestations of affect. These novel sensors are like perceptual mechanisms. Examples include tiny video camcorders to record facial expression, head gesture and posture changes, microphones to record vocal inflection changes, skin-surface sensing of muscle tension, heart-rate variability, skin conductivity, blood-glucose levels, and other bodily changes. Although they started off as bulky, affective "wearables" are now embedded in jewelry or woven into clothing (Picard and Healey 1997). Affective wearables are different to existing medical devices that measure similar signals, in that the wearer is in control. The wearer can take it off, or turn it off, or leave it, choosing when and where to gather information. The analogy is with a hearing aid or a pair of spectacles.

We have developed several kinds of systems for communicating affective information at the MIT Media Laboratory. FIGURE 1 shows portable forms of affective sensors, from left to right: expression glasses, blood-volume pulse earring, pressure-sensitive mouse, galvactivator, chest-worn heart monitor, and skin-conductance shoe. Here are some brief highlights about some of the wearable or portable devices:

(i) *Expression glasses* discriminate facial expressions of interest or surprise from those of confusion or dissatisfaction, allowing students to communicate feedback anonymously to the teacher in real time, without having to shift attention from trying to understand the teacher (Scheirer *et al.* 1999).

(ii) The *Galvactivator* is a skin-conductance sensing glove that converts level of skin conductance to the brightness of a glowing LED (Picard and Scheirer 2001). Skin conductance increases with many kinds of autonomic arousal, especially ramping up with novelty, significance, and stress. Hirstein's team (Hirstein *et al.* 2001) highlighted differences in skin conductance patterns among many people with autism. This glove can help wearers reflect on their personal response patterns.

FIGURE 1. Portable forms of affective sensors.

(iii) *StartleCam* is a wearable camera system that saves video based on a physiological response, such as your skin conductance arousal response, tagging the data with information about whether or not it was exciting to you (Healey and Picard 1998).

(iv) Affective state can also be inferred from the way we interact with and manipulate objects. An increase in physical pressure applied to a *pressure-sensitive mouse* has been shown to be associated with frustration, caused by poor usability in a computer interface (Qi *et al.* 2001; Qi and Picard 2002; Dennerlein *et al.* 2003).

(v) Location, proximity, audio and motion sensors signal socioaffective displays, such as dominance, excitement, and nonaggression, across populations (Pentland 2006).

More recent wearables that are made by industry include:

(i) The *SenseWear Pro2 armband* measures changes in energy expended, energy balance and weight loss using a heat-flux sensor, skin temperature, galvanic skin response, an accelerometer, and an electrocardiogram (ECG) sensor attached on the upper arm. Even though the armband is not specifically being marketed as an affective technology, it could be modified to detect and communicate affect variables to the wearer and to others, for example, monitoring and analyzing patterns of stress, frustration, and productivity.

(ii) *EmSense Corporation* is developing small, wearable sensors including dry ECGs that create a model of a user's emotions.

(iii) *Fraunhofer* has developed a research prototype glove that senses heartbeat, breathing rate, blood pressure, skin temperature and conductance, and an ECG shirt using conductive yarn and flexible electronics.

(iv) Goodwin's team used a *wireless heart rate monitor* (LifeShirt, Vivometrics, Inc., Ventura, CA) to monitor the cardiac responses of low-functioning persons with autism under repeated conditions of environmental stressors (Goodwin *et al.* 2006).

The above technologies are all at varying degrees of development and availability. But we can also speculate about other possible technologies that could become available, such as *swallowable pills* or *implantable sensors*, that analyze bodily fluids for hormones and neurotransmitter levels. For example, levels of dopamine act on voluntary movement and emotional arousal, producing effects, such as an increased heart rate and blood pressure; serotonin affects sleep and temperature. Drawing on research that links food, affect, and cognition to circadian rhythm (Wurtman and Danbrot 1988), affect-sensing swallowable pills would measure hormone and neurotransmitter levels and then send the measurements wirelessly to on-body portable devices. While neurotransmitter levels are currently not easy to sense without drawing saliva or blood or using other invasive procedures, and the data is not made available wirelessly, new implantable and swallowable sensors are already in progress, exploiting nanoscale technology.

As with any wearable system however, there are design issues. Wearable systems are certainly becoming smaller, but there are still issues with the number of wires flowing in and out of the sensors and with sensors slipping off. Battery power is a challenging issue too. Finally, sensors-on-the-go need to be robust to noise that arises from activity unrelated to the signal being measured. Heart rate, for example, can increase significantly with physical exertion or with sneezing, as well as with anger. Addressing these challenges is a prerequisite for the adoption of these wearable systems in everyday applications.

AFFECT RECOGNITION, LEARNING, AND GENERALIZATION

In her doctoral dissertation, Rana el Kaliouby (2005) developed a computational model of mindreading as a framework for machine perception and mental state recognition. This framework combines bottom-up vision-based processing of the face (e.g., a head nod or smile) with top-down predictions of mental state models (e.g., interest and confusion) to interpret the meaning underlying head and facial signals over time. The framework comprises multilevel, probabilistic architecture which mimics the hierarchical way with which people perceive facial and other human behavior (Zacks *et al.* 2001) and handles the uncertainty inherent in mindreading. The output probabilities represent a rich modality analogous to the information humans receive in everyday interaction through mindreading. FIGURE 2 shows the real-time output of the mindreading software showing different granularity of head gesture and facial analysis. The horizontal bars show the probability of various head gestures and facial expressions. The bottom line graphs show the probabilities of the mental states; the radial chart summarizes an interaction, showing the most likely mental states over time.

This model allows also multiple asynchronous sensors to be combined. One view of autism, the "weak central coherence" theory, emphasizes the importance of sensory integration. The theory contends that people with ASC process information at the local (rather than the Gestalt) level, often failing to integrate multiple sources of sensory information (Happé 1966; Frith 2003). If the primary deficit in autism is indeed one of integrating information at a global level, it is easy to imagine how theory of mind or empathy would suffer. This is because different affective modalities often complement each other, or substitute for each other when only partial input is available, or may contradict one another as in deception. Thus, compared with unimodal systems that assume a one-to-one mapping between an affective state and a modality, multimodal systems yield a more faithful representation of the relationship between mental states and external behavior. Our MIT group continues to develop novel approaches to combine multiple modalities, such as face and

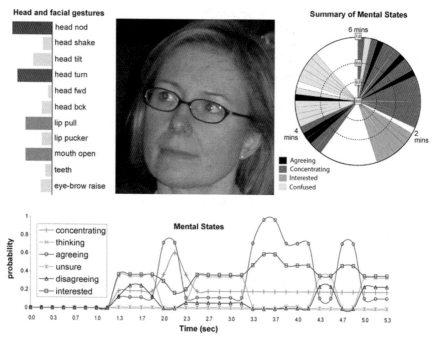

FIGURE 2. Real-time output of the mindreading software.

posture, to infer affective states, such the level of engagement (interest versus boredom), of learners (Kapoor *et al.* 2004, 2005).

Another challenge is generalization. Generalization is the capacity to apply knowledge from one context to new contexts. In autism, it is uncertain whether with existing interventions, individuals are able to successfully transfer the knowledge they acquire. Computers also have problems generalizing from the examples they were trained on, to the analysis of new unseen information. The field of machine learning is perpetually trying to improve the ability of computers to generalize. With the advent of more robots and agents that will interact with people, there is increased interest in enabling machines to learn better by learning from people in natural colearning situations, not just from people who "program" the computer or robot (Breazeal 2002). But such learning again requires socioemotional skills, such as the ability to see if the person teaching you is shaking their head and frowning.

As part of what we call the socioemotional intelligence prosthesis, we are exploring new kinds of systems that learn with people through natural interaction (el Kaliouby and Robinson 2005; el Kaliouby *et al.* 2006). The intelligent system we aim to build is a colearner with the person with ASC in trying to learn how to recognize and respond to socioemotional cues (Picard *et al.* 2004). One possibility for such a system is to exploit this common learning goal and perhaps play games with the individual, to assist him or her with continuously learning to generalize, occasionally bringing in non-ASC experts for corrective feedback and validation. The non-ASC person(s) could be present physically, or remotely connecting in through the technology, to help with the learning process. Social or emotion tagging, a situation where the parents and/or caregivers of a child with autism accompany the child and "tag" events with social labels, is a promising approach albeit expensive and impractical. Through the use of a head-mounted wearable camera/microphone, parents and caregivers could "eyejack" the child's visual field and tag the world remotely. This is both practical and cost-effective; it allows the child to be more independent, while continuing to enable parents and caregivers to share experiences with the child and help with learning.

TECHNOLOGIES THAT ENHANCE EMPATHIZING

Many persons with ASC prefer to communicate with and through computers because they are predictable and place some control on the otherwise chaotic social world (Moore *et al.* 2000). How can we harness their interest in technology to systemize the social world? For young children and those at the lower end of the autism spectrum, sociable robotics and dolls are a good approach to helping social interaction skills. The use of robots allows for a simplified, predictable, and reliable environment where the complexity of interaction can be controlled and gradually increased. It is also more realistic and engaging than interacting with a screen. The *Affective Social Quotient* project is one of the early projects at MIT Media Lab to develop assistive technologies for autism using physical input devices, namely four dolls (stuffed dwarfs), which appeared to be happy, angry, sad, or surprised (Blocher and Picard 2002). The system would play short digital videos that embody one of the four emotions, and then encourage the child to choose the dwarf that went with the appropriate emotion. When the child picked up the stuffed toy, the system identified its infrared signal and responded. Use of the dolls as physical input devices also encouraged development of joint attention and turn-taking skills, because typically another person was present during the session. Other robot platforms have been used for autism intervention, encouraging social behavior, such as turn-taking and shared attention (Dautenhahn *et al.* 2002; Scassellati 2005). Robotics may also be useful for individuals at the higher end of the autism spectrum, who would need help with the subtle, real-time social interactions. One can imagine a variation of LEGO—already known to be helpful as an intervention in autism (LeGoff 2004)—that combines rules and mechanics to allow for social explorations. Robotics could also be used by groups of children for improvisation, and directing play, encouraging turn-taking between children.

Affect sensing and affect recognition are technologies that are readily applicable to autism interventions. Affect sensing and recognition technologies can

FIGURE 3. The self-cam chest-mounted video camera.

help increase self-awareness, and provide novel ways for self-monitoring. One of the first problems we encountered when having a person wear a camera with software to interpret the facial expressions of a conversational partner was that the person with ASD might not even look at the face of the other person. Thus, the wearable camera might point at the floor or at a shirt pocket, or a nearby object instead of at the face that needs to be read. One possible solution is via a device, such as the *eye contact sensing glasses* (Vertegaal *et al.* 2001), wearable glasses that recognize when a user is in eye contact with another person. These glasses can be used to measure the magnitude and dynamics of eye contact in people with ASC. These patterns can then be compared to eye contact in people without ASC. It can also be used as an intervention to encourage people with ASC to pay more attention to the face.

   In some cases there are privacy concerns with wearing a camera that records those around you. Out of such concerns, Alea Teeters in our lab developed the *self-cam* shown in FIGURE 3 (Teeters *et al.* 2006). Self-Cam is a small, lightweight video camera that is worn over the chest and points at one's face.

The camera is connected to a small portable handtop that is belt-mounted on the hip, and has a built-in microphone for recording audio. Facial expression analysis software on the handtop identifies head and facial gestures (e.g., head nod and smile) and mental states (e.g., agreement, confusion and interest). In the real-time mode, the camera tracks and analyses the mental state of its wearer in real time, and communicates these mental state inferences to the wearer visually or via audio clips and/or tactile vibration. Self-Cam only records the face of the wearer, which solves privacy problems related to filming other people in the environment without their consent. If more than one person is wearing the Self-Cam, this information can be exchanged between different wearers. Thus, Self-Cam is a fun way for people to explore social situations that are relevant to them (e.g., the faces of family and friends) without accidentally recording data from people who do not want to be recorded. It also avoids the problems mentioned above of having to make sure the camera sees a face, because self-cam is almost always pointed directly at the wearer's face.

In a forthcoming collaboration between MIT Media Lab and the Groden Center—a school and intervention center for autism based in Providence, Rhode Island—we will evaluate the scientific and clinical significance of using Self-Cam to improve the recognition of emotions from faces in young adults with AS and high-functioning autism. In the study, the person with ASC as well as the interaction partner (a teacher) will each wear a Self-Cam, so that neither participant feels singled out. Wearers will review the videos recorded during the sessions and interact with the computerized facial analysis software at their own pace. This will enable the wearer to associate emotion and mental state labels, and to review specific social situations in slow motion (because people with ASC often report that nonverbal cues, such as facial expression, are too subtle and quick to discern in real time). Parents, teachers, and clinicians may play the video back for the wearer and provide feedback (e.g., help identify facial expressions and pair them with emotion labels) and reinforcement. With such a system we can also explore the question of whether looking at one's own facial movements (while of course knowing what one is personally feeling) will enhance interest in looking at faces in general. If people with ASC can start to associate their own facial expressions with their own feelings, this might enhance their natural interest in other people's faces.

MOVING UP THE AUTISM SPECTRUM

According to the E-S theory of sex differences, there are at least three types of brain, derived from two orthogonal dimensions—empathizing and systemizing (Baron-Cohen 2002), diagrammed in FIGURE 4 (numbers are standard deviations from the mean). The first is characterized by systemizing being stronger than empathizing, a profile more common in males. The second type has the profile of systemizing and empathizing being balanced. The third

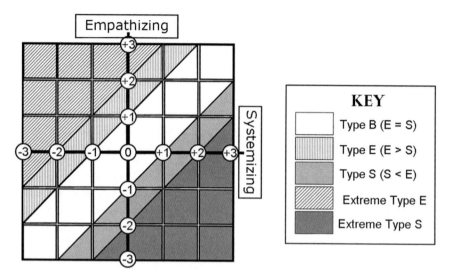

FIGURE 4. The main brain types.

involves empathizing being stronger than systemizing, a profile more common in females. Autism appears to correspond to an extreme of the male brain, with systemizing being intact or above average, alongside empathizing being impaired (Baron-Cohen 2006). One of the interesting aspects of this theory is that the brain types are continuous, blending seamlessly with normality. That is, we are all situated somewhere on the same continuum, and one's position on the continuum reflects a different cognitive style and inclination toward systemizing or empathizing. An important implication of this dimensional model is that the line between ability and disability is blurred. This view of autism as a different kind of mind is shared among an increasing number of individuals with autism and families (DANDA 2003), and is dubbed the neurodiversity model of autism.[1]

One's empathizing skills while in part genetically predisposed (Skuse 1997) and in part influenced by prenatal testosterone (Chapman *et al.* in press) are not fixed. Empathizing may vary as a function of the person's early experience (Bowlby 1982), current affective state, and the surrounding context. One factor that may improve or impede our ability to empathize is stress and anxiety. We have explored several approaches to measuring stress using physiological sensors, heart rate, pedometer, accelerometer, context beacons, and location (Picard and Du 2002; Healey and Picard 2005); other physical symptoms include blood pressure, muscle tension, and sleep problems. Affective state may also affect the ability to empathize. For instance, when angry, one's current emotional state might cloud the ability to see another person's perspective.

[1] http://www.neurodiversity.com.

Similarly, a person who is preoccupied may fail to notice the nonverbal cues of others, misreading their mental state.

The technologies that improve empathizing in autism should in theory also contribute to improvements in these skills in the general population. As Malcolm Gladwell shows in *Blink*, a person's knowledge base of people intuition can be broadened, affecting one's ability to make accurate snap judgments (Gladwell 2003). Technology may augment people's capacity to empathize and improve their people intuition (whether or not they are diagnosed with autism) in at least three ways: increased self-awareness, improved communication with others, and better social learning. For instance, a wearable system that continuously measures stress or anxiety signals can help the wearer regulate arousal, raising self-awareness and encouraging people to switch perspectives under conditions of high arousal. Another application is a personal anger management wearable system that would detect states, such as anger, and attempt to calm the wearer, perhaps even through empathizing verbally with the wearer (Klein *et al.* 2002). Technologies that sense various aspects of the person's affective and physiological state can be used for self-monitoring. Making this knowledge available in a simplified and easy to visualize manner is a good motivational factor to change habits. (It has been shown for instance, that daily self-weighing is a strong motivational factor for losing weight).

This information about oneself could also be selectively communicated to others to enhance group communication. An example is the *Communicator system* (Rubin *et al.* 2003) that uses a combination of nano/info technologies that allow individuals to carry with them electronically stored information about themselves, such as interests, background, and affective state, that can be broadcasted as needed in group situations. Participants would have the ability to define or restrict the kinds of information about themselves that they would be willing to share with other members of the group.

ETHICAL CONSIDERATIONS

Along with the potential benefits, we recognize that there are important ethical considerations that arise with the development of these technologies. An exhaustive discussion of these ethical considerations is beyond the scope of this article; instead, we will suffice with a few examples that highlight the importance of being sensitive to the needs of the end-users of this technology, be they autism researchers and practitioners, or individuals diagnosed with autism and their families.

Besides the privacy issues of sensing and broadcasting affective state information (Reynolds and Picard 2004), one issue to consider is whether individuals with autism need treatment or technology "fixes" at all. We agree that ASC involve a different cognitive style, allowing many individuals with autism to focus deeply on a given subject, which can lead to original thought.

We thus prefer to design technologies that do not try to "fix" people, but rather that can be used by individuals to augment or further develop their natural abilities. If these new technologies hold the promise of improving empathy, this should only be undertaken with the individual's consent, where it is possible to obtain it, or with their parent's consent in the case of a young child. Unlike medical interventions where there is a risk of unwanted side effects, affective computing based interventions may have highly specific effects (on empathy) while leaving other domains (e.g., systemizing) unaffected. We adopt a user-centered design and development approach to ensure that individuals with autism and their caregivers are involved in the development phases of intervention technologies that they need the most.

Another ethical consideration is whether exposing affective state information creates opportunities for others to manipulate one's behavior and thoughts using this information (see Reynolds (2005) for examples). Even in situations where the use of technology is honest, there are still potential concerns. If an individual with autism wears an assistive system that senses the affective state of others, then this would raise the expectations of interaction partners, increasing (rather than decreasing) the social pressures on the person with autism to respond to these cues in real time. Such a system might be more burdensome than helpful. It is essential that researchers address these considerations and explore the potential opportunities brought by a convergence in autism research and affective computing with open-mindedness about the possible successes or failures of such an approach.

CONCLUSION

This article highlights several opportunities for convergence between affective computing and autism, and presents some progress in that direction. The Department of Health and Human Services has called for new approaches that improve real-world functioning of individuals with autism, throughout their school-age years and beyond (Department of Health and Human Services 2004). The Cure Autism Now's Innovative Technology for Autism Initiative, intended to create a merger of technology with other fields, is yielding an interdisciplinary approach to the challenge of utilizing technology to improve the lives of people with autism (Cure Autism Now 2006). Industry funding too is on the rise. For instance, Motorola funded the "mood phone," a phone designed to interpret the mood of the person on the other end of the line, that is meant to help people with AS who are unable to recognize emotional cues in the speech of others.

In summary, this article presents affect sensing and recognition as core technologies, and describes their application as assistive and learning devices for individuals with autism. The opportunities for benefit are two way: helping people with autism, and helping technologies to be smarter about socioemotional interaction. People with autism, especially those who have developed solutions to systematize and understand social interaction can help technologists with their efforts to build systems that do exactly that. The opportunities are rich for two-way collaboration in technology-enhanced human interaction.

ACKNOWLEDGMENT

This work is supported by the National Science Foundation (NSF) SGER Award IIS-0555411 and by the MIT Media Laboratory Things That Think consortium. Rana el Kaliouby's doctorate research was supported by the Computer Laboratory, Cambridge University. SBC was supported by the Shirley Foundation during the Mindreading DVD project. We are grateful to Alea Teeters, Matthew Goodwin, Ofer Golan, and Peter Robinson for their contribution and valuable discussion of these ideas.

REFERENCES

AMERICAN PSYCHIATRIC ASSOCIATION. 1994. *The Diagnostic and Statistical Manual of Mental Disorders, IV*. Washington, D.C.: American Psychiatric Association.

ASPERGER, H. 1991. Autistic psychopathy in childhood. Pp. 37–92 in U. Frith (ed.), *Autism and Asperger Syndrome*. Cambridge, England: Cambridge University Press.

ATTWOOD, T. 1998. *Asperger's Syndrome: A Guide for Parents and Professionals*. Philadelphia: Jessica Kingsley Publishers.

BARON-COHEN, S. 1988. Social and pragmatic deficits in autism: cognitive or affective? *Journal of Autism and Developmental Disorders 18*(3), 379–402.

BARON-COHEN, S. 1995. *Mindblindness*. Cambridge, MA: MIT Press.

BARON-COHEN, S. 2002. The extreme male brain theory of autism. *Trends in Cognitive Science 6*, 248–254.

BARON-COHEN, S. 2003. *The Essential Difference: The Truth about the Male and Female Brain*. New York: Basic Books.

BARON-COHEN, S. 2004. Autism: research into causes and intervention. *Paediatric Rehabilitation 7*(2), 73–78.

BARON-COHEN, S. 2006. The hyper-systemizing, assortative mating theory of autism. *Progress in Neuro-Psychopharmacology and Biological Psychiatry 30*, 865–872.

BARON-COHEN, S., and S. WHEELWRIGHT. 2004. The Empathy Quotient (EQ). An investigation of adults with Asperger Syndrome or High Functioning Autism, and normal sex differences. *Journal of Autism and Developmental Disorders 34*, 163–175.

BARON-COHEN, S., S. WHEELWRIGHT, J. LAWSON, R. GRIFFIN, and J. HILL. 2002. The exact mind: empathising and systemising in autism spectrum conditions. Pp. 491–508 in U. Goswami (ed.), *Handbook of Cognitive Development*. Oxford: Blackwell.

BISHOP, J. 2003. The Internet for educating individuals with social impairments. *Journal of Computer Assisted Learning 19*, 546–556.

BLACKBURN, J., K. GOTTSCHEWSKI, E. GEORGE, and L. NIKI. 2000. A discussion about theory of mind: from an autistic perspective. *Proceedings of Autism Europe's 6th International Congress*, Glasgow May 19-21. Available online at http://www.autistics.org/library/AE2000-ToM.html.

BLOCHER, K., and R.W. PICARD 2002. Affective social quest: emotion recognition therapy for autistic children. Chapter 16 in K. Dautenhahn, A. Bond, L. Canamero, and B. Edmonds (eds.), *Socially Intelligent Agents—Creating Relationships with Computers and Robots*. The Netherlands: Kluwer Academic Publishers.

BOWLBY, J. 1982. *Attachment*. New York: Basic Books.

BREAZEAL, C. 2002. *Designing Sociable Robots*. Cambridge, MA: MIT Press.

CHAPMAN, E., S. BARON-COHEN, B. AUYEUNG, R. KNICKMEYER, K. TAYLOR, and G. HACKETT. 2006. Foetal testosterone and empathy: evidence from the Empathy Quotient (EQ) and the 'Reading the Mind in the Eyes' Test. *Social Neuroscience*, forthcoming.

CURE AUTISM NOW. 2006. Innovative technology for autism initiaive. Retrieved September 1, 2006, from http://www.cureautismnow.org/.

DANDA. 2003. The Developmental Adult Neuro-Diversity Association. Retrieved September 1, 2006, from http://www.danda.org.uk/pages/about.htm.

DAUTENHAHN, K., A. BOND, L. CANAMERO, and B. EDMONDS, eds. 2002. *Socially Intelligent Agents—Creating Relationships with Computers and Robots*. The Netherlands: Kluwer Academic Publishers.

DAVIS, M.H. 1983. Measuring individual differences in empathy: evidence for a multidimensional approach. *Journal of Personality and Social Psychology 44*, 113–126.

DENNERLEIN, J., T. BECKER, P. JOHNSON, C. REYNOLDS, and R. PICARD 2003. Frustrating computer users increases exposure to physical factors. *Proceedings of the XVth Triennial Congress of the International Ergonomics Association* (IEA 2003), Seoul, Korea, August 24–29. Available online at http://affect.media.mit.edu/pdfs/03.dennerlein-etal.pdf.

DENNETT, D.C. 1987. *The Intentional Stance*. Cambridge, MA: MIT Press.

DEPARTMENT OF HEALTH AND HUMAN SERVICES. 2004. Congressional Appropriations Committee Report on the State of Autism Research. Retrieved August 29, 2006, from http://www.nimh.nih.gov/autismiacc/congapprcommrep.pdf.

EISENBERG, N. 2000. Empathy and sympathy. Pp. 677–692 in M. Lewis, and J. Haviland-Jones (eds.), *Handbook of Emotions*. New York: Guildford Press.

FLETCHER, P.C., F. HAPPE, U. FRITH, S.C. BAKER, R.J. DOLAN, R.S. FRACKOWIAK, and C.D. FRITH. 1995. Other minds in the brain: a functional imaging study of "Theory of Mind" in story comprehension. *Cognition 57*(2), 109–128.

FRITH, U., ed. 1991. *Autism and Apserger Syndrome*. Cambridge, England: Cambridge University Press.

FRITH, U. 2003. *Autism: Explaining the Enigma,* 2nd ed. Oxford: Blackwell.

GLADWELL, M. 2003. *Blink: The Power of Thinking without Thinking*. New York: Little Brown.

GOLAN, O., S. BARON-COHEN, J.J. HILL and Y. GOLAN. 2006. Reading the Mind in Films—testing recognition of complex emotions and mental states in adults with and without autism spectrum conditions. *Social Neuroscience 1*(2), 111–123.

GOODWIN, M.S., J. GRODEN, W.F. VELICER, L.P. LIPSITT, M.G. BARON, S.G. HOFMANN, and G. GRODEN. 2006. Cardiovascular arousal in individuals with autism. *Focus on Autism and Other Developmental Disabilities 21*(2), 100–123.

HAPPÉ, F. 1966. Studying weak central coherence at low levels: children with autism do not succumb to visual illusions: a research note. *Journal of Child Psychology and Psychiatry 37*, 873–877.

HARRIS, J.C. 2003. Social neuroscience, empathy, brain integration, and neurodevelopmental disorders. *Physiology and Behavior 79*, 525–531.

HEALEY, J., and R.W. PICARD 1998. StartleCam: a cybernetic wearable camera. Pp. 42–49 in *Proceedings of the International Symposium on Wearable Computers*, Pittsburgh, October 19–20.

HEALEY, J., and R.W. PICARD. 2005. Detecting stress during real-world driving tasks using physiological sensors. *IEEE Transactions on Intelligent Transportation Systems 6*, 156–166.

HILL, E.L., S. BERTHOZ, and U. FRITH. 2004. Brief report: cognitive processing of own emotions in individuals with autistic spectrum disorder and in their relatives. *Journal of Autism and Developmental Disorders 34*, 229–235.

HIRSTEIN, W., P. IVERSEN, and V.S. RAMACHANDRAN. 2001. Autonomic responses of autistic children to people and objects. *Proceedings of the Royal Society 268*, 1883–1888.

JOLLIFFE, T., and S. BARON-COHEN 1997. Are people with autism and Asperger syndrome faster than normal on the Embedded Figures Test? *Journal of Child Psychology and Psychiatry 38*(5), 527–534.

JOSEPH, R., and H. TAGER-FLUSBERG 1997. An investigation of attention and affect in children with autism and Down syndrome. *Journal of Autism and Developmental Disorders 27*(4), 385–396.

EL KALIOUBY, R. 2005. Mind-reading machines: automated inference of complex mental states. Computer Laboratory, University of Cambridge.

EL KALIOUBY, R., and P. ROBINSON. 2005. The emotional hearing aid: an assistive tool for children with Asperger Syndrome. *Universal Access in the Information Society 4*(2), 121–134.

EL KALIOUBY, R., A. TEETERS, and R.W. PICARD. 2006. An exploratory social-emotional prosthetic for Autism Spectrum Disorders. Body Sensor Networks, MIT Media Lab. Available online at http://affect.media.mit.edu/pdfs/06.kaliouby-teeters-picard-bsn.pdf.

KANNER, L. 1943. Autistic disturbance of affective contact. *Nervous Child 2*, 217–250.

KAPOOR, A., H. AHN, and R.W. PICARD. 2005. Mixture of gaussian processes for combining multiple modalities. Pp. 86–96 in N.C. Oza, R. Polikar, J. Kittler, and F. Roli (eds.), *Multiple Classifier Systems: 6th International Workshop*, MCS 2005, Seaside, CA. Berlin: Springer.

KAPOOR, A., R.W. PICARD, and Y. IVANOV. 2004. Probabilistic combination of multiple modalities to detect interest. *International Conference on Pattern Recognition*, Cambridge, U.K., August 23–26. Available online at http://affect.media.mit.edu/pdfs/04.kapoor-picard-ivanov.pdf.

KLEIN, J., Y. MOON, and R.W. PICARD. 2002. This computer responds to user frustration: theory, design, results, and implications. *Interacting with Computers 14*, 119–140.

KLIN, A., and F.R. VOLKMAR 1995. Asperger's Syndrome: guidelines for assessment and diagnosis. Learning Disabilities Association of America. Available online at http://www.aspennj.org/guide.html.

KLIN, A., W. JONES, R. SCHULTZ, and F. VOLKMAR. 2003. The enactive mind, or from actions to cognition: lessons from autism. *Philosophical Transactions of the Royal Society B*(358), 345–360.

KLIN, A., W. JONES, R. SCHULTZ, F. VOLKMAR, and D. COHEN. 2002. Visual fixation patterns during viewing of naturalistic social situations as predictors of social competence in individuals with autism. *Archives of General Psychiatry 59*, 809–816.

LECOUTEUR, A., M. RUTTER, and C. LORD. 1989. Autism diagnostic interview: a standardized investigator-based instrument. *Journal of Autism and Developmental Disorders 19*(3), 363–387.

LEGOFF, D.B. 2004. Use of LEGO© as a therapeutic medium for improving social competence. *Journal of Autism and Developmental Disorders 34*(5), 557–571.

LESLIE, A.M. 1987. Pretense and representation: the origins of "theory of mind." *Psychological Review 94*(4), 412–426.

LORD, C., M. RUTTER, and A. LE COUTEUR. 1994. Autism diagnostic interview—revised: a revised version of a diagnostic interview for caregivers of individuals with possible pervasive developmental disorders. *Journal of Autism and Developmental Disorders 24*(5), 659–685.

LORD, C., M.L. RUTTER, S. GOODE, J. HEEMSBERGEN, H. JORDAN, L. MAWHOOD, and E. SCHOPLER. 1989. Autism diagnostic observation schedule: a standardized observation of communicative and social behavior." *Journal of Autism and Developmental Disorders 19*(2), 185–212.

LORD, C., S. RISI, L. LAMBRECHT, E.H. COOK, Jr., B.L. LEVENTHAL, P.C. DILAVORE, A. PICKLES, and M. RUTTER. 2000. The Autism Diagnostic Observation Schedule—generic: a standard measure of social and communication deficits associated with the spectrum of autism. *Journal of Autism and Developmental Disorders 30*(3), 205–223.

MEHRABIAN, A., and N. EPSTEIN 1972. A measure of emotional empathy. *Journal of Personality 40*, 525–543.

MIXING MEMORY BLOG. 2005. Autism and theory of mind. Retrieved September 1, 2006, from http://mixingmemory.blogspot.com/2005/08/autism-and-theory-of-mind.html.

MOORE, D., P. MCGRATH, and J. THORPE. 2000. Computer-aided learning for people with autism—a framework for research and development. *Innovations in Education and Training International 37*(3), 218–228.

OMDAHL, B.L. 1995. *Cognitive Appraisal, Emotion, and Empathy*. Mahwah, NJ: Lawrence Erlbaum Associates.

PELPHREY, K.A., J.P. MORRIS, and G. MCCARTHY. 2005. Neural basis of eye gaze processing deficits in autism. *Brain 128*(5), 1038–1048.

PENTLAND, A. 2006. Are we one? On the nature of human intelligence. *Fifth International Conference on Development and Learning*, Bloomington, IL, May 31–June 3. Available online at http://web.media.mit.edu/šandy/Are-We-One-2-13-06.pdf.

PICARD, R. 1997. *Affective Computing*. Cambridge, MA: MIT Press.

PICARD, R., and J. SCHEIRER 2001. The Galvactivator: a glove that senses and communicates skin conductivity. Pp. 1538–1542 in *Proceedings of the International Conference on Human-Computer Interaction*, New Orleans, August.

PICARD, R.W., and C. DU. 2002. Monitoring stress and heart health with a phone and wearable computer. *Motorola Offspring Journal 1*. Available online at http://affect.media.mit.edu/pdfs/02.picard-du.pdf.

PICARD, R.W., and J. HEALEY 1997. Affective wearables. *Personal Technologies 1*(4), 231–240.

PICARD, R.W., S. PAPERT, W. BENDER, B. BLUMBERG, C. BREAZEAL, D. CAVALLO, T. MACHOVER, M. RESNICK, D. ROY, and C. STROHECKER. 2004. Affective learning—a Manifesto. *BT Technical Journal 22*(4), 253–269.

POST-AUTISTIC ECONOMICS NETWORK. 2000. Post-autistic economics review. Retrieved September 6, 2006, from http://www.paecon.net/.

PRATT, C., and P. BRYANT 1990. Young children understand that looking leads to knowing (so long as they are looking into a single barrel). *Child Development 61*(4), 973–982.

QI, Y., and R.W. PICARD 2002. Context-Sensitive Bayesian Classifiers and Applications to Mouse Pressure Pattern Classification. Proceedings of the 16th International Conference on Pattern Recognition (ICPR'02), Quebec City, Canada.

QI, Y., C. REYNOLDS, and R.W. PICARD. 2001. The Bayes point machine for computer-user frustration detection via pressure mouse. *Proceedings of the 2001 Workshop on Perceptive User Interfaces*, Orlando, FL, November 15–16.

REYNOLDS, C.J. 2005. *Adversarial Uses of Affective Computing and Ethical Implications*. Media Arts and Sciences. Doctoral dissertation, Cambridge, MA: Massachusetts Institute of Technology. Available online at http://alumni.media.mit.edu/~carsonr/phd_thesis/index.html.

REYNOLDS, C., and R.W. PICARD 2004. Affective sensors, privacy and ethical contracts. Pp. 1103–1106 in *Proceedings of the Conference on Human Factors in Computing Systems*, April 24–29, Vienna, Austria. New York: ACM.

RUBIN, P., M. HIRSCHBEIN, T. MASCIANGIOLI, T. MILLER, C. MURRAY, R.L. NORWOOD, and J. SARGENT. 2003. The Communicator: enhancement of group communication, efficiency, and creativity. Pp. 302–307 in M.C. Roco, and W.S. Bainbridge (eds.), *Converging Technologies for Improving Human Performance: Nanotechnology, Biotechnology, Information Technology And Cognitive Science*. Dordrecht, Netherlands: Kluwer.

SCASSELLATI, B. 2005. How social robots will help us to diagnose, treat, and understand autism. *12th International Symposium of Robotics Research (ISRR)*, October 12-15, San Francisco, CA. Available online at http://cs-www.cs.yale.edu/homes/scaz/papers/Scassellati-ISRR-05-final.pdf.

SCHEIRER, J., R. FERNANDEZ, and R.W. PICARD. 1999. Expression glasses: a wearable device for facial expression recognition. Pp. 262–263 in *Proceedings of the Conference on Human Factors in Computing Systems*, May 15–20, Pittsburgh, PA. New York: ACM.

SHAH, A., and U. FRITH. 1983. An islet of ability in autistic children: a research note. *Journal of Child Psychology and Psychiatry 24*(4), 613–20.

SKUSE, D.H. 1997. Genetic factors in the etiology of child psychiatric disorders. *Current Opinion in Pediatrics 9*(4), 354–360.

SPIRO, H. 1993. Empathy: an introduction. Pp. 1–6 in H. Spiro, M. McCrea, E. Peschel, and D. St. James (eds.), *Empathy and the Practice of Medicine*. New Haven, Connecticut: Yale University Press.

TEETERS, A., R. EL KALIOUBY, and R.W. PICARD. 2006. Self-Cam: feedback from what would be your social partner. *Proceedings of the 33rd International Conference on Computer Graphics and Interactive Techniques (SIGGRAPH)*, July 30–August 3, 2006, Boston, MA. Available online at http://affect.media.mit.edu/pdfs/06.teeters-kaliouby-picard-siggraph.pdf.

VERTEGAAL, R., R. SLAGTER, G. VAN DER VEER, and A. NIJHOLT. 2001. Eye gaze patterns in coversations: there is more to conversational agents than meets the eyes. Pp. 301–308 in *Proceedings of the SIGCHI Conference on Human Factors in Computing Systems*. New York: ACM.

VOLKMAR, F., and A. KLIN 2000. Asperger's disorder and higher functioning autism: same or different? *International Review of Research in Mental Retardation 23*, 83–110.

VOLKMAR, F.R., and L. MAYES. 1991. Gaze behaviour in autism. *Development and Psychopathology 2*, 61–69.

WEGNER, P. 1997. Why interaction is more powerful than algorithms. *Communications of the ACM 40*(5), 80–91.

WELLMAN, H.M. 1992. *The Child's Theory of Mind.* Cambridge, MA: MIT Press.

WHITEN, A., ed. 1991. *Natural Theories of Mind: Evolution, Development, and Simulation of Everyday Mindreading.* Cambridge, MA: B. Blackwell.

WIMMER, H., and J. PERNER. 1983. Beliefs about beliefs: representation and constraining function of wrong beliefs in young children's understanding of deception. *Cognition 13*(1), 103–28.

WURTMAN, J.J., and M. DANBROT. 1988. *Managing Your Mind and Mood Through Food.* New York: Perennial Library.

ZACKS, J.M., B. TVERSKY, and G. IYER. 2001. Perceiving, remembering, and communicating structure in events. *Journal of Experimental Psychology 130*(1), 29–58.

Building Personal Maps from GPS Data

LIN LIAO, DONALD J. PATTERSON, DIETER FOX, AND HENRY KAUTZ

Department of Computer Science & Engineering, University of Washington, Seattle, Washington 98195, USA

ABSTRACT: In this article we discuss an assisted cognition information technology system that can learn personal maps customized for each user and infer his daily activities and movements from raw GPS data. The system uses discriminative and generative models for different parts of this task. A discriminative relational Markov network is used to extract significant places and label them; a generative dynamic Bayesian network is used to learn transportation routines, and infer goals and potential user errors at real time. We focus on the basic structures of the models and briefly discuss the inference and learning techniques. Experiments show that our system is able to accurately extract and label places, predict the goals of a person, and recognize situations in which the user makes mistakes, such as taking a wrong bus.

KEYWORDS: personal map; GPS; Relational Markov Network (RMN); dynamic Bayesian network (DBN)

INTRODUCTION

A typical map consists of significant places and road networks within a geographic region. In this article, we present the concept of a *personal map*, which is customized based on an individual's behavior. A personal map includes personally significant places, such as home, a workplace, shopping centers, and meeting places and personally significant routes (i.e., the paths and transportation modes, such as foot, car, or bus, that the person usually uses to travel from place to place). In contrast with general maps, a personal map is customized and primarily useful for a given person. Because of the customization, it is well suited for recognizing an individual's behavior and offering detailed personalized help. For example, in this article we use a personal map to:

An earlier version of this chapter appeared in the working notes of the *Workshop on Modeling Others from Observations* at the *International Joint Conference on Artificial Intelligence (IJCAI-2005),* Edinburgh, Scotland, 2005.

Address for correspondence: Lin Liao, AC101 Paul G. Allen Center, Box 352350, 185 Stevens Way, Seattle WA 98195-2350. Voice: 206-543-1795; fax: 206-543-2969.
e-mail: liaolin.cs.washington.edu

Ann. N.Y. Acad. Sci. 1093: 249–265 (2006). © 2006 New York Academy of Sciences.
doi: 10.1196/annals.1382.017

- Discriminate a user's activities (Is she dining at a restaurant or visiting a friend?);
- Predict a user's future movements and transportation modes, both in the short term (Will she turn left at the next street corner? Will she get off the bus at the next bus stop?) and in terms of distant goals (Is she going to her workplace?);
- Infer when a user has *broken his ordinary routine* in a way that may indicate that he has made an error, such as failing to get off his bus at his usual stop on the way home.

We describe a system that builds personal maps automatically from raw location data collected by wearable Global Positioning System (GPS) units. Many potential applications can be built upon the system. A motivating application for this work is the development of personal guidance systems that helps cognitively impaired individuals move safely and independently throughout their community (Patterson *et al.* 2004). Other potential applications include *customized* "just in time" information services (for example, providing the user with current bus schedule information when she is likely to need it or real time traffic conditions on her future trajectories), intelligent user interface (instructing a cell phone not to ring when in a restaurant or at a meeting), and so on (Golledge 2003).

Our work spans two of the four areas that have been highlighted in the Converging Technologies conferences, information technology and cognitive science (Roco and Bainbridge, 2002). Because cognitive disabilities are usually biological in origin, the envisioned application of the work touches upon a third area, biotechnology, as well.

This chapter is focused on the fundamental techniques of learning and inference. We develop probabilistic models that bridge low-level sensor measurements (i.e., GPS data) with high-level information in the personal maps. Given raw GPS data from a user, our system first finds a user's set of significant places, then a Relational Markov Network (RMN) is constructed to recognize the activities in those places (e.g., working, visiting, and dining out); as discriminative models, RMNs often outperform their corresponding generative models (e.g., hidden Markov models) for classification tasks (Taskar *et al.* 2002). The system then uses a dynamic Bayesian network (DBN) model (Murphy 2002) for learning and inferring transportation routines between the significant places; such a generative model is well suited for online tracking and real-time user error detection.

RELATED WORK

Over the last years, estimating a person's activities has gained increased interest in the artificial intelligence (AI), robotics, and ubiquitous computing communities. One approach learns significant locations from logs of GPS measurements by determining the time a person spends at a certain location (Ashbrook and Starner 2003; Hariharan and Toyama 2004). For these locations, researchers use frequency counting to estimate the transition parameters of Markov models. Their approach then predicts the next goal based on the current and the previous goals. Our system goes beyond their work in many aspects. First, our system not only extracts places, but also recognizes activities associated with those places. Second, their models are not able to refine the goal estimates using GPS information observed when moving from one significant location to another. Furthermore, such a coarse representation does not allow the detection of potential user errors. In contrast, our hierarchical generative model is able to learn more specific motion patterns of transportation routines, which also enables us to detect user errors.

In the machine learning community, a variety of *relational probabilistic models* were introduced to overcome limitations of propositional probabilistic models. Relational models combine first-order logical languages with probabilistic graphical models. Intuitively, a relational probabilistic model is a *template* for propositional models such as Bayesian networks or Markov random fields (similar to how first-order logic formulas can be instantiated to propositional logic). Templates are defined over object classes through logical languages such as Horn clauses, frame systems, Structural Query Language (SQL), and full first-order logic. Given data, these templates are then *instantiated* to generate propositional models (typically Bayesian networks or Markov random fields), on which inference and learning is performed. Relational probabilistic models use high-level languages for describing systems involving complex relations and uncertainties. Because the structures and parameters are defined at the level of classes, they are shared by the instantiated networks. Parameter sharing is particularly essential for learning from sparse training data and for knowledge transfer between different people. As a popular relational probabilistic model, RMNs define the templates using SQL, a widely used query language for database systems, and the templates are instantiated into (conditional) Markov networks, which are *undirected* models that do not suffer the cyclicity problem and are thereby more flexible and convenient. Since their introduction, RMNs have been used successfully in a number of domains, including web page classification (Taskar *et al.* 2002), link prediction (Taskar *et al.* 2003), and information extraction (Bunescu and Mooney 2004).

In the context of probabilistic plan recognition, Bui and colleagues (2002) introduced the abstract hidden Markov model, which uses hierarchical representations to efficiently infer a person's goal in an indoor environment from camera information. Bui (2003) extended this model to include memory nodes, which enables the transfer of context information over multiple time steps. Bui and colleagues introduced efficient inference algorithms for their models using Rao-Blackwellised particle filters (RBPF). Because our model has a similar structure to theirs, we apply the inference mechanisms developed by Bui. Our work goes beyond the work of Bui's group in that we show how to learn the parameters of the hierarchical activity model, and their domains, from data. Furthermore, our low-level estimation problem is more challenging than their indoor tracking problem.

The task of detecting abnormal events in time series data (called *novelty detection*) has been studied extensively in the data-mining community (Guralnik and Srivastava 1999), but remains an open and challenging research problem. We present the results on abnormality and error detection in location and transportation prediction using a simple and effective approach based on comparing the likelihood of a learned hierarchical model against that of a prior model.

EXTRACTING AND LABELING PLACES

In this section, we briefly discuss place extraction and activity labeling. Full technical details of the activity labeling are provided elsewhere (Liao *et al.* 2005).

Place Extraction

Similar to the work of Ashbrook and Starner (2003) and of Hariharan and Toyama (2004), our current system considers significant places to be those locations where a person typically spends extended periods of time. From the GPS data, it first looks for locations where the person stays for a given amount of time (e.g., 10 min), and then these locations are clustered to merge spatially similar points. An extension of the approach that takes into account more complex features is discussed later.

Activity Labeling

We build our activity model based on the RMN framework (Taskar *et al.* 2002). RMNs describe specific relations between objects using clique templates specified by SQL queries: each query C selects the relevant objects and their attributes, and specifies a *potential* function, or clique potential, Φ_C, on the possible values of these attributes. Intuitively, the clique potentials measure the "compatibility" between values of the attributes. Clique potentials are usually defined as a log-linear combinations of *feature* functions, that is, $\Phi_C(\mathbf{v}_C) = \exp\{\mathbf{w}^T_C \cdot \mathbf{f}_C(\mathbf{v}_C)\}$, where $\mathbf{v}_C$ are the attributes selected in the query, $\mathbf{f}_C()$ is a feature vector for C, and $\mathbf{w}^T_C$ is the transpose of the corresponding weight vector. For instance, a feature could be the number of different homes defined using aggregations.

To perform inference, an RMN is *unrolled* into a Markov network, in which the nodes correspond to the attributes of objects. The connections among the nodes are built by applying the SQL templates to the data; each template C can result in several cliques, which share the same feature weights. Standard inference algorithms, such as belief propagation and Markov Chain Monte Carlo (MCMC), can be used to estimate the conditional distribution of hidden variables given all the observations.

Relational Activity Model

Because behavior patterns can be highly variable, a reliable discrimination between activities must take several sources of evidence into account. More specifically, our model defines the following templates:

i. *Temporal* patterns: Different activities often have different temporal patterns, such as their duration or the time of day. Such local patterns are modeled by clique templates that connect each attribute with the activity label.

ii. *Geographic* evidence: Information about the types of businesses close to a location can be extremely useful to determine a user's activity. Such information can be extracted from geographic databases like http://www.microsoft.com/mappoint. Because location information in such databases is not accurate enough, we consider such information by checking whether, for example, a restaurant is within a certain range from the location.

iii. *Transition* relations: First-order transitions between activities can also be informative. For example, going from home to work is very common while dining out twice in a row is rare.

iv. *Spatial* constraints: Activities at the same place are often similar. In other words, the number of different types of activities in a place is often limited.

v. *Global* features: These are soft constraints on the activities of a person. The number of different home locations is an example of the global constraints. Such a constraint is modeled by a clique template that selects all places labeled as home and returns how many of them are different.

Inference

In our application, the task of inference is to estimate the labels of activities in the *unrolled* Markov networks. FIGURE 1 offers an example with six activities. Solid straight lines indicate the cliques generated by the templates of temporal, geographic, and transition features; bold solid curves represent spatial constraints (activity 1 and 4 are associated with the same place and so are 2 and 5); dashed curves stand for global features, which are label-specific cliques (activity 1 and 4 are both labeled as "AtHome" or "AtWork" at this moment).

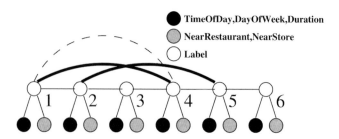

FIGURE 1. An example of unrolled Markov network with six activities.

Inference in our relational activity models is complicated by the fact that the structure of the unrolled Markov network can change during inference. This is due to the fact that, in the templates of global features, the label of an object determines to which cliques it belongs. We call such cliques *label-specific cliques*. Because the label values are hidden during inference, such cliques potentially involve all the labels, which makes exact inference intractable.

We perform approximate inference using MCMC (Gilks *et al.* 1996). We first implemented MCMC using basic Gibbs sampling. Unfortunately, this technique performs poorly in our model because of the strong dependencies among labels. To make MCMC mix faster, we developed a mixture of two transition kernels: the first is a block Gibbs sampler and the second is a Metropolis sampler (see Liao *et al.* 2005 for details). The numbers of different homes and workplaces are stored in the chains as global variables. This allows us to compute the *global* features *locally* in both kernels. In order to determine which kernel to use at each step, we sample a random number u between 0 and 1 uniformly, and compare u with the given threshold γ ($\gamma = 0.5$ in our experiments).

Learning

The parameters to be learned are the weights **w** of the features that define the clique potentials. To avoid overfitting, we perform maximum a posterior (MAP) parameter estimation and impose an independent Gaussian prior with constant variance for each component of **w**. Because the objective function for MAP estimation is convex, the global optimum can be found using standard numerical optimization algorithms (Taskar *et al.* 2002). We apply the quasi-Newton methods to find the optimal weights because they have been found to be very efficient for conditional random fields (Sha and Pereira 2003). Each iteration of this technique requires the value and gradient of the objective function computed at the weights returned in the previous iteration. Elsewhere (Liao *et al.* 2005) we presented an algorithm that *simultaneously* estimates at each iteration the value and its gradient using MCMC.

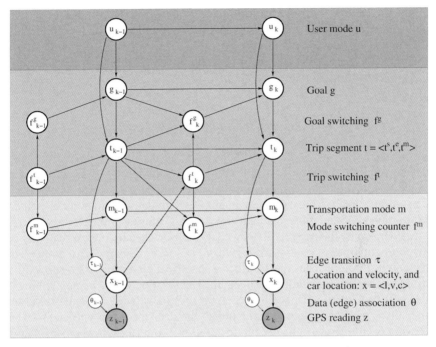

User mode u

Goal g

Goal switching f^g

Trip segment $t = <t^s, t^e, t^m>$

Trip switching f^t

Transportation mode m
Mode switching counter f^m

Edge transition τ
Location and velocity, and
car location: $x = <l, v, c>$

Data (edge) association θ

GPS reading z

FIGURE 2. Hierarchical activity model representing a person's outdoor movements.

Although parameter learning in RMNs requires manually labeled training data, parameter sharing makes it easy to transfer knowledge. For example, in our system, we can learn a *generic* model from people who have manually labeled data, and then apply the model to people who have no labeled data. Generic models in our system can perform reasonably well, as we will show in the experiments.

LEARNING AND INFERRING TRANSPORTATION ROUTINES

We estimate a person's activities using the three-level DBN model shown in FIGURE 2 (Liao *et al.* 2004). This is an hierarchical activity model representing a person's outdoor movements during everyday activities. The upper level estimates the user mode, the middle layer represents goals and trip segments, and the lowest layer is the flat model, estimating the person's location, velocity, and transportation mode. The individual nodes in such a temporal graphical model represent different parts of the state space, and the arcs indicate dependencies between the nodes (Murphy 2002). Temporal dependencies are represented by arcs connecting the two time slices $k-1$ and k. The highest level of the model indicates the user mode, which could be typical behavior, user error, or deliberate novel behavior. The middle level represents the person's goal (i.e., next significant place) and trip segment (defined below). The lowest level is the *flat* model, which estimates the person's transportation mode, location and motion velocity from the GPS sensor measurements. In this section, we explain the model from bottom up.

Locations and Transportation Modes

We denote by $\chi_k = (l_k, v_k, c_k)$ the location and motion velocity of the person, and the location of the person's car (subscripts k indicate discrete time). We include the car location because it strongly affects whether the person can switch to the car mode. In our DBN model, locations are estimated on a graph structure representing a street map. GPS sensor measurements, z_k, are generated by the person carrying a GPS sensor. Because measurements are given in continuous *xy*-coordinates, they have to be "snapped" to an edge in the graph structure. The edge to which a specific measurement is "snapped" is estimated by the association variable θ_k. The location of the person at time k depends on his previous location, l_{k-1}, the motion velocity, v_k, and the vertex transition, τ_k. Vertex transitions τ model the decision a person makes when moving over a vertex in the graph, for example, to turn right when crossing a street intersection.

The mode of transportation can take on four different values $m_k \, \varepsilon \, \{BUS, FOOT, CAR, BUILDING\}$. Similar to (Patterson *et al.* 2003), these modes influence the motion velocity, which is picked from a Gaussian mixture model. For example, the walking mode draws velocities only from the Gaussian representing slow motion. *BUILDING* is a special mode that occurs only when the GPS signal is lost for significantly long time. Finally, the location of the car only changes when the person is in the *CAR* mode, in which the car location is set to the person's location.

An efficient algorithm based on RBPFs has been developed to perform online inference for the flat model (Doucet *et al.* 2000). In a nutshell, the RBPF samples transportation mode $m_k^{(i)}$, transportation mode switch $f^m{}_k^{(i)}$, data association $\theta_k^{(i)}$, edge transition $\tau_k^{(i)}$, and velocity $v_k^{(i)}$, then it updates the Gaussian distribution of location $l_k^{(i)}$ using a one-dimensional Kalman filter. After all components of each particle are generated, the importance weights of the particles are updated. This is done by computing the likelihood of the GPS measurement z_k, which is provided by the update innovations of the Kalman filters.

We apply expectation maximization (EM) to learn the model parameters. Before learning, the model has no preference for when a person switches mode of transportation, or which edge a person transits to when crossing a vertex on the graph. However, information about bus routes, and the fact that the car is either parked or moves with the person, already provide important constraints on mode transitions. At each iteration of EM, the location, velocity, and mode of transportation are estimated using the RBPF of the flat model. In the E-step, transition counts of a forward and a backward filtering pass through the data log are combined, based on which we update the model parameters in the M-step. In our Rao-Blackwellised model, edge transitions are counted whenever the *mean* of a Kalman filter transits the edge. The learned flat model encodes information about typical motion patterns and significant locations by edge and mode transition probabilities.

After we estimate the mode transition probabilities for each edge, we find *mode transfer locations*, that is, usual bus stops and parking lots, by looking for those locations at which the mode switching exceeds a certain threshold.

Goals and Trip Segments

A trip segment is defined by its start location, $t^s{}_k$, end location, $t^e{}_k$, and the mode of transportation, $t^m{}_k$, the person uses during the segment. For example, a trip segment models information such as: "She gets on the bus at location $t^s{}_k$ and takes the bus up to location $t^e{}_k$, where she gets off the bus." In addition to transportation mode, a trip segment predicts the route on which the person gets from $t^s{}_k$ to $t^e{}_k$. This route is not specified through a deterministic sequence of edges on the graph but rather through transition probabilities on the graph. These probabilities determine the prediction of the person's motion direction when crossing a vertex in the graph, as indicated by the arc from t_k to τ_k.

A goal represents the current target location of the person. Goals include the significant locations extracted using our discriminative model. The transfer between trip segments and goals is handled by the boolean switching nodes $f^t{}_k$ and $f^g{}_k$, respectively.

To estimate a person's goal and trip segment, we apply the inference algorithm used for the abstract hidden Markov memory models (Bui 2003). More specifically, we use an RBPF both at the low level and at the higher levels. Each sample of the resulting particle filter contains the discrete and continuous states described in the previous section, and a joint distribution over the goals and trip segments. These additional distributions are updated using exact inference.

Because we have learned the set of goals using the discriminative model and the set of trip segments using the flat model, we only need to estimate the transition matrices at all levels: between the goals, between the trip segments given the goal, and between the adjacent streets given the trip segment.

Again, we use EM in the hierarchical model, which is similar to that in the flat model. During the E-steps, smoothing is performed by tracking the states both forward and backward in time. The M-steps update the model parameters using the frequency counts generated in the E-step. All transition parameters are smoothed using Dirichlet priors.

User Modes

To detect user errors or novel behavior, we add the variable u_k to the highest level, which indicates the user's behavior mode ε {*Normal,Novel,Erroneous*}. Different values of u_k instantiate different parameters for the lower part of the model. When user mode is typical behavior, the model is instantiated using the parameters learned from training data. When a user's behavior is *Erroneous*, the goal remains the same, but the trip segment is set to a distinguished value "unknown" and as a consequence the parameters of the flat model (i.e., transportation mode transitions and edge transitions) are switched to their *a priori* values: An "unknown" trip segment cannot provide any information for the low-level parameters. When a user's behavior is *Novel*, the goal is set to "unknown," the trip segment is set to "unknown," and the parameters of the flat model are again set to their a priori values.

To infer the distribution of u_k, we run two trackers simultaneously, and at each time their relative likelihood is used to update the distribution. The first tracker uses the hierarchical model with learned parameters and second tracker uses the flat model with a priori parameters. When a user is following her ordinary routine, the first tracker has higher likelihoods, but when the user makes error or does something novel, the second tracker becomes more likely. Unless the true goal is observed, the system cannot distinguish errors from novel behavior, so the precise ratio between the two is determined by hand selected prior probabilities. In some situations, however, the system knows where the user is going, for example if the user asks for directions to a destination, or if a caregiver indicates the "correct" destination, and thus the goal is fixed, treated as an observed, and therefore *clamped*. After we have clamped the goal, the probability of novel behavior becomes zero and the second tracker just determines the probabilities of an error.

EXPERIMENTS

To evaluate our system, we collected two sets of location data using wearable GPS units. The first data set contains location traces from a single person over a time period of 4 months. FIGURE 3 shows part of the locations contained in the data set of a single person, collected over a period of 4 months, the x-axis is 8 miles long. It includes about 400 activities at 50 different places. The second data set consists of 1 week of data from five different people. Each person has 25–30 activities and 10–15 different significant places. We extracted from the logs each instance of a subject spending more than 10 min at one place. Each instance corresponds to an activity. We then clustered the nearby activity locations into places.

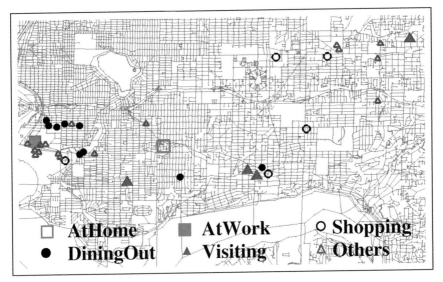

FIGURE 3. Some of the locations contained in the data set of a single person.

Evaluating the RMN Model

For training and evaluation, the subjects manually labeled the data with their activities from the following set: {**AtHome, AtWork, Shopping, DiningOut, Visiting, Other**}. Then, we constructed the unrolled Markov networks using the templates described above, trained the models, and tested their accuracy. Accuracy was determined by the activities for which the most likely labeling was correct.

In practice, it is of great value to learn a *generic* activity model that can be immediately applied to new users without additional training. In the first experiment, we used the data set of multiple users and performed leave-one-subject-out cross-validation: We trained using data from four subjects, and tested on the remaining one. FIGURE 4 A shows error rates of cross-validation of the generic models and customized models using different feature sets. The average error rates are indicated by the white bars. By using all the features, the generic model achieved an error rate of 20%. Note that the global features and the spatial constraints are very useful. To gauge the impact of different habits on the results, we also performed the same evaluation using the data set of single subject. In this case, we used 1-month data for training and the other 3-month data for test, and we repeated the validation process for each month. The results are shown by the gray bars in FIGURE 4 A. In this case, the model achieved an error rate of only 7%. This experiment shows that it is possible to learn good activity models from groups of people. It also shows that

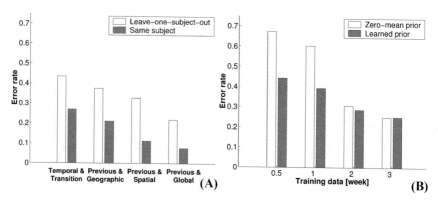

FIGURE 4. Results showing improvement in the error rates.

if the model is learned from more "similar" people, then higher accuracy can be achieved. This indicates that models can be improved by grouping people based on their activity patterns.

When estimating the weights of RMNs, a prior is imposed in order to avoid overfitting. Without additional information, a zero mean Gaussian is typically used as the prior (Taskar *et al.* 2002). Here we show that performance can also be improved by estimating the *hyper-parameters* for the means of the weights using data collected from other people. Similar to the first experiment, we want to learn a customized model for a person **A**, but this time we also have labeled data from others. We could simply ignore the others' data and use the labeled data from **A** with a zero-mean prior. Or we can first learn the weights from the other people and use that as the mean of the Gaussian prior for **A**. We evaluate the performance of the two approaches for different amounts of training data from person **A**. FIGURE 4 B shows results, zero-mean prior versus learned model as prior mean (showing the error rates over the new places only). We can see that using data from others to generate a prior boosts the accuracy significantly, especially when only small amounts of training data are available.

Using the Bayesian prior smoothly shifts from generic to customized models: On one end, when no data from the given subject is available, the approach returns the generic (prior) model; on the other end, as more labeled data become available, the model adjusts more and more to the specific patterns of the user and we get a customized model.

Evaluating the DBN Model

The learning of the generative model was done completely unsupervised without any manual labeling. FIGURE 5 shows the learned trip segments and

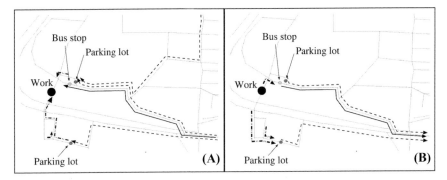

FIGURE 5. Learned model in the area around the workplace.

street transitions zoomed into the workplace, and the very likely transitions (probability above 0.75). Dashed lines indicate car mode, solid lines indicate taking a bus, and dashed-dotted lines indicate foot travel. In FIGURE 5 A, the goal is the workplace, whereas in FIGURE 5 B the goal is home. The model successfully discovered the most frequent trajectories for traveling from home to the workplace and vice-versa, as well as other common trips, such as to the homes of friends.

As we described, an important feature of our model is the capability to capture user errors and novel behavior using a parallel tracking approach. To demonstrate the performance of this technique, we did the following two experiments.

In the first experiment, shown in parts (A) and (B) of FIGURE 6, a user took the wrong bus home. For the first 700 s, the wrong bus route coincided with the correct one and the system believed that the user was in $\{u_k = Normal\}$ mode. But when the bus took a turn that the user had never taken to get home, the probability of errors in the clamped model dramatically jumped (FIG. 6 A). In contrast, the unclamped model cannot determine a user error because the user, while on the wrong bus route, was on a bus route consistent with other previous goals (FIG. 6 B). When the goal is unclamped, the prior ratio of typical behavior, user error and novel behavior is 3:1:2. When goal is clamped, the probabilities of novel behavior are always zero.

The second experiment was a walking experiment in which the user left his office and proceeded to walk away from his normal parking spot. When the destination was not specified, the tracker had a steady level of confidence in the user's path (FIG. 6 D), because there are lots of previously observed paths from his office. But when the goal was specified, the system initially saw behavior consistent with walking toward the parking spot, and then as the user turned away at time 125, the tracker's confidence in the user's success dropped (FIG. 6 C).

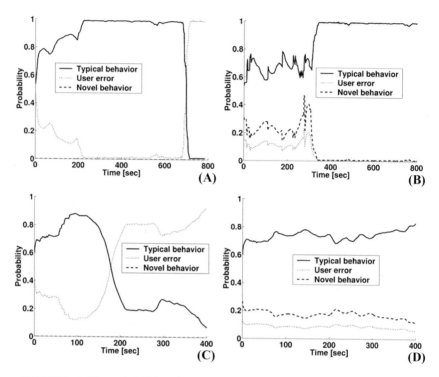

FIGURE 6. The probabilities of user mode in two experiments.

CONCLUSIONS AND FUTURE WORK

In this chapter we have described a system that can build personal maps automatically from GPS sensors. More specifically, the system is able to: recognize significant locations of a user and activities associated with those places, infer transportation modes and goals, and detect user errors or novel behavior. The system uses an RMN for place classification and a hierarchical DBN for online tracking and error detection. This technique has been used as the basis for both experimentation and for real context-aware applications including an automated transportation routing system that ensures the efficiency, safety, and independence of individuals with mild cognitive disabilities (see Patterson *et al.* 2004).

In our future work we plan to improve the place extraction. The current approach relies only on measuring the time periods a person stays at each place and uses a fixed threshold to distinguish significant places from insignificant ones. However, it is hard to find a fixed threshold that works for all significant places. If we set the threshold too big (say 10 min, as in our experiments), some places could be missed (e.g., places a user stops by to get coffee or pick up his kids); if we set the value too small (e.g., 1 min), some trivial places (such as traffic lights) may be considered significant. Therefore, to extract more places accurately, we will take into account more features besides stay duration. For example, transportation mode is a very useful indicator: If a user switches to *foot* at some place during a *car* trip, that place is likely to be significant. Because transportation mode itself has to be inferred, we must design a model that considers all these uncertainties comprehensively. In order to do that, we plan to extend the existing relational probabilistic languages so that we can model complex relations and still perform efficient inference and learning.

The application of this work to personal guidance systems for persons with cognitive disabilities is only one example of what can be called an "assisted cognition system" (Kautz *et al.* 2003). Assisted cognition systems, in general, combine artificial intelligence and ubiquitous sensing technology to create systems that observe and understand human behavior, infer and predict a person's needs and difficulties, and provide proactive guidance, prompts, and other forms of help. We believe that systems that provide such cognitively-aware assistance will play a vital role in the future of healthcare, and enable many individuals to lead active and productive lives (Turkle 2003; Wolbring and Golledge 2003).

ACKNOWLEDGMENTS

This research is supported in part by NSF under grant number IIS-0433637 and SRI International subcontract 03–000225 under DARPA's CALO project. We also thank anonymous reviewers for their helpful comments.

REFERENCES

ASHBROOK, D., and T. STARNER. 2003. Using GPS to learn significant locations and predict movement across multiple users. In *Personal and Ubiquitous Computing*. Available online at http://www.springerlink.com/content/t41dukuu8p2ulek9/fulltext.html.

BUI, H.H. 2003. A general model for online probabilistic plan recognition. In *Proceedings of the International Joint Conference on Artificial Intelligence (IJCAI)*; August 9–15, Acapulco, Mexico.

BUI, H.H., S. VENKATESH, and G. WEST. 2002. Policy recognition in the abstract hidden Markov models. *Journal of Artificial Intelligence Research, 17*. Available online at http://www.jair.org/.

BUNESCU, R., and R.J. MOONEY. 2004. Collective information extraction with relational Markov networks. In *Proceedings of the 42nd Annual Meeting of the Association for Computational Linguistics (ACL)*. East Stroudsburg, Pennsylvania: Association for Computational Linguistics.

DOUCET, A., N. DE FREITAS, K. MURPHY, and S. RUSSELL. 2000. Rao-blackwellised particle filtering for dynamic Bayesian networks. In *Proceedings of the Sixteenth Conference on Uncertainty in Artificial Intelligence (UAI2000)*, June 30- July 3, Stanford California: Stanford University. Available online at http://www.auai.org/.

GILKS, W.R., S. RICHARDSON, and D.J. SPIEGELHALTER. 1996. *Markov Chain Monte Carlo in Practice*. Boca Raton, FL: Chapman and Hall/CRC.

GOLLEDGE, R. 2003. Spatial cognition and converging technologies. Pp. 122–40 in M.C. Roco and W.S. Bainbridge (eds.), *Converging Technologies for Improving Human Performance*. Dordrecht, Netherlands: Kluwer.

GURALNIK, V., and J. SRIVASTAVA. 1999. Event detection from time series data. Pp. 33–42 in *5th ACM SIGKDD International Conference on Knowledge Discovery and Data Mining*, San Diego, California, August 15–18.

HARIHARAN, R., and K. TOYAMA. 2004. Project Lachesis: parsing and modeling location histories. In M.J. Egenhofer, C. Freksa, and H.J. Miller (eds.), *Proceedings of the Third International Conference on Geographic Information Science*, Adelphi, Maryland, October 20–23. Available online at http://research.microsoft.com/~toyama/hariharan_toyama_GIScience2004.doc.

KAUTZ, H., O. ETZIONI, D. FOX, and D. WELD. 2003. Foundations of Assisted Cognition Systems. University of Washington Department of Computer Science & Engineering Technical Report. Available online at http://www.cs.washington.edu/homes/kautz/papers/ac03tr.pdf.

LIAO, L., D. FOX, and H. KAUTZ. 2004. Learning and inferring transportation routines. In D.L. McGuinness and G. Ferguson (eds.), *Proceedings of the National Conference on Artificial Intelligence (AAAI)*, San Jose, California, July 25–29. Available online at http://www.cs.washington.edu/homes/kautz/papers/gps-tracking.pdf.

LIAO, L., D. FOX, and H. KAUTZ. 2005. Location-based activity recognition using relational Markov networks. In *Proceedings of the International Joint Conference on Artificial Intelligence (IJCAI)*, Edinburgh, Scotland, July 30 – August 5. Available online at http://www.cs.washington.edu/homes/kautz/papers/ijcai05-rmn-liao-fox-kautz.pdf.

MURPHY, K. 2002. *Dynamic Bayesian Networks: Representation, Inference and Learning*. Ph.D. thesis, Berkeley: University of California.

PATTERSON, D.J., L. LIAO, D. FOX, and H. KAUTZ. 2003. Inferring high-level behavior from low-level sensors. In *International Conference on Ubiquitous Computing (UbiComp)*. Available online at http://www.cs.washington.edu/homes/kautz/papers/High-Level-140.pdf.

PATTERSON, D.J., L. LIAO, K. GAJOS, M. COLLIER, N. LIVIC, K. OLSON, S. WANG, D. FOX, and H. KAUTZ. 2004. Opportunity knocks: a system to provide cognitive assistance with transportation services. Pp. 433–350 in I. Siio, N. Davies, and E. Mynatt (eds.), *Proceedings of UBICOMP 2004: The Sixth International Conference on Ubiquitous Computing*. Berlin: Springer. Available online at http://www.cs.washington.edu/homes/kautz/papers/UBICOMP2004Patterson.pdf.

ROCO, M.C., and W.S. BAINBRIDGE, eds. 2002. *Converging Technologies for Improving Human Performance: Nanotechnology, Biotechnology, Information Technology and Cognitive Science*. Arlington, Virginia: National Science Foundation. Available online at http://www.wtec.org/ConvergingTechnologies/Report/NBIC_report.pdf.

SHA, F., and F. PEREIRA. 2003. Shallow parsing with conditional random fields. In *Proceedings of the Conference of the North American Chapter of the*

Association for Computational Linguistics on Human Language Technology, Edmonton, Canada, May 31.

TASKAR, B., P. ABBEEL, and D. KOLLER. 2002. Discriminative probabilistic models for relational data. In *Proceedings of the Conference on Uncertainty in Artificial Intelligence (UAI).* Available online at http://ai.stanford.edu/~koller/Papers/Taskar+al:UAI02.pdf.

TASKAR, B., M. WONG, P. ABBEEL, and D. KOLLER. 2003. Link prediction in relational data. In *Advances in Neural Information Processing Systems (NIPS).* Available online at http://ai.stanford.edu/~koller/Papers/Taskar+al:NIPS03b.pdf.

TURKLE, S. 2003. Sociable technologies: enhancing human performance when the computer is not a tool but a companion. Pp. 150–158 in M.C. Roco, and W.S. Bainbridge (eds.), *Converging Technologies for Improving Human Performance.* Dordrecht, Netherlands: Kluwer.

WOLBRING, G., and R. GOLLEDGE. 2003. Improving quality of life of disabled people using converging technologies. Pp. 270–273 in M.C. Roco, and W.S. Bainbridge (eds.), *Converging Technologies for Improving Human Performance.* Dordrecht, Netherlands: Kluwer.

Embodiment Awareness, Mathematics Discourse, and the Blind

FRANCIS QUEK[a] AND DAVID MCNEILL[b]

[a]Virginia Polytechnic Institute and State University

[b]University of Chicago

ABSTRACT: Blindness might be described as a biological condition, and thus remedies could be in the realm of biotechnology. However, the convergence of information technology and cognitive science offers great opportunities for understanding and helping blind children as they learn mathematics, the crosscutting discipline most important for all branches of science and engineering. This article outlines our logic and approach for providing blind students with awareness of the embodiment of their teachers to maintain situated communication. First, we shall show that math discourse is inherently spatiotemporal, and that this information is carried by gesticulation in conjunction with speech. Second, we shall explore the capacity of those who are blind for the imagism necessary for mathematics reasoning. Third, we shall advance a set of augmentative devices suggested by our analysis. Finally, we shall outline our ongoing experiments to validate our rationale.

KEYWORDS: assistive technologies; biotechnology; blindness; comprehension

Humans are embodied beings. When we speak, our embodied behavior of gesture, gaze, posture, and facial expression are brought into the service of the communicative process. The communication of mathematical concepts seems especially to engage such cospeech behavior. The extent to which one's interlocutor is aware of such embodied behavior and utilizes it to maintain the interaction and comprehend the material conveyed is still an open question. We use the loose sense of "aware" not to indicate that one is "consciously attentive to," but only that one is able to derive information from the behavior, whether one is fully conscious of the behavioral carrier of the information or not. Students who are blind, in particular, have the capacity to conceptualize and access mathematical material (at their own level of competence), but have no visual awareness of a math instructor's embodied behavior. This affords us an opportunity to study the changes that accrue when such students are given

Address for correspondence: Francis Quek, Center for Human-Computer Interaction, 2202 Kraft Drive, Virginia Tech, Blacksburg, VA 24061. Voice: 540-231-8453; fax: 540-231-6075.
e-mail: http://www.hci.vt.edu

Ann. N.Y. Acad. Sci. 1093: 266–279 (2006). © 2006 New York Academy of Sciences.
doi: 10.1196/annals.1382.018

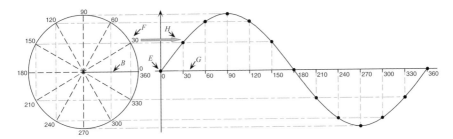

FIGURE 1. A mathematical sine function illustration.

some awareness of the instructor's physical actions, and how the behavior of the instructor may alter concomitantly. This article lays out the rationale for providing this awareness, and our approach to providing the affordances for such embodiment awareness.

To motivate our ensuing discussion, consider a teacher explaining the concept of a sine waveform to sighted high-school students using the locus traced by the elevation of a circumference point of a rotating unit circle. She utilizes a graphic (see FIG. 1) and gestures as she discusses the function. The teacher may say (pointing gestures shown as superscripts, and the duration of the deictic is marked by brackets): "The [sine function][A] {*points at the sinusoid*} traces the height of the end of a [rotating arm][B] {*points at B in the figure—Note that the italicized deictic markers do not appear on the illustration used by the teacher*} as it swings around [a circle][C] {*deictic gesture tracing the circumference of the circle in the counterclockwise direction*}. When the arm is [at zero degrees][D] {*points at the zero on the circle*}, the [value of the sine function is zero][E] {*points at E*}. When the arm is [at thirty degrees][F] {*points at F*}, the value of the sine function [at thirty degrees][G] {*points at G*} [is this][H] {*deictic gesture traces the path shown as a grey arrow*} ..." The teacher continues in her discussion showing that the arm traces the waveform shown.

Although, for simplicity, this example is a rather contrived monologue (as opposed to a more desirable discussion with the students), it serves to illustrate that math instruction discourse is a complex social interaction involving the speech of teacher and students, artifacts employed in the instruction like our graphical illustration, and the embodied behavior of both teacher and students. Much of math conceptualization is intimately tied to spatial reasoning and visualization. The dynamics of the interaction between the teacher and students requires the maintenance of a situated discourse stream that is at the same time grounded with any illustration that may be employed.

In our example monologue, the student would find it difficult to follow her teacher without access either to the graphic or the embodied deictic activity that is cotemporal with the speech stream. One can imagine the difficulty a visually impaired student may have in acquiring the sense of the function without visual access to either. This is possibly a key reason that visually impaired students typically lag their seeing compatriots in math and science education (Williams 2002). One might imagine employing multimodal communication approaches to provide the student with alternate spatiotemporal cues that seeing students derive naturally from the visual access to the embodied expressions of teachers.

ABOUT MATHEMATICS DISCOURSE

We begin our discussion with a foundational discussion of the theory of human discourse that allows us to understand the role multimodality (gesture and speech) in language and ideation. These theories of the "growth point" and the "catchment" have been developed for speech production will be extended here to speech reception, via analysis of math instruction uptake by blind students.

A *growth point* is a psycholinguistic unit in which linguistic categorial content and coexpressive gestural imagery, taken jointly, occur at the same slice of processing time. Being coexpressive and synchronous, the two forms of information—imagery and linguistic-categorial—can combine into a single processing unit. A growth point is a minimal unit of the thought process that becomes engaged during speech, and it implies that imagery is an integral part of verbal thought (a great deal of evidence has been gathered in support of this theory (Beattie and Shovelton 2000; McNeill and Duncan 2000; McNeill 2002; Beattie 2003).

A *catchment* is a related concept applying at the level of discourse—the realm beyond the single sentence. A catchment is a discourse segment based on gesture imagery. It is a collection of recurring gesture features that provide a thread of spatial cognition tying together possibly discontinuous elements of the discourse stream. A catchment can be seen to embody thematic content, and this content provides the unifying glue for thought and discourse. The concept of *embodiment awareness* refers to the ability of the recipients of communications to take in the full range of multimodal elements of the communication, specifically the coordinated speech–gesture components of growth point and catchments. By studying blind students, we can start to extend these hitherto production-based models to reception.

In this extension, reception is conceptualized, at least initially, as a kind of analysis by synthesis. A recipient generates her *own* growth points and catchments, in parallel with those of the producer whose communication she is comprehending (Furuyama 2000). Such a process leaves an observational trace of comprehension. The recipient's own speech–gesture productions can be studied, both concurrently with the teacher's and separately during self-guided math speech, as reflecting comprehension.

Gesture in Mathematics Discourse

In "The Emperor's New Mind," Roger Penrose, mathematician and physicist wrote: "almost all my mathematical thinking is done visually and in terms of nonverbal concepts, although the thoughts are quite often accompanied by inane and almost useless verbal commentary, such as 'that thing goes with that thing and that thing goes with that thing'" (Penrose 1989, p. 424). Penrose emphasizes the close psychological link between imagistic and mathematical thinking. The thinking is not entirely nonverbal, because all those "that things" could play a role in pointing to the references in an intricate line of thinking, especially with written expressions. Gestures also can pack imagery with math content, and gestural pointing can perform a function as "that thing" may have for Penrose. Our earlier studies (McNeill 1992) and new studies by Nathaniel Smith (2003) on math gestures show that gestures can be imbued with math content and this phenomenon appears on all levels of knowledge, from professional to student.

The remainder of this section applies these concepts to the speech and gestures of mathematicians, both professionals and advanced students. The aim is twofold. First, to demonstrate that math content is naturally expressed in spatial form, via gestures. Second, that catchments with math content play a role in math reasoning, by providing what can be termed "objects for contemplation" that can foster math reasoning. The gesture becomes the embodiment of a math concept that can be observed by the speaker herself and also by recipients. Such gestures show the close linkage of visualization and math understanding, a linkage that we propose to tap in the case of blind children exposed to math instruction, drawing on the visual cognition abilities of even the congenitally blind.

Gestures by Math Professionals and Students

The mathematician on the right below is saying, "*so the continuous line*ar dual," and performs a circular loop with his right hand (4 panels, one gesture, coinciding with the italic-boldface), as shown in FIGURE 2. Such a gesture demonstrates a growth point in math discourse. The analysis is that the idea of a

FIGURE 2. Mathematics professional's gesture: "so the continuous linear dual."

FIGURE 3. Examples of catchment-holds.

dual exists in two simultaneous forms—as a linguistic category ("a continuous linear dual") and an image (of circling), and implies that, for this mathematician at the moment of speaking, the math concept was embodied in this image as well as being identified as a dual.

Smith (2003) describes many examples of gestures with math content in videos of advanced undergraduate and early graduate student math majors at Berkeley. The gestures demonstrate growth points, comparable to the example just described, and also provide examples of gestural catchments. Many are "catchment-holds" in which the hand(s) move into the gesture space before the body, adopt a pose, and then remain motionless; the extent of the hold demarcates a period of thematic cohesion around some concept. Such catchment-holds provide "objects for contemplation." FIGURE 3 shows two examples. The speaker says "on both sides of zero—and so everything in the middle." The two illustrations on the left occurred as speaker endured a period of confusion during which she stared at her own gesture in the form of the two hands held apart motionlessly (FIG. 3-left). This hold then was animated and formed a new gesture in FIGURE 3-middle, when the source of the difficulty and its solution become clear to her. The hold served (successfully) as an object for contemplation.

This example also shows a possible case of embodiment awareness on the part of the interlocutor. The interlocutor (not shown) was engaging in conversation with the illustrated student and reacted to the first student's catchment-hold by saying "if it contains the point zero one" (line 7); it was this that triggered the illustrated student's insight in line 8 (R is the illustrated student, L is the interlocutor; from Smith 2003):

1	L	and it's going to be the complement . . .
		to a closed and bounded set . . .
		R's hands drift to her left
		which will be compact . . .
2	R	<XXX>
		rotates further to the left, still staring blankly at hands
3	L	plus infinity . . .
		so

4	R	what about, okay . . .
		except yeah,
		hands shift again, still held still and stared at (FIG. 3-left).
5	L	You see how it's the complement to a closed and bounded set
6	R	but, except that, umm
7	L	if it contains the point zero one
8	R	[oh, yeah, because it has to contain something on the other side –
		hands are released from hold, move around to indicate places on line
		on both sides of zero one,
		two parallel hands to indicate both sides
		and so everything in the middle]
		both hands sweep out, scoop, and then back in again (FIG. 3-middle).

An even more striking example of a catchment-hold providing an object for contemplation occurred on an earlier occasion (FIG. 3-right), when the same student was writing notes, looked up from the page, formed a gesture that she experienced only proprioceptively (her gaze was not at the gesture), and then returned to her writing—all without a word. It is hard to escape the impression that the gesture embodied math content. It is noteworthy that the experience of the catchment-hold was entirely actional; an experience a blind student also could access.

In general, at both the professional and student levels, we see that imagery is inherent to math reasoning, and that gestures play a part in this reasoning by creating images of math concepts that can serve as "objects of contemplation." Gestures can also make (albeit simpler) math concepts accessible to visually disabled students. Blind children are capable of visual imagery, and naturally create gestures. Deixis or pointing is an important subset of natural gestural behavior (McNeill 1992). Pointing in particular can be useful for keeping track of the components of a problem. Having access to both visual imagery and gesture, blind students could profit from the capacity to reason with images, if the technological issues of presenting accessible imagistic forms of math concepts and math gestures are solved.

STUDENTS WHO ARE BLIND AND MATHEMATICS DISCOURSE/INSTRUCTION

Numerous psychological studies show the blind to possess a surprising capacity for visual imagery and memory (Landau *et al.* 1984; Millar 1985; Haber *et al.* 1993). Kennedy (1993) observes even the ability to draw objects in three dimensions, among blind research subjects. Such capacities can be harnessed for mathematical thought.

Blind children also produce gestures, including gestures to other blind children (Iverson and Goldin-Meadow 1998). An example is tilting over a C-shaped hand in midair while describing how a liquid had been poured into a container—not a math concept but a gesture not unlike those in math discussions. Research using tactile displays even indicate that the congenitally blind is able to understand perspective graphics (Heller 2002).

Instructional Interaction in Mathematics and Science Education

Given the role of visual imagery and memory in math and science, the maintenance of grounded instructional communication between the instructor and student who is blind is a significant challenge. We shall illustrate this challenge by describing a characteristic scenario where an instructor discusses the sine wave in FIGURE 1 with a class of four in a school for the blind. The teacher begins by having the instruction material (graphic) reproduced as a tactile image. Typically, the graphic is first scanned and enlarged. Next, the enlarged graphic is edited on a computer to insert Braille annotations. Some systems employ a Braille extension specialized for mathematical notation known as the *Nemeth Code* (Craig 1980). The Braille-annotated graphic is transferred to a thermally sensitive paper and passed through a machine known as an image enhancer that heats the darkened pattern to make it rise. This produces a tactile image where the darkened areas are raised.

Returning to our sine wave example, the teacher might begin by first giving an overview of the graphic—that there is a x–y plot of an "up-and-down" curve on the right side and a circle with radii shown at 30° intervals on the left side—and then giving the students some time to familiarize themselves with the illustration. The teacher may then say: "Find the zero radius on the circle on the left" [*She gives students some time to do this and visits each student's desk to see if the correct radius is found—if not, she physically positions the student's reading hand on the appropriate portion of the graphic*]. "This point corresponds to the 'zero' point on the x axis on the plot" [*The students are expected to trace the corresponding point on the graphic*]. "Now go to the 30 degree radius of the circle" [*The teacher repeats the process to see if the students find the point and assisting as needed*]. "Good . . . now the height of the end of the radius is projected to the 30 degree point of the x–y graph—find the 30 degree point and the height of the curve is the height of the 30 degree radius on the circle" [*The teacher observes the motion of the reading hand of her charges and provides help as necessary*]. The instruction continues with the teacher giving the students a sense of the sine wave.

This example gives a sense of the communicative dynamic that must take place between the teacher and student, and difficulty in maintaining a situated communication flow with respect to the graphic that serves as the locus of the discourse. Clearly two elements are necessary. First, the communication requires the provision of the graphical material in a tactile format. Beside the tactile images described earlier, there is research in a variety of dynamic tactile display devices (Eramian *et al.* 2003). While there are still outstanding research questions for this in the domain of disabilities/rehabilitation research, this is not the focus of our present proposal. The second necessary element is the need to provide situated-grounded discourse. This involves the instructor, student, and the artifact.

Embodiment as a "Visual Cue"

Our basic hypothesis is that embodied communication plays a critical role in the complex spatiotemporal conceptualization of mathematics (Behr *et al.* 1984). We have shown that gesticulation and gaze play a critical role in communication between sighted individuals discussing math concepts. We posit that the interlocutor in such math discourse assimilates the visual information conveyed in this embodied behavior and fuses it with the information carried in the speech stream to comprehend the communication. If this is so, one might expect that deprivation of this embodied information in students who are blind contribute significantly to the difficulty such students have with math and science instruction. This gives us a significant "experiment in nature" that permits the study of how provision of embodied information might change the dynamic of this social interaction.

Static media alone is not able to express the spatiotemporal communication of even the simple example given earlier. A touch-based medium necessarily requires the student to scan the document as she attempts to follow the flow of the instruction. An analogous impediment that one might place on a seeing student is that she follows the same instruction with one eye looking through a tube.

In our sine wave discussion example for sighted students, we see that situated deixes into graphic are necessary to maintain discourse situatedness. We posit that sighted students employ the entirety of their experience in observing human multimodal communication in classroom and tutorial engagement. The student observes the location of the instructor, and the movement of her arms/hand/writing implement as a cue of where to look, and how the illustration/gesticulation is temporally and spatially situated with the instructor's vocal utterance. Without the embodiment cues, the student would be constantly searching for the attentional focus on the visual illustration. This is no different than the difficulty a distance-learning student encounters when trying to follow an illustrated discussion on a computer monitor with access only to a disembodied flying cursor. She will lose track of it the moment her attention is not fixed on the cursor. She will then have to search for the deictic point, expending valuable cognitive and attentional resources. Having access to the instructor's body will help in directing the student's attention and cueing her to the spatial presentation of the material. This will permit the student to devote more cognitive resources to the substance of the tutorial and not to the pragmatic task of trying to follow the disembodied cursor. This "disembodied" cursor phenomenon is a constant reality for the visually disabled student.

DEVICES FOR EMBODIMENT AWARENESS

Our preceding analysis suggests that embodied expression is critical in mathematics discourse, especially because it is bound to the imagism of the subject matter. Math discourse and instruction is rich in spatiotemporal imagery that is carried in the embodied behavior of the speaker. Our analysis also suggests that students who are blind have some capacity for mental imagery. Furthermore, tactile graphical material is readily available through such technology as the timely and cost-effective production of raised line drawings. This suggests that a solution space involving providing students who are blind with access to gesture of instructors produced cotemporally with instruction discourse will augment the students' ability to take in mathematics instruction. Individuals who are blind do not normally have access to such embodied interaction that is typically visually perceived. Even when math graphics/illustrations are displayed on media that are accessible to the blind, this lack of embodiment awareness severely impedes the critical need to maintain situated communication and comprehension.

Embodiment Cues for the Blind

We apply various tactile approaches to provide the blind student with cues for the embodied behavior of the instructor. Given the importance of the class of deictic gestures in math instruction, our approaches focus on giving the student a sense of the deictic behavior of the instructor. The purpose of these is to facilitate discourse maintenance between the teacher and student when using a graphic for instruction. We define two foci that must be detected and represented. The first is the *point of instructional focus, PIF*. This is the "zero point" of reference of the instructor's discourse and is detected by visually tracking the teacher's pointing hand. The video stream of a camera trained at the graphic will be processed to track the teacher's deixis. Various visual tracking algorithms are available to track both the pointing hand (Quek and Bryll 1998; Quek *et al.* 1999; Wu *et al.* 2003; Bryll 2004). In a similar fashion, we track the student's *tactile point of access, TPA*, on her raised line illustration. This is the location of the student's "reading hand" on the raised line graphic. We shall call the difference between the point on the student's graphic corresponding to the *PIF* and the *TPA* is the *focal disparity, FD*. Hence, the *FD* is a two-dimensional vector from the student's point of access to the current point of instruction focus.

FIGURE 4. Reverse joystick devices.

Our modes of interaction are intended to inform the blind student of the *FD* (and hence permit her to track the *PIF*). We posit that the student may employ this to target her *TPA*, or if she has already familiar with the graphic, to mentally track the point of reference. In either case, the effect is that the common ground of situated discourse with respect to the illustration is maintained between the student and instructor.

A vector may be conveyed by means of two primitives: direction and magnitude. Our devices support three tactile modes to convey the *FD* vector. In the first mode, the student reads the raised line diagram with her preferred hand, and the other hand is placed on a *reverse joystick*. This device is a handle mounted on an active motorized *x–y* table, as shown in FIGURE 4. The displacement of the ball from the center of the table indicates both the magnitude and direction of the *FD* (by the equivalent magnitude and direction deflection of the ball from center). As the instructor's *PIF* and the student's *TPA* change, the joystick moves to track the changes. This provides dynamic feedback to the student to remain grounded in the discourse.

The second tactile mode is a ring of vibro-tactile devices mounted on the inside of a skin-tight cut-off (fingers exposed to permit reading of the raised line drawing) glove (see FIG. 6). These devices vibrate with an intensity proportional to the voltage applied to them. The glove will convey the *FD* to the student by vibrating the group of devices with a Gaussian intensity distribution centered in the direction of the *FD*, and with an intensity or repetition rate proportional to the *FD* magnitude. The top of the glove will be marked with fiduciary markers to permit rapid video-based tracking of the *TPA*. The final mode of tactile interaction involves the production of *apparent motion* on a grid of vibro-tactile devices mounted on a cut-off glove similar to the second tactile mode (see FIG. 5). The direction of the apparent motion is motivated by activating the vibro-tactile devices in successive lines normal to the direction of the *FD*, and moving in the direction of the *FD*. The magnitude of the *FD* is conveyed by the speed of the apparent motion.

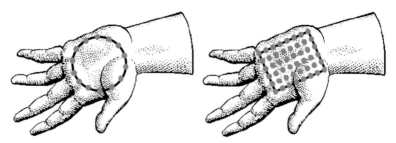

FIGURE 5. Vibro-tactile glove ring and glove array.

Device Fabrication and Experimentation

At the time of this writing, we have completed the development and testing of the devices and their drivers: two joysticks and three vibro-tactile gloves. FIGURE 4 shows the two joysticks. These devices utilize a two degree of freedom joystick driven by a pair of stepper motors. The difference between the devices is that the one on the left has a greater physical range than the other. The relative advantages of each will have to be determined empirically.

FIGURE 6 shows the construction of the vibro-tactile glove pad for a 5 × 4 rectangular actuator array, with a "closed-up" version on the right. Each device

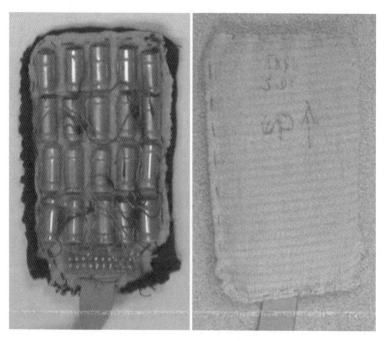

FIGURE 6. Vibro-tactile devices in 5 × 4 rectangular arrays.

TABLE 1. Firing pattern for east wave pattern for 5 × 4 glove pad

Column 1			Column 2			Column 3			Column 4			Column 5		
0	100	5	100	100	5	200	100	5	300	100	5	400	100	5
0	100	5	100	100	5	200	100	5	300	100	5	400	100	5
0	100	5	100	100	5	200	100	5	300	100	5	400	100	5
0	100	5	100	100	5	200	100	5	300	100	5	400	100	5

is an off-balanced motor that vibrates at a frequency proportional to the speed of the motor. The controller for all our glove pads is a simple microcontroller-based device that takes input through a RS-232 serial port. The actuators in each pad can be individually addressed to produce vibration patterns in any spatiotemporal configuration. Each device can vibrate at 16 different frequencies.

TABLE 1 shows a pattern that activates all devices by columns from left to right to convey a [E]ast signal. In the leftmost column, the devices fire up at time 0 and vibrate for 100 ms at a frequency value of 5. Devices in the second column begin at 100 ms and fire for another 100 ms. Similarly devices in the third, fourth, and fifth columns fire for 100 ms at times 200 ms, 300 ms and 400 ms, respectively. This pattern takes 500 ms to complete.

We are experimenting with several array configurations, including a 3 × 5 actuator array that is probably more suited to smaller hands, and a circular glove pad with eight vibro-tactile actuators arranged in a "star" configuration. As with the rectangular arrays, each actuator can be independently controlled and fired at 16 frequency levels for specified durations at specified times.

We are in the process of testing these devices to determine their efficacy in conveying directional information. We are also testing if the blind can read with their fingertips while receiving directional information via the devices, and whether they are able to integrate the directional and tactile reading information together with a cotemporal speech stream.

CONCLUSION

Humans gesture when we speak. One path from multimodal behavior to language is bridged by the underlying mental imagery. This spatial imagery, for a speaker, relates not to the elements of syntax, but to the units of thought that drive the expression (vocal utterance and visible display). Hence, gestures reveal the focal points of the accompanying utterance, and relates to the meaning of the newsworthy elements of the unfolding discourse. We advance the concept of "embodiment awareness" by which one's interlocutor accesses the situated communication, maintains the communicative context, and comprehends the material conveyed. In mathematical and scientific discourse, this relation between speech and gesture is of great importance because the underlying content is inherently spatial and imagistic. If a graphic is available to aid the communication, deictic activity into the illustration cotemporally with speech plays an important role in maintaining the imagistic discourse content.

We present the theoretical underpinnings for an approach to assistive technologies for the blind that reside in the psycholinguistics of language production. We focus these theories on math discourse, showing examples of how gesture reveals the imagery of mathematical reasoning and has the capacity to create images of the math concepts that serve as "objects of contemplation." Research with individuals who are blind suggest that they have remarkable capacity for visual imagery, memory, and conceptualization. However, students who are blind tend to lag sighted students in mathematics education. We posit that a significant impediment to math instruction for students who are blind lies in the lack of visual access to the embodiment of the instructor. We have in such students, a population that is able to access the graphical content (through tactile image technology) but are not visually aware of the embodied behavior of their interlocutor. Hence, we propose a research approach to understanding the role of embodiment awareness in maintaining situated math discourse and understanding by enabling blind students a sense of embodiment awareness.

We frame a set of augmentation approaches that employs tactile devices to provide elements of embodiment awareness. At the time of this writing, the devices and drivers have been developed, and we are beginning a series of "perception and action" experiments to assess the efficacy of these devices. Once the capacity of these devices to convey spatial information is known, we shall engage in a series of experiments with blind and sighted students in mathematics instruction.

REFERENCES

BEATTIE, G. 2003. *Visible Thought: The New Psychology of Body Language*. New York: Routledge.

BEATTIE, G., and H. SHOVELTON. 2000. Iconic hand gestures and the predictability of words in context in spontaneous speech. *British Journal of Psychology 91*, 473–491.

BEHR, M.J., I. WACHSMUTH, *et al.* 1984. Order and equivalence of rational numbers: a clinical teaching experiment. *Journal for Research in Mathematics Education 15*, 323–341.

BRYLL, R. 2004. A Robust Agent-Based Gesture Tracking System. Doctoral dissertation, Computer Science and Engineering. Dayton, Wright State University. Available online at http://vislab.cs.vt.edu/rbryll/PAPERS/Bryll-PhD-Dissert.pdf

CRAIG, R.H. 1980. *Learning the Nemeth Braille Code: A Manual for Teachers*. Salt Lake City: Brigham Young University Press.

ERAMIAN, M.G., H. JURGENSEN, H. LI, and C. POWER. 2003. Talking tactile diagrams. Pp. 1377–1381 in *Universal Access in HCI: Inclusive Design in the Information Society, Proceedings of HCI International 2003, Hersonissos, Crete, Greece*. Mahwah, New Jersey: Lawrence Erlbaum Associates.

FURUYAMA, N. 2000. Gestural interaction between the instructor and the learner in origami instruction. Pp. 99–117 in D. McNeill (ed.), *Language and Gesture*. Cambridge, England: Cambridge University Press.

HABER, R.N., L.R. HABER, C.A. LEVIN, and R. HOLLYFIELD. 1993. Properties of spatial representations: data from sighted and blind subjects. *Perception and Psychophysics 54*, 1–13.

HELLER, M.A. 2002. Tactile picture perception in sighted and blind people. *Behavioural Brain Research 135*, 65–68.

IVERSON, J.M., and S. GOLDIN-MEADOW. 1998. Why people gesture as they speak. *Nature 396*, 228.

KENNEDY, J.M. 1993. *Drawing and the Blind*. New Haven, CT: Yale Press.

LANDAU, B., E. SPELKE, *et al.* 1984. Spatial knowledge in a young blind child. *Cognition 16*, 225–260.

MCNEILL, D. 1992. *Hand and Mind: What Gestures Reveal about Thought*. Chicago: University of Chicago Press.

MCNEILL, D. 2002. Gesture and language dialectic. *Acta Linguistica Hafniensia 34*, 7–37.

MCNEILL, D., and S. DUNCAN. 2000. Growth points in thinking-for-speaking. Pp. 141–161 in D. McNeill (ed.), *Language and Gesture*. Cambridge, MA: Cambridge University Press.

MILLAR, S. 1985. Movement cues and body orientation in recall of locations by blind and sighted children. *Quarterly Journal of Psychology A 37*, 257–279.

PENROSE, R. 1989. *The Emperor's New Mind*. New York, NY: Oxford University Press.

QUEK, F., X. MA, and R. BRYLL. 1999. A parallel algorithm for dynamic gesture tracking. Pp. 64–69 in *Proceedings of the International Workshop on Recognition, Analysis, and Tracking of Faces and Gestures in Real-Time Systems, September 26–27, Corfu, Greece*. Washington, DC: IEEE Computer Society.

QUEK, F.K.H., and R.K. BRYLL. 1998. Vector coherence mapping: a parallelizable approach to image flow. Pp. 591–598 in *Proceedings of the Third Asian Conference on Computer Vision*. London: Springer.

SMITH, N. 2003. Gesture and Beyond. Undergraduate thesis, Program in Cognitive Science, University of California at Berkeley.

WILLIAMS, J.M. 2002. Nationwide shortage of teachers for blind students must be corrected. National Federation of the Blind: Advocates for Equality, Canadian Blind Monitor 14. Available online at http://blindcanadians.ca/publications/index.php?id=64

WU, S., F. QUEK, and L. HONG. 2003. Image based hand tracking via interacting multiple model and probabilistic data association algorithm. 1st IEEE Workshop on Computer Vision and Pattern Recognition for Human Computer Interaction, Madison, WI.

Nanotechnology and the Human Future

Policy, Ethics, and Risk

NIGEL M. DE S. CAMERON

Center on Nanotechnology and Society, Illinois Institute of Technology, Chicago, Illinois 60661, USA

ABSTRACT: The extraordinary potential of nanoscale research and development has yet to be matched in the growth of public awareness of the technology and its implications for society. Groups have emerged that are highly critical of the technology, and others that see it as the key to the radical transformation of human nature itself. Between these extremes, the direction of federal policy has been to encourage the technology while respecting the integrity of the human condition. Experience with genetically modified foods in Europe, where they are widely known as "Frankenfoods," suggests that wide public acceptance of a new technology is crucial to its economic success. A focus on the ethical, legal, and societal implications of the technology, and especially respect for human nature, is therefore prudent. But it is not enough to fund research on societal questions; respect for the human condition must frame the development of nanotechnology. This article draws upon our experiences with biotechnology to better understand the issues we face as developments in nanotechnology begin to impact society.

KEYWORDS: nanotechnology; ethics; ELSI; genetically modified organisms (GMOs)

As the discoveries of modern science create tremendous hope, they also lay vast ethical mine fields. As the genius of science extends the horizons of what we can do, we increasingly confront complex questions about what we should do. We have arrived at that brave new world that seemed so distant in 1932, when Aldous Huxley wrote about human beings created in test tubes in what he called a "hatchery" . . .. The most noble ends do not justify any means.

—President George W. Bush, August 9, 2001 [1]

Address for correspondence: Nigel M. de S. Cameron, Center on Nanotechnology and Society, Illinois Institute of Technology, 565 W. Adams Street, Chicago, IL 60661. Voice: 312-906-5337; fax: 312-906-5388.

e-mail: ncameron@kentlaw.edu

[1] http://www.whitehouse.gov/news/releases/2001/08/20010809–2.html

Ann. N.Y. Acad. Sci. 1093: 280–300 (2006). © 2006 New York Academy of Sciences.
doi: 10.1196/annals.1382.019

INTRODUCTION

Public awareness of nanotechnology is out of step with the level of federal funding, and the vigor with which the potential of the technology is being debated. The workshop that generated these papers and the conferences and associated publications commissioned by the National Science Foundation (NSF) are themselves notable ventures into promoting awareness of the technology, its promise, and its pitfalls. They are joined by the efforts of think tanks and pressure groups devoted to the nanotechnology agenda that range from the (Canadian) ETC group, to the long-standing Foresight Institute and the Center for Responsible Nanotechnology (CRN). Yet, as Adam Keiper (2003) has noted in his recent wide-ranging review of nanotechnology issues in *The New Atlantis*, there has yet to emerge any potentially critical interest group with traction in federal policy circles.

Many factors have contributed to this slow diffusion among the American public, including the abstract nature of the term "nanotechnology," and the wide set of applications. Meanwhile, the science space in the public mind has been filled by embryonic stem cell research and cloning. And the press, with its tendency to characterize potentially controversial questions in either/or terms, has yet to find good copy in the nanotechnology agenda. The finer points of argument that separate the Foresight Institute and the CRN on one side, and Greenpeace and ETC on the other, and distinguish them both from the discussions that have been cultivated by the NSF, have failed to grasp the public imagination. At some stage, perhaps very soon, a tipping point will be reached. When it is, the reports that break the story could have a powerful role in shaping public perception of the technology, perhaps for years to come. Policy makers and investors alike must recognize the risk implications of public disinterest, and the anticipated rapid dissemination of awareness of the technology. Already there is evidence that it is not only the environmental "left" that has found a place for the social and ethical implications of nanotechnology on its agenda. In early 2005, nanotechnology featured alongside cloning on a panel on technology and values at the Conservative Political Action Conference, one of the major events of the GOP political year. Unlike the various environmental groups that have been critical of the technology, the Family Research Council, which hosted the panel, is a high-profile leader among social conservatives. There is no question that the risk profile of a technology is strongly correlated with the social and ethical issues that will encourage or subvert its acceptance in the culture.

Part of the value of the "Converging Technologies" concept lies in its focusing not simply the technical connection of these particular technologies at the nanoscale, but the unified opportunities and challenges they present to human nature and our values. Leon Kass, chairman of the President's Council on Bioethics, has noted the interconnections of these technologies, such that advances in genetics "cannot be treated in isolation" but must be correlated with "other advances in reproductive and developmental biology, in neurobiology, and in the genetics of behavior—indeed, with all the techniques now and soon to be marshaled to intervene ever more directly and precisely into the bodies and minds of human beings" (Kass 1999, pp. 34–35).

It was in the context of the human genome project (HGP) that the acronym "ELSI" was coined for the "ethical, legal and social issues" raised by that technology, with the dual function of ensuring early awareness of problems and, in the process, aiding in the cultural acceptance of the technology, and thereby reducing its risk profile. Since in every respect the stakes are higher for nanotechnology, the development of an effective nano ELSI (NELSI) process is central to a strategy for its success.

The "NELSI" concept raises many kinds of question. Ethics is of course primary, and there is no question that addressing ethical issues early and candidly is central to the long-term acceptance of the technology. Legal questions include regulation, intellectual property, and a host of possible implications in areas, such as privacy. "Social issues" is a broad term, intended as a catch-all for other nontechnical questions. Indeed, problems of terminology and standards in the technical aspects of nanotechnology are paralleled by variety and latitude in the nontechnical categories. For example, the term "social" or "societal" sometimes encompasses educational and environmental issues within the ELSI package. It would be more logical to see environmental aspects as safety issues intrinsic to the technical side of the agenda, and educational aspects in the context of training and public information. Their inclusion with the NELSI questions may suggest that, in the initial development of nanotechnology policy, enthusiasm for technique and its transformative possibilities has pushed diverse considerations into a single category, and commingled the potentially critical NELSI function with technical safety assessment and the advocacy and training role of education. It is important that they be distinguished.

Societal issues could be defined to cover every nontechnical question. In the "NELSI" formulation the implication is that legal and ethical issues are distinct. It is also notable that "ethical" comes first. The tendency to subsume the NELSI disciplines under "societal" is regrettable since it takes the focus off the two sharpest sets of questions that are raised by any emerging and transformative technology, those of ethics and law. As the "NELSI" component of the National Nanotechnology Initiative proceeds, it will be important to monitor the funding for research in ethics and in law, and to consider the establishment of ethics and law centers. The question of the human condition lies at the heart of the ethical agenda, and is widely agreed to be of such fundamental importance to the human community that it must frame the development of the technology itself.

THE POLICY CONTEXT FOR THE DEVELOPMENT OF NANOTECHNOLOGY AND "CONVERGING TECHNOLOGIES"

In a speech intended to set the tone for the NSF's first conference on Converging Technologies, Undersecretary Phillip Bond (2003), who headed the Technology Administration in the Department of Commerce, laid out a luminous threefold charge to the conference: to achieve the human potential of everybody; to avoid offending the human condition; to develop a strategy that will accelerate benefits.

These goals are not, of course, discrete. Indeed, the challenge we confront lies precisely in the fact that they are competing. A technology that contains the seeds of incalculable economic benefit will require commensurable constraints if it is to be developed in a responsible manner. Yet, economic benefit does not always prove congruent with the human good. Therefore, economic benefits should be determined by public policy rather than steered by trends in research and development. Furthermore, we must not assume that the choices of individuals, as to where they see their "human potential" to lie, will combine in the market in a manner that does not threaten the "human condition." Such sunny assumptions would seem to get leaders, policy makers, and regulators off the hook. But it does not take much reflection to realize the unwisdom of a purely *laisser-faire* approach. When the human condition is threatened by the development or use of a technology, we have a well-established tradition of raising fundamental questions—whether in relation to hallucinogenic drugs, doping in sports, nuclear proliferation, or the shipping and shackles of slavery—that are widely agreed to be unsuitable for resolution by the market.

Addressing the high-profile science controversy that announced the opening of what has been called the "biotech century," President Bush addressed a White House audience on science, medicine, and human cloning in programmatic terms[2]:

> All of us here today believe in the promise of modern medicine. We're hopeful about where science may take us. And we're also here because we believe in the principles of ethical medicine. As we seek to improve human life, we must always preserve human dignity. And therefore, we must prevent human cloning by stopping it before it starts.

He continued, in somber terms:

> Our age may be known to history as the age of genetic medicine, a time when many of the most feared illnesses were overcome. Our age must also be defined by the care and restraint and responsibility with which we take up these new scientific powers.

---

[2] Remarks by the President on Human Cloning Legislation, Apr. 10, 2002, *available at* www.whitehouse.gov/news/releases/2002/04/20020410-4.html.

Advances in biomedical technology must never come at the expense of human conscience. As we seek what is possible, we must always ask what is right, and we must not forget that even the most noble ends do not justify any means. Science has set before us decisions of immense consequence. We can pursue medical research with a clear sense of moral purpose or we can travel without an ethical compass into a world we could live to regret.

The basic ethical question is that of the human condition itself. But it is framed by two other sets of concerns. On the one hand, we confront the traditional ethical questions that are concentrated on the application of technology to individuals, whether in clinical or, perhaps, commercial situations. On the other hand, we face the challenge that these new technologies present for the social order and the good of the human community, including those of "distributive justice." Perhaps the most telling lies in our human freedom, with the prospect of large-scale diffusion of RFID chips, retinal scanning, and so far undeveloped technologies that may render privacy the scarcest of all commodities. The central question, of course, is that of the human condition, and the conditions under which it may flourish and individuals, and the community as a whole, develop their full human potential.

Yet there are other interrelations in Undersecretary Bond's three principles. For one thing, it is impossible to speak of the fulfillment of human potential unless there is some degree of clarity and consensus on the nature of the human condition. Such clarity does not impede, it facilitates, the fulfillment of human potential, by declaring off-limits that which is not germane to the human, and declaring uncontroversial that which is. To the extent to which clarity as to the "human condition" may be attained, and public confidence secured, the unleashing of the new technology as an economic driver is enabled—and the risk of continual controversy over the development of individual manufacturing applications of the technology is lessened. By the same token, the focus on the "human potential of *everyone*" addresses in principle the global ethical dimensions of these technologies, and their transformative capacity to benefit not simply those who develop them—an important counterweight to anxieties that have been expressed about the emerging "nano divide" that threatens to exacerbate global economic inequities.

The HGP's ELSI Program

This approach follows the example set by the HGP, although in that case a set-aside proportion of congressionally appropriated resources was devoted to "ethical, legal and social" questions (this option was rejected in congressional consideration of the nanotechnology act, and should perhaps be revisited; it is hardly prudent to have ELSI projects compete with technical projects for funding, and place on the shoulders of science administrators the decisions involved). In the case of the genome project, the Department of Energy (DOE) and the National Institutes of Health (NIH) allocated 3–5% of their annual HGP budgets toward the ELSI component. The ELSI working group held its first meeting in September 1989 and defined the function and purpose of the ELSI program as follows:

1. To anticipate and address the implications for individuals and society of mapping and sequencing the human genome.
2. To examine the ethical, legal, and social consequences of mapping and sequencing the human genome.
3. To stimulate public discussion of the issues.
4. To develop policy options that would assure that the information be used to benefit individuals and society.

The ELSI Research Program was organized into four primary program areas[3]: (1) Privacy and Fairness in the Use and Interpretation of Genetic Information (privacy and confidentiality of genetic information, ownership and control of genetic information, consent to disclosure and use of genetic information, fair use of genetic information, conceptual and philosophical implications raised by genetics research); (2) Clinical Integration of New Genetic Technologies (informed consent in genetic testing, effect of prenatal genetic information, release of information to healthcare services); (3) Issues Surrounding Genetics Research (informed consent in genetics research, privacy, and confidentiality of genetic information about individuals and families participating in genetics research, commercialization of the products from human genetics research); and (4) Public and Professional Education (education for health professionals, policy makers, and the general public). Significant ELSI HGP challenges included safeguarding the privacy and confidentiality rights of human subjects who contribute DNA samples for large-scale studies, anticipating how genetic data will be used in various institutions and commercial ventures, and predicting how data may affect ideas of race, personal responsibility, and humanity.

NELSI in the 21st Century Nanotechnology Research and Development Act

The 21st Century Nanotechnology Research and Development Act repeatedly addresses the nano ELSI agenda. Similarly, the NNI's strategic plan identifies key research areas (economic, legal, ethical, cultural, science and education, quality of life, and national security) and divides the "responsible development of nanotechnology" into two categories: (1) environment, health, and safety implications; and (2) ethical, legal, and all other societal implications.

---

[3] *Available at* http://www.genome.gov/10001793.

Furthermore, the Act calls for a program that provides "public input and outreach to be integrated into the Program by the convening of regular and ongoing public discussions, through mechanisms, such as citizens' panels, consensus conferences, and educational events, as appropriate" (Sec. 2 (10)(D)). In an effort to encourage effective public engagement, the NNI plans to support forums for dialogue with the public and stakeholders (at museums, science centers, and other agency outreach mechanisms), disseminate information to the public, and evaluate public perceptions of nanotechnology. In particular, the NNI intends to encourage interdisciplinary dialogue and to incorporate research on societal implications at university-based nanotechnology centers. Additionally, the NNI anticipates funding for research involving the identification and assessment of barriers to the adoption of nanotechnology in commerce, healthcare, and environmental protection. The Act singles out for special consideration "the potential use of nanotechnology in enhancing human intelligence and in developing artificial intelligence which exceeds human capacity" (Sec. 2 (10), Sec. 9 (b)(10)).

While the HGP ELSI example is instructive, the focus of developments in human genetics is much narrower than the prospects of nanotechnology. A reading of the "points to consider" statement that has governed research within the ambit of the HGP shows this clearly (National Institutes of Health 1997). The many questions raised in the "points to consider" focus on the clinical application of human genetics. By comparison, the agenda raised by nanotechnology, especially set in the context of "converging technologies," extends ultimately to most, perhaps all, aspects of human society and the far reaches of "the human condition." This suggests that rolling an ELSI-type research component into federal nanotechnology policy, while it offers a starting-point, may not be adequate as a context for the identification, exploration, and resolution of such fundamental questions.

As the cloning debate has already shown, the new technologies raise questions of another kind than those that have traditionally divided our politics. The fact that opposition to cloning has come from both sides of the prolife and prochoice divide illustrates this forcefully (Andrews and Cameron 2001). "Conservatives" and "progressives" share a respect for human nature and a distrust of manipulative interventions. This pits political progressives against the mainstream "liberals" who are often their political allies, and conservatives who stress the dignity of life against both libertarians and others who uncritically favor corporate interests. While this process is more dramatic in the United States than elsewhere, there is an evident global move toward collaboration on particular technology issues—in defense of "the human condition"—and, beyond that, to the development of common ideas. The potential of nanotechnology, biotechnology, and cognitive science to bring about basic shifts in human nature has served as a common point of concern for persons of conscience from across the culture. This is particularly striking in biotechnology, where the policy debate is at its most advanced. Decisions during 2004 in both Canada and France to prohibit all forms of human cloning illustrate the multifaceted nature of the cultural debate about technology and the human condition. The remarkable vote of the United Nations General Assembly (by nearly 3–1), in March 2005, to urge a global ban on all forms of cloning, in response to a plea from President Bush though with support from nations as diverse as Germany, Russia, Saudi Arabia, and much of the developing world, illustrates how diverse are the cultural and ethical sensibilities shaping public responses to new technologies, and indicates the emergence of new fault-lines in the global community.

THE HUMAN ANALOGY

We have noted that at the heart of this discussion lies the question of what has variously been described in such terms as the human condition, human dignity, and the integrity of human nature. With the exception of self-described transhumanists, who share an ideological commitment to reshape or altogether supplant human nature, there is widespread agreement that the baseline policy question in the development of nanotechnology and "converging technologies" lies in ensuring the integrity of the human condition. Yet this concept, while simple to state, is not susceptible of simple definition. The explication of certain of its entailments, especially in the domain of human rights, has played a major role in shaping the modern world. But we do not have an equivalent idea of the meaning of "human nature" itself—and what it would mean to cross the line into effacing the essential humanness of our being. That does not render the question meaningless. We may readily intuit conditions that we would generally regard as effacing, in one measure or another, our humanness—all the way from the radical inhumanity of chattel slavery, and "crimes against humanity," to the abuse of hallucinogens and a life lived in frivolity and mere entertainment. The challenge we face in going beyond such intuitions and examples is vast. But it is the challenge we must take up if we are to ensure that our emerging technologies serve and do not subvert our human potential, and it is therefore the greatest question of our day.

In illustration of the importance and also the intractability of this challenge, the President's Council on Bioethics has recently devoted two volumes to the question. One volume explicitly addresses the problem of technology and its capacity to "enhance" human capacities and, thereby, to enhance or, perhaps, to degrade the human condition. The other brings together readings from the greatest of our literature to give pointers to the answer to the question by means of illustrations of what it does indeed mean to be human.

The report, *Beyond Therapy*, sets out a comprehensive reflection on the move from "therapy" to "enhancement" in the new technologies. Their point of departure is the "therapy/enhancement" dichotomy, though they recognize its problems. The Council set out the agenda in these terms:

> We want better babies—but not by turning procreation into manufacture or
> by altering their brains to give them an edge over their peers. We want to
> perform better in the activities of life—but not by becoming mere creatures
> of our chemists or by turning ourselves into tools designed to win or achieve in
> inhuman ways. We want longer lives—but not at the cost of living carelessly
> or shallowly with diminished aspiration for living well, and not by becoming
> people so obsessed with our own longevity that we care little about the next
> generations. We want to be happy—but not because of a drug that gives us
> happy feelings without the real loves, attachments, and achievements that are
> essential for true human flourishing (Kass 2003, p. xvii).

There is an intentional ambivalence in each of these statements, since while
something in each of us would seek the end without regard for the means, in
most of us there is a stronger intuition that declares the means to be central
to the proper attainment of the end. We reflect on the stories of the heroic
and the defiant that we wish our children to read, on the lives of courage and
accomplishment that we seek for them. We muse on the accolades that we
covet for ourselves. We discover that whatever our religious or nonreligious
understanding of the world, whichever location we find for ourselves on the
cultural spectrum, and whether we tend to favor or suspect the latest in technology, there is in most of us a hard core of commonality. We admire striving; we
despise those who cheat; we applaud the extraordinary achievements of those
who triumph over adverse and desperate circumstances; we seek an understanding of our own lives in heroic terms, as those who might one day be said
to have fought the good fight, and kept the faith—whatever that faith may have
been. We touch bottom in a common acknowledgement, for all our diversity,
of what human greatness might mean. We hold Mother Teresa and Abraham
Lincoln among our heroes. We watch Tolkien's *The Lord of the Rings*, and Mel
Gibson's *Braveheart*, and Liam Neeson's *Michael Collins.*

What we might call the narrative key to human nature, potently illustrated
in the vision of human greatness in the life story of great women and men, and
its counterpart in the striving and achievement of countless other members of
our species, both underscores the significance of the question, and warns us
against any expectation of a formulaic account of what it is that makes us who
we are. So, the President's Council on Bioethics report continues:

> In enjoying the benefits of biotechnology, we will need to hold fast to an
> account of the human being, seen not in material or mechanistic or medical
> terms but in psychic and moral and spiritual ones. As we note in the Conclu-
> sion, we need to see the human person in more than therapeutic terms:
>
> as a creature "in-between," neither god nor beast, neither dumb body nor
> disembodied soul, but as a puzzling, upward-pointing unity of psyche and
> soma whose precise limitations are the source of its—our—loftiest aspira-
> tions, whose weaknesses are the source of its—our—keenest attachments, and
> whose natural gifts may be, if we do not squander or destroy them, exactly
> what we need to flourish and perfect ourselves—as human beings.

And the Council, like President Bush in the epigram we set at the head of this essay, goes back to Aldous Huxley as its point of reference, with its intuition that the naïve predictions of bliss that will result from an unfettered application of new technologies will come unstuck in "the humanly diminished world portrayed in Aldous Huxley's novel *Brave New World,* whose technologically enhanced inhabitants live cheerfully, without disappointment or regret, 'enjoying' flat, empty lives devoid of love and longing, filled with only trivial pursuits and shallow attachments" (Kass 2003, p. 7).

Yet to speak simply in terms of "therapy" versus "enhancement" does not seem to work. The line is too blurred, as one person's therapy becomes another's enhancement (whether growth hormone, or neuroprosthesis). Yet the line is also fundamental, in sketching the point at which the human condition begins to come under threat. One way in which we may articulate the question of human nature that recognizes the blurring of therapy and enhancement is in terms of analogy. Technological interventions, if they are to sustain and not compromise the human condition, need to retain congruence, as it were, with the human, and not trespass upon its analogical integrity. The analogy of human nature offers a means of construing the given-ness that we inherit as biological, psychosocial beings who are members of the species *Homo sapiens.* While a comprehensive definition of what it means to be human escapes us, that does not render us unable to address the question. We may not comprehend, but we may seek to apprehend, the human. Just as we can identify the essential dogness in dogs, and catness in cats, without which we would cease to recognize our pets for who they are (and might instead, if their properties were radically changed, confuse them either with each other, or with the vacuum cleaner), we share substantial intuitions as to what it is to be human. While they may not amount to the kind of tight definition that would be required in legislation, our stories of heroism and tragedy—from Shakespeare to the news reports of *New York Times* and the all too human quirkiness of the cartoons of the *New Yorker*—afford us powerful defining marks for our common humanity. This central recognition on our part, bounded on one side by our shared notions of heroism and achievement, and on the other by the ambiguity of such subhuman exigents as steroids in sports or Viagra for performance, helps frame the human question.

In a plenary panel discussion at the 2004 International Congress on Nanotechnology in San Francisco I made the same point in terms of the idea of convergence. The powerful model of "converging technologies," with its concept of enabling technologies that catalyze change in others, needs to go further if we are to grasp the final significance of these developments for the human good. Alongside technological convergence must be placed the convergence of technology with the humanities and the arts; not the convergence of the human and the technological, but the convergence of our spheres of knowledge, of what have been famously called the "two cultures" (Snow 1959). For the final object of convergence is not the respective technologies that are mutually enabled, it is humankind and the impact they have on our nature and that of our communities. Technology ultimately enables humans. We must therefore find the primary context for our assessment of converging technologies not simply in "the human condition," abstractly conceived; but in the warp and woof of the humanities and the arts, and our induction of the given-ness of human nature, and the conditions needed for its flourishing. This is the most important of all conversations, and it must frame every consideration that touches on the role of these technologies, if we are to find a human future that is not that of the Lotos Eaters or, perhaps, the Borg.

In fact, our human nature is susceptible to the ambiguous technological benefits of enhancement in two fundamental ways. One would focus on the consciousness, through the manipulation—mechanical or pharmaceutical—of memory and the mind, generating intrinsic "enhancements" to our nature that have the effect of enhancing our experience while leaving the outside world untouched. As we know from the use and abuse of Prozac and other mood influencing drugs, "enhancements" in the subjective world can lead to powerful effects through behavioral changes in the world at large. Yet their focus is subjective. The second is the extrinsic, the objective, in which what is "enhanced" is not our affect but our capacities for reason and action. Between them, these two would seem to encompass the universe of possibility.

The Lotos Eaters

As we read Tennyson's poem *The Lotos-Eaters* and reflect on his encapsulation of the ancient vision of human life corrupted by drug-induced and contentless contentment we are uneasy, even as we acknowledge that such a life could sometimes have appeal. The active ingredient in the Lotos plant has similar, if perhaps more morose, effects to that of Huxley's happy drug "soma" nearly a century later.

Such concerns may perhaps be most starkly illustrated with reference to the "pursuit of happiness" by means of cognitive "enhancements" that involve the manipulation of perception and memory, whether through neuropharmaceuticals or cognitive prostheses. The President's Council on Bioethics' report avers that "the emotional flourishing of human beings in this world requires that feelings jibe with the truth of things, both as effect and as cause." This is the kernel of the case against all eaters of the Lotos and soma. The report continues:

> under conditions of psychic health, the moods of the mind and the experienced pleasures, both of soul and body, are neither primary nor independent aspects of our lives. They are rather derived from and tied to the things we do and encounter: the people we meet, love, and lose, and the children we rear; the activities we pursue and the successes and failures we encounter; the thoughts we have and the judgments we make; the beauty we admire and the evils we abhor... We do not really want the pleasure without the activity: we do not

want the pleasure of playing baseball without playing baseball, the pleasure of listening to music without the music, the satisfaction of having learned something without knowing anything. . ... We embrace neither suffering nor self-denial by suggesting that disconnected pleasure (or contentment or self-esteem or brightness of mood) produced from out of a bottle is but a poor substitute for happiness. (Kass 2003, pp. 264–265).

The Lewis Paradox

Whether subjective or objective, every technological intervention that is reflexive (focused on ourselves) and not unambiguously "therapeutic" raises a principle that is not widely acknowledged. In a famous essay memorably titled "The Abolition of Man," first published as far back as 1943, English literary scholar, novelist, and lay theologian C. S. Lewis addresses from afar the coming challenges of reflexive, transformational technologies. His essay opens by noting the *prima facie* appeal of these new technologies with a poignant quotation from John Bunyan's *Pilgrim's Progress*: "It came burning hot into my mind, whatever he said and however he flattered, when he got me home to his house, he would sell me for a slave." That, in embryo, is Lewis' response to the prospect of human technological enhancement.

His argument opens with a consideration of the fact that technology, which is always said to extend the power of the human race, is in fact a means of extending the power of "some men over other men." He instances the radio and the airplane as typical products of technology that like all other consumer goods can be bought by some, not afforded by others, and could be withheld by some from others who have the resources to buy. Writing 4 years into total war in Europe, Lewis is peculiarly aware of the capacity of these technologies to be used to subject some to the power of others, whether in the dropping of bombs or the broadcasting of propaganda. But his third example, the bridge to the potentials of the new technologies, lies in the eugenic use of contraception. Here some special features attach to the more general problems of use and abuse, since "there is a paradoxical, negative sense in which all possible future generations are the patients or subjects of a power wielded by those already alive." In the eugenic project, "by contraception used as a means of selective breeding, they are, without their concurring voice, made to be what one generation, for its own reasons, may choose to prefer." In light of the pervasive influence of eugenic thinking and practice, in the United States and the United Kingdom as well as Germany, in which enforced sterilization was widely employed for selective breeding purposes, Lewis is building his argument on the technology of the early 20th century even as he anticipates that of the 21st.

As a result, he continues, "From this point of view, what we call Man's power over Nature turns out to be a power exercised by some men over other men with Nature as its instrument." He hastens to add that while it can be easily said that "men have hitherto used badly, and against their fellows, the powers that science has given them," that is not his point. He is not addressing "particular corruptions and abuses which an increase of moral virtue would cure," but rather "what the thing called 'Man's power over Nature' must always and essentially be." For "all long-term exercises of power, especially in breeding, must mean the power of earlier generations over later ones."

In the nature of the case, the genetic accounting is of an even higher level of significance than economic relationships run through time, although the principle of intergenerational economics is the same: the impact of one generation's decisions on subsequent generations. So Lewis states: "We must picture the race extended through time from the date of its emergence to that of its extinction. Each generation exercises power over its successors: and each, in so far as it modifies the environment bequeathed to it and rebels against tradition, resists and limits the power of its predecessors." There can be no actual net "increase"

> in power on Man's side. Each new power won *by* man is a power *over* man as well. Each advance leaves him weaker as well as stronger. In every victory, besides the general who triumphs, he is a prisoner who follows the triumphal car... *Human* nature will be the last part of Nature to surrender to Man. The battle will then be won. We shall have 'taken the thread of life out of the hand of Clotho' and be henceforth free to make our species whatever we wish it to be. The battle will indeed be won. But who, precisely, will have won it?

Because "the power of Man to make himself what he pleases means, as we have seen, the power of some men to make other men what *they* please... Man's final conquest has proved to be the abolition of Man." While much of Lewis' analysis is directed at the possibility of inheritable genetic interventions, his thesis is of general application to the dynamic relation between technology and human nature. And his key perception is that the employment of radical manipulative powers upon our own selves, the seeming triumph of technological ingenuity, entails in truth the turning of human nature into one more manufacture, another artifact of human design.

While therefore the therapy/enhancement distinction is problematic, the line to which it draws attention—between the medical model and the manufacturing model—is central to distinguishing humane technological interventions from the ultimately inhumane, in which the human analogy is dislodged and the transformative potential of technology results in the fundamental reshaping of the human condition, which thereby loses its given-ness and begins a fateful move into the category of our projects; subject to the "degradation in the designed" (Kass 2003, p. 290).

TECHNOLOGY AND DEMOCRACY

The task is daunting. In a context bounded on one side by rapid research and development and high economic expectation, and on the other by general public disinterest and potential for disquiet, the direction for nanotechnology research and development needs to be based unambiguously on the threefold charge of Undersecretary Bond, focusing at a single point strategic technological advance, the development of human potential, and the safeguarding of the human condition. It is plain that this will require constant effort, both in articulating the strategic direction of the NNI in line with these lofty goals, and in applying them to research and development projects—in the context of fast-moving technology and, undoubtedly, rising public and political interest.

There is no question but that developing and applying science policy will be exacting and require hard choices as the direction of technological advance becomes evident. In the nature of the case, many projects could lead either to therapeutic applications (such as the restoration of sight to the blind) or to efforts at radical enhancement (such as granting humans the eyesight of an eagle, or radar). There may well be a need for recourse to legislation to prevent, for example, designer interventions in babies, and the use of enhancements in sports and examinations. Meantime, some prudent process steps could prove helpful.

Discussion in the United States has tended both to touch on the science fiction scenarios and at the same time to underplay the many elements of risk in the development of nanotechnology. That is partly because the environmental movement is much weaker as a political and cultural force than it is in Europe, and partly because there has yet to be generated a level of public interest comparable with that of the European nations in genetically modified organism (GMO) foods, or Americans in stem cell research. So nanotechnology researchers and advocates have been free to go about their work and press their claims without accountability to serious public questioning. This is true in relation to safety issues as well as broader ethical and societal concerns. While this may in the short term have made things easier for researchers, in the longer term its net effect is to raise the risk associated with the technology. One of the clear lessons of the European GMO debacle is that efforts on the part of the agricultural biotechnology sector and its government supporters backfired. They failed to convince the public that they had engaged critical concerns early in the development of the technology. This had the effect of raising the risk exposure, and helped precipitate the disastrous collapse of 1999.

Undersecretary Bond has emphasized the importance of our learning this lesson. At the World Nano-Economic Congress meeting in Washington, DC, in September of 2003, he both stressed the need to focus on ethical and societal issues as "the right thing to do," and added that it is also "the necessary thing to do":

> Societal resistance can create substantial barriers to technology adoption and diffusion. It can deter or delay the entry of new technology, its economic and social benefits, and its return on investment. In recent years we have seen such

concerns play out with respect to nuclear power, genetically modified organisms (GMOs), and other fields. We cannot allow irrational fears to prevent the adoption of technology-enabled products that—like today's GMOs — offer the potential to feed the hungry and alleviate human suffering.[4]

Moreover, as my colleague Vivian Weil has argued in her paper in the earlier NSF volume on *Societal Implications of Nanoscience and Nanotechnology,* it is important that those engaged in the technology (whether as researchers, investors, or public science administrators) do not assume that their own vision for the technology and its transformative possibilities for society is shared by the public. This caveat is central to the healthy development of public science: "[W]e should. . . try to avoid taking it for granted that there is wide agreement on the desirable consequences of various nanotechnology options." She later comments: "Experience with biotechnology shows the costliness of proceeding with mistaken assumptions about what are desirable outcomes and products" (Weil 2001, p. 247).

There is a close relationship between the public's confidence in a technology, and the likelihood of commercial success for its development. That is to say, in a market economy, ethics and risk are strongly correlated. This offers a strong argument for those whose interest is chiefly in the economic success of the technology to be open to ethical and wide societal reflection—more open than has been typical, either among corporate promoters of new technology or the engineers, other scientists, and science administrators whose role in the research and development enterprise is at the moment very great.

The cautionary tale, alluded to by Vivian Weil and Undersecretary Bond, lies in the story of agricultural biotechnology in Europe. There is much less awareness of the significance of these developments in the United States, and it is worth setting out the basic facts. Those in the nanotechnology business community have already registered its significance. So *Business Week,* in a cover story on the move from the lab to the marketplace, after discussing potential supply chain problems with such sophisticated products, noted the "GMO foods" parallel: "An even greater challenge for nano industries is to ensure that their new materials are safe in the human body and in the environment. Setbacks could sink nano companies and even lead to a global backlash among the same activists who are raging against genetically modified food" (Baker and Aston 2005, p. 68). It is worth reviewing what happened.

Technology and Risk: The Cautionary Tale of GMOs

In the speech quoted above, Undersecretary Bond noted that "Societal resistance can create substantial barriers to technology adoption and diffusion. It can deter or delay the entry of new technology, its economic and social

---

[4] http://www.technology.gov/Speeches/p‑PJB‑030909.htm

benefits, and its return on investment." He goes on to instance the example of so-called GMOs in agricultural biotechnology, and the way in which, especially in Europe, they met wide scale social rejection that resulted, *inter alia*, in very large corporate losses.

In 1998, Monsanto CEO Robert Shapiro declared the launch of GM seeds in the United States "the most successful launch of any technology ever, including the plow." Just 1 year later, Deutsche Bank announced in a research report that *GMOs Are Dead*; "[t]he term GMO has become a liability... [and that] GMOs, once perceived as the driver of the bull case for this sector, will now be perceived as a pariah" (Brown and Vidal 1999).

In fact, by 1999, U.S. soy exports to Europe were down from $2.1 billion (1996) to $1.1 billion. *Fortune* magazine's February 2001 issue noted overwhelming investor rejection of GM crops: "Spooked by the ruckus about... GM crops, investors have valued Monsanto's profitable $5 billion-a-year agricultural-business unit at less than zero dollars during the past few weeks, according to Salomon Smith Barney..." (Stipp 2001). Monsanto's stock had lost 35% in a year in which Wall Street as a whole rose 30%.

Evidently, the public held

> "...widespread distrust and suspicion" for decision-makers "especially government and companies such as Monsanto" (McCarthy 2003). Deutsche Bank's Washington analysts, Frank Mitsch and Jennifer Mitchell, explained that "[d]omestic concerns regarding ag-biotechnology are clearly on the rise. For the most part, though, it has not gotten the attention of the ordinary US citizen, but when it does—look out" (Brown and Vidal 1999). The situation has remained remarkably stable since then. As recently as September, 2003, in a government-commissioned UK poll, 86% was unhappy with eating GMO food, 93% believed GMO food driven by profit rather than the public interest, and only 2% were happy with GMO food "in all circumstances" (Coghlan 2003).

While the United States has not seen a similar rejection of GM products, Starlink corn, approved by the U.S. Environmental Protection Agency in 1998 for use in animal feed, was banned from any use after being found in the human food supply. In September, Kraft Foods recalled its taco shells that had been found to contain Starlink; on October 11, Safeway followed suit; and on October 12, Aventis canceled its license under EPA pressure—"the first time a biotechnology license had been effectively revoked" (Pollack 2000). In response to customers' refusal to buy GM foods and concerned about global markets, both North Dakota and Montana considered legislation to ban GM crops from their states for a period. Bills were defeated after lobbying by Monsanto and others (Anonymous 2001).

In July 1999, the Monsanto board met with Gordon Conway, president of the Rockefeller Foundation, who stated: "Admit that you do not have all the answers .... This is not the time for a new PR offensive but for a new relationship based on honesty, full disclosure, and a very uncertain shared future." Later that year, Robert Shapiro addressed the conference of the environmentalist group Greenpeace and publicly apologized for ignoring the concerns of Europe's consumers: "We forgot to listen" (Vidal 1999).

Vicki Colvin, director of the Center for Biological and Environmental Nanotechnology at Rice University, made this statement to a recent congressional hearing:

> In fact, I argue that the lack of sufficient public scientific data on GMOs [genetically modified organisms], whether positive or negative, was a controlling factor in the industry's fall from favor. The failure of the industry to produce and share information with public stakeholders left it ill-equipped to respond to GMO detractors. This industry went, in essence, from "wow" to "yuck" to "bankrupt." There is a powerful lesson here for nanotechnology.

> In contrast, the Human Genome Project provides a good model for how an emerging technology can defuse potential controversy by addressing it in the public sphere. Mapping of the human genome carries with it many of the same potential concerns as do other fields of genetic research. The increased availability of genetic information raises the potential for loss of privacy, misuse by the police and insurance companies, and discrimination by employers. The founders of the Human Genome Project did not try to bury these legitimate concerns by limiting public discourse to the benefits of this new knowledge. Instead, they wisely welcomed and actively encouraged the debate from the outset by setting aside 5% of the annual budget for a program to define and address the ethical, legal and other societal implications of the project (Colvin 2003).

This is an important contrast, although there are substantial distinctions between the HGP and nanotechnology, chiefly in the very wide range of potential applications, and the short- and medium-term nature of anticipated economic benefit. Moreover, while there was proper public anxiety in the early stages of developments in work on recombinant DNA, the potential scale of public unease in respect of the implications of nanotechnology could be much greater, since the manipulative capacities of nanotechnology have already been tied to the possibility of changing human nature itself.

SOME CONCLUSIONS

There is therefore a strong risk management argument for a clear repudiation of the transhumanist and "techno-utopian" visions for nanotechnology, since they have the effect of raising the element of risk associated with the technology without any countervailing economic or other benefit. It is vital that a prudent approach be taken to the development of the technology that carefully distinguishes the policy and expenditures of the federal government and its agencies from the aspirations of fringe philosophers and social thinkers. At the same time, it is equally important that those responsible for the development of the technology take pains to ensure both safety and the appearance of safety in their project funding and their adjustment and development of regulatory regimes, so that, insofar as possible, social acceptance of the technology is not undermined by scare stories. In safety and regulatory matters, the temptation to take chances, accept optimistic assumptions, or allow lobbyists for the business or the scientific communities to short-circuit prudent policies or play down difficulties must be resisted. Aside from the intrinsic importance of these questions, any other approach to the risk profile of the technology could prove disastrous.

An influential recent report from Swiss Re, the global reinsurer, sets out an approach to nanotechnology and risk that is characterized by prudence in the face of many unknowns (Hett 2004). There is a clear coincidence of interest between economic expectations for the technology, a prudent approach to both regulation and safety, and the integrity of the human condition. Indeed, one might go so far as to suggest that the economic success of nanotechnology may prove to be crucially dependent on an approach to safety and human nature issues that is both transparent and grounded in caution. As we have noted, it was the combination of unresolved safety concerns and anxiety about interventions in the natural order that led the Europeans to name GMO crops "Frankenfoods," and in the process destroy the European markets for these products.

Both transhumanists (who have commented that it "stunned even the most optimistic techno-utopians,"[5]) and critics (such as the European Commission's High Level Expert Group) have interpreted the first *Converging Technologies for Improving Human Performance* report as encouraging transhumanist approaches to the potential of nanotechnology to bring about fundamental changes in human nature. While this may have been unintended, it is necessary to find the most effective way to open clear blue water between a policy that affirms the primacy of the human condition, and the bizarre desires of those who seek in these technologies a *modus operandi* for their "techno-utopian" reconstruction of human nature itself. Whatever utility the phrase "improving human performance" may once have had is now lost in the extremism of some of the contributions to the first *Converging Technologies* report and the manner in which both enthusiasts and critics have now defined the meaning of the term.

So while it is hard to define the human condition and therefore to lay out in a systematic fashion what would detract from its dignity, it would not be possible to overstate the importance of the question. For the first time, humankind is

---

[5] "The NBIC's initial report stunned even the most optimistic techno-utopians with its predictions of rapid human enhancement, life extension and nano-neural interfaces in the coming decades. Turns out that when people on the cutting edge of the molecular, information and cognitive sciences begin to talk about merging their fields and applying them to extending the human body and brain, things get very transhumanist very fast—nanobots or no nanobots." James Hughes, World Transhumanist Association listserv posting, Mar. 9, 2004.

beginning to take possession of new powers over our own nature and our social order that hold the seeds of radical transformation. Any suggestion that these challenges are somehow peripheral, that those who raise them must be unsympathetic to technology, or that they may be left to resolve themselves in the sweep of the coming technological transformation, is naïve. Our new manipulative powers over human nature and the social order require the full glare of public debate, the application of the keenest minds, a conversation that draws on the centers of conscience in our culture and its grounding in the humanities, and policies that are as unfriendly to transhumanists and "techno-utopians" as they are to Luddites.

As we have noted, this is a global discussion—not simply because European and Asian governments and corporations are also embarked on the same enterprise, but because it is a discussion about the future of the human species and its global community. It is interesting to note that that community has begun to address the ethical and legal questions raised by the NBIC technologies, beginning with biotechnology. Both UNESCO (the United Nations Educational, Social and Cultural Organization) and the United National General Assembly (UNGA) have been engaged in developing instruments designed to set global standards for biotechnology—the UNGA in respect of the prohibition of human cloning, and UNESCO a "universal instrument on bioethics," setting questions of bioethics within the framework of "fundamental human rights and freedoms." Both these documents, in seeking to set the pace in global biopolicy for the 21st century, take as their point of departure the United Nations Universal Declaration on Human Rights, written in the aftermath of the Second World War, which has proved one of the foundation stones of the modern world. They seek specifically to set new technology questions in the framework of human values, and especially in the context of human dignity.

The Way Ahead

It is important to recognize that simply funding ELSI research in individual institutions and groups of institutions is not what is required. If the integrity of human nature is to be safeguarded in the face of the transformative implications of nanotechnology, and if public confidence is to be maintained in a manner that will ensure economic success within stable markets, a concerted effort will be needed that will involve government and civil society institutions, as well as business and other sectors of society. Energetic prosecution of technical research and development must be matched by an equally vigorous ELSI process that is visible to the public, credible—not seen as a marketing effort for the technology, and committed to the integrity of human nature.

As policy moves forward, some *desiderata* would seem clear:

1. Nanotechnology and converging technologies policy needs to be carefully inclusive of the NELSI agenda and, especially, the concern to enable the

flourishing of human potential without breaking the mold of human nature. To that end, *a policy statement needs to be crafted* that moves from the three-line charge of Undersecretary Bond to the kind of detail needed to guide decisions and expenditures, in line with the "points to consider" document that has governed the ethics of human gene experiments although, of course, on the wider scale appropriate to nanotechnology and its interrelations with other converging technologies.

2. This "points to consider" document should then become the basis for an NELSI audit process, including a NELSI statement in each grant proposal and project report, which would be appropriately evaluated by NELSI scholars. This would enable investigators to build on the principle of including NELSI components in each project.

3. A national NELSI oversight board should be established with responsibilities including the review, application, and revision of the "points to consider" document, which will require updating from time to time, as well as ensuring transparent public discussion, and advising and reporting on NELSI issues. This board should include nanotechnology experts but consist primarily of NELSI scholars and policy experts. Its mandate should include the development of links with similar bodies in other jurisdictions toward the end of developing global NELSI policies and standards.

ACKNOWLEDGMENT

The author would like to thank Dawn M. Willow, Legal Fellow at the Center on Nanotechnology and Society for her help in the preparation of this essay.

REFERENCES

ANDREWS, L.B., and N.M.de S. CAMERON. 2001. Cloning and the debate about abortion. *Chicago Tribune*, August 8, online at http://www.genetics-and-society.org/resources/items/20010808_chicagotribune_cameron.html

ANONYMOUS. 2001. North Dakota effort to ban altered wheat is set back. *New York Times*, March 31, online at http://query.nytimes.com/gst/fullpage.html?sec=health&res=9C07E7DC133FF932A05750C0A9679C8B63

BAKER, S., and A. ASTON. 2005. The business of nanotech. *Business Week*, February 14, online at http://www.businessweek.com/magazine/content/05_07/b3920001_mz001.htm

BOND, P.J. 2003. Converging technologies and competitiveness. Pp. 33–35 in M.C. Roco and W.S. Bainbridge (eds.). *Converging Technologies for Improving Human Performance*. Dordrecht, Netherlands: Kluwer.

BROWN, P., and J. VIDAL. 1999. GM investors told to sell their shares. *The Guardian*, August 25, online at http://www.guardian.co.uk/gmdebate/Story/0,,201282,00.html

COGHLAN, A. 2003. UK public strongly rejects GM foods. *NewScientist.com*, September 24, online at http://www.newscientist.com/channel/life/gm-food/dn4191

COLVIN, V.L. 2003. Testimony of Dr. Vicki L. Colvin in regard to Nanotechnology Research and Development Act of 2003. U.S. House of Representatives, Committee on Science, online at http://www.house.gov/science/hearings/full03/apr09/colvin.htm

HETT, A. 2004. *Nanotechnology: Small Matter, Many Unknowns*. Zurich, Switzerland: Swiss Reinsurance Company (Swiss Re).

KASS, L. 1999. The moral meaning of genetic technology. *Commentary Magazine* *108*(5), 32–38.

KASS, L.R., ed. 2003. *Beyond Therapy: Biotechnology and the Pursuit of Happiness*. Washington, DC: President's Council on Bioethics, online at http://www.bioethics.gov/reports/beyondtherapy/beyond_therapy_final_webcorrected.pdf

KEIPER, A. 2003. The nanotechnology revolution. *The New Atlantis*, August, online at http://www.thenewatlantis.com/archive/2/keiper.htm

LEWIS, C.S. 1943. *The Abolition of Man*. London: Oxford University Press. Also online at http://www.columbia.edu/cu/augustine/arch/lewis/abolition1.htm

McCARTHY, M. 2003. GM crops? No thanks. *Independent*, September 25, online at http://news.independent.co.uk/environment/article88426.ece

NATIONAL INSTITUTES OF HEALTH. 1997. Recombinant DNA research: actions under the guidelines. Pp. 171–185 in L. Walters, and J.G. Palmer (eds.), *The Ethics of Human Gene Therapy*. New York: Oxford University Press.

POLLACK, A. 2000. Aventis gives up license to sell bioengineered corn. *New York Times*, October 13, online at http://query.nytimes.com/gst/fullpage.html?sec=health&res=9F04EFDD153FF930A25753C1A9669C8B63

SNOW, C.P. 1959. *The Two Cultures and the Scientific Revolution*. New York: Cambridge University Press.

STIPP, D. 2001. Is Monsanto's biotech worth less than a hill of beans? *Fortune*, February 19, online at http://money.cnn.com/magazines/fortune/fortune_archive/2000/02/21/273844/index.htm

VIDAL, J. 1999. How Monsanto's mind was changed. *The Guardian*, Oct. 9, online at http://www.biotech-info.net/mind_change.html

WEIL, V. 2001. Ethical issues in nanotechnology. Pp. 244–251 in M.C. Roco, and W.S. Bainbridge (eds.), *Societal Implications of Nanoscience and Nanotechnology*. Dordrecht, Netherlands: Kluwer.

Rethinking Enhancement in Sport

ANDY MIAH

University of Paisley, KA8 0SR, Scotland, UK

ABSTRACT: This article explores the arguments surrounding the use of human enhancement technologies in sport, arguing for a reconceptualization of the doping debate. First, it develops an overview and critique of the legislative structures on enhancement. Subsequently, a conceptual framework for understanding the role of technological effects in sport is advanced. Finally, two case studies (hypoxic chambers and gene transfer) receive specific attention, through which it is argued that human enhancement technologies can enrich the practice of elite sports rather than diminish them. In conclusion, it is argued that elite sports are at a pivotal moment in their history as an increasing range of enhancements makes less relevant the protection of the natural human through anti-doping.

KEYWORDS: sports; enhancement; ethics; hypoxic training; gene doping

INTRODUCTION

As we improve our machines they will become more organic, more biological, more life like, because life is the best technology for living ... Some day the difference between machines and biology will be hard to discern. Yet "pure" life will still have its place ... because of its autonomy ... the organic and the machine are merging. (Kelly 1994, p.165.)

Recent events in the sporting world have made explicit the moral, political, and cultural characteristics of discussions surrounding the use of enhancement technology in sport. Within the last 5 years, the landscape of sport technologies and policy has changed dramatically and it is reasonable to consider that further innovations are imminent. Elite sports constitute arenas for convergent technological applications where a range of applications demonstrates the embeddedness of sports within technological structures. The prospects for even more radical technologies to influence athletic performance grow continually as progress in nanotechnology, stem cells, and genetics gain strength.

Address for correspondence: Andy Miah, School of Media, Language and Music, University of Paisley, Ayr Campus, KA8 0SR Scotland, United Kingdom. Voice: +44(0) 7962 716 616; fax: +44(0) 1292 886371.

e-mail: email@andymiah.net

Ann. N.Y. Acad. Sci. 1093: 301–320 (2006). © 2006 New York Academy of Sciences.
doi: 10.1196/annals.1382.020

This growing role of technology within sport raises questions about its future direction, particularly how, as Kelly describes it, biology will relate to the "new biology of machines."

One of the more volatile debates that surrounds enhancement in sport has been the application of gene transfer and genetic technology more generally. In 2003, the World Anti-Doping Agency (2003) instituted a policy prohibiting the use of "gene doping" and yet there is still considerable lack of clarity over whether it will ever be possible to detect all kinds of genetic enhancement. These debates have engaged the mainstream of bioethicists where controversies relating to human enhancement abound. Sport, it would seem, has become an exemplar case study for investigations into the ends of technology in society. One of the pivotal questions surrounding sports is whether the approach to doping needs radical transformation, as the age of enlightenment gives way to an age of enhancement.

This article aims to reconstitute the debate surrounding enhancement issues in sport. First, I outline the recent legislative context surrounding the regulation of enhancement in sport, which draws attention to the political nature of the issue and the tensions between individual liberties and social justice. Subsequently, I develop a conceptual framework for analyzing the effects of technology in sport, each of which reveals varying ethical connotations but, collectively, they demonstrate the convergent role of technology in sport and its multifarious moral value. Finally, I consider two case studies that, together, engage the complex ethical arguments arising from the use of enhancement but, which also both demonstrate the case for rethinking how enhancement technologies are limited by sports authorities.

LEGISLATIVE STRUCTURES ON ENHANCEMENT

Since the early part of the 20th century, various sports organizations have employed an anti-doping policy, though it was 1967 when the International Olympic Committee first organized a Medical Commission whose primary role was to address the use of doping substances. The main concern of this committee involved the risks to health that doping entailed for athletes, which, expectedly, was also seen to diminish the values of Olympism. In particular, the televised death of Tommie Simpson in the Tour de France in 1967 began a cultural turn in how the doped athlete was represented. His image of a doped athlete has become characteristic of the abjection associated with unnatural enhancements, which, I suggest, sustains part of the political will surrounding anti-doping. In 1998, the Tour de France again was monumental in transforming this political landscape. The images of athletes under siege by police provoked the world of sport to rethink its approach to doping and the World Anti-Doping Agency (WADA) was born soon after.

The current international standard for doping technologies is the World Anti-Doping Code, which indicates that two of three conditions must be met in order for a technology to be considered for prohibition from sport. These consist of the following:

1. Is the technology harmful to health?
2. Is it performance enhancing?
3. Is it against the "spirit of sport?"

It is widely recognized that determining whether these conditions are engaged is not simple and requires some form of discursive process to resolve. However, this process does not apply to all forms of enhancement technology, which are not considered in relation to the Code. For instance, when a new design element of a tennis racquet is introduced—such as the use of piezo-electric dampening technology—the anti-doping code is not engaged. Rather, the specific sport's federation will consult its own guidelines on technical specifications to determine whether the innovation is acceptable.

Since its beginning, WADA's role has been to harmonize policy and it has gradually worked toward independence from the International Olympic Committee at a time when the International Olympic Committee was under scrutiny for allegations of corruption. During this time, it has succeeded in working with UNESCO to develop a Convention on doping and its relocation to Montreal has been accompanied by renewed efforts from a range of countries whose recent actions suggest greater, rather than less controls over athletes' actions. In particular, President George W. Bush has included references to the "war on drugs" within his two most recent State of the Union addresses (2004 and 2005). Also, over the last 3 years, a series of congressional hearings have taken place in relation to doping within baseball, which aim to address the prevalence of substance use within youth culture. Yet, also during this time, critics have alluded to a need for more careful consideration on how best to tackle the use of performance-enhancing substances in sport. At a time when the United States is beginning to introduce anti-doping tests within a number of high schools, it is pertinent that the American Academy of Pediatrics (AAP 2005) published a statement questioning the effectiveness of such tests as a deterrent.

Other activities within the United States have also been relevant for raising the political profile of sports enhancement issues. For instance, during 2002 the U.S. President's Council on Bioethics received two sessions, which discussed enhancement in sport (2002a, 2002b). Also, the leading bioethics institute, The Hastings Center, has undertaken continual research in this area since the 1980s (Murray 1983, 1984, 1986a, 1986b; Parens 1998). Projects taking place at the Hastings Center during these years have been pioneering in terms of sport's commitment to funding ethical research. In 2006, Murray was also appointed as Chair of the new WADA Ethical Issues Review Panel, which, also in 2006, made its first substantive intervention by concluding that the use of hypoxic environments (also known as altitude chambers) should be deemed an infraction of the WADA Code because they violate the "spirit of sport."

Other, recent historical moments have been critical in shaping the current political landscape of anti-doping. In 2003, the now infamous Bay Area Laboratory Co-Operative (BALCO) affair reminded anti-doping authorities that designer substances are completely unknown and it will be near impossible developing direct tests for them in advance. Indeed, the challenge of proving positive doping cases has been one of the major obstacles for anti-doping authorities. This challenge has also recently given rise to changes in the law, where the emergence of a nonanalytical positive—a doping infraction without the need for a urine or blood test—means that athletes now face possible disqualification (and sometimes prosecution) based on evidence other than unequivocal facts. These circumstances are also accompanied by an emerging willingness to criminalize doping infractions and to discuss doping as underpinned by an international criminal drug mafia (see Donati 2005). These terms reshape what is at stake in the issue of doping, transforming a matter related to fairness and ethics in sport to a moral panic over drug use. An additional facet to this debate is also greater willingness to recognize the broader use of illicit substances, which are typically associated with sports performance. The AAP notes that many users are not elite athletes at all, but young people who are preoccupied with body image.

This final point alludes to the relevance of broader cultural studies of body modifications when considering the use of enhancement technologies in sport. While it is tempting to believe that the rationale for any athlete's use is merely to gain an edge over other competitors, other values are at stake. Yet, related studies of the cultural context of performance enhancement are often overlooked in the debate about the ethics of sporting performance (Denham 1999a, 1999b).[1] For instance, while there is considerable reference to how the media characterize the doping debate, very rarely is this media presentation taken into account in policy discussions. Thus, one could be skeptical of the claim that society broadly is unhappy about *enhanced* athletes. Rather, one might more adequately claim that the media discourses surrounding the *doped* athlete generate a justification for a culture of anti-doping (Magdalinski 2000).

The recent discussions on the ethics of hypoxic chambers in elite sport demonstrate how technology gives rise to a mixed reception and that the ethical stance taken by athletes or lay spectators or sports fans is malleable. In short, there is no ethical view "out there" that can, without qualification, justify the current approach to evaluating the role of technology in sport. However, concerns about doping in sport also reveal a rhetoric of "dehumanization" (Hoberman 1992) in sport, where technology might reduce the athlete's role in performance and, in so doing, diminish the value of competition. This view of dehumanization also emerges from a "mechanization" thesis that describes the scientification of sport as bringing about feelings of alienation—the manufacturing of athletes, for instance. Such an evaluation of contemporary, elite

---

[1] In 2006, WADA opened a tender for social science studies of doping.

sports, describes the athlete as a product of a scientific or technological process, somehow automated in performance.

Elsewhere, I have argued that the "dehumanization" thesis about sport and technological progress is neither accurate nor critical, but is a historical consequence of disenchantment with grand, technological progress (Miah 2004). Thus, one might describe a sense of anxiety over tampering with biology on a global scale. Yet, even in these cases, it is unclear why such tampering should matter morally. A further example that raises questions about whether there is a broad social concern about enhancement technologies is *cosmetic surgery* (or more broadly body modification). Very little is known about whether athletes would use elective reconstructive surgery for sports performance. While one might consider aesthetic interventions given the importance of gaining sponsorship within the sports world, one might also envisage other surgical procedures that could enhance the body. Indeed, there is some evidence of athletes undertaking risky, experimental surgical procedures when injured, hoping that their ability will be restored. In particular the so-called "Tommy Johns" surgery to rehabilitate the shoulder of baseball pitchers has shown anecdotal evidence that the recovered athlete is even stronger after the intervention. A related case that has been discussed widely is LASIK eye surgery to attain perfect vision, which was used by the champion golfer Tiger Woods. Such enhancements are not prohibited by sports governing bodies, which further emphasize how blurred the boundaries are between legitimate and illegitimate enhancements. These examples also raise questions about the appropriateness and capacity of sporting authorities to legislate in respect of personal biological modifications.

CONVERGENT TECHNOLOGICAL SYSTEMS IN SPORT

The suggestion that sport enhancement issues are converging with broader medical enhancement debates is reflected in the activities of key legislative agencies and advisory committees. The current U.S. President's Council on Bioethics (2003) has focused considerably on "enhancement" or, perhaps more accurately, emerging technology issues. Its landmark publication *Beyond Therapy* engages with some of the issues faced by the world of sport in the context of enhancements. Alternatively, the Australian Law Reform Commission (2003) published an extensive document on the use of genetic information within a range of social contexts, one of which includes sport. More recently, the UK Government Select Committee for Science and Technology launched a public inquiry into the use of Human Enhancement Technologies in Sport (Science and Technology Select Committee 2006). To this extent, it is useful to employ our convergent metaphor in the analysis of converging legislation surrounding human enhancement technologies. Nevertheless, of critical value is to understand how a range of technological systems affects social practices. The following section outlines various forms of technology within sport, which establishes a critical response to how technology is framed by sports authorities as a diminishing influence.

Making Sport Possible

An initial category of effect for technology involves the constitutive function of technology within sports. The category raises questions about the politics of defining technology, since it reminds us that sports have always been technological and the moral evaluation of this relationship shifts over time. Technology (primitive or sophisticated, premodern or post, recent or ancient) is unequivocally a necessary characteristic of many sports without which they would not be possible. It is thus, no surprise to notice that, as the technology evolves, so too do the sports. In Formula One motor racing, it is possible to see this most clearly where advances in motor engineering vastly affect the outcome and demands upon a driver and race team. In such a performance-driven sport, the technology has often been argued as being the determining factor of success, where the driver plays merely a secondary role (Aveni 1976). Yet, such a view would be naïve or, at least, incomplete since even those who reject the most recent advances in technology that they consider to have reduced the skills required to be a driver, no such views would argue for a return to cars from the earlier parts of the 20th century. To this extent, one might describe that the relationship between technology and sports has an optimal limit beyond which something critical about the sports particular character is compromised. One important conclusion that must be drawn from this is to realize that technologies are not antithetical to sports and that it can only be the way in which they develop—rather than their very existence in sport—that raises ethical problems.

Safety and Harm

One of the central aims of technological change in sport has been to improve safety and reduce the risk of harm. Many rule changes within sports can be viewed as *technologies of knowledge* that aim to restructure the range of technological interactions—such as the foot against the floor or a shoulder's movement when swinging a racket. Other examples include the redesigning of the javelin in the 1980s, when athletes were throwing dangerously close to the spectators. The only reasonable solution to this impending problem was to change the specifications of the javelin so that the athletes could not throw it as far. This resulted in a change in the kinds of athlete that were successful as javelin throwers, from the strongest to the technically proficient. Other examples include:

1. Improved floor surfaces within sports halls to reduce shock to athletes when landing or bounding (Bjerklie 1993).
2. Introduction of plastic helmets in American Football to reduce head injury (Gelberg 1995).
3. More sophisticated shoe design for more support to foot during athletic events.
4. Increased wicking qualities in clothing to protect climber or mountaineer from the cold and rain.
5. Spring board surface in diving to prevent slip and increase resiliency of board tips to reduce injury (Bjerklie 1993).
6. Sturdier epee and foil in fencing, as well, Kevlar jackets for more protection but with no loss to movement (Tenner 1996).
7. Navigational equipment in sailing (Inizan 1994; Tenner 1996).
8. Carbon composite Poles in Pole Vaulting and enhanced safety pits, allowed more daring contest and higher vaults (Bjerklie 1993).

These examples identify the imperative for sports federations or governing bodies of sport to strive for their practices to be less dangerous for the competitors by introducing new technological measures. Their ethical justification derives from an interest in athlete safety and, generally, allowing the athlete to perform at an optimal level without placing undue stress on the body. However, these examples are controversial since their implementation can change the kind of test that is constituted by the competition.

Deskilling and Reskilling

Technological innovations can alter the way that sports are played. They can change the conditions of training that are required to be successful at a particular skill, and can even make it easier to perform the required skills. Examples of such technologies include:

1. U-groove golf clubs that allowed greater accuracy on stroke (Gardner 1989).
2. Depth finders in fishing to make it easier to locate large schools of fish to enhance prospects of catching (Hummel and Foster 1986).
3. Superman cycling position that allowed more streamlined position for greater speed (Fotheringham 1996).
4. Breathable clothing material used to regulate body temperature in extreme climates (Miah 2000a).

The PGA's reasons for disallowing the "square" or "U-grooved" irons from golf in 1990 reflect how technology can alter the kinds of skill required of an athlete (Gardner 1989). Gardner describes how tour players considered that the clubs gave the golfer an advantage by creating a higher spin rate, which translated into better ball control. Some tour professionals had been opposed to their use because of a concern that they "devalue true golf skill and consolidate their talent" (p. 69). Similarly, Hummel and Foster (1986) recognized that the "spinning reel" in fishing "virtually eliminated backlash in casting and thus the necessity of an 'educated thumb' to act as a drag on line being cast" (p. 46). Thus, the innovation was considered to have democratized the skills of the sport and had devalued or deskilled the activity. While these devices would seem quite useful for a novice who may require assistance to engage in the activity in a meaningful way, their application to competitive sports is implied—yet, it is unclear that such things are beneficial within elite competition.

Additionally, it is not representative to argue that these technologies necessarily deskill a sport. It may also be argued that technological changes in sports "reskill" an activity. In explanation of "reskilling" one may consider the controversial "superman" cycling position introduced by Graeme Obree in 1995. The position entailed the arms of the cyclist being placed in front of the face and the seating post being unusually high, thus making the position more aerodynamic. Thus, while the skill had not been made any easier, it had altered the bicycle such that it did not resemble conventional cycling positions (it had been reskilled and it made it possible to achieve more without any greater physical capability). Interestingly, the International Cycling Union (ICU), made this very argument when legislating against the use of the position. In concluding their stance on the "superman" position, the ICU argued that the technical developments had "obscured the physical demands made by cycling, and had made it harder for the man on the street to identify with elite cyclists" (Verbruggen cited in Fotheringham 1996, p. 23). Despite such claims, it might be wondered how the ICU justify the acceptance of methods of design and construction of bicycles that are more comparable to the design of an aircraft than an "everyday" bicycle. It would seem possible to argue that, on similar grounds, the use of such materials also makes the bicycle unacceptably different from a preconceived notion of what is a bicycle.

Dehumanizing and Superhumanizing

The cycling example raises a more complicated question about whether an athlete can claim responsibility for any performance achievement and puts into question whether the human athlete or the technology has achieved the performance. However, to answer such a question requires being able to make clear distinctions between each. This category presumes that something clear can be said about humanness that is lessened or removed by the use of some technology. This categorization might be criticized for bringing together two quite different claims about a technology, which are not at all oppositional. Indeed, the elite athlete might both be dehumanized and superhumanized by a technology.

Nevertheless, the purpose of this categorization is to demonstrate ideas about the moral implications of technology so as to identify the kinds of argument that are being made about the effects of technology. In this sense, dehumanization is justified inasmuch as researchers of technology have made such claims. Some examples that have been (and might be) seen as reflective of dehumanizing/superhumanizing technologies are as follows.

- Doping and drug taking (Fraleigh 1984; Hoberman 1992).
- Genetic enhancement (Miah 2000b, 2004; Munthe 2000).
- Springboard in diving allowed divers to gain more height on dive (Bjerklie 1993).
- Fiberglass archery bows, more resilience and more consistency (Bjerklie 1993).
- Plastic/metal composite discus allows longer throw.
- Barbells are now stronger with some flexibility to allow the lifter to use more technique when lifting and drop bar at end of lift to save strength (Bjerklie 1993).
- Kevlar and carbon fiber kayaks are lighter, more sturdy and easier to maneuver.

While various authors discuss how these technologies alter what it means to be human, adding content to such claims is more problematic as identifying the salient characteristics of humanness that are removed or lessened by such technology is not easy. Nevertheless, if one is to place any credit at all in these, at least, intuitions about technology, then it is worth considering the possibility that they are not consistent with the characteristics of humanness. If one is not convinced that these technologies do, in fact, dilute human qualities, then it can be useful to discuss whether any kind of technology could be a threat to humanness. Would, for example, a human that is largely a mechanoid be a challenge to humanness? If not, then is a robotic human, one whose mental capacities are formed by some artificially intelligent computer, a threat to humanity? If such beings can be seen as a challenge to humanness, then there might be some grounds for concern. Where this line is drawn is less important than the possibility that it could be crossed, which I suggest, is often the basis on which anti-doping policy is justified (i.e., there is an imperative to draw a line somewhere).

Increase Participation and Spectatorship

One of the major interests of a sport governing body is to maximize the breadth of inclusion within the given sport. This ambition often translates into the development of technology that can allow a sport to become more accessible to prospective participants. The example is slightly different from developing technologies to make the sport easier, as the main aim here is the maintenance of standards, with the broadening of participation. Alternatively, equipment is often developed that can even exclude particular kinds of individual from participation. For example, the sophistication of technology demands a level of finance that is beyond many individuals. Examples of such technology include the following:

1. Artificial turf for field sports (Tenner 1996).
2. U-grooved golf clubs (Gardner 1989).
3. Carbon composite tennis racquets and mass production of other kinds of equipment (Brody 2000).
4. The carving ski (alpine) that makes it easier to learn skiing.
5. Different-sized tennis balls (Miah 2000c).
6. Varying speeds of squash ball for different levels of competence.

The benefits of such technology are not complex. The ability to reach a wider audience can seem a worthwhile ambition. However, the ends of such ambitions can be problematic for the sport. For example, in sports, such as climbing or skiing, there exist limited natural resources, the overuse of which could seriously damage the environment and lessen the aesthetic experience of the performance. If mountains were overrun with climbers and skiers, they could lose their tranquil characteristics, which would seem to entirely contradict what is valuable about these activities. Along these lines, it is not at all clear how big would be big enough for sports. While the ambition for widening participation is admirable, its justification tends to be more financial than moral. Yet, the exploitation of a sport simply to widen participation and generate more financial resources seems ambiguously beneficial.

These varied examples provide some basis for understanding the complexity and effect of technologies in sport and the range of values that are engaged when considering the ethical implications of any proposed technological innovation. In addition to these effects, one must also recognize that there are further concerns about the unknown consequences of new technologies. Indeed, it is crucial to recognize how anti-doping authorities develop policy on the basis of lacking scientific evidence that can demonstrate safety.

Alternate Conceptualizations

Within this brief conceptualization there is the degree of overlap among the different technological effects. For example, the improvement of floor surfaces within sports halls that can significantly reduce injury and which would thus, fit within the safety category, also reskills the activities. As such, the categorization vastly simplifies any single example of technology within sport and, therefore, does not suitably characterize it. Consequently, it is tempting to draw some further categorization about them in an effort to find some conceptual framework that demarcates technologies from nontechnologies. Thus, one might separate them into such categories as body, external, internal, environment, or something similar. However, this categorization would not yield any further critical edge to the main task, which is to demonstrate the broader performative role of technology as a way of reconceptualizing the role and ethics of enhancement within sport. It is not reasonable to expect that the categorization alone will yield answers to which ones are acceptable or not. Instead, the reason for undertaking this conceptualization is to reveal the range of technological effects that arise within sport and to demonstrate the range of moral narratives that they provoke. In short, the present approach to enhancement technology within the structures of sports administration, where, for instance, the performance-enhancing capacities of the Speedo FastSkin swimming suit are completely separate from debates over the ethics of blood doping creates a limited environment for ethical debate. Rather than an anti-doping policy, a "performance policy" (Miah 2005a) is necessary to develop so that this broader range of ethical discussions can take place.

The final substantive sections of this article will explore two case studies of human enhancement technology in sport. I have already mentioned the recent discussions surrounding the use of hypoxic chambers within elite sports. It is useful to focus on this technology as a specific case study, because it is an instance of technological enhancement whose ethical status remains in great doubt and because it does not easily fall within a specific kind of categorization. Subsequently, I will discuss the emergence of gene doping within sport, outlining some of the crucial ethical problems it provokes.

THE ETHICS OF HYPOXIC TRAINING

Unlike many forms of doping, the use of hypoxic chambers within sports does not involve synthetic substances that can easily be characterized as artificial or unnatural. Moreover, it cannot easily be aligned with the antisocial connotations of drug abuse, which are so effective at garnering political sport. At most, the arguments surrounding its use involve its effect as a form of cheating or as a health risk. Yet, for some time now it has not been possible to describe the use of such chambers as a form of cheating since they have been legal. Moreover, a number of high profile athletes have used them extensively without any moral outrage reported.

The science of hypoxia involves changes in the partial pressure of oxygen within an environment, which increases the body's hematocrit level. These changes reduce the partial pressure of oxygen in the pulmonary capillaries, which leads to an increased need to breathe. In turn, the body senses the changes and increases the production of red blood cells, which are rich in oxygen carrying protein (hemoglobin). This enhanced production leads to a greater aerobic potential for the individual.

In the same way that I allude to the importance of Tommie Simpson's tele-vised death, one might also draw attention to the visual presence of hypoxic chambers. It was not so long ago that the pop singer Michael Jackson was pho-tographed within such a chamber. Such a context easily frames this technology as something alien to "normal" human practices. Indeed, the characteristics of the technology tend to have required obstructive practices for athletes who will need to spend extensive time in these isolated booths. Such spaces conjure up images of athletes as rats in laboratories simply growing stronger almost by magic (Stivers 2001). Such images forces one to question whether the WADA Code seeks to protect an athletically *moral* way of life more than an *ethical* practice. Hypoxic training has also been particularly interesting because it seems to have divided the scientific community and its support for WADA's work.

Yet, the more intriguing characteristics of this issue relate to the ethical de-bate that has ensued. During 2006, the ethical status of hypoxic chambers was put to the recently formed Ethical Issues Review Panel in WADA, which is chaired by Thomas H. Murray. The Panel's report raises a number of specific arguments as critical to the ethical status of hypoxic training, beginning its discussion paper by asking what it is about sport that people find honorable, admirable, and beautiful. Their position concludes that hypoxic training is a violation of the "spirit of sport" (WADA Code) insofar as it does not require the "virtuous perfection of natural talents" matters to sport. In short, their view was that the use of such chambers was "passive" requiring no skill, knowl-edge, or effort on the part of the athlete. They state: "my responsibility for my performance is diminished by technologies that operate upon me, indepen-dent of any effort on my part." As was mentioned earlier, the "spirit of sport" concerns constitute only one element of the process by which a technology might be deemed a doping technology. Yet, in this case, it was the first major case where the ethical perspective was seen as being potentially decisive to the overall outcome, since the health risks surrounding hypoxia were unproven. The final outcome of this inquiry made in September 2006 was that the hy-poxic chambers should remain legal, which seems satisfactory to a number of commentators who challenged the proposal to prohibit their use (Levine 2006). However, an exploration of its reasoning elaborates on how categories of effect are articulated in moral language within discussions surrounding performance enhancement in sport.

The Nonvirtuous Perfection of Natural Talents

The Panel's view indicates that only virtuous nurturing of natural talents is valued in sports. To this extent, they note that an athlete who benefits from the knowledge of an excellent coach, engages with some form of relationship that implies their interacting. Yet, is such a view a reasonable articulation of the athlete–coach relationship? The athlete will not have undertaken any virtuous sacrifice to access such knowledge. To illustrate this, let us compare two athletes, one who has an international coach and another who has a regional coach. While each of these athletes might engage with some process of learning to gain insights into training and so on, the crucial point seems to be whether the difference in what they gain is attributable to the athlete's virtuous perfection of natural talents. I suggest it does not and, for this reason the argument from virtuous perfection would require that all athletes are similarly privileged in the expertise of their entourage. In anticipation that this would not be a sufficient rejection of the position, I also suggest that the mere conscientious following of advice and accepting it, does not, in my view constitute or imply virtue. Indeed, as is often the case in the world of sport, an athlete will follow the advice of the coach, doing precisely what they are told to do. Moreover, they will continue with such behavior providing that performance improves. If it fails to improve, then the athlete may switch coaches with nearly no care about the virtuous relationship they will have cultivated. The role of virtuous action here is unclear but doubtful. Nevertheless, if virtue were present here, one would not expect the dismissal of a coach merely due to failure to deliver results. Yet, this is the established ethos of sports practices. To this extent, it is false to suggest that the spirit of sport necessitates that *only* virtuous action is valued. Consequently, one can accept without controversy that nonvirtuous action—actions lacking virtuous content, rather than unvirtuous acts, such as cheating—can also have value in sport. By proposing a virtue theoretical view of ethics, it neglects other ways in which people value sport—for instance the value of witnessing misbehavior on a playing field.

Further examples challenge the importance of *virtuous* perfection as a limiting ethical criterion. The Panel mentions that use of "improved running shoes. . .requires interactions between the athlete and the technology; the human athlete utilizes, masters and controls the technology, not the other way round" (Ethical Issues Review Panel, World Anti-Doping Agency 2006). It seems unusual that one would talk about new running shoes as having been mastered by the skills of athletes. It is more likely that good performance technology is "seamless" for athletes; it appears as an extension of one's body that demonstrates its synergy with sporting actions by evidence that it is making the body perform better. Consider the use of piezoelectric technology within skis. In this case, it is, again, a stretch of the word virtue to suggest athletes become better by any special moral commitment. More likely, the accomplishment or enhancement in performance will arise quite easily. If the response to this argument is that knowledge of one's body is itself a form of virtuous perfection, then this seems a strange conceptualization of the word "virtue," which should imply some attribute of moral character.

While this response to the Ethics Panel position does not reject the claim that "the means" are ethically relevant in sport, it does not accept the notion that *only* virtuous means are valued. The Panel concludes that the crucial test will be "whether it supports or detracts from sport as the expression of natural talents and their virtuous perfection" but neither might be affected by the introduction of a particular performance-enhancing technology. Requiring that any enhancement be earned through virtuous action is too great a requirement, which should not be interpreted as too high an ideal. Nonvirtuous action does not mean that it lacks value.

Technology, Expert Systems, and the Athlete

The Panel recognizes that *technology and expert systems* have improved sports (though their report does not say how), but that the *athlete's* performance is the crucial factor that gives sport value. Yet, it is necessary to tease out the distinction between these two concepts since their relationship, I suggest, plays a crucial part of framing the moral evaluation of technological enhancements. The concerns of the Panel in this area seem to involve claims over responsibility for the performance. Their view might be similar to the deskilling thesis noted earlier. The Panel presumes that the athlete is and should remain largely responsible for his or her achievements. Moreover, the expert systems that surround the athlete are mere supplements to this achievement. Yet, one of the crucial factors in the negative culture of anti-doping arises from such a separatist perspective. Instead, the athlete should be empowered to become part of the "expert systems" surrounding technological development in sport, making conscientious and active decisions in the process of developing greater achievements. Indeed, many athletes are experts in sports science, to the extent that their own educational formation involves studying this subject. In a broader context, there might be a number of concerns with conflating the collective and the individual that go beyond their mere attribution of achievement.

The appeal of making a clear distinction between the athlete and the supportive system through which an athlete journeys to become elite derives from concerns about athletes' vulnerability to the political will of such systems. We remain haunted by stories of the GDR (East Germany), where the political value of sporting success gave rise to unacceptable exploitation and manipulation of individual athletes. Moreover, we expect that any state-funded program to improve athletes will have such a character. This is more broadly contextualized within views about human enhancement more generally. Without a vigilant permissive environment for human enhancements, this will remain a prospect. As such, the burden must be on critically establishing the conditions through which legitimate human enhancements could be permissible. Yet, our model of the relationship between technology and the athlete might benefit by analogizing it to established medical practice, where the ethical emphasis should be on the individual's autonomy as a guiding determinant of acceptability. Perhaps a useful metaphor here is the driver in the seat of a racing car. In this case, we would not describe the driver as only partially responsible for the performance or, at least, we might recognize her/him as an integral part of a performance that involves a complex biotechnological interface.

Technology in Progress

It seems remarkable that, for so many years, athletes have used hypoxic training without it giving rise to moral outrage. In various presentations, I have heard that athletes do not much like the form of this kind of commitment. The idea of spending time locked in a room doing nothing cannot easily be associated with the practice ethos of sports. Yet, this view of what hypoxic training entails is also ambiguous or, at least, contingent. For instance, there already exist rooms, which resemble regular rooms within a home. Moreover, one could envision its construction as a space of reflection on an athletic life or for learning essential information about the practice of sports. The point is that a hypoxic chamber is a work in progress and that the moral judgment of this technology on how it seems to occupy a quite different social space compared with the idea of athletes running in mountains is neither accurate nor relevant. Moreover, the development of this technology is only likely to become more "seamless" in the way that I mentioned earlier.

The Panel rightly concludes by indicating that the spirit of sport cannot require "an absolute leveling of athletes' circumstances." Thus, athletes that live at sea level cannot claim an injustice just because they might be disadvantaged by their location. However, where positive action is required to prohibit a sufficiently safe technology that could allow a more egalitarian form of equality to emerge, then it is counterintuitive to undertake such action. For this reason, the claim that hypoxic chambers violate the "spirit of sport" is not proven. Moreover, I have argued how such use can quite comfortably correspond with the nonvirtuous actions of athletes, which are also constitutive of sports value.

In short, it is possible for a performance-enhancing technology to be of no detriment to the spirit of sport, but simply involve a reskilling of the activities an athlete undertakes in order to remain competitive. The intrinsic value of sports—the skills required to bring about sporting performance—are unaffected by hypoxic chambers. At the very most, their use will raise the standard of sporting achievements, which is precisely what gives elite sports their unique social value. Undertaking action that curbs such technological development within sport compromises the broader intrinsic value of the sports community, which themselves are undervalued within the Panel's report. As I mention earlier, the ideal to approach is one where technologists are seen not merely as auxiliary to athletes, but integral to bringing about the sport performance. While it is inevitable that circumstances arise where an athlete is simply introduced to a new performance-enhancing technology, it is crucial to remember that every part of that technology's development has involved members of the athletic community. Indeed, as is true of other technologies, it is likely that open access to this innovation will lead to a more nuanced culture of use.

GENETICALLY MODIFIED ATHLETES

While the hypoxic chamber issue involves a claim about the "passiveness" or less-skilled requirements of the sport, gene transfer technology in sport is prohibited largely for its being a form of experimental science. The most likely applications of gene transfer to sports involve manipulation to enhance endurance capacity or muscle mass. Currently, research implicated for gene doping includes modifications to growth factors, such as IGF-1 (Lamsam et al. 1997; Barton-Davis et al. 1998; Martinek et al. 2000; Goldspink 2001), PGC-1alpha (Lin et al. 2002), recombinant EPO (Svensson et al. 1997), and the so-called ACE gene (Gayagay et al. 1998; Montgomery et al. 1998, 1999; Brull et al. 2001).

Ethically, its application to sport is considered by officialdom as unacceptable since there is no protocol for such use, nor standards of efficacy or safety. To this extent, any attempt to genetically modify athletes would currently be seen as medical malpractice. As such, any argument in favor of gene doping will need to address the broader question about the limits of medicine, which will involve tackling fundamental matters of medical ethics. Specifically, an argument will be required to justify treating healthy humans (athletes) with medical technology.

The emergence of gene doping should mark a new paradigm for anti-doping policy makers, because it presents a new landscape of ethical issues, political views on enhancement and concerns. This position does not suggest genetic exceptionalism, but speaks specifically to the moral opinions surrounding genetics, which are rather more unresolved than one might say for doping generally. As a substantive response to the ethics of gene doping, it is doubtful that it would dehumanize the athlete or that it would be merely passive. Moreover, it only constitutes cheating in so far as it is against the rules. Yet, our question involves asking what the rules should be in the first place.

Objection to genetic enhancement must wrestle with the positive contribution of technological change in medicine and the possibility that genomics could confer a competitive advantage through therapeutic application alone, such as through attending to athletic injuries. The moral tension arising from the application of genetic engineering to sport reflects the crisis of authenticity in contemporary society, specifically, the demise of the natural human and the widespread ambivalence or *anthropic bias* (Bostrom 2002) over this. Fair play and health are secondary matters in this debate and, yet, they dominate, in part because they lend themselves to an artificial, but sincere moral intuitionism and paternalism that remains part of elite sporting culture.

Considerable clarification is needed on what constitutes the genetically modified athlete. Currently, sports authorities are interested only in the somatic cell doper, who themselves consent to using gene transfer to gain an edge over a competitor. Yet it is unclear what would happen if an individual is made to be "better than well" (Elliott 2003) through the same kind of use in a therapeutic context. Alternatively, are we interested in the athlete who has been born from parents that have, themselves, been modified? Last, does the ethical debate take into account the child born from parents who select a form of enhancement for their child, or perhaps select their preferred embryo on the basis of its propensity for elite sports competition? In 2004, the first genetic test for performance was made commercially available. One year later, the WADA (World Anti-Doping Agency 2005) announces in its Stockholm Declaration on gene doping that such tests are to be discouraged.

CONCLUSION

Each of the issues and effects that have been discussed are imbued with similar philosophical concerns about the human condition and the degree to which enhancement technology can alter it. The ethical debate must take into account the risks to vulnerable groups, such as children or athletes who enhance because they feel coerced *and* the liberties of adults who make lifestyle decisions about body modification (Miah 2005b). Yet, it must also consider the limits of ethical policy making within the world of sport and the relationship of this to broader structures of ethical governance within society. When considering what should be the strategy for anti-doping officials in relation to gene doping, it is necessary to return to fundamental questions about the value of sport, consider how these values might have changed, and recognize the broader bioethical context within which decisions about medical technology are made. This requires that elite sports organizations reevaluate established systems of rewarding excellence, in order to promote a moral climate in sport that takes into account inherent natural and social inequalities, which are constitutive of sports practices.

The conceptual framework of technological effects is useful for (*a*) establishing how ethical issues arise in the context of technological change, (*b*) clarifying the interrelatedness of effects arising from any one technology, and (*c*) revealing that the debate surrounding enhancement as a doping infraction is only one component of a broader relationship between sport and technology. The two case studies that have been discussed are perhaps the most controversial examples within anti-doping debates presently. Unlike performance-enhancing drugs, they do not encounter the same forms of resistance and, as such, the moral evaluation of them is unclear. I have suggested that more instances of human enhancement technologies are likely to emerge in sport, which further stretch the capabilities of restrictive approaches to such use. As human enhancements become a constitutive element of broader social circumstances—and as enhanced adults give birth to similarly enhanced children—the concept of enhancement and of the natural human will become even more difficult to sustain. In such a future, sports authorities might still attempt to protect a particular way of life for an athlete, though athletes—as humans—might no longer see either the need or the relevance.

REFERENCES

AMERICAN ACADEMY OF PEDIATRICS. 2005. Policy statement: use of performance-enhancing substances. *Pediatrics 115*, 1103–1106.

AVENI, A.F. 1976. Man and machine: some neglected considerations on the sociology of sport. *Sociology Bulletin 51*, 13–23.

AUSTRALIA LAW REFORM COMMISSION. 2003. *ALRC 96: Essentially Yours.* Canberra: Commonwealth of Australia.

BARTON-DAVIS, E.R., D.I. SHOTURMA, A. MUSARO, N. ROSENTHAL, and H.L. SWEENEY. 1998. Viral mediated expression of insulin-like growth factor I blocks the aging-related loss of skeletal muscle function. *Proceedings of the National Academy of Sciences, USA 95* (December): 15603–15607.

BJERKLIE, D. 1993. High-Tech Olympians. *Technology Review 96*, 22–30.

BOSTROM, N. 2002. *Anthropic Bias: Observation Selection Effects in Science and Philosophy.* London and New York: Routledge.

BRODY, H. 2000. An overview of racket technology. Pp. 43–48 in S.A. Haake and A.O. Coe (eds.), *Tennis, Science, Technology.* London: Blackwell Science.

BRULL, D., S. DHAMRAIT, S. MYERSON, J. ERDMANN, V. REGITZ-ZAGROSEK, M. WORLD, D. PENNELL, S.E. HUMPHRIES, and H. MONTGOMERY. 2001. Bradykinin B2BKR receptor polymorphism and left-ventricular growth response. *The Lancet 358*, 1155–1156.

DENHAM, B.E. 1999a. On drugs in sports in the aftermath of Flo-Jo's death, Big Mac's attack. *Journal of Sport and Social Issues 233*, 362–367.

DENHAM, B.E. 1999b. Building the agenda and adjusting the frame: how the dramatic revelations of Lylle Alzado impacted mainstream press coverage of anabolic steroid use. *Sociology of Sport Journal 16*, 1–15.

DONATI, A. 2005. Criminality in the international doping trade. *World Anti-Doping Agency.* Hypertext Document. Available Online at: http://www.wada-ama.org.

ELLIOTT, C. 2003. *Better Than Well: American Medicine Meets the American Dream.* New York and London: W.W. Norton & Company.

Ethical Issues Review Panel, World Anti-Doping Agency. 2006. Report on Artificially Induced Hypoxic Conditions to Modify Performance. Montreal: World Anti-Doping Agency (Available on request to the organization).

FOTHERINGHAM, W. 1996. Sept 6. Cycling: hour of pain, shame or glory. *The Guardian.* London: 14.

FRALEIGH, W.P. 1984. Performance enhancing drugs in sport: the ethical issue. *Journal of the Philosophy of Sport XI*, 23–29.

GARDNER, R. 1989. On performance-enhancing substances and the unfair advantage argument. *Journal of the Philosophy of Sport XVI*, 59–73.

GAYAGAY, G., B. YU, B. HAMBLY, T. BOSTON, A. HAHN, D.S. CELERMAJER, R.J. TRENT. 1998. Elite endurance athletes and the Ace I Allele—the role of genes in athletic performance. *Human Genetics 1031*, 48–50.

GELBERG, J.N. 1995. The Lethal Weapon: how the plastic football helmet transformed the game of football, 1939–1994. *Bulletin of Science, Technology, and Society 155–156*, 302–309.

GOLDSPINK, G. 2001. Gene expression in skeletal muscle. *Biochemical Society Transactions 30*, 285–290.

HOBERMAN, J.M. 1992. *Mortal Engines: The Science of Performance and the Dehumanization of Sport*. Reprinted 2001, the Blackburn Press. New York: The Free Press.

HUMMEL, R.L., and G.S. FOSTER. 1986. A sporting chance: relationships between technological change & concepts of fair play in fishing. *Journal of Leisure Research 181*, 40–52.

INIZAN, F. 1994. Masters and slaves of time. *Olympic Review 320*, 306–310.

KELLY, K. 1994. *Out of Control: The New Biology of Machines*. London: Fourth Estate.

LAMSAM, C., F.H. FU, P.D. ROBBINS, and C.H. EVANS. 1997. Gene therapy in sports medicine. *Sports Medicine 252*, 73–77.

LEVINE, B.D. 2006. Should "artificial" high altitude environments be considered doping? *Scandinavian Journal of Medicine and Science in Sports 16*(5), 297–301.

LIN, J., H. WU, P.T. TARR, C. ZHANG, Z. WU, O. BOSS, L.F. MICHAEL, P. PUIGSERVER, E. ISOTANI, E.N. OLSON, B.B. LOWELL, R. BASSEL-DUBY, and B.M. SPIEGELMANN. 2002. Transcriptional co-activator Pgc-1 drives the formation of slow-twitch muscle fibres. *Nature 418*, 797–801.

MAGDALINSKI, T. 2000. Performance technologies: drugs and fastskin at the Sydney 2000 Olympics. *Media International Australia 97*(November), 59–69.

MARTINEK, V., F.H. FU, *et al.* 2000. Gene therapy and tissue engineering in sports medicine. *The Physician and Sports Medicine 282*. Available online at http://www.physsportsmed.com/issues/2000/02_00/huard.htm.

MIAH, A. 2000a. Climbing upwards of climbing backwards? The technological metamorphoses of climbing and mountaineering. Chapter 27 in N. Messenger, W. Patterson and D. Brook (eds.), *The Science of Climbing and Mountaineering*. London: Human Kinetics.

MIAH, A. 2000b. The engineered athlete: human rights in the genetic revolution. *Culture, Sport, Society 33*, 25–40.

MIAH, A. 2000c. "New Balls Please": tennis, technology, and the changing game. Pp. 285–292 in S.A. Haake and A.O. Coe. (eds.), *Tennis, Science, and Technology*. London: Blackwell Science.

MIAH, A. 2004. *Genetically Modified Athletes: Biomedical Ethics, Gene Doping and Sport*. London and New York: Routledge.

MIAH, A. 2005a. From anti-doping to a 'performance policy': sport technology, being human, and doing ethics. *European Journal of Sport Science 51*, 51–57.

MIAH, A. 2005b. Doping and the child: an ethical policy for the vulnerable. *The Lancet 366*, 874–876.

MONTGOMERY, H., P. CLARKSON, M. BARNARD, J. BELL, A. BRYNES, C. DOLLERY, J. HAJNAL, H. HEMINGWAY, D. MERCER, P. JARMAN, R. MARSHALL, K. PRASAD, M. RAYSON, N. SAEED, P. TALMUD, L. THOMAS, M. JUBB, M. WORLD, and

S. HUMPHRIES. 1999. Angiotensin-converting-enzyme gene insertion/deletion polymorphism and response to physical training. *The Lancet 353*(13), 541–545.

MONTGOMERY, H., R. MARSHALL, H. HEMINGWAY, S. MYERSON, P. CLARKSON, C. DOLLERY, M. HAYWARD, D.E. HOLLIMAN, M. JUBB, M. WORLD, E.L. THOMAS, A.E. BRYNES, N. SAEED, M. BARNARD, J.D. BELL, K. PRASAD, M. RAYSON, P.J. TALMUD, and S.E. HUMPHRIES. 1998. Human gene for physical performance. *Nature 39321*(May), 221–222.

MUNTHE, C. 2000. Selected champions: making winners in an age of genetic technology. Pp. 217–231 in T. Tännsjö and C. Tamburrini (eds.), *Values in Sport: Elitism, Nationalism, Gender Equality, and the Scientific Manufacture of Winners*. London and New York: E & F.N. Spon.

MURRAY, T.H. 1983. The coercive power of drugs in sports. *Hastings Center Report* August, 24–30.

MURRAY, T.H. 1984. Drugs, sports, and ethics. Pp. 107–126 in T.H. Murray, W. Gaylin and R. Macklin (eds.), *Feeling Good and Doing Better*. Clifton, New Jersey: Humana Press.

MURRAY, T.H. 1986a. Guest editorial: drug testing and moral responsibility. *The Physician and Sportsmedicine 1411*, 47–48.

MURRAY, T.H. 1986b. Guest editorial: human growth hormone in sports: no. *The Physician and Sportsmedicine 145*, 29.

PARENS, E., ed. 1998. *Enhancing Human Traits: Ethical and Social Implications*. Hastings Center Studies in Ethics. Washington, DC: Georgetown University Press.

SCIENCE AND TECHNOLOGY SELECT COMMITTEE. 2006, March 1. *New Inquiry: Human Enhancement Technologies in Sport*. Select Committee for Science and Technology, British Government. Available online at http://www.parliament.uk/parlimentary_committees/sciences_and_technology_committee/het.cfm (last accessed November 15, 2006).

STIVERS, R. 2001. *Technology as Magic: The Triumph of the Irrational*. New York: Continuum.

SVENSSON, E.C., H.B. BLACK, D.L. DUGGER, S.K. TRIPATHY, E. GOLDWASSER, Z. HAO, L. CHU, and J.M. LEIDEN. 1997. Long-term erythropoietin expression in rodents and non-human primates following intramuscular injection of a replication-defective adenoviral vector. *Human Gene Therapy 815*, 1797–1806.

TENNER, E. 1996. *Why Things Bite Back: Predicting the Problems of Progress*. London: Fourth Estate.

THE U.S. PRESIDENT'S COUNCIL ON BIOETHICS. 2002a. *Session 4: Enhancement 2: Potential for Genetic Enhancements in Sports*. Washington, D.C.: The President's Council on Bioethics. Hypertext Document, available at http://www.bioethics.gov/200207/session4.html.

THE U.S. PRESIDENT'S COUNCIL ON BIOETHICS. 2002b. *Sixth Meeting: Session 7: Enhancement 5: Genetic Enhancement of Muscle*. Washington, DC: The President's Council on Bioethics. Hypertext Document, available at http://www.bioethics.gov/transcripts/sep02/session7.html.

THE U.S. PRESIDENT'S COUNCIL ON BIOETHICS. 2003. *Beyond Therapy: Biotechnology and the Pursuit of Happiness*. Washington, DC

WORLD ANTI-DOPING AGENCY. 2003. *Prohibited Classes of Substances and Prohibited Methods.* Montreal: World Anti-Doping Agency.

WORLD ANTI-DOPING AGENCY. 2005. The Stockholm Declaration. *World Anti-Doping Agency*. Hypertext document. Available online at http://www.wada-ama.org (last accessed November 15, 2006).

Justice, Fairness, and Enhancement

JULIAN SAVULESCU

Director, Oxford Uehiro Centre for Practical Ethics, Oxford University, Oxford OX1 1PT, United Kingdom

ABSTRACT: This article begins by considering four traditional definitions of enhancement, then proposes a fifth, the Welfarist definition. It then considers fairness-based objections to enhancement, using the example of performance enhancement in sport. In so doing it defines sport and the values proper to it, surveys alternative theories of justice, considers the natural distribution of capabilities and disabilities, and draws a distinction between social, psychological, and biological enhancement. The article advances a new argument that justice requires enhancement.

KEYWORDS: bioethics; cognitive enhancement; sports

ENHANCEMENT AND FAIRNESS

An often-stated goal of Converging Technologies is "improving human performance" (Roco and Bainbridge 2003), which is to say *human enhancement*, in terms of biological, psychological, or social attributes. One of the most common objections to the introduction of any enhancement technology is that it will create inequality, injustice, and unfairness (Annas 2002; McKibben 2003; Fukuyama 2004). It is no doubt true that enhancement technologies might create inequality and injustice. But their use may also *reduce* inequality, injustice, and unfairness. To see this, we must understand what an enhancement is and how we should understand fairness-based objections. There are strong fairness-based arguments to establish a moral obligation to employ enhancement.

Few people have attempted to define enhancement in debates about new technologies. Often discussion focuses on a particular application, such as muscle strength, memory or lifespan, or a definition of enhancement is implicitly assumed. I will consider four dominant approaches and then offer a more promising account.

Address for correspondence: Julian Savulescu, Director, Oxford Uehiro Centre for Practical Ethics, Oxford University, Littlegate House, 87 St. Ebbes St., Oxford OX1 1PT, United Kingdom. Voice: +44 1865 286888; fax: +44 1865 286886.
e-mail: Julian.savulescu@philosophy.ox.ac.uk

Parts of this article have appeared in different form in Savulescu 2006a and 2006b.

Ann. N.Y. Acad. Sci. 1093: 321–338 (2006). © 2006 New York Academy of Sciences.
doi: 10.1196/annals.1382.021

FOUR APPROACHES TO THE ETHICS OF ENHANCEMENT

In the literature there is a great deal of uncertainty and confusion about the term *enhancement*, based on what might be called the *sociologically pragmatic* approach. Erik Parens (1998) states that "some participants think the term *enhancement* is so freighted with erroneous assumptions and so ripe for abuse that we ought not even to use it. My sense is that if we didn't use the enhancement, we would end up with another term with similar problems."

Parens himself uses the term as a focus for a discussion of the goals of medicine and society. A similar pragmatic approach is taken by Paul Root Wolpe. He claims that enhancement is a slippery "socially constructed" concept: "Yet, ultimately, any exclusive enhancement definition must fail, in part because concepts such as disease, normalcy, and health are significantly culturally and historically bound, and thus the result of negotiated values" (Wolpe 2002).

James Canton (2003, p. 78) also claims that enhancement is a relative concept: "The future may hold different definitions of human enhancement that affect culture, intelligence, memory, physical performance, even longevity. Different cultures will define human performance based on their social and political values. It is for our nation to define these values and chart the future of human performance." This approach can be viewed as the sociologically pragmatic definition: enhancement captures a certain a value-laded domain of discourse related to human performance rather than having a substantive transcultural meaning itself.

A related approach, that might be considered *ideological*, is to avoid defining the term at all. This move is made both by proponents and opponents of enhancement. Typically enhancement is defined by reference to a list of technologies, or the goals of enhancement are stipulated and the field is defined or marked by them (cf. Naam 2005). For example, the President's Council on Bioethics delineates the domain of discourse, after stating the problems of definition and the smooth blending between therapy and enhancement, as one related to the human desires and goals. As stated by Kass (2003): "The human meaning and moral assessment must be tackled directly; they are unlikely to be settled by the term 'enhancement,' any more than they are by the nature of the technological intervention itself." This ideological approach employs enhancement as a rhetoric or practical means to reach ideological ends.

Another influential approach has been to define enhancement in terms of going beyond health-restoring treatment or health, based on a distinction contrasting *treatment versus enhancement*. Eric T. Juengst (1998) defines it: "The term *enhancement* is usually used in bioethics to characterize interventions designed to improve human form or functioning beyond what is necessary to sustain or restore good health." Edmund D. Pellegrino uses a similar definition just for the purpose of arguing against enhancement on the grounds that it is beyond medicine as a healing enterprise:

...my operating definition of enhancement will be grounded in its general etymological meaning, i.e., to increase, intensify, raise up, exalt, heighten, or magnify. Each of these terms carries the connotation of going 'beyond' what exists at some moment, whether it is a certain state of affairs, a bodily function or trait, or a general limitation built into human nature... For this discussion, enhancement will signify an intervention that goes beyond the ends of medicine as they traditionally have been held (Pellegrino 2004).

One problem with this approach is that the definition of medicine and treatment itself is contested. Even a maximally inclusive definition such as medicine being the "science and art of diagnosing, treating, curing, and preventing disease, relieving pain, and improving and preserving health" (McKechnie 1961) still leaves us to define disease and health, equally complex terms (Smith 2002). Norm Daniels, after Christopher Boorse, has argued for the use of "species-typical functioning" as the definition of normality. By determining the natural functional organization of members of a species it is possible to create a normal function model, and disease represents a statistical deviation from normal functioning (Sabin and Daniels 1994; Daniels 2000).

A fourth approach is the positive *functional* approach. Enhancement is defined in terms of enhanced functions. The archetypal example of this approach is Douglas C. Engelbart's *Augmenting Human Intellect*:

By "augmenting human intellect" we mean increasing the capability of a man to approach a complex problem situation, to gain comprehension to suit his particular needs, and to derive solutions to problems. Increased capability in this respect is taken to mean a mixture of the following: more-rapid comprehension, better comprehension, the possibility of gaining a useful degree of comprehension in a situation that previously was too complex, speedier solutions, better solutions, and the possibility of finding solutions to problems that before seemed insoluble. And by "complex situations" we include the professional problems of diplomats, executives, social scientists, life scientists, physical scientists, attorneys, designers—whether the problem situation exists for twenty minutes or twenty years. We do not speak of isolated clever tricks that help in particular situations. We refer to a way of life in an integrated domain where hunches, cut-and-try, intangibles, and the human 'feel for a situation' usefully co-exist with powerful concepts, streamlined terminology and notation, sophisticated methods, and high-powered electronic aids (Engelbart 1962).

Here cognitive enhancement is defined in terms of improved general information processing abilities.

All of these definitions, while having attractions, are deficient. The sociological pragmatic approach captures an important area of concern: how society should deal with these technologies, stressing the important roles played by culture and negotiation. But there is a lack of a clear definition. The ideological approach stresses the need for core human values in debate, but fails to convincingly argue for an operational set. Both the treatment-versus-enhancement and functional approaches have their own weaknesses which I will now briefly outline.

Enhancement is, indeed, a wide concept. In the broadest sense, it means "increase" or "improvement." For example, a doctor may *enhance* his patient's chance of survival by giving the patient a drug. Or a doctor may enhance the functioning of a person's immune system or memory (the functionalist account). These are no doubt enhancements of a sort—enhancements in an attributive sense. But enhancing a permanently unconscious person's chance of surviving might not be good for the person. It might not constitute *human* enhancement. It might not enhance intrinsic good.

As the example of life extension shows, these senses of enhancement can come apart. Consider memory. Genetic memory enhancement has been demonstrated in rats and mice. In normal animals during maturation expression of the NR2B subunit of the *N*-methyl-D-aspartate (NMDA) receptor is gradually replaced with expression of the NR2A subunit, something that may be linked to less brain plasticity in adult animals. Tsien's research team modified mice to overexpress the NR2B. The NR2B "Doogie" mice demonstrated improved memory performance, both in terms of acquisition and retention (Tang *et al.* 1999). This included unlearning of fear conditioning, which is believed to be due to learning a secondary memory (Falls *et al.* 1992). The modification also made them more sensitive to certain forms of pain, showing a potentially nontrivial trade-off (Wei *et al.* 2001). It is possible that even though memory is improved, their lives go worse.

The term *human enhancement* is itself ambiguous. It might mean enhancement of functioning as a member of the species *homo sapiens*. This would be a functionalist definition. But when we are considering human enhancement, we are considering improvement of the person's life. The improvement is some change in state of the person—biological or psychological—which is good. Which changes are good depends on the value we are seeking to promote or maximize. In the context of human enhancement, the value in question is the goodness of a person's life, that is, his/her well-being.

WELFARIST DEFINITION OF HUMAN ENHANCEMENT

Consider, therefore, a fifth possible definition of human enhancement:

Welfarist Definition of Human Enhancement: Any change in the biology or psychology of a person which increases the chances of leading a good life in circumstances *C*. On the Welfarist definition of enhancement, we can define an enhanced state as a capability.

Capability: Any state of a person's biology or psychology which increases the chance of leading a good life in circumstances *C*.

This is a stipulative definition of capability as "good ability." The opposite of a capability is a disability.

Disability: Any state of a person's biology or psychology which decreases the chance of leading a good life in circumstances *C*.

Much debate about enhancement draws a mutually exclusive distinction between medical treatment and enhancement. This is a narrow definition of enhancement.

Naturalistic Conception of Disease: Any state of a person's biology or psychology which reduces species typical normal functioning below some statistically defined level.

Narrow Definition of Enhancement: Any change in the biology or psychology of a person which increases species typical normal functioning above some statistically defined level.

For example, low intelligence is defined as intellectual disability and treated as a disease when IQ falls below 70. On the naturalistic conception of disease and the narrow definition of enhancement, raising someone's IQ from 60 to 70 is treating a disease and raising someone's IQ from 70 to 80 is enhancement.

There are other normative and social constructivist accounts of disease besides the naturalistic conception of disease. However, on all concepts of disease, the mutually exclusive distinction between treatment and enhancement is a false one. Treatments are enhancements. Treatments are a subclass of enhancements. Diseases are a subclass of disabilities. Folk usage of the term "enhancement" supports this account. Pellegrino in fact gestured toward this definition in his account (Pellegrino 2004). According to the *Oxford English Dictionary* (Simpson and Weiner 1991, p. 315):

Enhancement: The action or process of enhancement: the fact of being enhanced.

> **Enhance:** to raise in degree, heighten, intensify (qualities, states, powers, etc)
>
> to raise (prices, value)
>
> to raise or increase in price, value, importance, attractiveness, etc.
>
> (Formerly used *simply*, = to increase in price or value; *esp.* to raise the intrinsic value of (coin). Also *(rarely)* = to increase in attractiveness, to beautify, improve.)

The spirit of all these definitions is that *to enhance is to increase in value.* In the context of human enhancement, to enhance is to increase the value of a person's life. Henceforth, I will refer to human enhancement simply as enhancement for brevity's sake. Enhancements include a family of different kinds of improvements, such as:

(i) Medical Treatment of Disease
(ii) Increasing Natural Human Potential—increasing a person's own natural endowments of capabilities within the range typical of the species *homo sapiens*, for example, raising a person's IQ from 100 to 140.
(iii) Superhuman Enhancements (sometimes called posthuman or transhuman)—increasing a person's capabilities beyond the range typical for the species *homo sapiens*, for example, giving humans bat sonar or the capacity fully to read minds.

By accepting the Welfarist definition of enhancement, the question of when should we enhance becomes: When should we increase human well-being?

One of the advantages of a Welfarist account of enhancement is that it reframes existing debates in a more productive manner. The ideological approach is really a debate about what constitutes a good life and resistance to enhancement is not really resistance to enhancement *per se*, but resistance to accepting an overly narrow or mistaken conception of human well-being.

When enhancement is understood as an intervention which increases the chances of a person having a good life, it is hard to see how there could be any objections to trying to make people's lives go better. Indeed, the fact that enhancements increase well-being provides a strong moral obligation based on beneficence to provide them. One class of objections relates to what constitutes a good life, and so what constitutes enhancement. Another relates to the risks or side effects of enhancement, and whether the risks outweigh the benefits. I will not address either of these. I will consider a class of objections that while enhancements may be good for individuals, they introduce inequality, injustice, and unfairness.

Sometimes a distinction is made between positional and nonpositional goods (Buchanan *et al.* 2000). Positional goods confer a relative advantage, like height, and only have value if not everyone has them. Nonpositional goods are goods which are good for people regardless of whether everyone has them, like sense of self-identity. Fairness-based objections are strongest in relation to positional enhancements in some competitive activity. I will take the example of performance enhancements in sport because it is clear that there are large numbers of effective performance enhancements, such as anabolic steroids, growth hormone, and erythropoietin, which are regularly used by professional athletes as positional enhancements.

ENHANCEMENT, FAIRNESS, AND SPORT

Dick Pound is the head of the Worldwide Anti-Doping Agency (WADA). In an interview with CBC Sports, Online, he was asked, "What drives you in the fight against drugs in sports? Why do you feel this is such an important issue?" His reply reveals much about the motivation of the antidoping campaigners:

Well, sports is so important to so many people, particularly young people, and it's a precursor to how you're going to behave in other aspects of social intercourse. You look around the world today and what have you got? The accounting profession is in the tank. You've got the business community in the tank. You've got the Enrons. You've got political shortcuts and all these kind of things, that it's very important to have some kind of activity where you can say to people 'this is on the level.' You respect the rules, you respect your opponents, you respect yourself. You play fair. I think that bleeds over into life as well.

I don't want my grandchildren to have to become chemical stockpiles in order to be good at sports and to have fun at it. Baseball, take your kid out to the ballpark some day and you say, 'Son, some day if you ingest enough of this shit, you might be a player on that field, too.' It's a completely antithetical view to what sport should have been in the first place. It's essentially a humanistic endeavor to see how far you can go on your own talent (CBC Sports Online 2003).

One of the main objections to enhancement of human beings is that it would be unfair. As Pound says in relation to drugs in sport, "You [should] play fair." Considerations of fairness play a prominent part in the regulation of drugs in sport. The WADA, which defines which drugs will be banned in international athletics, bans a drug if it has at least two out of three of the following criteria (WADA 2003, pp. 15–16):

(i) 4.3.1.1 Medical or other scientific evidence, pharmacological effect or experience that the substance or method has the potential to enhance or enhances sport performance.
(ii) 4.3.1.2 Medical or other scientific evidence, pharmacological effect, or experience that the *Use* of the substance or method represents and actual or potential health risk to the *Athlete*.
(iii) 4.3.1.3 WADA's determination that the *Use* of the substance or method violates the spirit of sport described in the Introduction to the *Code*.

WADA (2003, p. 3) defines the "spirit of sport" using a long list of words: ethics, fair play, and honesty; health; excellence in performance; character and education; fun and joy; teamwork; dedication and commitment; respect for rules and laws; respect for self and other participants; courage; community and solidarity. Enhancement can be unfair either because it violates the rules or violates the spirit, and the spirit may consist of internal or implicit rules.

If one person has access to an enhancement intervention (biological, pharmacological, technical, or other) which is banned by the rules governing that activity, then that is cheating and gives an unfair advantage. The student who takes Ritalin to improve study and performance in an exam when it is banned is cheating. The use of performance-enhancing drugs in sport would not be unfair in this sense if drugs were legal. Thus one way to eliminate cheating is to legalize enhancement. Students who drink coffee are not cheating.

In competitive activity, competitors are often driven by the rewards and permitted by the low penalties to seek unfair advantage. Even if safe performance enhancement were allowed, competitors would push the limits and seek out illegal but unsafe enhancement which provides a competitive advantage. However, the gap between the cheaters and the honest athletes would be narrowed as a market is created for safe performance enhancers because honest athletes could benefit from safe performance enhancement. Allowing safe performance enhancement reduces unfairness in competitive situations.

In 1979, the World Series Cup introduced many innovations into the sport of cricket, including a revolutionary one-day series. In the 1980–1981 final, the third final of its kind, New Zealand needed six runs off the final ball to tie the match. Six runs can be scored by an enormous hit of the ball over the boundary fence. Australian captain Greg Chappell ordered his younger brother, Trevor, to bowl the final ball underarm (instead of the usual overarm) along the ground to batsman Brian McKechnie. This made it impossible to hit the ball in the air over the boundary. It gave McKechnie no chance. Though legal at the time, this act was widely regarded as extremely bad sportsmanship, against the spirit of the game and unfair. Such tactics were subsequently banned.

There is a sense in which there is a spirit of any competitive activity and that everyone should start with a fair chance or a sporting chance. This is the concept of "against the spirit of sport" employed by WADA. In nonhandicapped foot races, everyone starts from the same place. There is a sense, attractive to many, in which performance enhancement would be against the spirit of sport, even if it were permitted for all and there was no cheating. Is performance enhancement against the spirit of sport?

WHAT IS SPORT?

There are many different senses of "sport." For example, the *Oxford English Dictionary* (Simpson and Weiner 1991, p. 517) defines sport as: "pleasant pastime; entertainment or amusement; recreation or diversion. . . . pastime afforded by the endeavor to take or kill wild animals, game or fish. . . participation in games or exercises, esp. those of an athletic character or pursued in the open air. . ."

Now the issue of performance enhancement does not normally arise in fishing, though fisherman might use caffeine or other enhancers occasionally. There is a relevant distinction between recreational sport and competitive sport. Questions of performance enhancement arise in the arena of competitive sport, especially professional competitive sport where livelihood, reputation, and money are at stake.

According to the Encyclopaedia Britannica (2006), sport has the following features: "recreational or competitive activities that involve a degree of physical strength or skill. . . sports are an invention" by *homo sapiens* comparable to play or hunting; "physical contests performed for their own sake and not for some ulterior end. . . Since sports are an invention, a part of culture rather than an aspect of nature, all definitions of sports are somewhat arbitrary."

We can define *competitive* sport as the pursuit of human physical excellence (skill or strength), generally in a rule governed activity. The rules of sport are arbitrary in the sense that they are defined by human beings. The rules define the nature of the activity to bring out the display of certain skills or strengths. They allow for meaningful comparison in competitive sport to determine who is better. They ensure that competitors are performing the same or relevantly similar activities and that a specific set of capabilities is being tested or exercised.

While the rules are arbitrary in one sense, there are reasons why each sport comes to have its own set of rules:

(i) To bring out or develop a particular set of skills, strengths or physical excellences
(ii) To facilitate meaningful and interesting competition
(iii) To promote or protect health
(iv) To provide spectator interest
(v) To increase its lucrativeness
(vi) According to some cultural or historical precedent
(vii) To allow historical comparison

The human excellence in sport has typically been biological endowment plus training and mental application to realize ones own innate biological potential. If competitive sport is meant to be a test of *natural physical talent*, then one might think that performance enhancement is against the spirit of sport. However, there are two reasons to think this does not preclude performance enhancement.

First, human sport is different from sports involving other animals, like horse or dog racing. The goal of a horse race is to find the fastest horse. Horses are lined up and flogged. The winner is the one with the best combination of biology, training, and rider. Basically, this is a test of biological potential. This was the old naturalistic Athenian vision of sport—find the strongest, fastest, or most skilled man. This is what Dick Pound appealed to when he said "[Sport is] essentially a humanistic endeavor to see how far you can go on your own talent" (CBC Sports Online 2003).

Training aims to bring out this potential. Drugs which improve our natural potential are against the spirit of this model of sport. But sport is not only a test of biological potential. Central to human sport is the competitive spirit. Humans are not horses or dogs. We make choices and exercise our own judgment and other mental abilities. We choose what kind of training and how to run our race. We can display courage, determination and wisdom. We are not flogged by a jockey on our back but drive ourselves. It is this judgment that competitors exercise when they choose diet, training, and whether to take drugs. We can choose what kind of competitor to be, not just through training, but through biological manipulation. Human sport is different from animal sport because it is creative. Far from being against the spirit of sport, biological manipulation embodies the human spirit (Savulescu *et al.* 2004)—the capacity to *improve* ourselves on the basis of reasons and judgment. When we exercise our reason, we do what only humans do. Even if sport is primarily a test of physical excellence, it is not only a test of physical excellence. While sport might be predominantly a test of natural physical talent, it is not entirely or exclusively a test of natural physical talent.

Second, if enhancement is permitted, sport will remain a test of natural physical talent. If everyone takes an enhancer, then the base line for all is raised. Competition is still possible and sport remains a test of physical talent. Indeed, this is what happens when enhancers have been permitted. When fiberglass poles were allowed in pole vault, everyone jumped higher. When large head racquets were introduced into tennis, everyone hit the ball harder and more accurately. Pole vault and tennis were still determined by the competitor's physical abilities. The introduction of caffeine or creatine means everyone runs longer or harder—but sport remains primarily a test of biological talent.

Sport is not a test of biological potential when some competitors enhance their biology while others do not. This enables the biologically inferior cheaters to win. But that can happen only when enhancement is not permitted.

Moreover, success at sport requires mental as well as physical abilities and exercises. The result will be that the winner is not the person who was born with the best genetic potential to be strongest. Sport would be less of a genetic lottery. The winner will be the person with a combination of the genetic potential, training, psychology, and judgment. Olympic performance would be an exercise of human creativity and choice, not a very expensive horse race.

RADICAL ENHANCEMENT

We have allowed changes to sport over the years. In tennis, large head tennis racquets changed the game. This allowed players to hit the ball harder from a wider range of places on the court. Ultimately, this, together with other changes to game, reduced the spectacle as male players were hitting, particularly serving, the ball so hard that there were no rallies. Subsequently, the pressure of the balls was reduced.

The increase in the size of the racquet head was allowed because it was thought to be in the spirit of tennis at the time. However, double strung tennis racquets which significantly increased spin were never permitted. They would have allowed too much spin and would have radically changed the game.

In swimming, skins or suits have been permitted because whatever advantage they confer is relatively small. We would not allow swimmers to take drugs which cause webbing of the hands and feet because that change would be too radical. (Although, interestingly, webbing is natural during fetal development, and it is possible a person could naturally exist with a genetic mutation resulting in webbing of the hands and feet. Presumably, if this were natural, such a person would be allowed to compete in swimming competitions, albeit as a genetic freak.)

In general, as human beings, we are biased in favor of small, gradual change and against large or dislocated changes. We are likely to accept small, gradual enhancements rather than radical and profound ones. There may be no moral reason for this but it seems important to people to keep some thread of continuity in the nature of a particular support. However, such a thread can be maintained while allowing small to modest enhancements. Classical musicians commonly use beta-blockers to control their stage-fright. It has been shown that the quality of their performance is improved by these drugs (Brantigan *et al.* 1982). We do not think less of the violinist or pianist who employs them. If the audience judges the performance to be improved with drugs, then the drugs are enabling the musician to express him or herself more effectively. Such enhancements are consistent the spirit of fine music.

THE GAME OF LIFE AND THE SPIRIT OF LIFE

Performance enhancement is not against the spirit of sport. So too human enhancement does not violate the rules of the game of life. To be human is to seek to have a better life.

But of course life is different to sport in one way. It is not a competition or a race to see who gets there first. The point of life, or the spirit of life, is to have a good life. The prize of the game of life is well-being, which is a complex result of co-operation, individual development and competition. On a Welfarist account of enhancement, enhancements increase the chance of having a good life and so embody the spirit of life. Human enhancement is not somehow "cheating."

INJUSTICE

Another kind of fairness-based objection is that enhancement will create injustice. There is a straightforward sense in which this could be true. If limited resources are directed to developing or buying enhancements, at the expense of other technologies such as medical technologies, which improve well-being more, then that is a violation of distributive justice. So when considering limited community resources, then those resources should not be directed to enhancements like providing better than 20/20 vision at the expense of life-saving cancer treatments. Of course, where enhancements are purchased or developed with private funds in a legal and legitimate way, there is no violation of the requirements of distributive justice. If certain enhancements provide significant increments in well-being, for example, by providing greater impulse control or significantly better memory, and these are equivalent to or greater than the benefits of certain medical treatments or other uses of community resources, then they should have priority.

Another sense in which enhancement may create injustice is by exacerbating inequality. According to free-market or libertarian theories, the rich may buy enhancements which the poor cannot afford provided that their assets have been justly and legally acquired. Those with the highest levels of well-being and privilege will be able to buy even greater happiness and opportunity. This, according to some, is unfair. It is worth stressing that on libertarian accounts of justice, like that of Nozick (1974), this is not unfair.

But let us for a moment, grant that it is unfair that the rich get richer or at least happier and better off, and the poor get poorer. Is enhancement *inevitably* or *necessarily* unfair in this sense? To answer this question, we must understand what these theories of justice require. When we understand the nature of justice, we see that justice and fairness may require enhancement.

Theories of justice include Utilitarianism, Egalitarianism, Rawl's Maximin (or Justice as Fairness), and Prioritarianism (Savulescu 2006a).

According to Utilitarianism, goods, such as enhancements, should be distributed to provide the maximize the good or increase in well-being, that is, to bring about what Jeremy Bentham famously said was "greatest good to the greatest number." Utilitarianism employs a principle of equality, as Bentham put it: "Everybody to count for one, nobody for more than one." That is, provided that enhancements are allocated strictly to maximally promote well-being, with no eye to existing social privilege, status, wealth or other irrelevant consideration, the resulting distribution is just (Savulescu 2003).

According to Egalitarianism, the proper ground for distribution of resources is need (Williams 1962). "Equal treatment for equal need." Enhancements should be provided to alleviate need in individuals as much as possible. The greater a person's need, the greater that person's entitlement to resources.

According to Rawls' Justice as Fairness, we should distribute enhancements so that the worst off in society are as well off as they can be (Rawls 1971). According to Prioritarians (Parfit 1997), we should give priority to those who are worst off, but we should also aim to maximize well-being of all members of society.

Which view of justice we accept does not matter for the purposes of this argument. John Mackie once suggested, against Utilitarians, that everyone has a "right to a fair go" (Mackie 1984). This an attractive principle. According to a maximizing version of this principle, we should give as many people as possible a decent (reasonable) chance of having a decent (good) life. This has also been called "sufficientarianism."

A fair go entails that each person has a legitimate claim to some enhancement or medical intervention when that intervention provides that person with reasonable chance of reasonable extension of a reasonable life and/or a reasonable improvement in its quality. Comparable legitimate claims are those referring to similar needs. As many comparable legitimate claims should be satisfied as possible. Provided as many comparable legitimate claims are being satisfied as possible, there should be equality of access.

It is an empirical fact that our biology and psychology can influence how well our lives go. Certain biological or psychological states can be capabilities or disabilities depending on the social or natural environment. Aggressiveness may be a capability in a hunter society but may be a disability in a dense urban society requiring close social co-operation. We are all disabled in the sense that some features of our biology or psychology make it more difficult for us to live well.

Some qualities are likely to be capabilities, in most likely environments or circumstances. Buchanan *et al*. (2000) call these "all purpose goods." Some all-purpose goods might include: intelligence, memory, self-discipline, foresight, patience, sense of humor, and optimism. Autonomy-enhancing traits include concept of self, capacity to form and act on conceptions of the good life, and the ability to predict consequences of behavior. Among social capabilities are the ability to make friends, form close personal relationships, and understand others' feelings. Moral capabilities are virtues such as empathy, imagination, sympathy, fairness, and honesty.

Other specific examples notably include impulse control. Walter Mischel placed 4-year-old children in a room with one marshmallow and told them that if they did not eat the marshmallow, they could later have two. Some children would eat the marshmallow as soon as he left the room. Others would devise strategies to help control their behavior and ignore the temptation of the single marshmallow. A decade later, Mischel found that those who were better at delaying gratification had more friends, better academic performance and more motivation to succeed. Whether the child had grabbed the marshmallow had a much stronger bearing on their SAT scores than did their IQ (Mischel *et al*. 1988). Poor impulse control is a disability.

Laziness is another notable example of how biology can influence behavioral capabilities. Gene therapy has been used to turn lazy monkeys into workaholics by altering the reward center in the brain (Liu *et al*. 2004). This suggests that there might be some biological basis to how hard primates work.

Not surprisingly, patterns of sexual behavior also have biological roots. Scientists used gene therapy to introduce a gene from the monogamous male prairie vole, a rodent which forms life-long bonds with one mate, into the brain of the closely related but polygamous meadow vole (Lim *et al*. 2004). Genetically modified meadow voles became monogamous, behaving like prairie voles. This gene, which controls a part of the brain's reward center different to that altered in the monkeys, is known as the vasopressin receptor gene. It is possible that in the future, our sexual behavior might be amenable to biological and psychological modification. Hormonal castration to reduce sex drive is already offered to some pedophiles in some US jurisdictions.

NATURAL DISTRIBUTION OF CAPABILITIES
AND DISABILITIES

Nature allots capabilities and disabilities unequally, with no mind to fairness. The "normal distribution" of IQ is an example. Other capabilities are similarly distributed across a range, even if it is not a statistical "normal distribution." Capabilities and disabilities are also distributed socially: self-inflicted or other-inflicted injuries, institutions, culture, and education all advantage some and disadvantage others.

For a fair society, as many people as possible should be given a decent chance of a decent life. We already try to use social determinants of good life, such as laws, attitudes, and practices to ensure that women, different races, and disabled people are given a "fair go." By manipulating the biological determinants of the good life, we could ensure that people have the capacity to have a good life in the way the world is likely to be.

For example, IQ is distributed according to a bell curve. Low intelligence is arbitrarily defined as a disease when it falls below 70. That is, intellectual disability is arbitrarily defined as an IQ less than 70 because IQs less than that, although within the normal distribution, severely affect people's chances, historically, of leading a good life. Medical research is directed to treating intellectual disability through biological or pharmacological means. Social resources are provided to support people with an IQ of 70.

But what IQ is necessary for a decent chance of a decent life? Perhaps, in a technologically sophisticated society, people would significantly benefit from a higher IQ. An IQ of 120 is needed to be able to complete tertiary education.

Justice/Fairness requires we get as many people as possible up to the minimum IQ necessary for a decent chance of a decent life. Fairness thus requires enhancement. Far from being opposed to enhancement, justice requires enhancement. It is on these grounds that we choose to treat those currently with an IQ less than 70. But where we set the minimum threshold for treatment or enhancement is up to us. It depends on how we define a decent chance of a decent life in the way society and the world are likely to be.

This is a general point. The need to provide as many people as possible with a decent chance of a decent life does not apply only to the enhancement of IQ. Any biological property which can constitute a capability or disability is suitable for enhancement. This includes: cognitive abilities, social abilities, impulse control, physical abilities, and more. In so far as these contribute to a reasonable chance of leading a reasonably good life, they are candidates for enhancement on the grounds of justice.

McKibben (2003) claimed that enhancement should not be permitted because it will be used to increase inequality. According to this kind of argument, enhancement technologies will be available primarily to the wealthy, and so the rich get richer, the rich get smarter, the smarter get smarter, and the smarter get richer. But this is not necessarily so—how enhancement technologies are made available is up to us. They could be made available free, or only to the poor, or to promote equality or to achieve justice. We have the power to dictate policy on the employment of enhancement technology.

A related claim is that allowing enhancement will result in discrimination against the unenhanced. This again assumes a crude form of what I have called "social determinism"—that we have no control over social attitudes and practices. But we have free will and a sense of responsibility; it is up to us how we choose to use this technology and how we treat those who are not enhanced. Which laws and policies we form to protect the opportunities of the unenhanced is up to us. Whether someone is treated with concern and respect is completely independent of their biology—enhanced or unenhanced. It is a function of our attitudes and motivation to treat others with concern and respect. Discrimination is our choice—not written into biology.

SOCIAL NOT BIOLOGICAL ENHANCEMENT?

Sometimes it is claimed that we should alter society to improve people's lives, and not employ enhancement technologies that are owned by or affect individuals. First, many enhancements, such as advances in nanotechnology or information technology, could change the structure of society.

Second, when we are considering "private" enhancements, whether we should permit individuals to access these or alter social structures depends on whether there are good reasons to prefer social rather than private interventions. Such reasons might be, for example:

(i) If it is safer
(ii) If it is more likely to be successful
(iii) If justice requires it (based on the limitations of resources)
(iv) If there are benefits to others or less harm

When there are good reasons to prefer social enhancement rather than direct private enhancement, then we can say that disability is "socially constructed"; it is caused or upheld by social structures or beliefs. However, the range of disabilities includes biological and psychological elements as well as socially constructed elements. It is possible to remove or alleviate disability at all levels, and we must consider reasons for and against biological and psychological intervention as well as the more commonly acceptable social interventions.

We have seen that Nature allots advantages and disadvantages with no regard to fairness, and that enhancement improves people's lives. The best way to protect the disadvantaged from the inequalities that bioconservatives like McKibben (2003) believe will follow from enhancement is not to prevent enhancement, but to ensure that the social institutions we use to distribute enhancement technologies work to protect the least well off and to provide everyone with a fair go. People have disease and disability, and egalitarian social institutions and laws against discrimination are designed to make sure everyone, regardless of natural inequality, has a decent chance of a decent life. Enhancement to remove the disability and disease would be an effective way of achieving a laudable aim.

CONCLUSION

Fairness and justice require enhancement. Which enhancements and how depends on which theory of justice we subscribe to. Failure to enhance may result in significant injustices. It is within our power to use technology and enhancement to bring about a more just society, where everyone has a fair go. Many technological enhancements, such as nanotechnology and information technology, will operate at a social level. Biological and psychological enhancements, especially those associated with cognitive science, will represent more private enhancements, as will technology that can be privately owned and employed. Conservatives who oppose the use of biological, internal technological, and other private enhancements are guilty of a crude form of social determinism, predicting some adverse social consequence of allowing enhancement when it is within our power to prevent these adverse social consequences and reduce inequality.

We can allow our lives to be determined by the natural lottery, or by wealth. Both of these lead to injustice. Judicious use of enhancement, based on a rational policy can ensure that each of us, regardless of genetic or financial inheritance, has "a fair go." Human enhancement is not cheating: the spirit of humanity is to seek to have a better life.

ACKNOWLEDGMENT

I would like to thank Anders Sandberg for research assistance.

REFERENCES

ANNAS, G. 2002. Cell division. Available online at http://www.genetics-and-society.org/resources/items/20020421_globe_annas.html.

BRANTIGAN, C.O., T.A. BRANTIGAN, and N. JOSEPH. 1982. Effect of beta blockade and beta stimulation on stage fright. *American Journal of Medicine 72*(1), 88–94.

BUCHANAN, A., D.W. BROCK, N. DANIELS, and D. WIKLER. 2000. *From Chance to Choice.* Cambridge: Cambridge University Press.

CANTON, J. 2003. The impact of convergent technologies and the future of business and the economy. Pp. 71–78 in M.C. Roco, and W.S. Bainbridge (eds.), *Converging Technologies for Improving Human Performance: Nanotechnology, Biotechnology, Information Technology and Cognitive Science.* Dordrecht, Netherlands: Kluwer Academic Publishers.

CBC Sports Online. 2003. The Enforcer [online]. Available from http://www.cbc.ca/sports/indepth/drugs/stories/qa_dickpound.html (accessed October 6 2006).

Daniels, N. 2000. Normal functioning and the treatment-enhancement distinction. *Cambridge Quarterly 9*(3), 309–322.

Encyclopaedia Britannica. 2006. Encyclopaedia Britannica Online. [Online] Available at http://search.eb.com/eb/article-9108486. Accessed October 6, 2006.

Engelbart, D.C. 1962. *Augmenting Human Intellect: A Conceptual Framework*. In Summary Report AFOSR-3223 under Contract AF 49(638)-1024, SRI Project 3578 for Air Force Office of Scientific Research, Stanford Research Institute, Menlo Park, CA, October 1962. Available online from http://www.bootstrap.org/augdocs/friedewald030402/augmentinghumanintellect/1introduction.html [Accessed October 6 2006].

Falls, W.A., M.J.D. Miserendino, and M. Davis 1992. Extinction of fear-potentiated startle: blockade by infusion of an NMDA antagonist into the amygdala. *Journal of Neuroscience 12*, 854–863.

Fukuyama, F. 2004. Transhumanism. Foreign Policy (September/October) 144:42–44. Available online at http://www.foreignpolicy.com/story/files/story2667.php.

Juengst, E.T. 1998. What does enhancement mean? In E. Parens (ed.), *Enhancing Human Traits: Ethical and Social Implications*. Washington, D.C.: Georgetown University Press.

Kass, L. 2003. Biotechnology and the pursuit of happiness. Pp. 1–8 in L. Kass (ed.), *Beyond Therapy: Biotechnology and the Pursuit of Happiness*. Washington, D.C.: The President's Council on Bioethics.

Lim, M.M., Z. Wang, D.E. Olazábal, X. Ren, E.F. Terwilliger, and L.J. Young. 2004. Enhanced partner preference in a promiscuous species by manipulating the expression of a single gene. *Nature 429*, 754–757.

Liu, Z., B.J. Richmond, E.A. Murray, R.C. Saunders, S. Steenrod, B.K. Stubblefield, D.M. Montague, and E.I. Ginns. 2004. DNA targeting of rhinal cortex D2 receptor protein reversibly blocks learning of cues that predict reward. *Proceedings of the National Academy of Sciences of the United States of America 101*(33), 12336–12341.

McKechnie, J.L., ed. 1961. *Webster's New Twentieth Century Dictionary of the English Language, Unabridge*d, 2nd ed. New York: The World Publishing Company.

McKibben, B. 2003. Designer genes. *Orion* (May-June). Available online at http://www.orionsociety.org/pages/om/03-3om/McKibben.html.

Mackie, J. 1984. Rights, utility and universalization. Pp. 86–105 in R.G. Frey (ed.), *Utility and Right*. Minneapolis: University of Minnesota Press.

Mischel, W., Y. Shoda, and P.K. Peake. 1988. The nature of adolescent competencies predicted by preschool delay of gratification. *Journal of Personality & Social Psychology 54*(4), 687–696.

Naam, R. 2005. *More Than Human: Embracing the Promise of Biological Enhancement*. New York: Broadway Books.

Nozick, R. 1974. *Anarchy, State and Utopia*. New York: Basic Books. Pp. 233.

Parens, E. 1998. Is better always good? The Enhancement Project. Pp. 1–28 in E. Parens (ed.), *Enhancing Human Traits: Ethical and Social Implications*. Washington, D.C.: Georgetown University Press.

Parfit, D. 1997. Equality or priority? *Ratio 10*(3), 202–221.

Pellegrino, E.D. 2004. *Biotechnology, Human Enhancement, and the Ends of Medicine*. In The Center for Bioethics and Human Dignity Website. Available online from http://www.cbhd.org/resources/biotech/pellegrino_2004-11-30.htm. [Accessed October 6 2006].

RAWLS, J. 1971. *A Theory of Justice*. Cambridge, MA: Harvard University Press.

ROCO, M.C., and W.S. BAINBRIDGE, eds., 2003. *Converging Technologies for Improving Human Performance: Nanotechnology, Biotechnology, Information Technology and Cognitive Science*. Dordrecht, Netherlands: Kluwer Academic Publishers.

SABIN, J.E., and N. DANIELS 1994. Determining medical necessity in mental health practice. *Hastings Center Report 24*(6), 5–13.

SAVULESCU, J. 2003. Bioethics: utilitarianism. In D. Cooper (ed.), *Nature Encyclopedia of the Human Genome*. New York: Nature Publishing Group.

SAVULESCU, J., B. FODDY, and B. CLAYTON. 2004. Why we should allow performance enhancing drugs in sport. *British Journal of Sports Medicine 38*, 666–670.

SAVULESCU, J. 2006a. Enhancement and Fairness. Forthcoming in James Martin World Forum Publication. Submitted to Earthscan Science in Society Series. London: James and James.

SAVULESCU, J. 2006b. Genetic interventions and the ethics of enhancement of human beings. Forthcoming in B. Steinbock (ed.), *The Oxford Handbook on Bioethics*. Oxford: Oxford University Press.

SIMPSON, J.A., and E.S.C. WEINER, eds. 1991. *Oxford English Dictionary*, 2nd ed. Oxford: Clarendon Press.

SMITH, R. 2002. In search of "non-disease." *British Medical Journal 324*, 883–885.

TANG, Y.P., E. SHIMIZU, G.R. DUBE, C. RAMPON, G.A. KERCHNER, M. ZHUO, G. LIU, and J.Z. TSIEN 1999. Genetic enhancement of learning and memory in mice. *Nature 401*, 63–69.

WEI, F., G. WANG, G.A. KERCHNER, S.J. KIM, H. XU, Z. CHEN and M. ZHUO 2001. Genetic enhancement of inflammatory pain by forebrain NR2B overexpression. *Nature Neuroscience 4*, 164–169.

WILLIAMS, B. 1962. The idea of equality. Pp. 121–122 in P. Laslett, and W.G. Runciman (eds.), *Philosophy, Politics and Society*. Oxford: Basil Blackwell.

WOLPE, P.R. 2002. Treatment, enhancement, and the ethics of Neurotherapeutics. *Brain and Cognition 50*, 387–395 389.

WADA (WORLD ANTI-DOPING AGENCY). 2003. *World Anti-Doping Code*. Montreal: World Anti-Doping Agency.

Regulation

Threat to Converging Technologies

ALAN S. ZIEGLER

*Institute of New Dimensions, Fair Lawn,
New Jersey 07410, USA*

ABSTRACT: This article discusses two competing principles underlying efforts to regulate technological developments converging at the nanoscale that are intended to promote human health: the internalization of social cost by use of economic cost–benefit analysis and the precautionary principle by implementation of preventative safety standards. Overemphasis of the former may lead to potential unacceptable political and ethical effects while narrow focus on the latter may lead to potential retardation of innovation by deterring private risk capital investment. Suggestions are made for reconciling these principles through legislative initiatives.

KEYWORDS: ESH regulations; converging technologies

REGULATION: THE THREAT TO CONVERGING TECHNOLOGIES (CT)

The focus of this article is not the many challenges posed by the terra incognita of CT for the improvement of human performance to specific current environmental, safety and health (ESH) regulations. Rather, it is to raise for further discussion the appropriateness of two currently competing movements for change in the principles underlying our regulatory structure for the regulation of technological developments in area of human health. They are the principle of internalization of social costs and the precautionary principle. Each comes from different and sometimes contending major philosophic underpinning of ESH regulations, respectively, utilitarian cost–benefit analysis and Enlightenment/religious values of individual intrinsic worth. Underlying my argument are three assumptions:

1. The promise of technological convergence to change significantly society and humanity for the better for the most part is justified and not just special interest hype.

Address for correspondence: Alan S. Ziegler, Institute of New Dimensions, 7 Beekman Place, Fair Lawn, NJ 07410. Voice: 201-797-7465.
e-mail: aziegler@sweeneylev.com

Ann. N.Y. Acad. Sci. 1093: 339–349 (2006). © 2006 New York Academy of Sciences.
doi: 10.1196/annals.1382.022

2. The time frame for achieving the fruits of such change depends in significant part on the availability of private risk capital.

3. The availability of risk capital depends in part on the investor's perception of the probability and magnitude of liability incurred by the activities financed. A corollary to this assumption is that unwise regulation can increase the perception of uncertainty, which will then retard technological development based on private capital.

THE PRINCIPLE OF INTERNALIZATION OF SOCIAL COSTS

John Stuart Mill said that there are some limits to the freedom of a rational person to act as he or she pleases: when these actions impinge on others' ability to act as they choose (Mill 1869). Thus a rational person should take some care or precaution to avoid harming others. This standard is embodied in law, either in the common law traditions relating to negligence and reasonable care or more recently in our regulatory precautionary framework erected on a statutory base.

All legal systems, with the exception of those that are arbitrarily imposed by force on others for the sole benefit of some tyrant or kleptocracy, provide for the protection of individuals from the harmful effects of the actions of other people. Protection from intentional injury by other individuals is the function of criminal law. In common law countries, there is a second line of defense against injury and other harms to specific individuals: civil suits grounded in the law of torts either for specified intentional acts or for unintentional actions, which harm others due to negligence or other fault. In other noncommon law countries, these types of actionable activities from private commercial activities may be specifically codified. This both remedies the wrong to the individual but also creates an incentive to change the actions or methods used by businesses in the future.

There is a third layer of protection through regulation of activities that are recognized as likely to cause harm or injury to the general public or to identifiable groups but whose geographic or temporal causal connection to identifiable individuals is nebulous. To protect the general public as opposed to specific individuals, these activities may be proscribed in advance or they may be otherwise regulated to reduce the overall incidence of harm.

The amount of precautionary care deemed rational care is often set forth in economic terms, using a cost–benefit analysis. The idea is that a rational person takes precautionary action up to the point where the cost of the harm he is trying to avoid is less than the cost of the additional effort to avoid it. This amount is termed *efficient caution*. The barebones rational economic basis underlying this concept (Posner 1986) is that:

1. If prices rise, people seek substitutes or buy less. For example, when the price of home heating oil goes up, more people either switch to natural

gas heating or lower the setting on their thermostats. When the price of gasoline goes up and mass transit is an available option, more people may choose to take the train or bus or even bike or walk. If it is not available, they may car pool.

2. People do not engage in business that loses money—they will reallocate their investment resources to other activities where their costs will be lower.
3. In a free market these resources tend to go toward their most valuable use.
4. Prices are signals of consumer preferences or social valuation.
5. Value is the sum of individual decisions signaled by price—what people are willing to pay.

When resources have shifted to the highest priced or most valuable use in an economy, then they are considered to be employed efficiently. The basic underlying concept, at least in a free society, is that no one knows better than the individual as to what should be produced. There may be other social goals, but economic efficiency, representing maximal individual choice, is a very important component of a free society.

While of value to the parties directly involved, many transactions may cause harm or injury to third parties. If enough people are affected, these transactions are called social costs. The broader version of the efficiency of a transaction or activity (a "potential Pareto superior transaction") is generally measured by determining the increase in value to the seller and to the buyer compared to the harm done to the third party. If the economic measurement of that harm is less than the amount of gain to the other two parties, then the two should be able to compensate the third party and still be ahead of where they would have been had they not entered into the transaction. Thus the total costs are internalized to the original transaction.

When the costs of an economic activity are not reflected by the market (i.e., included in the product price) but instead are borne by the wider community, then the costs are considered to be externalized. If prices do not reflect the true social costs of production (including accidents and environmental degradation), this externalization of costs leads to economic inefficiency, and there will be an increase in choices to use or purchase a product over those that would be chosen if the price reflected the true cost. If activities that produce harm bore their full cost that included the cost of these harms, that is, the costs were internalized, there would be less of such activity and hence less harm. Socials costs would, in the aggregate, be reduced.

This can be illustrated by the following example: If the price of a car and driving bore all the costs of accidents and the pollution effects of automobile production and use, whether through an increase in the cost of insurance, an increase in the cost of petroleum products, or an increase in the cost of the auto components that contaminate land fills, then some people might choose not to buy a second car or even forgo the car for public transportation, where it conveniently exists. Fewer drivers might mean fewer vehicle-related injuries and fewer cars might mean less air pollution-related health problems. The manufacturer/seller would also make a cost decision as to whether to include a safety feature in the cost of production of a car. The producer would spend money to the point of efficient caution. That is, he would choose to increase his cost of production by adding safety features that reduce his cost of compensating third parties to the point where additional safety yield no longer exceeds the cost of this feature. This would be the point of maximum net benefits to individual seller and to society.

Thus at least for economists, harms can and should be viewed in economic terms, so that social costs of accidents and other harms will be internalized (Calabresi 1970).[1] Some argue that the real role for government regulation is to internalize social costs so that they are part of the cost–benefit calculus (Stewart 1993). The hoped for result is that social costs will be automatically optimized by price through market transactions just like Adam Smith's invisible hand that cumulatively optimizes the supply and demand of goods through the expression of individual choices.

But if regulation or user fees or taxes supposedly can be used to internalize at least some of these costs (e.g., the "polluter pays" principle now being favored in Europe), why are some if not most regulations not based on an economic cost–benefit analysis that incorporates the principle of internalization of social costs?

CRITIQUE OF COST–BENEFIT ANALYSIS
AS A BASIS FOR REGULATION

There are many criticisms to the use of utilitarian cost–benefit analysis to reduce the level of harm or the social cost of accidents. Some are economic. Others are more philosophic or ethical (Keating 2002). Some of the more common justifications for the use of outright regulation prohibitions as a substitute for the use of market cost internalization to reduce the level of accidents or harmful activities are:

1. Individuals really do not know what is best (for themselves).
2. There are some important costs and benefits that must be compared, which cannot be monetized through the market.
3. Moral or ethical concepts besides costs should be considered.
4. Resource allocation theory has some inherent limitations that necessitate collective or centralized decision making.

---

[1] Starting with Calabresi, Guido, *The Costs of Accidents*, Yale Univ. Press (1970). See also Appendix Economic Analysis of Tort Law in Henderson and Pearson, *The Tort Process*, 3rd ed. Little Brown & Co. (1988).

5. Deterrence through the market does not work efficiently for some categories of activities and for individual acts.

The resistance to the acceptance of the legitimacy of relying solely on internalization of social costs to reduce accidents and other harm can be shown by real world examples in my own profession. Even where internalization is feasible without regulation or user fees through cost shifting, tort litigation based on enterprise or strict liability, this explicit cost–benefit approach is usually deemed fatal in negligence jury cases where the standard of care is reasonableness. Research has shown that juries punish companies that do a cost–benefit analysis (Keating 2002). Jury awards against companies that ignore the issue of the calculation of cost of harm to third parties in the decision to produce a product or method of manufacture fare better than those that go through a deliberative cost–benefit process, particularly if they place a value for life in the calculus of the cost as opposed to the economic benefit. Clearly, in a juror's mind, utilitarian economic rationalism is not equated with reasonableness.

In my opinion, the main objection to the principle of internalization of social costs is philosophical or ethical. Individuals differ and must be recognized as being more than just interchangeable parts of a group. Opponents of the private use of cost–benefit analysis think that not all benefits and harms are equivalent; that is, in reality they can be qualitatively different. The economic cost–benefit approach minimizes the distinction between people. It assesses total value of the benefits and costs or harms over the entire population. The actual burdens to be shouldered by an individual can be swamped by the incremental gains over the entire population sample. Thus a devastating injury to one or a few can be overwhelmed by the trivial gains to large numbers of people.

To be tradable under a cost–benefit approach, benefits and costs should be comparable—and it is unjust and unfair to consider harm comparable to benefits unless they burden or impair individual lives in comparable ways—whether the impact is major or minimal.

Let us consider two hypothetical examples. First, a new hair product is developed that only requires one application to continually change gray hair to its original natural color. Preliminary tests suggest that a small but measurable percentage of people who will use this hair dye will develop a fatal cancer—maybe one in ten thousand or five hundred in a pool of 5 million potential users. But almost 5 million people may feel younger and have better social lives with this dye. What if we could also show that users were able to keep their jobs to an older age and thus add to the gross national product in excess of any economically measured cost from the cancer victims? What if we added a label to the product that indicated its use could be dangerous to your health? Is one death in ten thousand comparable to improvement in the lives and economic situation of 5 million people? Would the calculus be different if some social research showed that the suicide rate among the graying population facing decreased job prospects might drop by a number comparable to the increase in cancer fatalities?

Second, during a major internationally televised event watched by a billion people, such as the Olympics or the international soccer championship, with billions of dollars invested in advertising and staffing, a spectator who sneaked in without a ticket and in an effort to find a place to watch the game, slips while attempting to sit on a ledge and falls over the edge. His leg is caught in some netting and he is seen in the video screen dangling over railing of an upper tier of the stadium. To bring him to safety, the event would have to be interrupted and maybe cancelled while rescue equipment is brought on to the field. Do we take a chance of leaving him dangling and hope he does not fall for the half hour or so until the conclusion of the event? Does it matter if the event is merely delayed during the rescue or whether it would have to be canceled entirely? Does it matter if there really is no risk of death or irreversible injury but he probably experiences the terror of dangling there 50 meters above a spiked fence? Is there any further mitigation in the latter situation if it could be shown that ratings would soar (with a subsequent significant upswing in economic activity and temporary drop in the crime rate in certain viewer areas) if the video cameras just prior to each commercial break switch to close-ups of his situation?

Most people viscerally reject this type of calculus that reduces life to the level of a commodity—the idea that there is a price on one's head that can be paid by others for their own gain. That is why I think regulation of activities with the potential social harm is grounded on an alternative approach to cost-justified precaution, namely, safety—the reduction or modification of risky activities themselves.

THE PRECAUTIONARY PRINCIPLE CHALLENGE

Let us turn to the other trend: the precautionary principle. Definitions of the precautionary principle differ, ranging from the relatively modest statement in Principle 15 of the Rio Declaration on Environment and Development: ("Where there are threats of serious or irreversible damage, lack of full scientific certainty shall not be used as a reason for postponing cost-effective measures to prevent environmental degradation.") to the 1999 Wingspread Declaration ("When an activity raises threats of harm to human health or the environment, precautionary measures should be taken even if some cause and effect relationships are not fully established scientifically. In this context the proponent of an activity, rather than the public, should bear the burden of proof."). Proponents want to apply a precautionary principle in all situations where sound scientific knowledge is not available to determine if a proposed activity will be harmless. In those situations of uncertainty, rather than permit continued development in tandem with assessments based on scientific studies and tests, the strong version of the precautionary principle would forbid development until an activity or product is proved safe regardless of the length of time or the financial practicability of trying to achieve such proofs. Thus the precautionary principle requires proactive intervention of protective measures in face of possible risk and in its robust form imposes a moratorium on development until clarification of all scientific uncertainties. In contrast, in the United States, while agencies, such as the Food and Drug Administration (FDA) and the Environmental Protection Agency (EPA), have been authorized by law to regulate activities to prevent harm in advance of any actual activity, the courts have interpreted their latitude to restrain activities or products theorized as hazardous to be constrained by the requirement that the agency first make some type of finding both of the significant threat of the perceived harm and also of the rational efficacious of the proposed regulations to address the problem. Both of these findings have to be based on scientific safety assessment. See, for example, *Industrial Union Department v. American Petroleum Institute*, 448 U.S. 607 (United States Supreme Court 1980). In that case, the Supreme Court invalidated OSHA regulations that imposed a zero standard without specific statutory authorization. This requirement has been followed in lower court decisions.

While the United States refused to sign the Rio Declaration, this principle has been more favorably received in Europe, and is being broadened to include more than just environmental concerns. The European Union (EU) is finalizing (at the time of this writing) a new but contentious approach to chemical regulations known as Registration, Evaluation, and Authorization of Chemicals (REACH).[2] REACH is expected to change a situation where only a fraction of the chemicals currently on the market in the Europe have undergone risk or hazard assessment to one requiring the pretesting of all substances. Invoking the precautionary principle, the EU will shift the burden of proof for a chemical's safety from the government to the manufacturer. The aim is to encourage the substitution of less hazardous chemicals and materials in products (either existing or through innovation) and thus reduce chemical-related health care costs.

In one sense, the precautionary principle certainly takes a strong stand in favor of the worth of the individual. The problems with the precautionary principle or even a less ideological but still very rigorous precautionary approach is that it poses a risk of stifling innovation or at least delaying of positive development not only of economically important technical advances but of advances vital for the health of individuals and the overall well-being of society, a subset of CT for improvement of human performance, which I will refer to as CT–Human Health. Regulations can have the effect of diverting venture capital that might have been used to fund research; changing the nature of the

---

[2] Set forth in "Strategy for a Future Chemical Policy," a white paper adopted by the European Commission in February 2001.

type of research undertaken; and causing firms to recalculate the payoff from investment in research and development and to diminish the amount (Eads 1980).

If the regulatory focus is on the CT–Human Health product rather than on deterring conduct (i.e., providing sanctions for the foreseeable negligent or quasi-criminal acts of the individuals involved, such as deliberate toxic waste dumpers), then such regulations could strangle in the cradle important innovations that might produce greater health and safety in the long run then the sum of any specific harm to specific individuals. I thus question whether specific centralized safety decisions made in advance on theoretical grounds are justifiable at the early stages of CT–Human Health development and implementation.

THE COST INTERNALIZATION CHALLENGE

Like the precautionary principle, there are potential negative effects of cost internalization on early stage CT–Human Health. There are at least four reasons why I think not all early-stage products in CT–Human Health will be able to internalize the ultimate cost of the harmful consequences of their production and use.

1. The ultimate consequences of such activities and products are unknown and not estimable at this time. It is hard enough to reliably determine such things for conventional products. CT–Human Health is qualitatively different and immensely more complicated. Synergistic effects from the cumulative use or exposure to multiple products may be beyond current human predictive powers.
2. Under our current technology, not all biological/pharmacologic products can be made safe for everybody—there is too much genetic variation in people. Even as the concept of strict liability evolved in our tort law, it was always judicially recognized that there were classes of products or procedures considered unavoidably unsafe (such as the use of diagnostic X rays). This exception is incorporated into section 402A of the Restatement (Second) of Torts (American Law Institute 1977). That there is always a subset of people who react badly even to conventional drugs, therapies, or vaccines is recognized in tort law and thus strict liability is considered not to be applicable (Fox and Traynor 1991).
3. CT–Human Health holds out the promise to narrow the range of adverse effects by customizing treatment to individuals—but there is always a needed period of trial and error in such developments. The product or therapy has to get out there in actual use before we can really know its adverse effects and then how to circumvent or ameliorate them.
4. There may be no practical way to internalize social costs through use of liability insurance, which may be either unavailable or insufficient

(through limits and exclusions). In the United States, the legal doctrine of enterprise liability, which through variations of the principle of strict liability without ordinary fault can place responsibility for accidents on the producer even in the absence of traditional negligence, forces business to take out adequate liability insurance to avoid the risk of catastrophic judgments in favor of victim claimants that would otherwise bankrupt any single business entity. The risk of loss through the activity is thus spread over the entire production industry or business sector. Spreading loss, however, is only one function of such insurance. Insurers, through variable renewal/cancellation/deductible/premium incentives in conjunction with the dissemination of information on risk reduction practices and the development over time of standards enforced by inspections, act as a nongovernmental regulation of business designed to promote the overall reduction of injury and other harms from economic activities.

Fire insurance is a classic illustration of how insurance standards can be developed and used, through internalization of costs, to lower the incidence of accidents or harms to society. The very factors that make insurance cost-effective in fire casualty, however, are missing in the nascent CT–Human Health development, where there would be a uniqueness of output with an unpredictable nature of product interaction in a context where there are no applicable standard manufacturing techniques. The producer would also face an unlimited potential number of differently situated claimants who may claim diffuse symptoms (e.g., lower intellectual or artistic potential) (Katzman 1987)

5. The threat of bearing all of the costs may either make the products unaffordable or deter research into important areas all together. Yet these products could be critical to the welfare of society.

Even if merely delayed for an extra decade, there could be an enormous cost paid (through illness, disability and death, pain and suffering) by individuals who were denied the benefits during those additional 10 years—a cost that probably dwarfs the avoidance of harm to a few by the precaution of standing still. Thus it is reasonable to consider these CT–Human Health benefits as potentially offsetting the amount of harm when considering their potential risks to individuals.

But does not that bring us back to the equity issue—the lack of fairness to the individuals who will actually experience harm for an activity that has some positive societal benefit? I suggest that it is not unfair to permit CT–Human Health developers to externalize some of these injury costs.

Those harmed (the victims) are not identifiable before the fact by any party in advance in a manner that would lead to cost-effect change in harm-/accident-producing behavior. After the fact, when more is known based on scientifically acceptable evidence, regulations can step in to require additional safety procedures or warning labels.

The victims are part of the class that will share in the rewards—this is for a class of health products that go beyond mere cosmetic enhancement products. CT–Human Health promises increased longevity (for example, 20 years of additional productivity) or, farther in the future, rejuvenation.

EXTERNALIZATION OF SOCIAL COSTS IN A RESPONSIBLE REGULATORY FRAMEWORK

There are some actions that can be taken to ameliorate some of the negative effects of externalization of the cost without slowing down progress.

1. The impacts on individuals would be lessened in societies that have full or very broad medical coverage of its populace. In societies like the United States, where significant segments of the population do not have adequate health care, some type of compensation fund or use tax could be imposed once some causative association of unavoidable harm is identified. For example: The Vaccination Victims' Compensation Fund established by the Vaccine Victims Compensation Act recognized that where there is a judgment to permit and even to promote a product that has known dangers, there should nevertheless be some compensation available to the victims from the state rather than the producers. More recently, the federal government funded the 9/11 victims compensation plan to compensate victims in lieu of their suing and likely bankrupting the airlines.
2. Societies could adopt effective civil actions for negligence (either intentional/gross or plain negligence with no imputed enterprise liability or other strict liability in tort) and impose FDA-like postmarket reporting obligations and an evolving clear regulatory based external measure of care with no retroactivity. This would likely lead to the activities eventually becoming insurable and internalizable.

Can this work under the current statutory and regulatory framework? United States statutes and regulations provide some precedents that show a capacity to be stretched to accommodate CT–Human Health research and development.

Currently, the EPA makes a cost–benefit decision when it sets a de minimus standard for the level of harm from a toxic substance—that is, one death in a million. Then the agency embarks on risk assessment to determine what amount of exposure will produce this. One could similarly set a standard for CT–Human Health and a reporting structure to detect it, although this might be exceedingly complex and difficult to achieve.

In another regulatory context, antitrust, the National Cooperative Research Act of 1984 was designed to promote high technology and innovation. Among its other provisions was a limit to damages available for the competitive harm caused by certain promoted research and development joint ventures.[3]

---

[3] United States Code. §§ 4301-05 (Suppl II 1984).

There is also a trend toward restricting remedies through litigation; for example., the pending proposals in Congress to limit damages in malpractice suits in order to reduce dropouts from and encourage more new doctors to enter high-risk medical specialties, thus both expanding the availability of medical specialist services and also reducing medical malpractice insurance costs that would be passed through to the patient.

A major step to facilitating development without major negative social effects would be to reduce the availability of strict liability in selected CT–Human Health areas. This could be done by creating safe harbors for producers who comply with published standards or procedures based on empirical evidence, requiring a showing of gross negligence or case by case negligence for failure to exercise due care in compliance with existing norms. The norms can become more restrictive as more becomes known but would not apply retroactive liability. Insurance would probably become available and exercise its preventive cost internalization role if liability is solely based on faulty behavior based on established norms.

Thus it may be possible to have our cake (rapid CT–Human Health progress) and eat it too (fairness of application and risk reduction for individuals over time).

REFERENCES

AMERICAN LAW INSTITUTE. 1977. Section 402A of the Restatement (Second) of Torts.

CALABRESI, G. 1970. *The Costs of Accidents*. New Haven, Connecticut: Yale University Press.

EADS, G.C. 1980. Regulation and technical change: some largely unexplored influences. *American Economic Review 70*(2), 50–54.

EUROPEAN COMMISSION. 2001. Strategy for a Future Chemical Policy, a white paper adopted by the European Commission. Brussels.COM (2001) 88 final.

FOX, E.M., and M. TRAYNOR. 1991. Biotechnology for human life and health – the special case for a negligence-only rule to promote critical innovation. *Berkeley Technological Law Journal 6*(Fall), 2, online at http://www.law.berkeley.edu/journals/btlj/articles/vol6/Fox/html/text.html

HENDERSON, J., and R. PEARSON. 1988. Appendix Economic Analysis of Tort Law. *The Tort Process*, 3rd ed. Boston: Little Brown & Co.

KATZMAN, M.T. 1987. Environmental risk management through insurance. *The Cato Journal 6*(3), 775–799.

KEATING, G.C. 2002. Pressing Precaution Beyond the Point of Cost-Justification. USC Law and Economics Research Paper No. 02-2.

MILL, J.S. 1869. *On Liberty*. New York: Bartleby.com

POSNER, E.A. 1986. *Economic Analysis of Law*, 2nd ed. Boston: Little, Brown and Company.

STEWART, R.B. 1993. Environmental regulation and international competitiveness. *Yale Law Journal 102*(8), 2039–2106.

UNITED STATES CODE. 1984. 15 U.S.C. §§ 4301-05 (Supp. II).

UNITED STATES SUPREME COURT. 1980. Industrial Union Department v. American Petroleum Institute. 448 U.S. 607.

APPENDIX I

Convergence Glossary

WILLIAM SIMS BAINBRIDGE

*National Science Foundation**

Adaptive System: A complex set of interacting entities that adjust in some way to internal pressures or environmental influences, often with the assumption that it acts in some way to preserve its own equilibrium or to evolve in a particular direction.

Affective Computing: Designing computers or robots so they can correctly respond to human emotions, perhaps thereby taking on emotional qualities of their own.

AFM: Atomic Force Microscopy.

Assisted Cognition: The use of technologies to help cognitively disabled people, or indeed any people, deal with life's mental challenges better, currently based on cognitive-information convergences, in future supported by biotechnology and nanotechnology.

Autism: A set of human neurodevelopmental conditions characterized by social interaction and communication difficulties, as well as unusually narrow, repetitive interests.

BFM: Biological Force Microscopy.

Bioethics: Systematic consideration of the ethical implications of biotechnologies, often used as a model for exploration of the ethical implications of other technologies.

Biological Signal Transduction: The process by which one living cell influences another, often through the medium of hormones.

Biomimetic: Engineered structures or devices that imitate biology in their functions or methods of manufacture.

Bionic Technology: Engineered devices and systems that combine biology with electronics, including prosthetic devices and biosensors.

Biotechnology: Techniques for accomplishing practical goals based on biology and related sciences, from ancient methods like the cooking of food or fermentation of wine to modern genetic engineering.

Bottom-Up Approach: Creating nanoscale structures or devices by assembling atoms or molecules, for example by means of scanning probe techniques.

*The views expressed in this glossary do not necessarily represent the views of the National Science Foundation or the United States.

Ann. N.Y. Acad. Sci. 1093: 350–357 (2006). © 2006 New York Academy of Sciences.
doi: 10.1196/annals.1382.023

Boundary Work: Effort invested in defining fields of activity, delineating the differences between concepts, and locating things in a sociocultural context.

Character Displacement: The process in which competition between species, organizations, or cultures causes them to become more different from each other; product differentiation in marketing is an economic example.

Cloning: A variety of biotechnology methods for growing tissues from a single cell, much broader in techniques and applications than the popular image of it, which is more properly called "human reproductive cloning."

Coevolution: The simultaneous development of two different phenomena in interaction with each other, for example, the emergence of nanotechnology coupled with the emergence of research on its societal implications.

Cogniceuticals: Chemical agents that enhance brain performance.

Cognition: Mental processes of perception, analysis, and decision making, energized in human beings by emotion and in machines by human programming.

Cognome: The mental heritage of human beings, by analogy with the genome, based in culture as well as the brain.

Complementarity: Partial substitutability of two or more entities or analytical frameworks; especially: the situation when two incompatible theories are both needed to provide a full explanation of a phenomenon.

Complexity: The property of being composed of many interrelated parts, or a system of high entropy that cannot be reduced accurately to a very simple model.

Configuration: The detailed, dynamic structure of an object, such as a molecule, which determines its properties and behavior.

Conservation: The tendency of some properties of a system to remain stable over time, or to switch between well-defined states that possess some form of symmetry.

Consilience: Convergence of the natural sciences into one, unified body of knowledge.

Convergence: The tendency of two fields of technology to share progressively more similar methods, concepts, and goals, leading eventually to a merging of these fields.

Convergenist: An advocate for technological convergence.

Converging Technologies: Unification of nanotechnology, biotechnology, information technology, and cognitive technologies, based largely on the unity of nature at the nanoscale and on transforming tools for research and production.

Cost–Benefit Analysis: Rational, utilitarian calculation of the net balance of harms and benefits from a new technology.

Creole: A language, often simplified but combining words from two or more other languages, used to communicate across cultures.

Critical Zone: The place where the land converges with the hydrosphere and atmosphere, the interstitial region that humans inhabit.

CT: Converging Technologies; the combination of new technologies and more traditional technologies.

Cultural Genetics: Applying principles from biological genetics to the study, management, and creation of cultural products.

Cyberinfrastructure: A substantial investment in computing and communications facilities to serve as the platform for many different scientific projects.

Cyborg: Cybernetic Organism: a hybrid that is part biological organism and part engineered machine; metaphorically, people who are strongly in favor of technological enhancement of human nature.

Diffusion: The spread of a technical idea or other cultural element from one group, place, or application to another.

Digital Arts: An interdisciplinary convergence between the visual arts and computer science.

Distributive Justice: Theories of the proper distribution of goods and other values throughout society, focusing alternatively on an individual's needs or contributions.

Egalitarianism: The ethical view that the proper basis for distribution of resources is need, so that individuals receive equal treatment for equal need.

EHS: The Environmental, Health, and Safety implications of a technology.

ELSI : The Ethical, Legal, and Social Implications of a branch of technology, a component of government funding in the given area of research.

Empathy Enhancement: Technological methods, such as computer-assisted education or the use of affective computing aids, to help a person become more attentive to the needs and feelings of other human beings.

Entropy: A measure of disorder or of unavailable energy in a closed thermodynamic system; the information content of a message or system, or the irreducible complexity of a scientific model.

Epigenetic Rules: Genetically encoded regulations guiding the development of a cell, organ, or organism.

Evolution: Change marked by drift, natural selection, and a trend toward greater complexity, exploiting variation to develop new configurations that compete through interactions.

Evolutionary Trajectory: The likely course of development of a species or culture, for example, the probable future of humanity.

Exaptation: The phenomenon in which a characteristic that evolved to serve one function comes to serve a very different function.

Externalization of Costs: The situation in which some of the costs of a technology are not reflected by the market or in the product price, but instead are borne by the wider community.

Fluidics: An engineering discipline comparable to electronics, but controlling the flow of liquids, potentially even at the nanoscale.

Frankenfoods: A popular term for food produced from genetically modified organisms, especially when they are produced without proper concern for public safety and acceptance.

Genetic Algorithm: A specific technique in evolutionary computing that expresses potential solutions to a problem as byte strings then allows them to compete in a reproductive system incorporating recombination of bytes ("crossover") and selection on the basis of how well each string solves the problem.

Genetic Engineering: Intentional manipulation of an organism's genes, for example to improve agricultural products, by means of procedures such as gene splicing, mutation induction with selection, or other methods.

Genetic Enhancement: The use of gene therapy or genetic engineering to improve the capabilities or a human being or other living thing.

Genomics: The scientific study of an organism's entire genome (genetic code), or of the dynamics of large-scale genetic systems, whether representing part of a genome or an entire gene pool.

GMO: Genetically Modified Organism; a result of genetic engineering.

Governance: Setting the parameters of the system within which people and institutions develop new technologies, so that self-regulation achieves the desired outcomes.

GPS: Global Positioning System; a navigation technology that uses computation and communication with orbiting satellites to measure one's location on Earth with a high degree of precision.

Human Enhancement: Technological treatments or accessories that give a person abilities not naturally present or augment abilities beyond the normal range.

Human Nature: The proper, traditional, or fundamental characteristics of the human species; a contested concept used to anchor debates about the possibly radical impacts of new technologies on humans, usually invoked to resist change, but sometime supporting change in the argument that the nature of humans is to modify their environments and themselves.

Human Performance: The relative level of success with which a person achieves his or her goals.

Human Potential: An achievable high level of human functioning marked by improved abilities and sense of well-being.

Indecision: A summary term for situations in which some aspect of reality is fundamentally inconsistent, undecidable, uncertain, aleatoric, chaotic, or otherwise incapable of complete description and prediction.

Informatics: The science and engineering of information processing, especially in a specific domain, such as bioinformatics or nanoinformatics.

Information: Data that are potentially meaningful to human beings, in a pattern distinguishable from randomness, which could be used as knowledge to guide decisions if placed in a larger context.

Information Science: Often treated as synonymous with computer science, but actually much broader, encompassing mathematical information theory, computer science, library science, and multidisciplinary research on the structure and dynamics of human culture.

Information Technology: The computer and communications hardware, software, and networks that collect, store, retrieve, and analyze information automatically but under human control.

Interaction: Mutual influence among elements of a system, often generating higher-level dynamics and other emergent phenomena.

Interactional Expertise: The skill and experience required to pass information from one scientist to another, especially the ability to act as a cultural broker between significantly different fields.

Interdisciplinary: A field of endeavor that integrates principles from two or more disciplines.

Ion Channels: Membrane proteins that facilitate the transport of charged ions across a living cell's membrane.

Laser Tweezers: A device that holds and manipulates small particles by means of a finely tuned laser beam.

Libertarianism: A theory of justice that holds a person should receive in proportion to what he or she contributes in exchanges with other people.

Logical Positivism: A philosophical perspective that asserts any statement that cannot be tested through some at least conceivable scientific procedures is meaningless.

Luddites: An outbreak of collective behavior in early nineteenth-century Britain, in which labor disputes took the form of machine breaking; by extension (but not correct historically) any unreasonable opposition to technological progress.

Machine Learning: A very wide range of computational and statistical methods in artificial intelligence that employ iterative or progressive methods to develop a model of a particular kind of data.

Markov Model: A statistical or computational model of a process involving a number of states with a distinctive probability of transition from any one state to any other.

Mechatronics: An engineering design philosophy that integrates precision mechanical engineering, electronics, control theory, and computer engineering in the design of intelligent products, systems, and processes.

Metrology: The science of measurement, for example covering the theory and instrumentation required to describe nanoscale structures and determine their dimensions accurately.

Moral Imagination: The creative faculty displayed when a person conceives of a new way to benefit human beings or to resolve conflicts.

Multidisciplinary: Activity in which people with two or more different kinds of disciplinary expertise cooperate.

Nanogeoscience: The science of the nonliving, solid Earth, the hydrosphere, and the atmosphere in their relationship to nanoscale phenomena and nanotechnology.

Nanoscale: The size range of roughly 1 to 100 nm, where many of the fundamental structures of biology are formed, composite materials may take on their distinctive characteristics, and many important physical phenomena are found.

Nanoscience: The study of the unique properties of matter at the nanoscale; an interdisciplinary field of science combining physics, materials science, the chemistry of complex molecules, and related disciplines.

Nanotechnology: The ability to engineer at the molecular level, atom by atom, to build new structures, materials, and machines.

NBIC: The convergence of four engineering realms: Nanotechnology, Biotechnology, Information technology, and new technologies based on Cognitive science.

NELSI: Nanotechnology's Ethical, Legal, and Social Implications.

Network Analysis: Graphical or statistical analysis that describes the relationships among nodes in a network, such as between people in a social network.

Neuroethics: The philosophical study of or practical rules for deciding issues concerning transformation of the human nervous system, for example by mood-enhancing or ability-expanding medications.

Neuromorphic: Electronic circuitry (or potentially other technologies such as fluidic systems) that mimic the structure and function of neurons, such as digital neural networks or many kinds of very complex analog circuits.

Neurotechnology: Engineering methods for supplementing or improving the functioning of the human nervous system.

Nexialist: A skilled professional who works at the boundary between scientific fields, systematically combining knowledge from two or more areas; the opposite of a specialist.

Nonspatial Government: A new form of mutual obligation and authority that is not based on geographic residence and collective dominion over land, as has been the case in human history since the development of agriculture, facilitated by new information technologies.

Novelty Detection: Detecting abnormal events in time series data.

Patent Pool: An arrangement in which two or more patent holders aggregate patent rights into a package for licensing.

Patent Thicket: A dense web of overlapping intellectual property rights owned by different companies that can retard progress.

Personality Capture: The process of documenting the characteristics of an individual human personality for analysis or emulation within an information system.

Pervasive Computing: A European term meaning the same as "ubiquitous computing."

Polymath: An individual scholar, scientist, or engineer who possesses significant expertise in multiple fields.

Precautionary Principle: The ethical claim that a proponent for a new technology should bear the burden of proof in advocating its adoption, for fear of unrecognized or unfair risks.

Proteomics: By analogy with and extension from genomics, the study of the structures, functions, and origins of proteins.

Reasonableness: The legal or cultural standard of behavior reflecting what a reasonable person might do under the given circumstances, often quite different from a rational or cost-benefit analysis.

Recommender System: A cognitive technology widely used since the introduction of online businesses, advising the customer on the basis of the past behavior and preferences of this customer and of other, similar customers.

Semantic Architecture: The structure of related meanings in a culture, profession, or information processing system.

Semantic System: A set of concepts connected by meaningful relationships.

Sensory Substitution: Using one of the human senses for information input rather than another, to overcome either sensory disability or sensory overload.

Services Science: The systematic study and improvement of methods for managing service industries, including information services.

Signal Integration: In neurobiology, cognitive science, and information science, the process by which bits of information from two or more sources are combined.

Sociobiology: The study of the genetic and evolutionary basis of animal and human behavior, and the interaction between genetics and behavior in determining evolutionary fitness.

Spirit of Sport: A doctrine of competitive sports that extols the value of an athlete's virtuous perfection of natural talents, but potentially opposes artificial enhancement.

Systematics: Development of technical language, models, and theories to describe the behavior of a system, especially through the relationships among its parts.

Technology Transfer: The expansion of a technical idea, device, or new material from one area of application to another.

Technopolitics: The dimension of political debate that concerns public policy decisions about new technologies.

Therapy: Treatment intended to restore a person to natural functional health, contrasted with human enhancement.

Top-Down Approach: Creating nanoscale structures or devices by further miniaturization of larger-scale technologies, for example by means of photolithographic techniques.

Trading Zone: A metaphoric place, consisting of shared assumptions and terminology, where specialists from different fields can come together, communicate, and cooperate.

Transhumanism: An ethical perspective compatible with convergenism but not identical, stressing the right of all human beings to seek to improve themselves, especially through advanced technologies; only a small minority of convergenists are transhumanists.

Transilience: In technology, a revolutionary leap that renders older technology obsolete, often involving convergence of technologies and a new relationship between producers and customers.

Two Cultures: The theory propounded by C. P. Snow that the science and humanities in modern society are distinct cultures separated by a gulf of ignorance and misunderstanding.

Ubiquitous Computing: The emerging situation in which information technology is everywhere, mobile as well as embedded in a great variety of devices, communicating via the universal network and involved in all facets of human life.

Utilitarianism: The ethical view that goods should be distributed in such a manner as to increase total well-being, or the greatest good to the greatest number.

Variation: Statistical distributions of properties caused by the combination of chance and divergent processes of interaction.

Welfarist Definition: The view that human enhancement consists of any change in the biology or psychology of a person, which increases the chances of leading a good life.

APPENDIX II:

Annotated Convergence Bibliography

WILLIAM SIMS BAINBRIDGE

National Science Foundation, Arlington, Virginia 22230, USA

KEYWORDS: nanotechnology; biotechnology; information technology; cognitive science; bibliography

In recent years, many books and articles have discussed the importance of unification across scientific and technological fields and suggested means for achieving it. The following 25 books are a recommended library for students, scientists, engineers, policy makers, and other interested citizens, who wish to understand the reality and the implications of Converging Technologies.

CONSILIENCE

Wilson, Edward O. 1998. *Consilience: The Unity of Knowledge*. New York: Knopf.

The author is a noted entomologist who contributed to the development of the convergent field called *sociobiology*, then expanded its scope to include human culture as well as animal behavior. This book takes the progressive unification of the most rigorous physical sciences as its starting point, explains how biology and behavioral sciences are joining this consilience, then wonders how far into the social sciences and humanities this unification can go. The style of the book is literary and philosophical, raising deep questions like the possibility that religion might be left out in the cold when all the rest of human culture converges. Wilson acknowledges the religious influences that affected his early life, and the conclusion of the book suggests that scientific progress teaches us to be self-reliant Atheists: "...we have learned a great deal about ourselves as a species. We now better understand where humanity came from, and what it is. *Homo Sapiens*, like the rest of life, was self-assembled. So here we are, no one having guided us to this condition, no one looking over our shoulder, our future entirely up to us" (p. 297).

The views expressed in this essay do not necessarily represent the views of the National Science Foundation or the United States.

Ann. N.Y. Acad. Sci. 1093: 358–367 (2006). © 2006 New York Academy of Sciences.
doi: 10.1196/annals.1382.024

Damasio, Antonio R., Anne Harrington, Jerome Kagan, Bruce S. McEwen, Henry Moss, and Rashid Shaikh (eds.). 2001. *Unity of Knowledge: The Convergence of Natural and Human Science.* New York: Annals of the New York Academy of Sciences (volume 935).

This is the proceedings volume from a conference inspired by E. O. Wilson's *Consilience*, and Wilson himself gave the keynote address. The papers tend to be in the biomedical area, with some in psychiatry and others about biological factors shaping personality or similar topics in adjacent areas of psychology. Several authors discuss how to transcend the nature versus nurture debate, seeking ways to integrate heredity and environment in explaining human behavior. Authors differ in how enthusiastically they view the potential for unifying science, and the concluding essays address educational issues.

NANOSCALE SCIENCE AND TECHNOLOGY

Siegel, Richard W., Evelyn Hu, and Mihail C. Roco (eds.). 1999. *Nanostructure Science and Technology: A Worldwide Study.* Dordrecht, Netherlands: Kluwer. Online at http://www.wtec.org/loyola/pdf/nano.pdf.

In 1996–1998, a special eight-person panel of the Interagency Working Group on NanoScience, Engineering, and Technology conducted site visits and workshops in the United States, Japan, Germany, Sweden, and Russia, to determine the state of advancement in nanoscience around the world. The editors then collated and analyzed information from these sources and others to produce this book, with the following four goals (pp. xvii-xviii): (1) provide the worldwide science and engineering community with a broadly inclusive and critical view of this field, (2) identify promising areas for future research and commercial development, (3) help stimulate development of an interdisciplinary international community of nanostructure researchers, and (4) encourage and identify opportunities for international collaboration.

Roco, Mihail C., R. Stanley Williams, and Paul Alivisatos (eds.). 2000. *Nanotechnology Research Directions: IWGN Workshop Report.* Dordrecht, Netherlands: Kluwer. Online at http://www.wtec.org/loyola/nano/IWGN. Research.Directions/.

This is the report of a workshop held on January 27–29, 1999. It provided a number of recommendations to guide the National Nanotechnology Initiative, based on a comprehensive survey of research needs and opportunities. One chapter looks at applications in the biological, medical, and health areas. Connections to information technology are evident in the book's extensive sections on computer simulation and nanoelectronics. Early parts of the book introduce fundamental concepts of nanotechnology to a broad audience, and later parts describe related activities at a number of federal government agencies.

Postek, Michael T., and Robert J. Hocken (eds.). 2006. *Instrumentation and Metrology for Nanotechnology*. Arlington, Virginia: National Nanotechnology Coordination Office.

This is the report of a National Nanotechnology Initiative Workshop, January 27–29, 2004, organized by the National Institute of Standards and Technology, which has an extensive mission in setting standards for measurement and encouraging the development of new and more accurate measurement instruments. Chapters cover five main measurement domains: (1) Nanocharacterization (description of nanoscale structures and materials), (2) Nanomechanics (determining the dynamic properties of nanostructures), (3) Nanoelectronics (including nanophotonics and nanomagnetics, employing the optical and magnetic properties of materials), (4) Nanofabrication (making individual structures or parts), and (5) Nanomanufacturing (making useful quantities of nanoscale devices and materials). A final section is devoted to the convergent topic of computational science issues in nanoscale metrology.

SOCIETAL IMPLICATIONS OF NANOTECHNOLOGY

Roco, Mihail C., and William Sims Bainbridge (eds.). 2001. *Societal Implications of Nanoscience and Nanotechnology*. Dordrecht, Netherlands: Kluwer. Online at http://www.wtec.org/loyola/nano/societalimpact/nanosi.pdf.

This is the book-length report of the first major conference about the societal implications of nanotechnology, held at the National Science Foundation, September 28–29, 2000. The report considers not only the intended benefits of the technology, but also the wider economic and political implications, including management of unintended and second-order consequences. Among the application areas considered were those in the medical, environmental, space exploration, and national security areas. Nanotechnology has implications for a range of sciences, and for science education, as well as potentially influencing the wider culture. Recognizing that research on the social, ethical, and legal implications had hardly begun, contributors examined methodologies for social science research and public involvement in policy making. The book contains recommendations, reports of working groups, and individual scientific or policy-oriented essays.

Roco, Mihail C., and William Sims Bainbridge (eds.). 2006. *Nanotechnology: Societal Implications—Maximizing Benefit for Humanity*. Berlin: Springer. Online at http://www.nano.gov/nni_societal_implications.pdf.

An official report of the Nanoscale Science, Engineering, and Technology (NSET) subcommittee, this short book communicates the observations and recommendations of participants in a major conference held December 3–5, 2003, at the National Science Foundation. In addition to an overview and introductory remarks by policy leaders, the book reports the conclusions of 10 thematic task forces: (1) Productivity and Equity, (2) Future Economic Scenarios, (3) The Quality of Life, (4) Future Social Scenarios, (5) Converging Technologies, (6) National Security and Space Exploration, (7) Ethics, Governance, Risk, and Uncertainty, (8) Public Policy, Legal, and International Aspects, (9) Interaction with the Public, and (10) Education and Human Resource Development.

Roco, Mihail C., and William Sims Bainbridge (eds.). 2006. *Nanotechnology: Societal Implications—Individual Perspectives*. Berlin: Springer.

Although not an official NSET report, this is the second, large volume in a pair that resulted from NSF's December 3–5, 2003 conference on the societal implications of nanoscience and nanotechnology. It collects 48 chapters written by the scientists, engineers, and policy leaders in seven broad areas: (1) Economic Impacts and Commercialization of Nanotechnology, (2) Social Scenarios, (3) Converging Technologies, (4) Ethics and Law, (5) Governance, (6) Public Perceptions, and (7) Education. The section on Converging Technologies contains seven essays on implications for the quality of life, technology, and conceptualization of the self, management, and legal issues of innovation, the use of cross-discipline analogies to promote convergence, benefits, and hazards for environmental protection, and the immediate impact of convergence on scientific and engineering disciplines themselves.

CONVERGING TECHNOLOGIES CONFERENCE VOLUMES

Roco, Mihail C., and William Sims Bainbridge (eds.). 2003. *Converging Technologies for Improving Human Performance*. Dordrecht, Netherlands: Kluwer.

This is the public version of the original government report based on a conference co-sponsored by the National Science Foundation and Department of Commerce, held December 3–4, 2001. A natural extension of work on the societal implications of nanotechnology, this book shows that the unification of science has become possible through the use of transforming tools, based on the unity of nature at the nanoscale. Fundamental to this approach are the concept of reality as closely coupled complex, hierarchical systems, and the goal to improve human performance. This report covers five major application areas: (1) expand human cognition and communication, (2) improve human health and physical capabilities, (3) enhance group and societal outcomes, (4) strengthen national security and competitiveness, and (5) unify science and education. In addition to reports of task forces in these five areas, the book contains many scientific essays by participants, both well-grounded statements of near-term opportunities and more visionary projects for the more distant future.

Roco, Mihail C., and Carlo D. Montemagno (eds.). 2004. *The Coevolution of Human Potential and Converging Technologies*. New York: New York Academy of Sciences (Annals of the New York Academy of Sciences, volume 1013).

This book developed out of NBIC Convergence 2003, the second Converging Technologies conference, held February 5–7, 2003, at the University of California, Los Angeles. The 17 chapters are contributions from individual authors. Three chapters are overviews of the field, and the others are research contributions at the intersections of two or more fields, or analyses of ethical, legal, and social implications of convergence. Most of the authors participated in the first NBIC conference and book, so this volume is very much an addendum to the first. It ends with an appendix describing early convergence research projects funded by, the National Science Foundation.

Bainbridge, William Sims, and Mihail C. Roco (eds.). 2006. *Managing Nano-Bio-Info-Cogno Innovations: Converging Technologies in Society*. Berlin: Springer.

This book grew out of NBIC Convergence 2004, the third Converging Technologies conference held February 25–27, 2004 in New York City. The 19 chapters and 3 appendices build on the earlier work and begin to expand the community of scientists and scholars involved in the movement. In addition to overviews, chapters cover such important specific issues as convergent education, convergence in developing countries, neuroethics and neuropolicy, cognitive technologies, services science, technopolitics, and the coevolution of social science and emerging technologies. One of the appendices is the report of a smaller workshop, Commercializing and Managing the Converging New Technologies.

SPECIFIC CONVERGENCE AREAS

Bainbridge, William Sims (ed.). 2004. *Encyclopedia of Human-Computer Interaction*. Great Barrington, Massachusetts: Berkshire.

This two-volume reference work primarily emphasizes the convergence between information technology and cognitive science, in essays on such topics as psychology and HCI, social psychology and HCI, artificial intelligence, smart homes, social informatics, personality capture, and the design method called "cognitive walkthroughs." Several essays add biology to the convergence: anthropometry (computer measurement of the human body), brain-computer interfaces, cyborgs, physiology, repetitive strain injury, and universal access, which refers to the challenge of designing systems to empower disabled people. Computer vision systems that interpret human physical movement are described in essays about eye tracking, facial expressions, gesture recognition, and motion capture. Another essay explains how evolutionary engineering uses computers to design products following the biological principle of natural selection from random variation, and the essay on computer viruses draws parallels with their biological cousins. A long essay by the editor introduces the concept of Converging Technologies and explains the central role that science and engineering in the human–computer interaction area can play in advancing convergence.

Vogel, Viola, and Barbara Baird (eds.). 2005. *Nanobiotechnology.* Arlington, Virginia: National Nanotechnology Coordination Office.

This is the report of a workshop held October 9–11, 2003, and cooperatively organized by the National Institutes of Health and the National Science Foundation. The executive summary (p. v) makes clear the convergent and progress-oriented nature of this area: "Scientists, engineers, and physicians assembled to identify groundbreaking scientific opportunities for research at the intersection of nanotechnology and biology." Specific topic areas include advanced imaging technologies to study how biological processes work at the nanoscale, *in vivo* analysis of cellular processes at the nanoscale, assembly of nanosystems that duplicate biological functions and thus increase our understanding of them, and applications of nanotechnology to human health.

Meyyappan Meyya and Minoo Dastoor (eds.). 2006. *Nanotechnology in Space Exploration.* Arlington, Virginia: National Nanotechnology Coordination Office.

This is the report of a National Nanotechnology Initiative Workshop, held August 24–26, 2004, supported by the National Aeronautics and Space Administration. After a general introduction, six chapters cover nanomaterials, nanosensors and instrumentation, nano-enabled microcraft, nano-enabled robotics, nano-micro-macro integration (including nanomanufacturing), and astronaut health management. Given the very stringent performance demands of space technology, nanotechnology may be a cost-effective option in many cases. Among other benefits, it can provide structural materials with improved strength at lower mass, electronics with reduced power demands, and more efficient solar power generation.

Gilbert, Nigel, and Klaus B. Troitsch. 2005. *Simulation for the Social Scientist.* Maidenhead, Berkshire, England: Open University Press.

This is a textbook showing how many kinds of computer simulation can be used to model social phenomena. In addition to linking social science to information technology, partly through cognitive science, the book explains simulation methods that are also used in the physical and biological sciences. Examples include system dynamics, queuing models, multilevel models, cellular automata, multi-agent systems, genetic algorithms, and neural networks. Several of the approaches illustrate the dynamics of complex systems, some of which are hierarchical in nature, thus illustrating the fundamental principle that much convergence in science and technology will require analyzing reality as a complex, hierarchical system.

Bainbridge, William Sims. 2006. *God from the Machine: Artificial Intelligence Models of Religious Cognition*. Lanham, Maryland: AltaMira.

Published in a cognitive science series, this book uses information technology to develop theories of human social behavior and cultural evolution. Firmly rooted in traditional literature in the social science of religion, it employs a novel methodology. A comprehensive computer simulation program models communication among the 44,100 people living in an imaginary town, as they influence each other, exchange values with each other, and collectively develop theories about the nature of the world they inhabit. The problem employs both rule-based and neural net artificial intelligence methods.

HUMAN ENHANCEMENT

Fukuyama, Francis. 2002. *Our Posthuman Future: Consequences of the Biotechnology Revolution*. New York: Farrar, Straus, and Giroux.

Although this book emphasizes biotechnology, it also refers to the three other NBIC fields and offers principles that could apply to the impact of all four technologies on human nature. The emphasis is on the ways that morality could be undermined by sciences of the brain, pharmaceuticals that affected human behavior, the prolongation of life, and genetic engineering. Fukuyama contrasts different theories of the source of ethics, arguing that pure pragmatism will not work and that in the absence of a religious consensus there must be a shared, stable notion of human nature. Readers who disagree with Fukuyama's premises or conclusions may still find this book useful as an introduction to philosophical issues salient for ethical application of NBIC technologies.

Hughes, James H. 2004. *Citizen Cyborg: Why Democratic Societies Must Respond to the Redesigned Human of the Future*. Cambridge, Massachusetts: Westview Press.

The first section of this book summarizes some of the ways the technology may enable humans to be smarter, healthier, and happier in the 21st century, and the third section suggests the kind of thinking we need to build a better future. The middle section, on which the analysis of the book turns, considers the "biopolitical landscape" where the important policy decisions will be made. Hughes argues that politics has been two-dimensional in the past, focusing on economic and cultural issues, but the new century adds the dimension of technological politics. Like Fukuyama, Hughes tends to focus on examples from biotechnology, but his more recent work extends the same analysis explicitly to Converging Technologies.

ORGANIZATION OF CONVERGENCE

Sigma Xi. 1995. *Vannevar Bush II: Science for the 21st Century*. Research Triangle Park, North Carolina: Sigma Xi.

These are the proceedings from a conference marking the 50th anniversary of the report Vannevar Bush delivered to President Truman that set the course federally funded science was to take during the Cold War. About 350 scientists and engineers sought a new rationale for government support of scientific research and outlined the proper responsibilities of scientists to society. Among noteworthy contributions were an essay by Donald Stokes, "Renewing the Compact Between Science and Government," suggesting that much support should be in *Pascal's quadrant*, use-inspired basic research. Others included "Reinventing the Research University" by Kumar Patel, "Partnerships Between Government and Industry" by Graham Mitchell, and "Public Funding of Scientific Research" by Lewis Branscomb. Both Neil Smelser and William Bainbridge argued that science needed to understand better the democratic institutions that encourage discovery, and the entire volume considered the social, economic, and cultural situation in which all the sciences exist.

Gray, Denis O., and S. George Walters (eds.). 1998. *Managing the Industry/University Cooperative Research Center: A Guide for Directors and Other Stakeholders*. Columbus, Ohio: Battelle.

This is an extremely detailed, practical guide for managing research centers that connect academic and industrial organizations, based on the extensive experience of the National Science Foundation's I/UCRC program. Although it does not belabor the point, the centers it describes are of necessity multidisciplinary, and a constant theme is communicating across organizational and disciplinary boundaries. Especially relevant to NBIC are the chapters titled "Communications," "Knowledge and Technology Transfer in Cooperative Research Settings," and "Planning the Cooperative Research Program." Although the book offers much very specific advice, it is probably most useful as a stimulus to brainstorming about whatever convergence issues need to be addressed in one's own situation, whether or not anything so large as a multi-million-dollar research center is involved.

GENERAL CONVERGENCE THEORY

Wheeler, John Archibald. 1994. *At Home in the Universe*. Woodbury, New York: American Institute of Physics.

This collection of essays by an innovative physicist was written over a period of more than three decades and approaches the unification of science from a number of directions. Wheeler is especially famous for having suggested that information, not energy or matter, is the primary constituent of the universe, notably in the essays "Beyond the Black Hole" and "It from Bit." He offers seven principles on which concepts from one field may be applied to another, in "A Septet of Sibyls: Aids in the Search for Truth." In "Einstein and Other Seekers of the Wider View," he offers seven more principles for gaining a broader scientific perspective. Other essays touch upon the unity of scientific knowledge, the distinction between convergent and divergent phenomena, and the proper perspective on humanity's place in the universe.

Simon, Herbert A. 1996. *The Sciences of the Artificial*. Third edition. Cambridge, Massachusetts: MIT Press.

This classic work by a pioneer of artificial intelligence advocates computer simulation as a profound but practical way of modeling complex systems across the sciences, but especially for complex economic, social, and technical systems. After a chapter on economic rationality, the book offers two chapters in psychology, one on the thinking process and the other on memory. These present the traditional but currently controversial artificial intelligence assumption that intelligence consists in the rule-based manipulation of well-defined symbols. A chapter on the science of design presents the influential idea that engineering and software design can be codified, followed by a chapter that asks whether social planning also can be rationalized. The book concludes with two chapters on complexity, insightful for understanding complex systems in any field of science or engineering.

Dennett, Daniel C. 1995. *Darwin's Dangerous Idea: Evolution and the Meanings of Life*. New York: Simon and Schuster.

A professor of philosophy and cognitive studies at Tufts University, Dennett has written extensively about evolution, human intelligence, and the need to discard old superstitions in favor of fresh ideas based on scientific research. This book explicitly connects the biological process of evolution by natural selection to principles of computer science and cognitive science. A theme that runs throughout this book is the fear many people have that Darwin's theory of evolution diminishes human hope and dignity. He acknowledges that "Darwin's idea is a universal solvent, capable of cutting right to the heart of everything in sight" (p. 521). However, Dennett believes that humans can lead fulfilling, hopeful lives without the need for illusions, and that this universal solvent does not in fact ruin humanity's best ideas.

FUTURE OF SCIENCE AND TECHNOLOGY

Horgan, John. 1996. *The End of Science: Facing the Limits of Knowledge in the Twilight of the Scientific Age*. Reading, Massachusetts: Addison-Wesley.

The author is a journalist who worked for Scientific American magazine and uses that background to interview a large number of famous, senior scientists.

The book has five themes, some more explicit than others: (1) the impression that most of the major discoveries have already been made in some sciences, (2) the possibility that some important scientific questions may be beyond our ability to answer, (3) the dispute over whether some questions that science cannot answer could be addressed successfully by nonscientific modes of knowing, (4) the progress that can be achieved by taking ideas or methods from one field and applying them in another, and (5) the hope that advances in technology will pose new questions for science that it is able to answer.

Barrow, John D. 1998. *Impossibility: The Limits of Science and the Science of Limits*. Oxford, England: Oxford University Press.

This book is a serious attempt to locate the boundaries of scientific progress, and thus the limits to technological innovation, written in a nontechnical but logically developed manner. Although physics and the neighboring fields are the prime focus of attention, the analysis often involves principles of cognition or information processing. At times, the book considers topics that appear to be remote from technology, including cosmology and number theory. However, that may be a virtue, because it suggests that the limits of technology may be very far beyond current work in the NBIC fields. The book gives many examples in which a general intellectual principle is applied across two or more distinct scientific fields, such as uncertainty, paradox, and complexity.

Index of Contributors